Counselling, Psychotherapy and the Law

PROFESSIONAL SKILLS FOR COUNSELLORS

The *Professional Skills for Counsellors* series, edited by Colin Feltham, covers the practical, technical and professional skills and knowledge which trainee and practising counsellors need to improve their competence in key areas of therapeutic practice.

Titles in the series include:

Medical and Psychiatric Issues for Counsellors
Brian Daines, Linda Gask and Tim Usherwood

Personal and Professional Development for Counsellors
Paul Wilkins

Counselling by Telephone
Maxine Rosenfield

Time-Limited Counselling
Colin Feltham

Client Assessment
Stephen Palmer and Gladeana McMahon (eds)

Counselling, Psychotherapy and the Law
Peter Jenkins

Counselling, Psychotherapy and the Law

Peter Jenkins

SAGE Publications
London • Thousand Oaks • New Delhi

SAGE Publications Ltd
6 Bonhill Street
London EC2A 4PU

SAGE Publications Inc.
2455 Teller Road
Thousand Oaks, California 91320

SAGE Publications India Pvt Ltd
32, M-Block Market
Greater Kailash – I
New Delhi 110 048

British Library Cataloguing in Publication data

A catalogue record for this book is available
from the British Library

ISBN 0 8039 7986 X
ISBN 0 8039 7987 8 (pbk)

Library of Congress catalog record available

Typeset by Mayhew Typesetting, Rhayader, Powys
Printed in Great Britain by Biddles Ltd, Guildford, Surrey

Contents

Foreword

Tim Bond

Talking with Kenneth Cohen, a solicitor who pioneered writing about British law for counsellors (Cohen, 1992), I suggested that attempting to persuade counsellors to take an interest in the law was like trying to swim against a powerful current. I had found that, in the main, counsellors both resented the intrusion of law into the therapeutic relationship, and felt antagonistic towards the legal way of thinking. Ken expressed his disappointment, observing that the law has much to offer counsellors and their clients. He suggested that by working within the legal framework, counsellors are better able to establish and protect both the respective rights and responsibilities of their clients and themselves, not only in relation to each other, but also against the unwanted intrusion of others.

Since the early 1990s, counsellors' resistance to learning about the law appears to have faded. Counselling as a profession is maturing from what may be characterised as its more adolescent phase, and in its young adulthood is much more interested in rights and responsibilities. I am sure that this book will make an important contribution to these changing attitudes. By setting out the law in a lively and accessible manner, Peter Jenkins shows that the law is not primarily a source of onerous liability for counsellors, but instead can be used to the advantage of counsellors and clients alike.

There are good reasons why counsellors need to know the law relating to counselling. Firstly, it is an ethical requirement of the leading professional organisations. The British Association for Counselling, the largest counselling organisation (outside the United States), requires its members to 'work within the law' and that they should 'take all reasonable steps to be aware of the current law affecting the work of the counsellor' (BAC, 1993: B.2.7.1–2). Similarly, counselling psychologists in membership of the British Psychological Society are bound by a code of conduct which requires them to take account of their obligations under the law (BPS, 1993: sections 1, 3.4–5, 4). Secondly, it is a basic legal principle that everyone in Britain, counsellors included, is bound by the law of the United Kingdom. These obligations have been recently extended to include obligations created by European and international law. Ignorance of the law is no defence. For counsellors to remain in ignorance of the law is to place themselves and their clients in unnecessary jeopardy.

Whilst the above are important reasons for counsellors to inform themselves about the law, they may not be the most persuasive reasons for doing so. In my experience as a trainer, counsellors collectively are suspicious of obligations especially when expressed in terms of 'oughts' and 'shoulds'. On the other hand counsellors, like most professionals, are alert to arguments based on enlightened self-interest, and especially receptive to anything which enhances the best interests of their clients.

With my interest in ethics for counsellors, I am struck by the extent to which ethical standards adopted by counsellors prior to any extensive knowledge of the law correspond to the general legal requirements. A counsellor who is conscientious in achieving a clear agreement with a client about the basis on which they are working together, who works within the client's informed consent in ways consistent with the counsellor's competence, and who is rigorous over confidentiality, will have satisfied not only the ethical standards of best practice, but also some of the most important legal requirements. This coincidence of ethical standards and law is significant. It provides an important source of protection for clients and counsellors alike, thus increasing the security of the therapeutic space which is essential for successful counselling. Attentiveness to these basic requirements may be all that is required in most counselling situations with adults.

Inevitably, from time to time, difficult situations arise which require a more extensive knowledge of the law. Some of these situations are associated with particular client groups, such as young people, which are considered extensively in this book. Other difficulties arise because of conflicts between a client's rights to confidentiality and the rights of people who the client may be threatening to harm, a situation which has been considered by the courts. Sometimes the conflict arises between an individual's rights, such as control over their own life and death, and a public policy committed to the reduction in numbers of suicides. In many of these circumstances, there remains a degree of legal uncertainty. The law is evolving rapidly so that it may be impossible to give definitive legal guidance to a concerned counsellor. However, a counsellor who has taken the appropriate legal principles into account in their decisions about the management of the case is in the best possible position to defend those decisions in the courts and in professional adjudications. Some situations may have such important consequences or be so complex legally that the wisest course of action is to seek the advice of a lawyer or professional organisation. A working knowledge of the relevant legal principles and current legal debates can make such advice much more meaningful to both the counsellor and the client.

Increasing numbers of counsellors are finding that they have occasional direct contact with the law. Perhaps the most likely reason for this direct contact is a client's request that a counsellor appears as a witness on their behalf, often to testify in a claim for damages which might be boosted by evidence of emotional trauma. Counsellors are sometimes asked to appear in a Coroner's Court following a client's suspicious death in which suicide is a possibility. Increasingly, counsellors are required to testify in criminal hearings where a client alleges sexual assault and rape, especially if the account given to the counsellor precedes any statements given to the police. Counsellors can also be called to provide evidence to courts considering the welfare of children. Over the past five years, I have encountered hundreds of counsellors faced with one or more of these situations. Some prior knowledge of the law and the way the legal process works is a considerable advantage in facing these professionally challenging situations. The growth of counselling has made our work much more visible and it is inevitable that we shall be expected to respond more frequently to requests, and sometimes to orders, to appear as witnesses. For most counsellors, these demands may arise only a few times during their professional lifetime and prior knowledge of how they might arise is valuable and reduces the element of surprise.

The appearance of this book suggests that a debate, within professional bodies representing counselling, about the legal knowledge which is considered essential to a basic professional training is now due. Peter Jenkins' book is an important stepping stone towards a greater level of professional sophistication and general competence in the formal management of counselling relationships, and deserves to be widely read by counsellors.

References

BPS (1993) 'A code of conduct for psychologists', *Code of Conduct, Ethical Principles and Guidelines*. Leicester: British Psychological Society, pp. 1–5.

BAC (1993) *Code of Ethics and Practice for Counsellors*. Rugby: British Association for Counselling.

Cohen, K. (1992) 'Some legal issues in counselling and psychotherapy', *British Journal of Guidance and Counselling*, 20(1): 10–26.

Acknowledgements

I received help, interest, support and encouragement from a wide range of people in writing this book, which originally started out as a short article for the journal *Counselling*, and was later to take more rigorous shape as a dissertation for an M.A. in Counselling at Keele University. Amongst those I would like to thank are students and colleagues on the Manchester University Certificate in Counselling Skills and Diploma in Counselling. Linda Stone, Fred Wolstenholme, Pat Lockley, Wayne Poulsen, Margaret Wilson, Josie Lee, Peter Smith, Stephanie Danziger, and Hazel Batchelor have all helped in various, much appreciated ways. Other colleagues in the School of Social Work and Counselling at Stockport College, Ralph Barnett and Tina Miller, have also been supportive. Without the efficient and prompt service of the Inter-Library Loan Section at Stockport College, this book would not have been possible.

Thanks are due to my tutors in the Counselling Section at Keele University, Joyce Sharples, Professor John McLeod and Ray Woolfe, for encouragement and supervision with the original dissertation. Peter De Cruz from the Law Department, Brian Williams from the Social Work section, and Ursula Sharma from the Sociology Department, all at Keele University, also gave useful feedback.

A large number of people have helped with sources, advice or information for the book, including Jayne Zito, of the Zito Trust; Marjorie Orr, of Accuracy About Abuse; Kenneth Cohen, solicitor; Roger Scotford, of the British False Memory Society; Marche Isabella, Counselor, Washington, D.C.; Joanna Beazley-Richards, of Wealden College; Helen Shaw, of Inquest; Derek Hill, Head of Counselling at Relate; Simon Armson, Chief Executive of the Samaritans; Jenny Fasal, of POPAN; Paul Rice and Heather McCurry, of Manchester Medical Group; Susanna Stringer, of *Counselling News*; Dr Anne Hayman; Dr Ann Richardson and Sheila Richards, Department of Health; Phil Jones, Office of the Data Protection Registrar; and, not least, the clients and therapists who agreed to be interviewed about their experiences for this study.

Paul Rice, Lecturer in Law at Liverpool University (also mentioned above), kindly agreed to act as a reader for this book, and made useful and insightful comments on the text. Tim Bond, former Chair of the British Association for Counselling, and Tony Dugdale, Professor in Negligence Law at the Department of Law, Keele University, both provided detailed comments, for which I am more than indebted.

Special thanks to Colin Feltham, who returned edited scripts more quickly than I could write them, and to Susan Worsey, editor at Sage, whose persistence more than helped to shape the final product! Marion Steel provided excellent copy-editing.

The information and guidance contained in this book has been carefully checked, but the law is changing day by day even in the process of writing about it. This book is a general guide, but not a definitive statement of the law; anyone requiring legal advice should seek professional assistance. Any errors and omissions are my own.

Finally, I now understand why authors make a point of thanking their partners and families at the end of their acknowledgements. Without Jane's support and practical 'rescuing' in the final stages of the process of writing, this book would have remained just another interesting idea. Words are inadequate in expressing my gratitude for her support.

Hodder Headline are gratefully thanked for their permission to reproduce the diagram on page 179, which originally appeared in J. Rozenberg (1994) *The Search for Justice: An Anatomy of the Law*. London: Hodder and Stoughton, p. 124.

Introduction

This is not a law book in the usual sense, but a book *about* the law for therapists written *by* a therapist. The starting point for this book was my growing puzzlement as to why so little had been written on the relationship of therapy in the UK to the law. My previous training as a social worker had emphasised the legal framework which enveloped practice, and gave it a foundation for making decisions. This approach seemed very alien to counselling, as I soon discovered when I became involved in working as a part-time counsellor, in training on counselling courses, and in undertaking my own professional development. Counsellors I met seemed either to dismiss the law as irrelevant, to see it as a threat of some kind, or to be rather unnecessarily in awe of it as an omnipotent power. These responses appeared to gather force as lawsuits about false memory cases in the USA started to surface, and a more general concern about therapists' vulnerability to legal action seemed to take root.

In a sense, the book is a response to a speaker at one conference on therapy and the law, who expressed the view that 'there is no case law on counselling in the UK'. This may be true in a strict sense, but this book is an attempt to describe the case law concerning counselling as far as it can be divined by looking at other comparable fields, such as medicine. It has been rather like trying to write a book about 'Pumas on Dartmoor'. Whether there are actually pumas on Dartmoor is a subject of fierce dispute – actual cases are either rare, or are tantalising in their lack of detail. However, enough is known about Dartmoor, and about pumas and large cats in other habitats, to be able to describe accurately what the characteristics of these animals would be like if they were living wild in South-West England. So, based on the example of medical case law, this is an attempt to read the main characteristics of the law as applied to therapy, in the absence, so far, of extensive case law. Hopefully, therapists may be able to avoid actually featuring in future case law by following some of the suggested guidelines included here.

If any lawyers read this book, they may be somewhat frustrated that it does not follow the format of a conventional law book. In addition, general statements are made about the application of the law which a trained legal eye will recognise as often containing exceptions which are hinted at, rather than fully explored. For every general legal principle, there seems to be an exception. One such example would be the principles about damages awarded for psychiatric injuries. The existence of exceptions to almost every general rule in law provides one of the reasons why this book cannot be taken as a definitive guide to the law, but is rather a general outline of the terrain. Advice to therapists is, in most cases, to stick to established paths. Therapists needing more detailed guidance on specific cases should seek legal advice, as the law is frequently changing, and no coverage of the law can be comprehensive in every respect.

Whilst on the topic of advice, therapists are often asked by clients what they should do, to which the classic response is for the therapist to turn the question round for the client to find their own preferred solution. However, when it comes to legal questions, it often seems the case that therapists become frustrated with the lack of certainty in the face of complicated and difficult legal issues. Responding to questions about what a therapist may do, or may not do, or must do or must not do, frequently depends upon the context in which they work, the nature of the client and the type of issue of concern. This is especially true of therapists working with children and young people, for example. Therapists may prefer certainty in the form of a straight answer, but often the legal position provides less than absolute certainty, and rather sets out the parameters within which decisions can be made. The paradox seems to be that as therapists we prefer certainty for ourselves on difficult legal issues, but meanwhile encourage our clients to learn to work with ambiguity and uncertainty in their own lives.

On the issue of therapists seeking an element of clarity about legal issues, it is perhaps worth pointing out the differences between *liability* and *risk*. Any lawyer is trained to identify liability in any transaction or responsibility. However, liability and risk may not necessarily belong to the same family of concepts. The liability of people being struck by lightning in the UK may be evenly spread across the population, but the actual *risk* incurred may be much more narrowly focused on a small proportion of people. In theory, therapists may be liable for a whole range of activities. In reality, the risks that they actually run in doing their work may be quite small. Few therapists are currently sued, and even fewer are *successfully* sued by clients. This may well change in the future, but the present culture both of therapy and the law would have to change to make this a more likely possibility.

One concern in writing this book has been to explore some of the current received wisdom often encountered amongst therapists in the UK about their legal liability, or about wider legal developments affecting therapy. In some cases, the views expressed by therapists as established truths appear to me to be wrong, and in others, they seem to be very debatable, at least. Some of the main contentious beliefs about therapists and the law might include the following:

- therapists are at high and increasing risk of legal action by dissatisfied clients
- legal action by third parties against therapists, such as in cases of alleged false memory, is likely to follow the US pattern where therapists have been successfully sued
- coverage by professional indemnity insurance is an absolute requirement for every practitioner
- therapists working with children under 16 are required to first obtain parental permission in order to do therapeutic work
- all therapists are legally obliged to report child abuse
- supervisers are liable for the mistakes and negligent actions of their supervisees
- 'private' confidential records of therapy sessions are exempted from demands for disclosure to the courts
- following a professional *Code of Practice* will provide a sufficient defence for therapists whose practice is legally challenged in a court of law
- the European Commission is actively considering policies to regulate and control access to practice by UK therapists
- regulation of therapists by the UK government is likely to follow on logically from the adoption of voluntary registers of practitioners.

For various reasons, each of these statements is open to debate. The reasons for doubting them are explored more fully in the text that follows.

There is, it seems, a fairly widespread perception of the law as a vague external threat to therapists, either in the form of unknown requirements concerning breaches of confidentiality, or for compliance with court-ordered demands for access to client information, along with the ever-present spectre of being sued by angry clients. This seems to have given way more recently to another, more optimistic construction of the relationship of therapy to the law. In some spheres of counselling and psychotherapy, the perception is emerging and gaining strength that therapy's relationship with the law is an opportunity to be grasped and explored in full. In part, this connects with the drive towards the statutory recognition of therapy, in the form of state-backed registers of practitioners, or via the expectation that European Directives may soon be in force to speed up this process. The recognition linked to this point is that therapists need to be better informed of their rights and responsibilities under the law as a starting point. This view has been illustrated by the conferences held by various groupings on legal issues within therapy, such as confidentiality, and the positive response to these made by practitioners (BCP, 1995b). Another example of the shift has been in the form of the acknowledgement of the law as a cornerstone of safe and ethical practice, made by Tim Bond, former Chair of the British Association for Counselling, and of the prominence of legal issues within the revised BAC *Code of Ethics and Practice for Counsellors* adopted in 1992. The *Code* shows the growing realisation of the need for practical and accurate guidance to counsellors in this area, and is based on the important work undertaken by Tim and members of BAC's Standards and Ethics Committee over the previous few years. The *Code* is frequently the main training resource in use by psychotherapy and counselling courses on this topic, along with Tim Bond's key book, *Standards and Ethics for Counselling in Action* (Bond, 1993a).

On the one hand, therefore, there is the possibly widespread concern amongst practitioners over the process of the creeping 'legalisation of therapy' that recent writers such as Christopher Bollas and David Sundelson describe. On the other hand, there is perhaps a realistic recognition that an informed understanding of the law, and a closer relationship with it, represent also something of an opportunity for therapists in the next stage of development of the therapeutic community. This book is intended as one contribution to that process, which therapists will hopefully find useful, and which will be improved upon by their future responses and contributions in the debate now opening up.

A note on how to use this book

In writing this book, I have tried to combine a *theoretical discussion about the law* affecting therapy, with more *practical information for therapists* facing legal issues involving their work. Thus the general outline of the law includes detailed reference to original sources, and to the relevant case law. Hopefully, these references will be useful for readers wanting to check original and more detailed sources, and will not break the 'flow' of the book for other readers. Legal references are written in a style which is probably unfamiliar to non-lawyers, so this style is briefly described at the beginning of the Table of Cases at the end of the book. This final section also contains an index of case law for the USA and UK, and Acts of Parliament referred to in the text, again for readers with a more specialist interest. The Glossary contains professional terms for which lawyers, therapists or clients may want brief definition or explanation.

For practitioners who may simply want to check the legal situation regarding a topic, such as defamation or contract for example, key points are displayed in summary boxes, together with sets of guidelines for professional practice for quick reference. Part of the therapist's role may be in passing on information to clients, or in gaining access to recent public documents, publications or legal advice. The Resources section at the end of the book contains a comprehensive list of organisations which can be contacted for further information by therapists or clients. For trainers and students, suggested questions are included at the end of each chapter, which identify key points for discussion.

In terms of its structure, the book begins with an outline of key terms relating to the law, and a survey of some of the main problematic issues facing therapists at present. This is followed by a description of the broad range of therapeutic work which contains a legal dimension. Current concerns about professional negligence are then explored in the third chapter.

The limits to confidentiality are then identified, with the focus on the therapist's role as custodian of sensitive client information. This is distinguished from the legal pressures to grant access to this information to outside agencies, such as the courts, which is the subject of the following chapter.

The chapter on the courts describes the structure of the courts system, provides information for therapists facing involvement in legal proceedings, and explores issues of compensation, particularly regarding psychological damages. Counselling children and young people is examined as a specialist area in its own right, albeit one with implications for other therapists as well.

Complaints systems are emerging as a contentious and challenging area for therapists and clients alike, and current systems are considered in comparison with those in use by other professional groupings. The final chapter explores tensions around the issue of professional status for therapists and the progress made towards achieving full statutory recognition and regulation.

The overall theme of this book is that the law is dynamic, fluid and rapidly changing, rather than being fixed for all time. Therapists need to be alert to those issues which have an impact on a broad spectrum of their work with clients. Hopefully, the style and content of this book will be of assistance in this process.

1

Therapy and the Law

Therapy and the law enjoy, at best, an uneasy relationship. They inhabit different spheres of emotion and logic. They employ contrasting languages of feeling and evidence. Each operates in a space that is either essentially personal and private, or is, by definition, highly formalised and public. The points of intersection between therapeutic practice and the law are often obscure, specialised and subject to nervous speculation by therapists about what is actually required of them. The areas of overlap tend to be seen as uncharted territory, full of hazards and pitfalls for unwary therapists, unschooled in the harsh world of litigation. All too often in this area, discussion by therapists is premised on an underlying and frequently unrealistic fear of being sued as a result of imperfect knowledge of the law, or inadvertent negligence. However, despite these misgivings and uncertainties, therapists are ultimately bound by the law. They clearly have a professional responsibility to be aware of their legal obligations and to work within the law (BAC, 1993a).

The starting point for an exploration of therapy and the law is to look at definitions of the basic building blocks of any discussion of the topic – **law, ethics and therapy**. Some of the **problem areas** associated with therapy are identified, such as those concerning practice, training and the problematic model of therapy and the law provided by the USA. The growth of **legal recognition for therapy** in the UK is centred around the examples of adoption and infertility counselling. This is followed by a broader survey of areas where law and therapeutic practice have implications for counsellors and psychotherapists, such as counselling in primary care and in work settings.

Law, ethics and therapy

The term law, as used here, includes all systems of civil and criminal law, including statute, common and case law. As the legal systems of Scotland and Northern Ireland have their own characteristics, the focus here will be on the law relating to counselling in England and Wales. The legal system is based on a mixture of *statute*, or laws passed by Parliament, such as the Children Act 1989 or the Mental Health Act 1983, and *common* law. The latter embodies long-established principles, regarding confidentiality or contract, which are not necessarily expressed in one single piece of law. *Case law* is the interpretation of the law made by judges on individual cases, often with far-reaching implications. The *Gillick* [1986] case, for example, gave legal backing to the provision of confidential contraceptive advice by doctors to young persons under the age of 16. The hierarchy of the courts system, described in Chapter 6, can also mean that decisions taken at one level of the legal system, for example, to refuse a child in care access to confidential files held on them, can be overturned by a decision in a higher court, such as the European Court of Human Rights. This decision then has a major effect on the law in the UK, prompting legislation which sets out the rights of citizens to have access to confidential files in a wide range of settings.

Ethics

Ethics provide the moral framework for counselling practice by providing 'normative standards of conduct or actions', or proposing what is 'right' or 'correct' (Austin et al., 1990: 242; Holmes and Lindley, 1989, 1994). The main ethical framework referred to in many discussions of therapy is one based on the concepts of autonomy, fidelity, justice, beneficence, non-maleficence and self interest (Daniluk and Haverkamp, 1993; Bond, 1993a). These ethical values seek to promote the well-being and self-determination of the client, to avoid harming the client or others, and to maintain the competence of the therapist. They underpin the published codes of ethics and practice, such as those of the British Association for Counselling (BAC), the British Psychological Society (BPS), and the United Kingdom Council for Psychotherapy (UKCP). These codes seek to anticipate and respond to the actual dilemmas that therapists may encounter with their clients or third parties (BAC, 1996; BPS, 1995b; UKCP,

1995). At certain points, ethical principles regarding client autonomy and avoiding harm may conflict, as in the case of suicide prevention, or avoiding intended harm by clients to third parties. The actual legal responsibilities of therapists may either be unclear, or may appear to conflict with the ethical principles underpinning good practice, as in the case of some aspects of counselling staff in organisational settings. (For a comprehensive discussion of ethical dilemmas facing therapists, see Bond, 1993a.)

Therapy

The terms counsellor, therapist, and psychotherapist are self-defined occupational terms, with, as yet, no legal restrictions on their current use.

> Only the titles of 'registered medical practitioner', 'chartered psychologist', and 'registered nurse' are protected. Anyone can call themselves a doctor, psychologist, nurse, counsellor, social worker, psychotherapist, sexual or marital therapist, or any other therapeutic title, providing they do not mislead patients by falsely claiming to have certain qualifications. (Jehu et al., 1994: 191)

There have been moves towards achieving full statutory recognition for psychotherapists since the 1970s, as recorded in the recommendations of the Foster Report (1971) and the Sieghart Report (1978). These developments and the subsequent setting up of voluntary registers for psychotherapists and counsellors are discussed in Chapter 9. There are proposals for the term 'psychologist' to be restricted by law, under legislation being worked on by the British Psychological Society. As opposed to psychologists, psychiatrists are qualified medical practitioners with the capacity to diagnose and prescribe medication and other forms of treatment, including electro-convulsive therapy.

The generic terms 'counselling' and 'therapy' are used here to include a wide variety of forms of therapeutic exploration and resolution of emotional distress and behavioural problems using psychological methods, primarily within a dyad or triad, but also in groups. The terms 'counsellors' and 'therapists' are used interchangeably here to denote persons carrying out these activities. The distinction between counselling and psychotherapy is one which is hotly debated in therapeutic circles, but carries no legal weight outside of these narrow confines, and the distinction is unlikely to interest or impress a court of law. The generic term 'therapist' will be used to describe both counsellors and psycho-therapists in this context (Jehu et al., 1994: xv). At another level, the British Association for Counselling has proposed a useful distinction between *counselling* as such and *counselling skills*, where the latter skills are used as part of another role, for example, as nurse, teacher or personnel manager (BAC, 1989). While many of those using counselling *skills* in their professional work are not accurately described as *counsellors* or *therapists*, for example psychiatric nurses, social workers or doctors, there will be material discussed here which will be of direct relevance to the work of these and other groups. It will not be assumed that all therapists are solely engaged in therapeutic work, to the exclusion of other roles and responsibilities, nor that they are primarily engaged in private practice. Research suggests that this is far from being true in the case of most therapists (BAC, 1993b: 243–4).

Current issues in therapy and the law

Discussion of the law and therapy is inseparable from the issue of professionalisation. Almost by definition, established professions such as medicine and the law, have a recognised status in legislation and case law. This authorises them to carry out certain activities, and delegates some of the responsibility for self-discipline and the maintenance of high standards of practice. Other occupational groups, such as teaching, nursing and social work, have sometimes been described as semi-professions. These groups possess some of the features of established professional groups, but lack unqualified acknowledgement of their professional expertise (Etzioni, 1969). However, unlike these semi-professions, therapists in the UK have been relatively slow to recognise the legal dimension of their practice. Establishing a clear relationship with the law is one of the elements which is associated with acquiring full professional status (Jenkins, 1996). Some of the implications of this process of professionalisation will be further outlined in Chapter 9.

Problem areas
Some of the areas in therapy which are particularly problematic for practitioners and their clients derive from the essentially 'private' nature of their practice, with resulting concerns over confidentiality, and over reported cases of bad practice. The search for statutory recognition of therapy is becoming increasingly

prominent, and with it, the requirements for training and a licence to practise. The growth of legislation from the European Community (EC) seems to present possibilities for the development of therapy as a profession. However, the Anglo-American heritage is still influential, and offers a widening body of case law and statute on therapy which may be both enticing and alarming to practitioners in the UK.

Private v. public arenas

Therapy is par excellence a *private* relationship between individuals. Apart from in training, supervised practice or directly recorded sessions, what the therapist does with his or her client is not usually directly observed or experienced by others. This presents both a power for promoting personal change, or, alternatively, a potential for the *abuse* of this power. Therapy, as the 'talking cure', can also be seen by lay persons, and by the legal system as being either arcane, or an overly complex presentation of what is only commonsense, namely talking to a sympathetic listener. The courts and the media, as public arenas, do not always deal sympathetically with the more private concerns and preoccupations of therapists.

Bad practice

The fundamental privacy of the therapeutic session can provide opportunities for bad practice to go unnoticed and unchecked, and the actual scale of this may be hard to assess. Sexual abuse of clients by therapists has emerged as a persistent theme of concern in recent explorations of unethical practice by therapists. For some critics, this provides proof of the essentially unequal and exploitative nature of the therapeutic relationship (Masson, 1992; Russell, 1993). There have also been allegations that therapists have fostered allegedly false memories of early childhood sexual trauma in clients as a routine diagnosis. Therapeutic influence, it is claimed, has inflicted adverse effects upon the affected third parties, such as the wrongly alleged abusing parents, and upon the extended family as a whole. The avenues open to clients to make complaints or bring legal action are looked at in Chapters 3 and 8.

Confidentiality

One of the major areas of difficulty for therapists in encountering the legal system, is the attempt to harmonise two competing approaches to confidentiality. Confidentiality is one of the first principles that therapists learn on any training course. They quickly go on to discover that this is not necessarily an *absolute* principle, but a guideline which can often be compromised by their professional role, and by organisational considerations, as in the case of social workers working with possible child abuse. (On issues concerning counselling children and young people, see Chapter 7.) Confidentiality within therapy is, in reality, enveloped by a much broader concept of *the public interest*. The law sees the benefits of one-to-one confidentiality as potentially out-weighed by wider considerations of what is deemed to be in the public interest. Hence the therapist's notes and recollections of sessions can be called into the witness box if need be. This aspect of the law will be addressed in Chapter 6.

Professional recognition
Therapy is currently striving for recognition of its particular exper-tise from the wider society, by seeking statutory acknowledgement of its role. Initially, it is attempting to do this by establishing voluntary registers of practitioners, and by drawing up tightly monitored processes for the accreditation of individuals, and for the validation of training courses. The role of counselling in society as a whole has been increasingly acknowledged, by refer-ence to the need for counselling of survivors of traumatic events, of juries in especially horrific trials, and as a means of coping with major life events such as bereavement and redundancy. The implicit irony has been noticed by sceptical observers, however, of seeking to reassure the doubtful or unconvinced by stating that the service is being staffed by 'trained counsellors'. The helpful term 'trained', intended to *dispel* doubts about their value or efficacy, actually confounds its purpose – after all, in comparable situ-ations, 'no one talks about trained pilots or trained dentists' (Bennett, 1994). The widespread cultural uneasiness about the proven value of counselling persists, expressed in a wide variety of ways, from magazine articles through cartoons to television documentaries.

Training
An emphasis on 'trained' therapists raises the question of the *nature* and *adequacy* of training for therapists. Moves have been made by the British Association for Counselling to validate

courses which meet set criteria (1993c), and the UKCP has sought to negotiate criteria for the recognition of registered practitioners with its component organisations (1995). The highly diverse nature of counsellor training, and the rich variety of approaches available to students and trainers make it hard and even undesirable to achieve uniformity in the specifics of training (Jenkins, 1995b). Buried within this eclecticism is also a very patchy coverage of the legal issues which confront future therapists. In a small sample survey of 60 counsellor training courses at Diploma level or above, a third had no specific coverage of legal issues (Jenkins, 1995c). There is a growing awareness, fuelled by fears of legal action in the USA on false memory claims, that this is an aspect of therapist training which now needs addressing more closely.

The American deluge
A complicating factor in this scenario is that while UK therapists increasingly look to their future under EC Directives, and UK statute, they also often look backwards over their shoulders to the USA. Here, therapists are, in part at least, licensed to practise and recognised in law. Within a different, but broadly comparable system of law, therapists have achieved a large measure of recognised legal status. The apparent cost has been a burden of statutory responsibilities such as the duty to report child abuse, and to warn third parties at risk, and an increasing deluge of litigation against therapists. The more visible therapists become through legal recognition, the more vulnerable they also seem to become in a litigious environment to being sued for malpractice. However, the reference to US precedent, frequently made by UK therapists in the case of *Tarasoff* (1976), can be both instructive and misleading. There are significant differences between the respective legal systems of the USA and UK. These may mean that the long expected American future of litigation against therapists may actually be slower to arrive here than is generally thought at the time of writing (see Chapter 3).

Statutory recognition of therapy

Since statutory recognition for therapy and counselling has emerged as a major goal for the future, it is worth looking at what has been achieved so far in this respect. Therapy has achieved well-established statutory reference in two main areas, adoption and infertility counselling, and degrees of recognition in a growing range of other areas of work, which will now be explored.

Specific areas of practice: adoption
The first statutory recognition of counselling in the UK is in s.51 of the Adoption Act 1976 (previously s.26 of the Children Act 1975; s.64 of the proposed Adoption Bill). As outlined in s.1 of the Adoption Act 1976, it is the duty of every local authority to establish a service for 'counselling for persons with problems relating to adoption'. Adoption has been legal in England and Wales since 1926. Scotland has had a legal form of adoption since 1930, but with the added possibility of adopted persons applying for information on their birth mother and father (if recorded) from the age of 17. The Houghton Committee, set up in 1969 to reform adoption law, was at first reluctant to change the law to widen access to records. It was swayed by the research into the Scottish system of access to birth records undertaken by John Triseliotis of Edinburgh University (Home Office/Scottish Education Department, 1972; Triseliotis, 1973). This demonstrated the value to individuals of acquiring knowledge of their origins, and suggested that the numbers coming forward to use the service would not be overwhelming. A major consideration was that birth mothers had been promised secrecy when initially placing their child for adoption. How would this rewriting of the contract of confidentiality now be managed to the mutual benefit of all parties concerned?

The answer to this difficult social and human problem was via the provision of counselling. The Act introduced the somewhat problematic concept of 'compulsory counselling' for those adopted before provision was introduced. For those adopted after 12 November 1975, the counselling was to be offered on a voluntary basis.

In the first place, the responsibility for providing the counselling service fell to local authority social services departments (DHSS, 1976a). The dilemmas facing the social worker in this counsellor role, as keepers of sensitive personal information, have been carefully noted by researchers such as Halmes and Timms. They identify 'the ambiguity inherent in the law: is the law on access and the provision of counselling a law for the provision of information, or a law for the protection of natural parents?' (1985: 27).

Counselling was designed here to serve a *protective* function, to balance the competing rights of the individual to birth record information, and of the birth mother or father to the original compact of confidentiality. Providing only partial access to information, namely information from *past* circumstances, rather than *current* information, has been one strategy used here to manage the release of information. The concept of compulsory counselling also underlined the confusing signals being given here to applicants. 'In effect a double message was being given to adopted people: they were entitled by law to the information, but the counselling implied that to use it may be unwise' (Hodgkins, 1991: 7). The counsellor's only statutory obligation is to help the applicant to obtain a birth certificate, and the name of the placing agency. Many will go well beyond this narrow remit, in order to help the individual to explore the *meaning* of their being adopted, and their expectations, if any, of reunion with birth parents.

The Children Act 1989 has since widened the individual's right of access to adoption counselling, in setting up a National Contact Register. Broader services for adoptive families have also been developed by social services departments in some areas (Phillips and McWilliam, 1995). The numbers of people coming forward for adoption records counselling were originally expected to be small, but the potential numbers of people affected could be high, according to NORCAP (The National Organisation for Counselling of Adoptees and their Parents). Approximately three-quarters of a million people have been adopted in England and Wales between 1926 and 1994. NORCAP estimates, extrapolating from current statistics, that approximately half of all adopted women and a third of adopted men will seek access to birth records information at some time, the majority of which will go on to trace members of their former families. '85% of adopted people who apply officially for access to information choose to receive the required counselling at their local social services department' (Burnell et al., 1990: 3).

Purposes of adoption counselling   The original purpose of adoption records counselling was seen in narrow terms, as a means of *controlling* the release of sensitive personal information, rather than as an enabling or empowering purpose for clients. According to the then DHSS, the aims were:

to ensure

(1)   that the adopted person has considered the possible effect of any enquiries both on himself and on others: and

(2)   that the information he seeks, and to which he now has a legal right, is provided in a helpful and appropriate manner. (DHSS, 1976b)

The original practice remit of adoption counselling was thus set in very narrow terms. The main providers – social services departments – have since been criticised by some voluntary organisations as providing a service which is often patchy and under-resourced (Marks, 1995). Other organisations such as the Post-Adoption Centre (PAC) have grown up, providing counselling to 2,000 adults since it was established in 1986. This group has focused on meeting a wider range of needs associated with this field. This includes facilitating post-adoption reunions, providing specialist counselling for inter-racial adoptions and for adoptees with special needs, and offering a broad overall level of counselling and support (Burnell et al., 1990). The PAC argue that 'birth records counselling should provide a continuity of service beyond the initial dispensing of information. The process of counselling should reflect the process of inquiry, meeting and post-reunion experience for all parties.' It has identified an agreed need by those involved for 'a national adoption register, counselling, intermediary services, support groups and, for some, therapy' (Burnell et al., 1990: 16).

The personal benefits of counselling and access to birth records information can be enormous, despite the problems detailed above. One adoptee explained that 'You want to know if you are a child of love or lust' (Halmes and Timms, 1985: 2). For another, the experience of being *heard* was crucial. 'For my part, being asked how it felt, over and over, by someone who looked genuinely interested, someone who didn't back off when I was not immediately able to respond, helped me to appreciate the significance of this process, and allowed me to connect with my feelings of outrage, pain, excitement and apprehension' (Marks, 1995: 49).

From the counsellor's point of view, the ethical and legal dilemmas may arise in the form of balancing of competing rights, namely the right of the individual to obtain birth records information, and the earlier, original right of the birth parent to privacy. In one case, explored in detail in Chapter 5, the counsellor was faced with the need to assess the degree of personal *risk* posed to the birth mother by the request for information. Here the rights of both parties were in direct conflict, with little in the way of precedent to guide the counsellor's final decision.

Infertility counselling

The second area of clear statutory recognition of counselling has been in the field of infertility treatment, in what is known in the popular press as the provision of 'test-tube babies' (Read, 1995). Rapid technological advances in the treatment of infertile couples prompted the setting up of the Warnock Committee. This took a positive and generally understanding view of the role that counselling could play in helping donors and couples make difficult emotional decisions. In contrast with the earlier approach to adoption counselling, this report made a number of striking recommendations, which clearly laid out a purposeful agenda for counselling. It argued for recognition of its distinct professional expertise, linked to appropriate training and qualification (Warnock, 1985: 16).

Under s.3 of the Human Fertilisation and Embryology Act 1990, an offer of counselling to potential donors or recipients of the service is mandatory. For example, under Schedule 3 of the Act:

(1) Before a person gives consent under this Schedule –
    (a) he must be given a suitable opportunity to receive proper counselling about the implications of taking the proposed steps, and
    (b) he must be provided with such relevant information as is proper.

Counselling is of key importance in establishing the necessary basis of *informed consent* by the donor or recipient to treatment. This issue is illustrated by the case of Diane Blood, who wished to use her deceased husband's sperm to have his child after his death. The Human Fertilisation and Embryology Authority (HFEA), while heavily criticised by the media for their stand, based their refusal of treatment on the absence of prior counselling, and on the lack of her deceased husband's full, informed and written consent to treatment (*Guardian*, 23 November 1996). (For discussion of the concept of informed consent, see Chapter 3.)

Code of practice   The details of *how* counselling is to be provided are set out in the *Code of Practice* issued by the Human
Fertilisation and Embryology Authority (Morgan and Lee, 1991:
113). In the *Code* (HFEA, 1993), counselling is distinguished from
other forms of helping in a way that is consistent with definitions
forwarded by organisations such as BAC (1993a). Counselling
should thus be distinguished from:

- giving information
- establishing the normal clinical relationship
- the process of assessing people for the service

It goes on to identify three different types of counselling:

- *counselling as information giving* about the implications of
  the proposed course of action. (Detailed guidance is given on
  this.)
- *supportive counselling*, through providing emotional support,
  for example when a client is failing to become pregnant.
- *therapeutic counselling*: 'this aims to help people to cope with
  the consequences of infertility and treatment, and to help them
  to resolve the problems which these may cause. It includes
  helping people to adjust their expectations and to accept their
  situation' (HFEA, 1993: 29).

The resources needed to achieve this are set out in detail.
'Centres should allow sufficient time for counselling to be conducted sensitively, in an atmosphere which is conducive to discussion. The length and content of counselling, and the pace at
which it is conducted, should be determined by the needs of the
individual concerned' (Para 6.6). Requirements for counselling
practice are specified to include either a social work qualification,
BAC accreditation, or chartered psychologist status. However,
these specifications are somewhat weakened by the provision that
such qualifications may be required of an *adviser* to those carrying
out the counselling work (Para 1.10). Relevant criminal convictions, for example, for violence, dishonesty, blackmail, sexual
offences against children, drugs offences and breaches of regulatory machinery are to be considered in making appointments.
    Several points stand out in the way that counselling is intro-
duced into the process of providing infertility treatment. Firstly, it

is identified as a distinct area of expertise, deliberately separated out from the clinical responsibilities of the doctor organising the treatment (Para 6.7). Secondly, the specific boundaries of counselling confidentiality, based on the primacy of information shared between client and counsellor, rather than information available to any member of the team as a whole, are carefully demarcated and preserved. Under Para 6.25: 'All information obtained in the course of counselling should be kept confidential, subject to Paragraph 3.27, above.' (HFEA, 1993: 33) In turn, the crucial reference to Para 3.27 elaborates:

> If a member of the team receives information which is of such gravity that confidentiality *cannot* be maintained, he or she should use his or her own discretion, based on good professional practice, in deciding in what circumstances it should be discussed with the rest of the team. (1993: 16)

The *Code*, which has statutory authority, sets out a distinct role for counsellors and establishes fresh boundaries for handling confidential information, based on a *counselling* rather than a *medical* model. In fact, the early predominating concern for absolute confidentiality of *medical* information, based on the concerns of inadvertent breaches of sensitive information about donors or recipients of services, proved to be unworkable. It required further legislation to correct the balance. Under the original s.33 of the 1990 Act, clinicians were not even allowed to disclose information to a patient's GP. Disclosure was only permitted by consent of the *patient*. This could obviously present problems where a patient was admitted to a hospital for emergency treatment, and the law was subsequently revised to broaden the scope for legitimate disclosure to third parties (McHale, 1993a).

Practice issues in infertility counselling From a practice point of view, the *Code* sets out an admirable standard to follow. The need for counselling within the treatment and decision-making process is set out as one which should not be restricted to the early contact with the service, but, as with adoption, needs to extend throughout the contact with the Centre. Thus 'it may be imperative for the counselling to which patients are likely to be directed . . . to apprise patients of the results which they are likely to meet, and for the counselling to be available throughout the treatment cycle programme, and even afterwards' (Morgan and Lee, 1991: 17). In addition, 'It is possible that after many repeated, unsuccessful attempts to establish a pregnancy, counselling is more necessary than at the beginning' (1991: 150–1).

Concerns have been expressed that these high standards are not always applied in reality. The British Infertility Counselling Association 'has reported that in practice very few infertility clinics have professionally trained counsellors available. Those that do, offer such a limited service that only a small minority of patients can benefit from it' (Morgan and Lee, 1991: 148). It has been suggested that the mandatory offer of counselling is less likely to be taken up by clients in receiving a service from the private sector (Naish, 1994: 5). Centres may also discriminate against lesbian couples or single women, on the grounds of needing to consider the statutory grounds of the child's welfare, including the need for a father (1994: 20).

The purpose of counselling is described as sharing 'the client's task of looking at current and future choices and helping them move towards healing and acceptance at their pace' (1994: 14). One practitioner has described the parallels within infertility counselling that exist to bereavement work, given the powerful mood fluctuations that can occur due to 'the switchback of hope and disappointment that continues month after month' (1994: 18). Practice dilemmas with a legal dimension can also be experienced:

> There are times too when the counsellor feels torn between the requirements of doctors, patients, society and the law. Perhaps s/he possesses a fuller picture of the client than the clinic. So where does the counsellor stand who knows:
>
> - of Schedule 1 offences in the client's history which suggest a child might be at risk within this family (*Author's note*: Schedule 1 offences are serious offences against children under the Children and Young Persons Act 1933), or
> - that children of either partner have been removed or are in care, or
> - of health factors, mental or physical, which suggest the client would be put at serious risk by pregnancy or parenting? (Naish, 1994: 20–1)

Unlike the more specific issue of surrogacy, these dilemmas are not exclusive to the field of infertility counselling, but are classic issues of third party risk which are discussed more fully in Chapter 4. They do, however, illustrate how counselling material quickly challenges the established boundaries of the actual practice setting regarding confidentiality, client rights and the therapist's liability.

Developments in the provision of therapy

The first full statutory recognition of counselling has been in the fields of adoption and infertility. Starting from a rather narrow conception of counselling in adoption, and moving towards a more rounded one in infertility counselling over a period of 15 years, the comparison also suggests how public perceptions of counselling are now more informed by the views of counsellors themselves, for example, regarding roles and confidentiality. Thus the legislation on adoption counselling was influenced by the views of the British Association of Social Workers, whereas the law concerning the provision of infertility counselling bore the stamp of the British Association for Counselling. In both cases, the potential for a widening of the original brief, or what sociologists call 'net-widening', has occurred. New needs are identified and the pressure for counselling to respond to a wider range of situations begins to develop. It is also striking that both instances of statutory counselling provision revolve around the processes of releasing information and of decision-making in the context of family relationships, either past or future. However, counselling has also established itself in a wider range of settings, with less clear-cut legal recognition, but with a growing appreciation of its value to society. These settings include psychiatric and forensic or criminal care, HIV counselling, marital therapy, counselling in social work and health care, and counselling at work, which will now be briefly covered.

Mental health practice

Psychiatric care is sometimes seen to be distinct from the provision of therapy and counselling, and even to be counterposed to it, given the degree of compulsion that it may contain. Psychiatry may also be seen as relying too heavily on medication and physical treatments like electro-convulsive therapy, rather than on psychotherapeutic approaches as such. In fact, psychiatric care under the National Health Service provides a substantial amount of psychotherapy, as opposed to purely physical methods of treatment such as ECT. Therapy is provided, albeit within the context of a statutory framework and within a medical model of diagnosis and treatment. Critics of psychiatric care may take the position of counterposing therapy to medication. However, this may not be a completely convincing stance to adopt, when the focus is shifted to the relative *balance* of psychological and medical therapies for *specific* types of problems such as depression. One survey reported that roughly one third of a sample of patients wanted psychotherapy or counselling, but were unable to obtain it. While scores of satisfaction for those who did obtain counselling were high, they were also high for anti-depressants, and remained significant for major tranquillisers (Rogers et al., 1993: 146–62). Counselling and psychotherapy are provided by the NHS, although they are not available on demand. Therapeutic work is done by a wide variety of practitioners, including GPs, general and psychiatric nurses, community psychiatric nurses, clinical psychologists, hospital doctors and psychiatrists.

The case for therapists outside the NHS to acknowledge the value of the psychiatric services is put by Owen (1993). He makes a strong case for therapists outside the mental health services to have an understanding of how the system works. He argues that:

- certain groups of clients may be beyond the therapist's level of expertise, for example, those presenting with severe depression, psychosis and attempted suicide
- referral to community or emergency mental health services can be in the client's interests, by preventing unnecessary harm to themselves or others
- a basic knowledge of emergency procedures for mental health admission is a necessary part of competent therapeutic practice, in order for therapists to work ethically and safely (1993: 287–9)

The provision of psychiatric care is governed by the Mental Health Act 1983. As with the 1959 Act which preceded it, the emphasis is on community rather than hospital care, and on voluntary rather than compulsory admission for treatment. The operation of the Act is guided by a statutory *Code of Practice*, which does not have the full force of law. However, failure to abide by it can be cited as evidence in legal proceedings (DoH/ Welsh Office, 1993: Para 1.1). The Act sets out a series of safeguards for the rights of patients, including procedures for complaints to Mental Health Review Tribunals. While these are intended to protect patients' rights, this protection does not always

---

Box 1.1

Main emergency provisions of the Mental Health Act 1983

s.2 *Admission for assessment:* where a patient is seen to be in need of protection from causing harm to themself or to others, and they require detaining on the grounds of mental disorder, they can be admitted for 28 days on a compulsory basis. The 'section', as it is called, or being 'sectioned', needs to be authorised by two doctors, such as a consultant psychiatrist and the GP.

s.3 *Admission for treatment:* authorised on a similar basis to the above, initially lasts six months, and is extendable for a further six months. It is thereafter renewable on an annual basis, subject to review by the Mental Health Review Tribunal.

s.4 *Emergency admission for assessment:* this to be used only where it is not possible to obtain a section 2 admission. Authorised usually by the patient's GP, the section can be applied for by the patient's 'nearest relative' (closely defined by the Act), or by an Approved Social Worker from the local authority social services department.

(Source: Bluglass, 1984)

---

extend to children and young people in psychiatric care (see Chapter 7).

Mental illness as such is not defined by the Act, but is diagnosed by clinicians such as general practitioners and psychiatrists. Mental illness constitutes one basis for compulsory detention under the Mental Health Act, together with the additional categories of mental impairment, severe mental impairment and psychopathic disorder. (Mental impairment is otherwise more usually described as learning disability or learning difficulties by other semi-professional groups such as social workers.) Wherever possible, mental illness is treated in the community, or on the basis of voluntary admission to psychiatric hospital. The grounds for compulsory treatment most relevant to the work of therapists are set out in Box 1.1

Many therapists will perhaps be critical of compulsory psychiatric care, as being incompatible with the ethical principles of promoting client autonomy. However, it would seem to be consistent with good practice that therapists are informed about the basic principles of mental health and mental illness, and have a working knowledge of the services available and how to access them. They should be able to make an appropriate referral to such services when a client is experiencing problems or behaviour beyond their competence or expertise to help. (For detailed commentaries on mental health law, see Hoggett (1996) and Jones (1997). Training and consultancy is available from the Institute of Mental Health Law – see Resources section for details.)

One example, unfortunately not a fictitious one, is provided by David Reed in his autobiographical description of an experience of mental illness, in his book *Anna*. This is a harrowing account of his wife going through a psychotic breakdown. She was anxious to avoid hospitalisation in order to pursue alternative methods based on the ideas of her therapist, Landis, a follower of R.D. Laing.

Case Study: Therapeutic work with a psychotic and suicidal client

During the night, while staying at the therapeutic community, Anna attempts to strangle one of the children, Thomas. Reed writes:

> *Ought I to have abandoned the 'holiday' then and there? There could be no mistaking the seriousness of Anna's condition. What had once been only a threat to the children (the night she reported to the police station that she had murdered them) had now been physically enacted – at least attempted. If I hadn't woken?*
>
> *It was not simple obstinacy that made me continue though. Perhaps it was, on the contrary, a* new *determination. On the one hand I saw remote ECT-favouring doctors, on the other the idealistic self-concern of Landis' Community. Between them there was Anna; and more then than at any other moment in her psychosis I felt her need. There could be no doubt that in attempting to kill Thomas she was reaching the brink of extinction – for Thomas she loved without anxiety, reserve or guilt. Thomas represented her loving, open self: 'moon-face' as she called him. To kill him meant surely to kill the most good thing within herself – I felt despair could go no further, no deeper, or be more cathartic than that. And I felt no one else could or was even willing to understand or to help. (Reed, 1976: 106–7)*

(Two days later, Anna set fire to herself, dying in hospital five weeks later from 75% burns.)

The example poses in an extreme form the limits of human responsibility for another's safety and protection. The therapist involved is not criticised in any way for the attempt to work with the client in this manner. There is obviously no guarantee that referral to psychiatric services or admission to a psychiatric hospital could have avoided this tragic outcome. But the case does raise uncomfortable questions about:

- what level of knowledge or expertise in psychiatric issues does a therapist need to have?
- to what extent are therapists and their supervisors prepared for this level of distress by their training and supervision?
- on what basis do therapists consider the risks to the client, or to third parties?
- what would a 'reasonably competent practitioner' need to do in this situation to minimise their legal vulnerability?

In the short term, a therapist clearly needs to know how to gain access to psychiatric services in their area via referral to a client's GP, and how to contact an Approved Social Worker via their local authority social services department in the case of needing an acute emergency admission. The broader questions raised above concerning working with suicidal clients will be explored in more detail in Chapters 3 and 4.

Forensic and criminal aspects of counselling provision

A further area of legal recognition of the value of therapy, partly linked to psychiatric care discussed above, is to be found in the area of criminal law (Williams, 1996). Certain recent cases have highlighted the position of offenders where the need for treatment and therapy is seen by the courts to outweigh the need for simple punishment. In one case, a former captive of the Iraqi regime immediately prior to the Gulf War, experienced severe trauma by being used as a 'human shield' to protect key military installations. After his return home to the UK, the former captive was later charged with arson. He was ordered by the court to undergo six weeks of in-patient treatment in a secure unit at a psychiatric hospital, rather than simply receiving a sentence for the offence. Another former prisoner in the Gulf War sympathised with his colleague's position:

> 'I have terrible flashbacks', he said. 'I can turn at any time, a streak goes through me and I want to kill someone. I've had no counselling or help since I was freed, sometimes something makes me just want to lash out and I don't even want to stop myself. I can't explain it.' (*Guardian*, 3 November 1994)

With the wider legal acknowledgement of the phenomena of post-traumatic stress disorder, such options have become more available to persons appearing before the courts for offences attributable to their psychiatric condition (Pugh and Trimble, 1993; Scott and Stradling, 1992). A remand for a hospital admission can be ordered by the court for a report, under s.35, or for treatment, under s.36 of the Mental Health Act 1983.

For non-custodial options, the main legislation for adults is the Criminal Justice Act 1991, which emphasises community-based sentences for minor offences. For children and young people, the relevant laws are the Children and Young Persons Acts of 1933 and 1969, and the Criminal Justice Act 1991. Therapy can be ordered via the courts via a Supervision Order for offenders under 18 years, lasting up to three years, monitored by a social worker, or by a Probation Order for adults. Such Orders may include a requirement for psychiatric treatment if medical evidence shows that he or she has a condition which requires, and is susceptible to, treatment. The person's consent is required only if the offender is 14 or over (Faulk, 1994: 23).

In another case coming before the courts, a young woman who had abducted a baby was sentenced to three years probation, rather than to imprisonment, with a requirement that she live at a psychiatric hospital specialising in an appropriate form of therapy. Such Probation Orders, lasting from six months to three years, can be made for young people over the age of 16, and for adults. They can include requirement for psychiatric treatment and for attending a probation centre, depending upon the local availability of resources. Therapy may be provided by taking part in groups, which is frequently the case for sex offenders. Alternatively, there are some therapies that aim to deal directly with the offender's behaviour – such as treatment for substance abuse or developing clients' skills in anger management (Faulk, 1994: 18).

HIV/AIDS counselling
Counselling in the field of HIV and AIDS is an area of growing recognition, without as yet possessing a clear statutory framework (Harris and Haigh, 1995; Kloss, 1989). Counselling is prescribed for HIV testing, but is not limited to advising clients on the options or alternatives available. Bond describes a wide continuum of counselling services related to AIDS and HIV, including pre- and post-test counselling for the 'worried well', and for the 'HIV and

well'; counselling for persons with HIV who have a treatable or chronic illness; preparation for dying and bereavement; counselling for partners/carers of the person with HIV; group counselling; and bereavement counselling (Bond, 1992c: 17). There is a range of important legal issues relating to this complex area of work, including that of clients making a will, for example (Bor et al., 1992: 137–8).

Confidentiality is another crucial issue for counselling in the field of AIDS and HIV, not least because the former is a contagious and life-threatening illness, with serious implications for the individual's emotional and physical well-being. It also affects their employment, financial and insurance prospects, because of the threat of the stigma, discrimination and even outright physical harassment which can accompany the diagnosis. The case of Doctors *X. v. Y.* [1988] has been the most public airing by the courts of the issues regarding confidentiality of medical information regarding a positive diagnosis of AIDS. This affirmed the right for individual privacy to override the conflicting right of newspapers to publish information of interest to the public. (For a fuller discussion of the case, see Chapter 4.)

The other manifestation of confidentiality related to AIDS and HIV concerns the therapist's responsibility to break confidentiality where a third party is seen to be at risk. The classic dilemma is where a client is known to be HIV or to have AIDS, but refuses to inform a current sexual partner or needle-sharer. Bond cites the example of the dilemma as explored by John Green, Chief Clinical Psychologist at St Mary's Hospital, London, where the latter describes his work with two separate individuals. Both of these were initially reluctant to tell their partner of their condition, but were assisted to do so via counselling. The focus of the therapeutic work in both cases was in identifying the underlying reasons or emotions for *not* telling, and in working through these feelings to reach a new perception of the possibilities of telling the partners concerned (Green, 1989). The cases do not resolve the ethical and legal dilemmas facing the therapist who is *unable* to achieve such a positive therapeutic outcome. Is the therapist then required by law to break confidentiality, where there is an appreciable risk to a third party which the client is unwilling to reduce or remove?

The US experience is instructive here. Given the huge impact of AIDS in the USA, the issue has been widely debated in the counselling press. Actual case law in the USA on the subject of counsellor liability for failure to warn a potential AIDS patient is rare. There is one reported case to date, where the outcome is still pending (ACA, 1995). Therapist liabilities and responsibilities in this area are explored further in Chapter 4.

Social work
Counselling has been explicitly identified as an essential part of the social worker's role by the Barclay Report (1982: 41). However, given the legal authority which is an inescapable part of the social worker's role, it may be more correct to describe the social worker as using counselling or therapeutic *skills*, according to the BAC definitions (1989). This is not to deny the range and value of the therapeutic work that many social workers provide. However, such therapy is increasingly being displaced by the priorities of child protection and case management. The time needed for therapeutic work with child and adult survivors of abuse is being put under pressure by an ever-growing range of additional statutory duties.

The Children Act 1989 has codified the responsibilities of social workers for children and families, focusing on the target group of 'children in need'. This includes children and young people under the age of 18 who

- suffer from disadvantage
- require services to avoid impaired development
- have a disability

Counselling as a service is directly linked to this group of 'children in need', with family centres intended to be the main providers of counselling (Jenkins, 1993b). Family centres are a progressive development away from more traditional child-centred nurseries, and a move towards a more open partnership with families requiring support. For children in residential accommodation, the need for skilled counselling to be provided for children and young people with distinct needs relating to disability, sexual orientation, race and culture has been explicitly recognised by the authorities (Department of Health, 1991b: Para 9.53).

For the therapist, some of the key issues relating to the Children Act 1989 may include those in Box 1.2.

The Children Act 1989, under s.8, also contains significant provisions for the court's decision-making regarding parental

---

Box 1.2

Children Act 1989

s.17   duty of the local authority to safeguard and promote the welfare of children in need

s.22   duty to give due consideration to the child's wishes and feelings in making decisions

s.26   duty to provide a complaints system for children and families

s.44   power to remove and retain a child in their care, on application to the court (Emergency Protection Order)

s.46   police powers to remove and detain a child 'at risk' in police protection for 72 hours

s.47   duty of the local authority to investigate cases where a child is likely to suffer 'significant harm'

---

responsibility, the residence of children, and other specific provision, which therapists may need to be aware of in working with complex divorce and contact cases (Allen, 1992). The Children Act 1989, taken together with the United Nations Convention on the Rights of the Child of the same year, marks a major extension of the rights of children and young people. It broadens the scope for counsellors working with them to treat the *child* as client, under the *Gillick* principle. Some of the practice dilemmas associated with this stance are considered in more detail in Chapter 7.

Community care
Another potentially relevant area of law for therapy concerns the provision of community care. Under s.47 of the NHS and Community Care Act 1990, there is a responsibility for local authority social services departments to assess the needs of persons requiring services in the community (Robertson and Tudor, 1993). Carers can also request assessment of their own needs for support services, under s.I of the Carers (Recognition and Services) Act 1995. These assessments could include a need for therapy. A social services department could contract a therapist to provide a set number of counselling sessions for a particular client under this provision, which is similar in some ways to the US system of insurance-funded 'managed care'. Therapists accepting such contracts for work need to be fully aware, and to inform their clients, that part of the contract with the local authority may require more or less detailed reports on the client's progress.

Client–therapist confidentiality may thus be extended to include passing information back to the agency funding the therapy. This suggests a need for clear contracting with all parties concerned at the outset. In the USA, the system of 'managed care' has brought a number of legal and ethical problems for therapists in its wake (Appelbaum, 1993).

The distinction between *assessment* of the need for therapy, and its *provision* is an important principle within the philosophy of community care. Assessment is meant to be needs-led rather than resource-led, although there is a tension here which many local authorities are finding hard to manage successfully, due to financial cutbacks and limited resources. Some service users have successfully challenged the results of assessments in the courts. These challenges have been based on principles drawn from public law, namely the law regulating the behaviour of public authorities (Mandelstam and Schwehr, 1995). This could include the use of judicial review, to request the courts to review a decision which is illegal, unreasonable or which has been improperly arrived at (Public Law Project, 1994). A body of case law regarding community care is developing, setting out key principles of client entitlement which can be consulted for guidance (*R. v. Gloucestershire C.C.*, (1995)).

Marital counselling

Counselling and therapy with couples is a long established area of practice in the UK, as shown by the activities of Relate and other relationship counselling organisations such as Marriage Care (Lewis et al., 1992). Couple therapy provides one of the closest connections existing between the worlds of therapy and the law, now formally acknowledged in the provisions of the Family Law Act 1996. The very nature of the work requires the development of an informed understanding of, and a close working relationship with, legal processes such as divorce and conciliation. Parkinson explains how bruising it can feel for couples to shift their private conflicts to a very public arena when considering divorce or separation.

> What feels like a state of anarchy at a personal level may then be exposed to an alien public world – a world in which lawyers communicate with each other about their clients' personal affairs in language that is unfamiliar, intimidating and, for some people, wholly incomprehensible. (1991: 217)

Box 1.3

Family Law Act 1996

s.1   support for the institution of marriage; parties to be encouraged to take all steps, including marriage counselling, to save a marriage

s.5   irretrievable breakdown of marriage signalled by either party making a 'statement of marital breakdown'

s.7   statement followed by nine months (15 months if children under 16 involved) 'period for reflection and consideration'

s.8   three months prior to making statement, parties to have attended 'information meeting' with an independent and qualified person. Couple may attend jointly or separately to obtain information about separation and divorce, marriage counselling and mediation. Marital counselling to be provided under prescribed provisions, and may be free

s.11 welfare of children to be paramount consideration of court

s.13 court power to direct parties to attend mediation meeting

---

The role of counsellors in this process can be to help couples resolve conflict within their relationship, or to find ways of separating which are least damaging for all parties concerned. The number of divorces in England, Wales and Northern Ireland rose to 167,000 in 1993 (CSO, 1996: 58). The human and social cost of divorce has increasingly focused government attention on the role of marital counselling, as a support for marriages under pressure, and as an acceptable form of social engineering (James and Wilson, 1991). The White Paper on divorce provided firm recognition of the value of mediation in divorce proceedings, as a valuable measure for couples, children and society generally. Family mediation is defined as 'a process in which an impartial third party, the mediator, assists couples considering separation or divorce to deal with the arrangements which need to be made for the future' (Lord Chancellor's Department, 1995: Para 5.4). Recognised as a valuable process for resolving difficult conflicts, amendments to the Family Law Bill were proposed to make this counselling a compulsory aspect of divorce procedure (*Guardian*, 1 May 1996). Specified provision is made for giving parties information on marriage counselling under the Family Law Act 1996 (see Box 1.3).

The actual terms used to describe the options available for couples considering divorce or separation can often appear to be

confusing. Parkinson (1991: 223–5) suggests useful distinctions
between:

- *conciliation*: voluntary settling of disputes over contact and
  custody concerning the couple's children
- *mediation*: voluntary settling of disputes over financial affairs
  such as maintenance, finances and property
- *arbitration*: disputes are resolved by couples agreeing to refer
  them to an independent third party

There has been a growth of skilled and experienced conciliation services at a local level (see addresses in Resources
section). One significant legal development has been the need to
actively consider the views and wishes of the children involved in
divorce proceedings, as required under the Children Act 1989.
Carolin (1995) describes child-centred ways of working with
children and young people which acknowledge their needs as
being separate from their parents. These approaches are based on
the notion of the child's right to have their voice heard according
to the *Gillick* principle.

Confidentiality is a concept of critical importance in marital
counselling. In therapeutic terms, it is vital for the therapist to
preserve a strict neutrality between couples who may be experiencing intense conflict with each other, and who may be actively
looking for allies and support within the counselling relationship
itself. As an agency, Relate, for example, has clear policy guidelines
and training for volunteers on the issue of confidentiality (Tyndall,
1986). From a legal perspective, marital counselling is unusual in
possessing a degree of 'privilege' for therapeutic activities which is
based in case law rather than statute. This 'privilege' protects the
therapist from being required to disclose confidential material to
the courts. This limited but important form of legal recognition for
therapeutic confidentiality is discussed in Chapter 4.

Counselling in primary care
A major growth area for counselling in the 1990s has been in the
field of General Practice and primary health care. While reflecting
a demand for responsive and accessible therapy at a local level, it
has also been possible due to changes in funding arrangements
for General Practices, allied to the reforms introduced by the NHS
overall. Funding changes include:

- the Practice Staff Payment Scheme, where the Family Health Service Authority reimburses the cost of GPs employing staff. Prior to the GP contract scheme, this used to be guaranteed at 70% of the cost, but now varies.
- the General Practice Fundholding Scheme: Fundholding practices can pay for a counsellor from practice staff funds. Since 1993, counselling has been added to the list of services which fundholders may purchase from their Hospital Services Budget (Ball, 1995: 10)

There is increasing interest in analysing the cost-effectiveness of counselling and other therapies within the NHS, with a major Review of Psychotherapy in the NHS due to report in 1996 (Roth and Fonagy, 1996; Tolley and Rowland, 1995). Practice issues for therapists working in primary health care and other medical settings can include:

- clarifying boundaries of counselling confidentiality as opposed to medical confidentiality
- recognising indicators of mental ill-health, self-harm and potential suicide
- maintaining appropriate liaison with other professionals, and making prompt referrals (CMS, 1995; Daines et al., 1996; East, 1995; Higgs and Dammers, 1992; SDHA/DCC, 1996)

Clarifying legal accountability for the work of counsellors in primary health care is a complex issue, which is discussed in Chapter 2.

Counselling at work

Counselling at work has emerged as another of the growth areas for therapy, against a background of rising job insecurity, and changing conditions of work and employment. According to the *Annual Report* of Kenneth Calman, Chief Medical Officer, unpublished research suggests that minor psychiatric disorder, associated with stress, is now the second most common cause of absence from work lasting more that 21 days (DoH, 1995b). Mental health problems as a whole are said to be costing industry as much as £26 billion a year (*Guardian*, 28 September 1995).

One of industry's responses has been to make increasing use of counselling, whether provided in-house, or via contracted

Employee Assistance Programmes (EAPs) (Reddy, 1987). This provision has grown particularly since the realisation by major employers that counselling is cost-effective in reducing employee dissatisfaction and labour turnover (Cooper et al., 1990). An additional factor has perhaps been the case of John Walker, who won damages against his employer, Northumberland County Council, following a second nervous breakdown caused by pressure of work. Employers, keen to avoid liability as well as motivated by a genuine concern for staff, have increasingly looked to counselling as an effective means of reducing stress levels amongst staff.

However, staff counselling comes with its own ethical and legal dilemmas for therapists (Sugarman, 1992; Wise, 1988). Sugarman identifies five ethical issues for the work-based counsellor:

- identifying the extent to which the aims of the organisation over and above the aims of counselling compromise counselling's ethical foundation
- identifying any points at which the counselling provision benefits the organisation at the individual's expense
- identifying any points at which the organisation exceeds its right to control aspects of the employee's behaviour
- negotiating what is understood by the term 'confidentiality' and the conditions under which it will and will not be maintained
- identifying whether the resources are sufficient and appropriate to doing more good than harm, and in what ways the origins of the resources compromise the aims of the service.
  (Sugarman, 1992: 72)

There is a useful distinction to be drawn between voluntary and mandatory referrals, in terms of clarifying any resultant limits to confidentiality. Employees may, as a consequence, have greater confidence in counselling provided by external agencies (Sugarman, 1992: 69–70). Employee Assistance Programmes may have greater appeal to staff, given that there may not be such immediate concerns from staff about confidentiality. However, the limits to confidentiality may still remain where the client's behaviour conflicts with the interests of the organisation. Megranahan gives the example of the limits to confidentiality where an employee is committing a serious offence, such as a bank clerk stealing cash, where the counsellor needs to inform the employee before breaking confidentiality. The preferred route is clearly for the employee themselves to take the issue up with the employer (Megranahan, 1989: 281–3). There may be a contractual require-ment for the counsellor to pass on information to the employer where the counsellor is working for an EAP. As will be explored in Chapter 4, this can put the counsellor in a difficult and legally vulnerable position, liable *both* to pass information on to the employer under contract, *and* potentially liable to the client for breach of confidentiality.

Working as a therapist for an Employee Assistance Programme can also bring ethical and legal problems of a different kind. One 24-hour EAP helpline covers relationship difficulties; parenting concerns; marital problems; substance abuse such as alcohol or drugs; stress; health or psychological problems; financial worries; legal disputes and career issues. Counsellors working on such a helpline may actually be dispensing information to clients about complex legal matters. Issues of liability for negligent advice can be readily identified here, which need further clarification (see Chapter 3).

Overall, despite the research evidence to the contrary, it may be perceived by some organisations that counselling is the last resort of underperforming staff. East gives the example in a health setting of a nurse teacher talking about counselling for staff: 'Managers sometimes try to ferret out information about staff. This has increased since the Clothier Report. Mental health problems are a real taboo subject' (1995: 60).

The reference to the Clothier Report might be little known outside the nursing profession. It refers to the inquiry into the deaths caused by Beverly Allitt, an enrolled nurse on a children's ward of a general hospital in 1991. Beverly Allitt was sentenced to life imprisonment for committing four murders and three attempted murders. She was diagnosed as suffering from a serious personality disorder, although the Inquiry took issue with the presumed diagnosis of 'Munchausen's Syndrome by Proxy'. The Report recommended 'that no candidate for nursing in whom there is evidence of major personality disorder should be employed in the profession' (Clothier, 1994: 129). While per-sonality disorder can be notoriously difficult to detect in some cases in the short term, the Report rang warning bells about maintaining an alert stance towards potentially dangerous staff.

In Para 5.5.16, 'Problems of diagnosing personality disorder in staff', it was suggested to the Inquiry that 'excessive absence through sickness, excessive use of counselling or medical facilities, or self-harming behaviour such as attempted suicide, self-laceration or eating disorder are better guides than psychological testing' (1994: 84). 'Excessive use of counselling' remains a worryingly subjective criterion for evaluating staff liability or underperformance. It remains to be seen how far this concept may be taken up by other organisations using counselling services to address problems in the workplace.

Summary

Legal recognition is a key element of the process of therapy achieving greater status as a profession or semi-profession. Areas which are problematic for therapy at present derive from the essentially 'private' and confidential nature of its work, which may mask bad or abusive practice on occasion. Wider social recognition also raises questions about the nature and adequacy of the training and qualifications required of therapists. To date, in the UK, statutory recognition has been achieved in the areas of adoption counselling and infertility counselling, with significant developments over time in terms of the different perceptions of its role and purpose. From more established areas of practice in psychiatric care, social work, and marital counselling, therapy and counselling have gained increasing recognition in the fields of primary health care, HIV counselling, sentencing by the courts and counselling at work. Clarifying the complex relationship of therapy to the law requires further exploration of the legal context in which therapists work, which will be outlined in the following chapter.

Discussion points

1   What options would you consider as the therapist in the case of 'Anna'? What ethical and legal factors would influence your choices?
2   Should the use of specific terms such as 'counsellor', 'psychotherapist' and 'therapist' be restricted by law? What positive or negative effects might this have on the status of therapeutic practice in society?

3 What does the comparison of adoption records counselling and infertility counselling suggest about the changing status of counselling and therapy? What other areas of counselling practice deserve specific recognition by the law?

4 The US example suggests that legal recognition for therapists carries with it an increased risk of hostile litigation by clients. Is this a price that therapists in the UK should be prepared to pay?

5 Where ethical principles and the law are in conflict, which should the therapist follow and why? Discuss an example relating to third party risk or child abuse or potential suicide.

2

The Legal Context of Therapy

The legal system in the United Kingdom is complex and many-sided. The first part of this chapter will offer a brief guide to some of the **content and structure of the law**, or rather to the main areas likely to be of interest to therapists, such as tort, contract and the responsibilities of service providers. This is followed by exploring issues of **communicating information**, such as data protection, copyright and defamation. A final section looks at responsibilities relating to **service provision and employment** regarding employers' liability, the status of past criminal convictions and legislation concerning discrimination. The structure of the court system and more practical aspects of going to court or claiming damages are dealt with in Chapter 6.

Content and structure of the law

The actual language used by the law gives a clue to the origins of the legal system. Thus, 'law' itself is a Norse word, as in the Danelaw from school history books. The terms 'jury' and 'verdict' come from Latin (*iuro*: I swear; *vere dicere*: to speak truly). The word 'tort' comes from French, meaning simply a civil wrong. Each of these terms provides a clue to the historical combination of different systems of law – Anglo-Saxon, Roman and Norman – into the current system of law.

It needs to be said at the outset that there are quite different systems of law in the UK for Scotland, Northern Ireland, England and Wales. The main focus of this chapter is on the law relating to England and Wales, with some reference to specific features of the law in Scotland where this is relevant. There is also some reference to the law relating to therapy in the USA, as this system has some similarities with law in the UK, being based on a mixture of statute and common law. However, US law possesses a very wide diversity of law at the level of the individual states, for example in terms of law regarding therapists' duty to warn third parties, the registration of therapists, and therapists' rights to privilege (Hay, 1991). Legal principles applying in some states in the USA are of interest to therapists in the UK, but often have no immediate relevance for law in England and Wales, except as a point for comparison and discussion.

Statute

The term *statute* refers to actual pieces of primary legislation passed by Parliament, such as the Mental Health Act 1983, Children Act 1989, Consumer Protection Act 1987 and Data Protection Act 1984, all of which have a bearing on the work of therapists in different ways. In some cases, secondary legislation operates in the form of Statutory Instruments, authorised by the relevant Minister.

Common law

Common law is a term used in contrast to *codes* of law. Codes seek to regulate a wide variety of circumstances on the basis of set principles. The European system of law is based on firstly Roman, and then Napoleonic codes of law, which both express this centralising principle. Arguably the European Union (EU) now picks up this mantle, hence some of the tensions evident between EC Directives and UK law. The latter is based more on a combination of statute and common law. Common law is often described as law made by judges, based on their practice and experience, so the law evolves on an empirical basis, adapting to new circumstances, without necessarily requiring fresh legislation. Hence, 'in common law countries judges adapt the past to the present from actual experience of cases, with a measure of legislative interaction' (Fleming, 1994: 210). The relevance of this to therapists is that large and important areas of law are not codified in statute in England and Wales, but operate on the basis of established principles evolved through common law. These areas include much of the law relating to contract, confidentiality, and tort.

Case law

The concept of case law is important both in relation to the evolution of common law, and in terms of influencing future legislation. Principles, for example, concerning the rights of mature children to confidential medical treatment, were expressed in the so-called *Gillick* case, which later influenced the Children Act 1989. Another lesser-known instance, the *Gaskin* case, helped establish the rights of a wide range of service users to their files, across the fields of health, education and social services. Statute will have greater weight than case law, unless the case in question, such as *Gillick*, clarifies an important principle of law for future reference.

Civil and criminal law

A useful starting point is the exploration of the fundamental differences between civil and criminal law, which are set out in Table 2.1.

In Scotland, there are certain differences from the outline in Table 2.1. Criminal cases are brought to the court by the Procurator Fiscal. The levels of the court system include District Courts at the local level, Sheriff's Court at regional level, and the High Court of Justiciary for appeals. In criminal trials, verdicts can include 'not proven' as well as guilty or not guilty.

Civil law provides remedies for resolving disputes between private individuals, such as those concerning property, child and family proceedings and the protection of the interests of individuals, such as privacy, personal reputation and confidentiality. The criminal law operates to punish breaches of the law within the wider community. Two key elements of the criminal law are proof of the committing of a guilty act (*actus reus*), and of the possession of *intent*, or of a guilty mind (*mens rea*). In rare cases, a person can be found not responsible for their actions by reason of insanity, under the McNaughten rules, based on the case of the individual who attempted to kill the Prime Minister, Sir John Peel, in 1843 (Faulk, 1994; Owens, 1995).

Tort law

The most likely area of relevance to therapists, generally speaking, will be in proceedings under the *civil* law, rather than the criminal law. In civil law, the question of *tort*, or *delict* in Scotland,

Table 2.1

Comparison of Features of Civil & Criminal Law
(England and Wales)

Civil Law	Criminal Law
Proceedings can be brought by private interest to secure a direct remedy	Prosecution normally brought by public agency, i.e. Crown Prosecution Service
Parties referred to as plaintiff and respondent or defendant	Parties referred to as prosecutor and the accused or the defendant
Courts include Tribunals, Magistrates, County and High Court, Court of Appeal, House of Lords	Courts include Magistrates, Crown and High Court, Court of Appeal, House of Lords
Case proven on 'balance of probabilities', i.e. it is *more* probable than not that this is true	Case proven to be 'beyond reasonable doubt', i.e. more stringent criteria of proof
Leads to judgement or order for:	Leads to acquittal or sentence, i.e.:
• unsuccessful party to pay damages • party to take action, e.g. comply with contract • party to stop activity, e.g. molesting another person	• fine, custody, etc. • criminal conviction

is a key area of law to understand. The term 'tort' simply means 'wrong' in French. In legal terms it refers to a civil wrong inflicted upon another person such as a neighbour, who wishes to correct this or to seek compensation. Thus 'the general gist is damage or injury arising to one person from unfair, careless or unreasonable action (or inaction) by another' (Fleming, 1994: 165). In England and Wales, the parties involved in tort cases are referred to as the plaintiff and defendant. In Scotland, the parties are known as the defender and the pursuer. This chapter will give a brief outline of the concept of tort, which will be explored more thoroughly with regard to professional negligence in Chapter 3, with specific reference to therapists.

Negligence law Within tort law, the concept of negligence derives from the landmark case of *Donoghue v. Stevenson* [1932], where the plaintiff found a decomposed snail in a bottle of ginger beer, and accordingly sued the manufacturer for damages. The case confirmed what is known as the 'neighbour' principle, namely that one should take care not to cause harm to one's neighbour through any positive act or omission. Proving a case based on tort requires the fulfilment of three conditions:

■ existence of a duty of care to the client
■ breach of that duty
■ resultant harm as a consequence of the breach

Professional negligence law Professional negligence relates to the specific application of this general principle to those working in a special, professional relationship, and the duty that follows from this to act with care regarding the client. It is interesting to note that, in the legal field, a barrister is immune from negligence while acting as an advocate. Solicitors who are in a contractual relationship with their clients are liable both in tort and in contract, except when directly acting as an advocate (Pannett, 1992, 44).

The notion of *fault* is a function of the *objective* standard of care which is required, rather than one based on the personal qualities of the individual. For example, in the case of *Nettleship v. Western* [1971], it was held that an inexperienced learner driver should be judged by the standards of the 'reasonable driver', despite lacking the experience of the reasonable driver. In this situation, a learner driver crashed into a lamppost, injuring the passenger in the front seat of the car. The learner driver was convicted of driving 'without due care and attention'. The Court of Appeal held that the standard required, even of a learner driver, was that of a reasonably competent driver (Pannett, 1992: 65).

Standard of care This standard of care is based on the idea of the 'reasonable man', or what is described as an *objective* standard (Pannett, 1992: 64–5). The implication for professional standards that derives from this, referring to the case of the learner driver above, is that 'the inexperienced professional is negligent if he does not achieve the standards of a reasonably competent and experienced person exercising the particular skill of his/her profession' (1992: 71). A further illustrative example here is that of the junior doctor in the case of *Wilsher v. Essex Area Health Authority* [1988]. Here, in looking after a premature baby in the special care unit, the junior doctor mistakenly injected a catheter into the plaintiff's umbilical vein, as opposed to his artery. This contributed to an overdose of oxygen, associated with the plaintiff's later development of blindness. However, the standard of care applied in establishing negligence was that of a *reasonably competent* doctor holding a post in a baby care unit, rather than simply that of an inexperienced junior.

So how is the standard to be expected of a *therapist* to be decided by a court, which may be unfamiliar with the reasonable expectations of a counsellor working, for example, with a suicidal client? The answer, as will be seen, is by determining the appropriate standard for the profession, or for a significant part of that profession, by calling expert witnesses, to establish the relevant standard to be applied by the court.

Problem of proving causation Breach of a duty of care may be one factor, but the real problem, in many tort cases, is resolving the issue of *causation*, or proving that the lack of care actually *caused* the client's worsened depression, or suicide attempt, or other adverse effect. For causation, the first test is that of the 'but for' test. In other words, *but for* this negligence, would this result have occurred? The second test is that of *foreseeability*, so that the consequences should be capable of having been reasonably *anticipated*. This does not exclude the 'eggshell-skull' rule, where the plaintiff is particularly susceptible to damage, unknown to the defendant, and suffers damage which makes worse a pre-existing condition, such as someone breaking their skull with a light blow. The defendant here is liable for the *additional, unforseeable* damage caused. This ruling has been applied to the idea of an 'egg-shell personality', where the injury to the plaintiff aggravates a pre-existing nervous condition (*Malcolm v. Broadhurst* [1970]). In this case, the husband and wife were injured by the defendant's negligent driving. The accident caused an adverse personality change in the husband, and worsened the wife's pre-existing nervous condition. The defendant was judged to be liable for the wife's loss of earnings, as the psychological injury was forseeable. (Damages are discussed in Chapter 6.)

This outline of tort law in Box 2.1 raises a number of issues of concern to therapists. The existence of a duty of care to clients is probably already well known by practitioners. What is less clear may be the actual *standard* of care or practice to be applied. This

---

Box 2.1

Action for tort against therapists

- proving a tort or civil wrong requires:
  - existence of duty of care, e.g. by therapist to client
  - breach of duty
  - resultant harm to client
- standard of care based on what it is 'reasonable' to expect
- standard established via evidence of expert witnesses
- standard expected of a trainee may be the same as for a competent practitioner
- damages awarded for foreseeable damage, as decided by the court
- damages may also cover additional, unforeseen damage, if client has vulnerable condition or personality

---

issue is explored in more detail in Chapter 3, with case examples. The possibility that the standard of a competent practitioner is still the one to be applied to a student or trainee therapist is perhaps of concern. The best measure to be taken here would be to ensure that students are closely supervised in their practice, and not given work far beyond their level of training or expertise. Finally, although it will be seen that proving a case brought under tort is difficult for the client, it needs to be borne in mind that many of the clients in therapy may well have a vulnerable personality, or have a predisposition towards anxiety or depression. Best practice and prudence in a legal sense would suggest that therapists avoid doing anything which would damage their clients, or which would cause additional damage to an already vulnerable person.

Assault, battery and harassment
It could be that followers of more physical or tactile methods of therapy may need to consider issues of trespass on the person, assault and battery, to avoid unnecessary complications arising later on. Trespass to the person may consist of:

- assault and battery, or
- false imprisonment

Assault and battery *Assault* can include a threat, or a reasonable fear and apprehension of immediate violence or battery. *Battery* must include some application of actual force. It involves the unlawful application of force to another, such as touching someone without their consent or making an uninvited sexual advance, even when the other person may be unaware of this, because of being asleep or drugged. Battery does *not* include the normal, unavoidable touching which is part of everyday life. *Reasonable force*, or what is seen to be necessary and proportionate, can be used by a person to defend themselves against unlawful violence, as in the example given below.

Recourse to the criminal law may be necessary where a therapist assaults a client, or where a client seeks to assault or harass a therapist in the course of his or her work. Assaults by clients on therapists may be rarely reported, but do sometimes occur. In psychiatric care, nurses and doctors are the subject of attack, as are social workers and probation officers going about their work. In March 1994, Georgina Robinson, a physiotherapist, was killed by a patient who was seeking revenge for his treatment by the medical profession. Therapists working in private practice may also be at risk. Bob Cooke, a psychotherapist, was subjected to an unprovoked attack at his clinic by the aggrieved partner of a client, who felt that the therapy being provided was breaking up the couple's relationship. The man attacked Bob Cooke with a spanner, badly bruising the therapist's head and shoulders, while accusing him of 'brainwashing' his client. The client's partner was later jailed for 14 weeks for this attack (*Guardian*, 15 March 1994).

False imprisonment Could be held to apply where a client is physically prevented from leaving a therapy session, as was alleged in the case of a group therapy meeting attended by a distressed client (BBC, 1992).

Harassment Harassment of therapists may also take other, less physically damaging, but equally threatening forms. In very rare cases, it may be that the client or patient is suffering from delusions about a fantasised romantic relationship with the therapist, defined as De Clerambault's syndrome, which leads the client to pursue and harass the therapist without due cause (Gelder et al., 1989: 337–8). In cases where a therapist is harassed by a current or former client, a civil procedure, such as obtaining a court injunction, will provide some degree of protection. One consultant psychiatrist received a stream of telephone calls at home at all hours, and a barrage of unordered taxis and parcels, from a patient with a grievance against her (*Observer*, 24 September 1995). Despite obtaining a court injunction, bricks were thrown through the doctor's windows, and fire engines were called to her home address. Ultimately, the patient was given a prison sentence of six months for breaking the court injunction. The prison sentence was suspended at first, but then enacted when further breaches of the injunction occurred (MPS, 1995).

The Medical Protection Society has developed substantial experience in advising practitioners in how to protect themselves from this situation. Sumerling (1996) indicates that police protection is unlikely to be provided unless there is an actual occurrence of violence against the therapist. Some of the possible defensive measures to be taken could include:

■ civil injunction, breach of which can be dealt with by the court
■ prosecution for assault or battery, which needs to be initiated within six months of an attack
■ action for nuisance such as 'watching and besetting', i.e. lying in wait for the therapist
■ action for obscene, annoying or offensive phone calls under Telecommunications Act 1984 and Criminal Justice Act 1991
■ action for sending indecent, grossly offensive, threatening or false information under the Malicious Communications Act 1988
■ action for using abusive or threatening words or behaviour under s. 4, Public Order Act 1986
■ action against 'stalking' under the Protection from Harassment Act (1997)

Hopefully, such responses will not be necessary in the vast majority of cases, but it is important that therapists know of the possible defences available to them under the law, to help protect their privacy and security in the face of an unreasonable and threatening client. Personal security for therapists is often not taken seriously enough. For example, in the related field of health care, one union survey found that more than half of employees interviewed had suffered violence, threats or serious abuse in the previous two years, with 7% needing medical aid (*Guardian*, 17 April 1996). It is worth considering advice from specialist organisations with expertise in the field, such as the Suzy Lamplugh Trust (see Resources section for address).

Gathering evidence of harassment may be an important step, either in convincing an employer of the threat, persuading the client to desist, or in preparing for possible legal action. Sumerling (1996) provides some useful suggestions, such as:

- keep any evidence, such as poison pen letters, messages left on answer machines
- carefully record events and incidents after they occur
- respond to threatening clients in a calm, professional manner
- seek expert professional advice without delay
- do not minimise or underestimate the personal risks involved

Using contracts

> *Driftwood*: . . . just you put your name right down there and the deal is – uh – legal.
>
> *Forelo*: I forgot to tell you. I can't write.
>
> *Driftwood*: Well, that's all right. There's no ink in the pen. But, listen, it's a contract isn't it?
>
> (Marx Brothers, *A Night at the Opera*, MGM/UA 1992)

Like the Marx Brothers, many therapists are more likely to deal with verbal rather than written contracts. Still, contract represents one of the key areas of law that therapists need to understand. Contracts have a purpose not only for setting out the respective obligations of therapist and client, but are increasingly used by voluntary organisations providing counselling and other services to local government, as part of the contracting out provisions of the Local Government Act 1988 (Woolf, 1991; 1992). As with all legal matters, there is a certain amount of mystique concerning the complexity of contract law, but the essentials can be stated fairly briefly (Adirondack and MacFarlane, 1992; Painter and Lawson, 1990).

Requirements of contract Contract is one of the areas covered largely by common law, rather than solely by statute. Contracts for the sale of goods have been regulated since the Sale of Goods Act 1893, a consolidating piece of legislation which tied together earlier legal enactments. There are four conditions required for a contract to exist:

- legal capacity of persons involved
- firm offer and unequivocal acceptance
- clear intention of parties to create a legally binding agreement
- contract is supported by consideration, an exchange of goods or services for payment

To explain these points in more detail, the persons involved must have legal capacity, so that they are not mentally disordered, drunk, or aged under 18 years. There must be a firm offer and unequivocal acceptance. The acceptance must be oral, written or implied by the contract. Any acceptance must be absolute and unqualified, and cannot be withdrawn once made. Making a counter offer or conditional offer rejects the first, which cannot then be revived by an attempt to accept the first offer. For example, a therapy centre is offered for sale, priced at £200,000. A potential buyer offers £180,00. If this is rejected, the seller is not then obliged to accept a second offer from the same person of £200,000.

A contract must be supported by *consideration*, or, in other words, each party must *give* something or *do* something to or for the other. The considerations provided do not necessarily have to be equal in value. It must be clear from the terms of the agreement that the parties intended to create a legally binding agreement. Where the intention is unclear, a court will decide. Informal agreements for purely social or domestic arrangements are excluded. A contract between businesses is intended to be binding, unless expressly agreed otherwise. As the rock star George Michael discovered in his legal dispute with the record company Sony, a contract, however irksome, is a contract.

The doctrine of 'privity of contract' means that those who are not actual parties to a contract have no right to sue on it. A third party affected by a contract, for example, the parents or partner of a client in therapy, cannot sue the therapist over contractual issues, but would have to find other means, perhaps via action in tort (see discussion on third party actions in Chapter 3).

Therapists' use of contracts   For therapists, there are a number of practical points to consider in using contracts. The same fundamental points will apply whether this is a contract between an individual therapist and client, or between a counselling agency and an employer. The fact that terms *appear on* a contract does not mean that they are *legally part of* the said contract. Terms need to be *incorporated* into the contract, which is usually done by each party signing the document which sets out the terms to be included. Presenting the other party with the terms *after* the contract is signed does not make for an enforceable agreement. Terms need to be made clear *before* agreement and signing takes place.

The terms of a contract, such as one between a therapist and client, would include *express* terms, or those specifically included, such as frequency of contact, length and cost of therapy sessions. The contract will also include *implied* terms, whether specifically mentioned or not, such as the maintenance of confidentiality (Eastman, 1987). Implied terms are those terms implied by law, or which are held to be customary in the trade, such as the exercise of reasonable care and skill by the provider of the service. Thus under s.13 of the Supply of Goods and Services Act 1982, the supplier must carry out the service with 'reasonable care and skill'. This is relevant to therapists because in s.18, 'business' is held to include a profession, and the activities of any government department or local or public authority. The professional person has to exercise the ordinary skill of an ordinary competent person exercising that particular art or skill (as with the *Wilsher* case referred to above). However, as commonsense would suggest, there is no implied guarantee that the service will necessarily achieve the desired result. Lord Denning expressed this with characteristic bluntness. 'The surgeon does not warrant that he will save the patient. Nor does the solicitor warrant that he will win the case' (*Greaves and Co. v. Baynham Meikle* [1975]). Nor, it could be added, does the therapist necessarily guarantee a positive outcome to the therapy.

Stuart Sutherland, a highly dissatisfied consumer of therapy and psychiatry, recounts one example where he considered taking legal action for breach of contract.

Case Study: Proposed action for breach of contract in therapy

My condition continued to deteriorate, but the decision about terminating analysis was for the time being taken out of my hands, since my second analyst announced that he was going on holiday. I never saw him again, although I had not yet quite escaped the lure of psychoanalysis.

I was so annoyed with him for what I regarded as very unhelpful treatment that I did not pay his bill. When many months later I received a peremptory letter from his solicitors, I took legal advice myself and wrote to him saying that I had no intention of paying. I contested the claim on the grounds that his treatment had been incompetent. In the state of desperate anxiety in which I then was, his threatening remarks had only increasèd my problems: to accept such observations as that at some level of the unconscious mind one has homosexual proclivities, that one's virtues stem from weakness, or that one has missed out on the best things of life, it is necessary to be in a much more robust state of mental health than I then was. I also alleged that he himself felt threatened by my own knowledge of the subject and my doubts about the efficacy of psychoanalysis, and consciously or unconsciously he had been attempting to punish me. Finally, I wrote that he had claimed to be able to make me feel much better within six months of commencing therapy, that this claim was fraudulent and that I had entered therapy only through false pretences on his part. Such was my fury that I think I would have been prepared to contest a legal action, but it never arose. (Sutherland, 1977: 22)

It seems a moot point as to who would have won if the case had actually gone to court, not least over whether the therapy was consistent with reasonable standards of care and skill in the practice of psychoanalysis. For his part, Sutherland appears to have been in breach of contract by not paying as required by the terms of the contract, if contract there was. His complaints about the therapist's sudden disappearance on holiday, and the therapist's alleged claims to guarantee a positive result within six months could have assisted the client in winning a potential case that the contract was unfulfilled. At best, the example illustrates the dangers of therapists making exaggerated claims for the effectiveness of their work, claims which may well come back to haunt them in the form of complaints or litigation by dissatisfied clients. (Action by therapist or client for alleged breach of contract is discussed in Chapter 6.)

Box 2.2

Elements of a model contract for therapy

- cost of sessions (if relevant)
- duration and frequency of sessions
- arrangements and charges (if relevant) for cancellation or holiday periods
- main characteristics of therapy to be provided
- total number of sessions, and arrangements for review
- limits to confidentiality
- arrangements for termination of therapy
- cover or substitution of therapist in case of illness
- date and signatures of both parties

Reasons for using contracts The use of contracts by therapists is promoted by Bond as a means of ensuring ethical practice and promoting the autonomy of the client (Bond, 1993a: 69–71). He suggests that 'legally, making a contract with fee-paying clients is a wise precaution' (1993a: 204). At minimum, it may reduce the likelihood of later misunderstanding, complaint or litigation by the client. Kitching argues that 'whilst a contract is not fool-proof it does by and large offer much more protection than nothing at all except some vague tacit agreement' (1995a: 10). It would at least clarify subsequent argument over what was originally offered and what was claimed for the therapy, if these points had been explicitly included as terms of the contract. The use of contracts has also been advised for organisations providing *training* in therapy, in order for students and tutors to be clear about their respective obligations in case of later confusion or dispute (Jakobi, 1995; Murray, 1995).

Several model contracts have been suggested for use by therapists (Kitching, 1995a; Syme, 1994: 46–47; 134–6). Drawing upon these examples, it would seem that a contract for therapy could usefully include the elements listed in Box 2.2.

The use of contracts can be linked to the issue of obtaining the client's informed consent to therapy, which is discussed in more detail in Chapter 3. A more contentious issue, perhaps, concerns the extension of the therapist's duty to the client after death. In an agency or organisation, continuity of care would presumably be taken as a responsibility held by the organisation. In the case of private or independent practice, it has been suggested that

---

Box 2.3

Using contracts with clients

- Valid contract requires:
  - legal capacity of parties
  - offer and acceptance
  - intention to make agreement
  - an exchange or consideration
- contract includes both express (explicit) and implied terms
- 'privity' prevents third parties from suing for breach of contract

---

therapists write a counselling will indicating the steps to be taken to conclude or transfer therapy with clients, destroy confidential client records and wind up the affairs of the practice (Kitching, 1995b; Trayner and Clarkson, 1992).

One of the concerns about using contracts in general is the mythology of falling foul of the 'small print'. Consumer rights have been significantly strengthened in this respect by the Unfair Terms in Consumer Contracts Regulations 1994 (SI 1994/3 159), arising from an EU Directive, which complements the Unfair Contract Terms Act 1977. Other consumer rights will be held to apply to a contract, even if not specifically mentioned as such. Thus, Part 2 of the Supply of Goods and Services Act 1982 regulates contracts for the supply of services under s.12. Under s.14 (2) 'there is an implied condition that the goods supplied under the contract are of merchantable quality', unless otherwise indicated. The term merchantable here means 'saleable' or 'marketable' (Leder and Shears, 1991: 49). Hence, any goods that a therapist supplies, such as relaxation tapes, electronic stress level monitors, aromatherapy oils, candles, meditation mats or whatever, need to be of a reasonable quality, again, as commonsense would no doubt suggest.

Strict liability and therapy   The concept of *strict liability* represents a form of liability which is relevant here, based on contract law. This was prompted by the European Union's Product Liability Directive (85/374), and introduced into UK law by the Consumer Protection Act 1987. Under s.2, the producer of goods which cause damage produced wholly or partly via a defect in the product, carries strict liability. This means that the affected consumer does not then have to prove *negligence* on the producer's part to succeed in a legal action for redress (Pannett, 1992: 178). The producer cannot escape liability by blaming the manufacturer of the goods. 'In contract, the liability is strict, in tort it is based in fault. That is, somebody must be blamed' (Leder and Shears, 1991: 56).

An important distinction to be kept in mind here is that strict liability normally applies to the sale of *goods*, rather than to the provision of *services*, such as therapy. Some critics in the USA have argued that applying a notion of strict liability to therapy would be a positive step, by providing an effective defence against malpractice (Otto and Schmidt, 1991). Despite concerns by BAC about the effect of EU Directives, strict liability has yet to be extended to cover the provision of therapeutic and other professional services (Palmer, 1991: 34). Discussion continues regarding EU legislation on introducing strict liability for the provision of professional services, but this principle is some way from being either fully accepted by member states, or from being codified as law (*Croner's Europe*, 1991; 1995).

False description and advertising Another relevant piece of legislation, the Trades Descriptions Act 1968, prohibits false trade descriptions about goods, and false or misleading statements about services, including professional services. One aspect of this would be relevant to therapists who, it is alleged, wrongly represent themselves as having certain qualifications or professional membership, accreditation and registration. It is, for example, an offence to impersonate a doctor, under s. 49 of the Medical Act 1983. In 1993, a hypnotherapist was arrested for sexual assaults carried out on patients during treatment. The therapist had used the title doctor, but held no medical qualifications (*Guardian*, 10 March 1993). In the case of *R. v. Breeze* [1973], the principle of false representation was held to apply regarding an architectural student who falsely described himself as fully qualified, and as a result, was employed to draw up plans (Leder and Shears, 1991: 230). A similar ruling could apply to therapists who make unsubstantiated claims for services offered or provided.

The public's uncertainty about relative value of qualifications in counselling and psychotherapy has led to guidance for members of some associations, such as BAC, *not* to advertise membership of the organisation, which might imply professional standing or status (BAC, 1996). The BPS provides detailed guidelines on what

---

Box 2.4

Guidelines on advertising counselling or therapy services

- do not make exaggerated and unjustified claims
- avoid advertising services in ways likely to encourage clients' unrealistic expectations of their effectiveness
- avoid misleading potential clients about the nature and likely outcomes of any therapy
- avoid playing on clients' fears
- never claim or imply certainty of cure or success in resolving clients' problems
- avoid the use of testimonials from clients
- avoid making offers to refund fees to dissatisfied clients

---

is acceptable for members to include in advertisements for their services (1995b) (see Box 2.4).

Communicating information

Therapists are inescapably involved in the business of handling and communicating sensitive personal information from the moment a client is referred, before setting up a contract. This section explores some of the legal issues concerning data protection, protecting copyright and defamation.

Data protection and record keeping

The use of computerised data is governed by the Data Protection Act 1984 (see Box 2.5). Many therapists use computers for keeping records of their work, and will therefore need to be aware of the principles of data keeping and the rights of subject access which are embodied in the Act. There are several exemptions which apply to the requirements of the Act, including that regarding information simply kept on computer for the purpose of wordprocessing a document (Data Protection Registrar, 1992a: 7). Similarly, personal data held by an individual, such as a home computer user, for personal, family, household or recreational purposes, is also exempt from the requirements of the Act.

The use of other personal data in computerised form requires registration with the Data Protection Registrar, an independent officer appointed by Her Majesty the Queen, reporting directly to Parliament. Personal data means 'data consisting of information

---

Box 2.5

Data Protection Principles: Data Protection Act 1984

Personal data shall be:

- obtained and processed fairly and lawfully
- be held only for the lawful purposes described in the register entry
- be used only for those purposes and only be disclosed to those people described in the register entry
- adequate, relevant and not excessive in relation to the purpose for which they are held
- accurate and, where necessary, kept up to date
- held no longer than is necessary for the registered purpose surrounded by proper security

---

which relates to a living individual who can be identified from that information (or from that and other information in the possession of the data user)' (DPR, 1992b: 6). Under s.5 of the Data Protection Act 1984, it is a criminal offence to hold data on a person without being registered with the Data Protection Register.

The current registration fee is £75 for an initial three-year period. The consequences of failing to register are serious. Data users who fail to register commit a criminal offence, as do those who knowingly or recklessly operate outside the descriptions in their data register entries. Despite this, 'the commonest problem is a failure to re-register after expiry of the initial three-year registration period' (Panting and Palmer, 1992: 6).

The Data Protection Act 1984 also opens doors to data subjects for compensation, where individuals have suffered damage as a result of data which is inaccurate, lost or disclosed without authority. Compensation may be available for such damage and for any distress they have suffered. 'As yet there have been no claims for damages under the Data Protection Act 1984 but experience in countries where similar legislation has been in force for some years shows that litigation follows as the population becomes more aware of its rights' (Panting and Palmer, 1992: 5). Concern has been expressed, for instance, about banks disclosing information on customers to other financial institutions, and about an organisation which holds a database of police officers involved in civil actions for assault or wrongful imprisonment (*Observer*, 27 August 1995). (The rights of individuals, or *data subjects*, to information held on them are discussed in Chapter 5.)

An EU Directive on the protection of personal data is due to come into force in 1998 (95/46/EC). This is primarily to regulate the flow of information in banking, insurance and distance selling. It is intended to harmonise EU arrangements for data exchange on the principle of fairness, so that data collection can be as transparent as possible. The current Data Protection Registrar, Mrs Elizabeth France, will put proposals to the Home Secretary regarding UK implementation. The EU proposals are designed to simplify registration, and to increase the number of exemptions. The Directive will also apply to *manual* records, unlike current UK law, and to smaller companies currently *not* included under the Data Protection Act 1984. The Institute of Personnel Development Directive has produced guidelines on the Directive's implications for records of employee counselling (IPD, 1995).

One issue of particular concern to therapists is that of *time limits for keeping client records*. Bond suggests a three-year time limit for keeping records, corresponding to the maximum time limit for starting an action for personal injury (Bond, 1993a: 178–9). This corresponds with the three-year time limit for complaints to be made under the BAC system. In contrast, Syme argues that 'counsellors must keep all records of their sessions with clients for at least six years' (1994: 52). This would conform with the Law Society's advice to solicitors to keep client records until six years from date of last contact. (It also corresponds to time limits for certain legal actions, such as those brought under tort: see Chapter 6.)

Protection of material via copyright, contract and trade marks

Besides data protection, therapists may also have an interest in legal aspects of *copyright*. To what extent can new ideas about therapeutic practice be protected from others who wish to copy them or reproduce them without acknowledgement? If a contract is signed, promising not to reveal the therapeutic secrets of a particular school or workshop, what status does this have in law?

The bald answer is that there is a basic rule of English law that *ideas* as such cannot be made copyright or patented. Thus, under s.1 of the Patents Act 1977, to be granted a patent, the invention in question must be new, and not merely part of the 'state of the art'. It must involve an inventive step not obvious to a person skilled in that art, and be capable of industrial application. This means that essentially intellectual inventions such as therapeutic approaches cannot be patented. 'An invention of a method of treatment of the human or animal body by surgery, therapy or diagnosis is not included as capable of industrial application' (Painter and Lawson, 1990: 72).

However, one way of protecting an investment of time, money and energy in the development of new approaches to therapy could be through the use of a *contract*. In this way, an author could protect their work by requiring persons attending a training school or workshop to sign a contract not to reproduce it, on pain of action for breach of contract. An alternative might be by taking action on the basis of *breach of confidence*, on the grounds that this was a private lecture, where a confidential relationship could be held to apply (Flint, 1990: 36). An action for breach of confidence requires three conditions to operate:

- information kept under protection which is confidential
- an obligation to keep the material confidential
- unauthorised disclosure, damaging to the communicator

Another possible approach for therapists is by using the defence of *copyright*. Copyright covers specific categories of work, the most relevant here being 'literary works', not so much in the sense of being great literature, but in terms of being *written* material. Copyright is a right derived from *actual works*, not solely from *ideas* as such. To obtain copyright in the manner of *expressing* an idea, the idea must be original, and the idea must have involved the use of skill and labour by the author. Copyright lasts for the life of the author, plus 50 years, now extended to 70 years by the EU.

The basic law here is the Copyright Act 1956, plus various amending Acts, such as the Copyright, Designs and Patents Act 1988. This created four 'moral rights', bringing UK law into line with the Berne Copyright Convention. Probably the most relevant one here is the moral right to be identified as the author of a particular work under ss. 77 and 78 of the Act, often now seen at the beginning of books. Thus, for example, it is no longer necessary to register work or use the © symbol in order to protect written material in the UK, or in other countries which follow the Berne Copyright Convention, rather than the competing Universal Copyright Convention (Flint, 1990: 32).

It is also possible to protect material communicated through lectures and workshops in this manner. Normally, workshop or training material is not covered by copyright unless the material is written down by the author, which then makes it into a literary work, or unless it is recorded on to tape (Robertson and Nicol, 1992: 216). For some lecturers and trainers, restrictions are placed on their use of educational and training material produced in the course of their employment. Contracts of employment should be carefully checked for any such restrictions on ownership or subsequent use of training materials or course designs which are covered in this way.

What are known as 'passing off' actions can be used under tort law, to protect works whose use is not specifically restricted by copyright. This could occur where a specific work is represented as having a spurious or unfounded connection with another unrelated business, for instance, the publishers of *Decorators and Painters* magazine preventing a new magazine being published under the title of *The Decorator*. Particular schools of therapy with a distinctive brand-name may be keen to seek protection for the use of a particular title in this way. Another option is for a school of therapy to register its brand-name as a *trade mark*. Neuro Linguistic Programming (TM) is thus protected. Trade marks need to be registered with the Registrar of Trade Marks, unlike copyright (Flint, 1990: 331).

Finally, breach of copyright is not a casual matter, and needs to be taken seriously by those therapists perhaps using 'bootleg' versions of training videos or other photocopied material such as psychological assessment questionnaires. In rare cases, private search warrants can even be authorised, under what are known as 'Anton Piller orders', to search for unauthorised material (Robertson and Nicol, 1992: 256). If successful in litigation, the plaintiffs can claim compensation under s. 96(2) for profits lost, or for the fee that could have been charged for use of copyright. In particularly serious cases, copyright breach is also a criminal offence, potentially leading to a fine or conviction, under s.108 of the 1988 Act.

Defamation, libel and slander
Another area of potential interest to therapists is *defamation*, covered by the Defamation Act 1996. This may be relevant in making or challenging statements, whether as client or as

therapist, about professional work, training establishments or in making allegations of malpractice. It has been suggested that fear of being sued for slander or libel may be an inhibiting factor for some clients and professionals, making them reluctant to report alleged malpractice, for example, such as another therapist's sexual relationships with current clients, or unsafe and unethical practice (Russell, 1993: 26).

Defamation is defined as a statement which injures the reputation of the plaintiff by tending to lower them in the thinking of right-minded members of society, or by causing the latter to shun or avoid them, or by bringing them into 'hatred, ridicule or contempt' (Pannett, 1992: 225). This does not include what goes under the label of an insult or general abuse, for example, calling someone a scoundrel. The statement must not only be untrue, but must be *damaging* as well. Taking legal action over defamation is a risky and expensive business, which should be carefully thought through before being embarked upon, given both the legal costs involved and the appreciable risk of failure.

Libel and slander There are two main forms of defamation, *libel* and *slander*. The difference is often assumed to be that existing between written and spoken forms of defamation, but the real difference is between *permanent* and *temporary* forms, so that libel can include words spoken in recorded form such as on TV, radio, or video. Thus, Victoria Gillick, campaigner for parental rights, has sought to bring a libel case against the BBC and a journalist speaking on one of its programmes. In the debate, the journalist was alleged to have referred to reported suicides following Victoria Gillick's earlier legal action, which restricted medical confidentiality in giving contraceptive advice to girls under the age of 16 years (*Guardian*, 20 October 1995). Libel may also be considered as criminal libel if seditious or obscene. Legal aid is not generally available for libel actions, which may well inhibit an individual from taking action. However, under proposed reforms of the law on defamation, there are plans for a cheaper procedure for less serious forms of libel, to be heard by a judge without a trial, for damages of up to £10,000 (*Guardian*, 20 July 1995). It is also likely that past 'excessive' libel awards, reaching a massive £1.5 million in the case of damages against Nikolai Tolstoy in 1989, will be sharply curtailed in future (*Guardian*, 14 July 1995; 13 December 1995).

In some situations, newspaper reporting may simply be intrusive rather than necessarily libellous. In one instance, an article revealed that a prominent feminist therapist had gone to Switzerland to have an abortion at the age of 15 (*Daily Mail*, 12 January 1996). Apart from a complaint to the Press Complaints Commission made by the UKCP, there is little protection available to individual therapists singled out in this way. As a number of commentators have pointed out, there is remarkably little protection of privacy for individuals under UK law (Robertson and Nicol, 1992: 40–1). In Scotland, it should be noted by way of contrast to the above, that the terms libel and slander are used somewhat differently, and are used almost interchangeably on occasion. Slander, for instance, is seen as a verbal injury which is comparable to battery in assault cases.

Slander consists of spoken or less permanent forms of defamation. This is actionable only if it causes *financial* damage to the individual concerned, as opposed to damages for injury to feelings. Another possibility is to take legal action for malicious falsehood, for which legal aid is available. 'In ordinary language 'malice' means 'spite' or 'ill will'. But in libel laws it generally refers to dishonest writing or reporting – the publication of facts that are known to be false or opinions that are not genuinely held' (Robertson and Nicol, 1992: 71). There are some odd and very specific grounds for legal action for slander where *no* financial damage has been incurred, relating to charges of being guilty of an imprisonable offence, having an infectious disease, or, for a woman, of being unchaste, adulterous or a lesbian. Such action is also possible for statements intended to disparage a person in any office, profession, calling, trade or business.

Defences against defamation can include:

- the statement is true (an absolute defence)
- it can be justified as 'fair comment'
- the consent of the person concerned was obtained
- offer of an apology and compensation
- a claim of privilege

The time limit for taking legal action for defamation or malicious falsehood has been reduced from three years to one year by the Defamation Act 1996.

Qualified privilege as defence against defamation charges The use of the defence of 'qualified privilege' is likely to be of particular interest to therapists, as a defence against potential defamation charges in reporting alleged malpractice by a colleague. The crucial elements for claiming a defence of qualified privilege are:

- a moral or social duty on the part of the person giving the information, or making the statement
- a corresponding duty on the part of the person receiving the information

This reciprocity is *essential* in legal terms in order to claim this defence (Pannett, 1992: 242; *Adam v. Ward* [1917]).

While a professional person may not possess full legal privilege, there is acceptance that, in some situations, this protection is needed for persons giving information of social value. This is described as a *qualified* form of privilege. 'Qualified privilege provides that where the retailer of the information has a duty or interest in passing it on, and the person to whom he gives it also has a duty or interest in receiving it, then provided it was not done with malice there is no liability' (Pearce, 1988: 4). This would cover stating a professional opinion, as when taking part in a child protection case conference. Qualified privilege has also been taken to include the process of giving references. However, there has been a recent case which now establishes a *duty of care* on the part of the person giving a reference to the person who is the *subject* of the reference (*Spring v. Guardian Assurance plc* [1994]). A therapist who gave an inaccurate and damaging reference about a colleague or student may no longer be able to depend upon the defence of qualified privilege to protect them from being sued for damages (see Chapter 3).

There is a degree of protection under qualified privilege for professionals who bring complaints against others for unprofessional conduct. In the past, professionals, therapists included, have often been reluctant to disclose information about a colleague's incompetence or abuse of clients for fear of counteraction for libel or slander (Jehu et al, 1994: 40). In the case of a psychiatrist in Burnley working with recovering drug users, concern about his abusive practices towards clients was widespread long before action was eventually taken. The *Report of*

Inquiry stressed that, within the health authority, an employee providing information given in good faith would be indemnified against the costs of any legal counter-action for defamation. The defence of qualified privilege would apply to a statement made in furthering a legal, moral or social duty to a person who has a corresponding duty to receive it (NHS NW, 1994; DHSS Health Circular (82)13).

Telecommunications and therapy
Therapy may be described as the 'talking cure', but it is increasingly affected in various ways by the new technologies. The Samaritans, for example, now provide a counselling service by e-mail, which meets a previously unrecognised demand. Pressure groups provide information on topics such as false memory via the Internet's bulletin boards. Each advance in technology raises new questions about ethics and the law in relation to communicating sensitive personal information (Rosenfield, 1996). An audio tape of a daughter's accusations of abuse against her father featured prominently in one TV documentary on recovered memories of abuse, with no indication of her permission having been obtained to broadcast it. In several TV documentaries, hidden cameras have been used to record therapeutic dialogue covertly for later broadcasting (BBC, 1994; 1996), with no clear acknowledgement of the ethical issues involved in breaching therapeutic privacy. While the possibility of the following measures being used may appear remote, there is provision under the law to limit or prevent some abuses of therapists' privacy and confidentiality:

■ 'hacking' into computer data is an offence under the Computer Misuse Act 1990
■ unauthorised interception or recording of phone conversations is an offence under s.45 of the Telecommunications Act 1984
■ the Home Office can stop programmes endangering the privacy of persons in vulnerable positions, under the Broadcasting Act 1990

Sometimes the disclosure of sensitive personal information via broadcasting can have unforeseen and serious consequences. R.D. Laing, well known as a critic of orthodox psychiatry, openly discussed his life-long struggle with alcohol dependency and depression on the radio programme *In the Psychiatrist's Chair*.

Prior to the interview, a former patient of Laing's had lodged a complaint against him with the General Medical Council. The transcript of the radio programme was then used as part of the examination of his practice by the GMC. Laing decided to withdraw voluntarily from the Medical Register, which did not, however, prevent him from continuing to practise as a psychotherapist (Clare, 1993: 203–4).

Law relating to service provision and employment

Understanding the law in terms of a wider set of responsibilities, such as those relating to employment and provision of a counselling or psychotherapy service, is also important for many therapists. Two areas to be covered here are the concepts of employers' liability for staff, and of supervisers' liability towards therapists under their supervision. There are also particular issues to be considered about rights to confidentiality and fair treatment for ex-offenders under legislation. Finally, issues of discrimination, at the core of much therapeutic work, also are at the forefront of employment law, needing consideration by therapists and agencies alike.

Liability of employers
Employers have what is known as *vicarious liability* for acts carried out by employees, or by others who carry out activities without necessarily being formally employed. To illustrate the former point, in medical cases, for example, action for negligence can be brought against an individual doctor. If the doctor is employed by the NHS, then the claim is more likely to be brought against the relevant health authority or NHS trust, from whom damages or compensation can be sought. In theory at least, the health authority could then sue the negligent doctor for costs and damages, although this is unlikely to happen in reality (Ham et al., 1988). This process is shown in the case of *Cassidy v. Ministry of Health* [1951]. In this instance, a patient had an operation on his hand, which was placed in a splint to overcome the likely contraction of two fingers. However, on removal of the splint, it was found that the plaintiff's whole hand had become paralysed. Given that all the staff involved in his care were NHS employees, the court found against the staff's *employer*, the NHS.

Vicarious liability The concept of vicarious liability is particularly relevant for therapists working in GP practice, where issues of clinical accountability and legal liability can sometimes seem complex and confusing. One recent discussion of this distinguishes in terms of liability between staff who are *employed* by the practice and those who are *self-employed* as the key factor in deciding where liability for negligence lies (Scott, 1994: 64–5). Where a therapist is employed or working as if employed by the GP practice, then the practice would hold vicarious liability for any mistakes or poor practice. Where the therapist was self-employed, but using an interview room for counselling clients referred by the GP, then the therapist would be liable him or herself for any action brought by a dissatisfied client. The confusion arising here is that the issue is often presented in terms of the doctor's overall *clinical* responsibility for overseeing patient care (CMS, 1996). This is not necessarily the crucial element for the courts in determining *legal liability*, which rests much more on the *employment status* of the therapist or other member of staff, and their *employment relationship* with the practice concerned.

Vicarious liability does not provide an endless chain of responsibility. For example, a college might require a lecturer to keep in practice in therapy in order to teach it as a subject. If a client then brought a legal action against the lecturer, the liability would be held vicariously by the *college* if the counselling was carried out, say as part of its student counselling service, as part of an agreed workload. If the lecturer was carrying out the counselling as private work, then the lecturer would be *personally* liable for his or her own practice, as any private practitioner would be liable. Vicarious liability does not *remove* the individual's liability as an employee, but *extends* it to the responsible employing organisation. In practical terms, lawsuits tend to be directed against an organisation, such as a hospital or NHS Trust, more often than against the individual practitioner concerned.

Employers' duties In terms of negligence liability, employers have a common law duty regarding employees, deriving from the *Donoghue* [1932] case, in addition to certain statutory duties under Health and Safety law (see Box 2.6). These common law duties cover doing what is reasonably practicable regarding provision of safe equipment, a safe system of work, such as a duty not to put the employee at risk of attack (*Charlton v. Forrest* [1980]), and

Box 2.6

Duties of employer

Health and Safety at Work Act 1974

s.2   to ensure the health, safety and welfare at work of employees
s.2(2)(e) to provide a working environment that is safe, without risks to
              health, and adequate for the welfare of employees

*Management of Health and Safety at Work Regulations 1992
(SI 1992/2051)*

3(1)   to make assessment of risks to the health and safety of
              employees and others at work
5   to ensure employees are provided with appropriate health
              surveillance

(Source: LRD, 1994)

provision of reasonably competent staff with whom the employee is required to work (Pannett, 1992: 124–7).

The growth of recorded stress levels at work, and the increasing use of Employee Assistance Programmes to try to respond to this phenomenon, have focused increasing interest on the issue of liability for stress-induced illness amongst employees. The case of John Walker, a social worker who successfully took legal action against his former employer, has been hailed as a landmark decision in this respect. The judge's decision confirms the employer's existing duty of care towards employees, but may be less radical than it seems at first sight.

Case Study: Employers' duty of care regarding stress-induced psychiatric illness

John Walker worked for Northumberland County Council as an Area Social Services Officer from 1970 to 1987. There was a high volume of work, often concerning problematic and stressful child protection cases. With no previous history of mental problems, Mr Walker suffered a nervous breakdown, namely mental exhaustion and stress reactions, in 1986. This recurred in 1987, despite his employer having been alerted to the problems he was experiencing at work. In 1988, he was dismissed by his employers on the grounds of permanent ill-health.

*Taking legal action against his employers, he was successful in winning his case. The judge noted the expert evidence which attested to the intrinsically stressful nature of much social work, but noted an additional factor, which was the structure and manning of the relevant social services department. In 1996, two years after winning the court case, Walker reached an out-of-court settlement with his former employer for a compensation payment of £175,000. (*Walker v. Northumberland C.C. *(1994))*

(Source: BASW, 1995; *Guardian*, 27 April 1996)

The case needs to be read carefully to follow the main lessons to be drawn from it. The action against Northumberland was based both in tort law, for negligence, and in contract. The employers were found *not* liable for causing the first nervous breakdown, because it was not reasonably foreseeable that the pressures of work and the staffing and management arrangements would carry a material or significant risk of a nervous breakdown. However, on the plaintiff's return to work, it *was* held to be clearly foreseeable that a continuation of these conditions would cause this to happen all over again.

Judge Colman held that 'when the plaintiff returned to work the defendants, knowing of his previous breakdown, ought to have taken steps, as the plaintiff had been led to believe they would, to alleviate his excessive work-load. They were therefore in breach of their duty of care as regards his second nervous breakdown' (BASW, 1995: 34). As the Law Commission has pointed out, it is worth noting that Mr Walker's psychiatric illness was not shock-induced, unlike the majority of cases in this field (Law Commission, 1995a: 34).

In a second case which is relevant, Chris Johnstone, a junior doctor, won £5,000 compensation in an out-of-court settlement from Camden and Islington Health Authority in April 1995 for working hours which he described as 'inhuman' (*Johnstone v. Bloomsbury Health Authority* [1991]). Dr Johnstone said he had suffered clinical depression and suicidal impulses as a result of working between 83 and 120 hours a week as a junior doctor in obstetrics. While the health authority concerned was at pains to point out that it did not admit liability, this was against a backdrop of policy reforms where the Government had made an agreement with the British Medical Association in 1990 to reduce junior doctors' working hours to 72 hours per week maximum. Clearly, as an out of court settlement, this does not set a legal precedent for others to follow.

In Scotland, Joan Ballantyne, a former residential social worker, won £66,000 damages from her employing authority. This was an out of court settlement for stress-related illness, which had caused her to take early retirement. Lorna Gunn has also brought a case against Highland Council for damages allegedly caused by an attack when counselling a 13-year-old girl (*Community Care*, 30 May 1996; 20 June 1996).

Employers' liability for workplace stress The optimistic view is that these cases illustrate a decisive shift in terms of establishing a wider principle of employer liability for their workers' well being. Professor Cary Cooper, of the University of Manchester Institute of Science and Technology, has claimed that, since the Walker case, 'employers now have a duty of care over the management of people – not just a duty of care over health and safety issues regarding machinery and the like' (Cooper, 1995: 14). A somewhat more sceptical view is that the *Johnstone* and *Walker* cases were settled out of court, without any admission of liability by the employers. Again, what seems to have been a crucial factor in the *Walker* case was the fact that the employers took no effective remedial action after the *first* breakdown, which should have been warning enough for them to become alerted to the problem.

The cases described above are relevant to therapists in several ways. They clearly illustrate the need for counselling in the workplace, and may provide encouragement to therapists concerned about rising or unrealistic caseloads in their own work setting. However, the message given by the judgements is not clear-cut. In the *Johnstone* case, the issue of hours and pressure of work was a national concern, with direct implications for patient care, with intense media publicity and the backing of a wide body of public and professional support. Others attempting to pursue this kind of action in the courts perhaps need to consider the possible outcomes carefully before launching into litigation against their employers.

Stress at work is rightly, however, an area of growing concern to therapists and many others, such as managers, staff and trade unions. There has been a major growth of Employee Assistance

Programmes (EAPs), where counselling is usually provided by external contracted agencies for work forces facing work-related stress, redundancy and the trauma of assault or robbery, such as in the banking industry (Reynolds and Allison, 1996). Standards of practice for EAPs have been published by the EAP Professional Association (EAPA, 1995).

Liability of supervisers

The potential legal liability held by *supervisers* for therapists under their charge seems to be a major area for misunderstanding and potential confusion (CMS, 1995: 6). In reality, as Page and Wosket suggest, the legal liability of supervisers in the UK for their supervisees is an untested area, where the likelihood of liability is probably rather limited (Page and Wosket, 1994: 151). Looking at other forms of commercial practice to get a wider perspective on this issue, it seems that some insurance firms have been able to deny liability for coverage where professionals were inadequately supervised, or were given responsibility beyond their experience or qualifications. This principle, however, has yet to be applied to therapeutic practice concerning counsellors or psychotherapists (McGee, 1992).

In the USA, the principle of superviser liability has been more firmly established in cases such as *Tarasoff*, where the therapist's superviser was held responsible, together with the employing institution, for failure to warn a third party of a serious threat to her life (see Chapter 4). Beyond this, there has also been the case in the USA of *Peck v. Counseling Service of Addison County* (1985), where the Counseling Service itself was found to be negligent, for failing to have any written policy for consultation procedures when a client presented a serious danger to life and property (Harrar et al., 1990: 40). Again, state licensing of therapists in the US may incorporate the formal liability of supervisers for their trainees' practice, specifically where the trainee is acting on a voluntary basis, within a defined scope, and under the immediate direction of the superviser (Harrar et al., 1990: 39).

There is, admittedly, an evident ambiguity inherent in the use of the term *superviser* in these cases. The term 'superviser' carries a very occupationally specific meaning in the world of therapy. Most therapists receive supervision in the form of *professional consultation* for their work, from a person who is usually explicitly required *not* to be a superviser in any formal managerial or organisational sense. It would follow, therefore, that such supervisers *do not* necessarily hold vicarious liability in the sense that an employer would. The liability of such professional consultants for the negligence of therapists in the UK therefore remains an untested and possibly unlikely development, which remains to be clarified by future judgements of the courts.

Criminal convictions

Turning to the issue of past convictions, the checking of prospective staff's backgrounds for criminal convictions is now standard procedure in statutory areas such as health, education and social services, but is less well-established in other fields where therapists may be working. The UKCP requires members to inform their organisation of any convictions (UKCP, 1995), and convictions are considered by the Human Fertilisation and Embryology Authority in making appointments (HFEA, 1993). According to the latter, 'relevant convictions will depend upon the particular post and the gravity of the particular offence, but may include any offence of violence or dishonesty, blackmail, sexual offences and offences against children, drugs offences and breaches of regulatory machinery' (HFEA, 1993: Para 1.18).

Provision for employers considering or setting aside past or 'spent' convictions is set out by the Rehabilitation of Offenders Act 1974. Under the Act, most types of previous criminal convictions become spent after a fixed period of time, in order to assist the re-entry of offenders back into society (Harris, 1976). Apart from specified exceptions such as medical, nursing and other professional posts, previous convictions with a prison sentence of 30 months become spent after 10 years, and do not have to be disclosed to employers when seeking employment. There are wide exceptions to this, however, and the 1986 Order SI 1249 extended the requirement of disclosure to *any* office or employment providing access to under 18-year-olds.

The changes in the law have raised a number of questions about the implications of such checks for voluntary agencies. In 1984, the conviction of Colin Evans for the murder of a young child, Marie Payne, raised concern about individuals gaining access to children through voluntary work. In fact, although Evans was involved in voluntary work, he actually came into contact with his victim through offering babysitting services to her mother (Gulbenkian Foundation, 1993: 132).

Criminal records checks   Practice concerning criminal record checks on staff and volunteers varies considerably in the voluntary sector. It is standard practice with agencies such as many volunteer bureaux and with Victim Support, which works closely with statutory agencies such as the police and the Home Office, but appears to be less widespread elsewhere. Checks are now being extended to cover priests in the Church of England, following concern about past cases of abuse of children in the UK and USA (*Guardian*, 16 August 1995). Earlier proposals for checks on all staff in voluntary organisations with access to children have now been modified, to focus particularly on 'substantial unsupervised access to children', as, for example, with telephone counsellors working with distressed children. Checks were seen to be important 'where the children being cared for were most vulnerable or where supervision was difficult or impossible, but [were] generally of less importance where adults were working together with larger groups of less vulnerable children' (HOC 93/47). The groups at most risk included children under 16, under 18 with special needs, or in residential care.

Following a pilot scheme, it is under consideration that this system be extended to voluntary organisations, and to wider groups of potentially vulnerable clients, such as older people, people with disabilities, and people with learning difficulties (Unell, 1992). However, the pilot research revealed some practical problems in undertaking record checks, including the cost of £15 per check, the mismatch between the gender profile of volunteers (55% female) and of sex offenders (98% male), and the concern about the possible deterrent effect on volunteers. Apart from specific groups of vulnerable children, there were no proposals until 1993 to extend the system of police checks to the voluntary sector as a whole (HOC 117/92). Voluntary organisations considering policy and practice on this issue should seek advice from the Voluntary Organisations Consultancy Service (see address in Resources section).

Proposed changes to criminal records checks   The Government has enacted changes to the law relating to access to criminal records (Home Office, 1993; 1996a). Based on new computerised systems, it has introduced three types of access to past records under the Police Act (1997).

- *Criminal Conviction Certificates*: available to individuals only, listing unspent convictions, similar to a 'certificate of good conduct' (s. 100)
- *Full criminal records checks*: including spent convictions for those working with children under 18, elderly, sick and handicapped people (s. 101)
- *Enhanced criminal records checks*: for prospective employees, trainees and volunteers having regular, unsupervised contact with children and young persons under 18. Enhanced checks include access to information known to the police, such as involvement in paedophile activity, which may need to be considered in making appointments for particularly sensitive posts (s. 102).

Initial response to these proposals by voluntary organisations has been cautious. It has been pointed out that one in three men have a criminal record by the age of 30, and that the proposed system might deter some potential volunteers who would suffer embarrassment at having to disclose past minor or irrelevant convictions. Mainly, the scheme is criticised on the grounds of the potential cost to either individual volunteers, or to small and often financially hard-pressed voluntary organisations. The Home Office measures are intended to strike a balance between protecting the civil liberties of past rehabilitated offenders, and the need to protect vulnerable members of the public from harm. Ellison, however, suggests that the scheme may be of doubtful value. 'The best defence against unsuitable volunteers remains good procedures for recruitment, selection, support and supervision' (1996: 4).

The issue of criminal convictions raises ethical questions for many therapists and agencies about achieving the correct balance between protecting potentially vulnerable clients, and preserving the civil liberties of past offenders, in terms of their right to be rehabilitated into society. The voluntary sector seems to be expressing a degree of caution about adopting a wholesale policy of instituting record checks for other than restricted areas of access to clients. The implications for counselling do not seem to have been widely considered, except that the British Association for Counselling now requires a declaration from applicants for membership regarding pertinent convictions, to be taken into account when the application is being considered.

Government proposals for criminal record checks to be privatised to a commercial firm have also raised concerns about breaches of confidentiality and a possible increase in discrimination against former offenders (*Guardian*, 10 May 1995). At present, employers and training organisations cannot require applicants to reveal 'spent' convictions, unless this disclosure is specifically required under the law.

Unlawful discrimination

Experience of stigma and discrimination is at the heart of many clients' life stories. Therapists are often made aware of these issues through their practice and training, if not through their own life histories. From the point of view of employment and providing a professional service, the main pieces of legislation covering discrimination are the Sex Discrimination Acts 1975 and 1986, the Race Relations Act 1976 and the Disability Discrimination Act 1995. The employment provisions of the Disability Discrimination Act 1995 will be limited to firms with 20 or more employees, although goods and services provided by smaller firms are covered by the Act (Gooding, 1996).

Discrimination on grounds of sex, race and disability   The Sex Discrimination Acts 1975 and 1986, incorporating the earlier Equal Pay Act 1970, make it unlawful for an employer to discriminate against men or women, either directly or indirectly, on grounds of sex or marital status. The Race Relations Act 1976 similarly makes it unlawful for an employer to discriminate, either directly or indirectly, on the grounds of colour, race, nationality or ethnic or national origin. Complaints within the public sector regarding racial discrimination have been increasing rapidly. The Commission for Racial Equality received 286 formal complaints in 1994 from local authority employees. In February 1993, two black trainers, Claudius Gayle and Claudia Webb, were awarded £25,000 for racial discrimination. Their training course on the Children Act 1989 had been temporarily closed down by Nottinghamshire Social Services Department, after workers had complained that there was an over-emphasis on race issues in the training (Francis, 1995).

The Department of Employment recommends that a clear and effective complaints procedure is available, which covers the possibility of *harassment* in the workplace, and which describes the steps to be taken by employers in the event of its occurrence

(DE, 1995). A *Code of Practice* concerning combatting sexual harassment at work has been issued to complement the EU Resolution (90/C 157/02) on the Protection of the Dignity of Women and Men at Work (CEC, 1993). Case law has recognised for some time that sexual harassment actions can successfully be brought under the Sex Discrimination Act 1975. Where an employee brings a valid complaint, but is victimised, and is forced to leave employment, they are also able to bring an action for constructive dismissal.

Attention has been focused recently on the implications of dual relationships in Higher Education where trainers, supervisers or lecturers may be engaged in consensual sexual relationships with students, trainees or practitioners. Clearly, relationships based on full agreement are not necessarily exploitative or detrimental to either party. However the often unequal power relationships and the potential for other parties to perceive the likelihood of favouritism or of a potential conflict of interests raises difficult issues about their advisability (BPS, 1995b). The BAC *Code of Ethics and Practice for Trainers* proscribes sexual relationships between trainers and trainees as being unethical (1995b).

In terms of disability, the Disability Discrimination Act 1995 makes it unlawful to discriminate *directly*, rather than indirectly, against a disabled person. The Act defines disability in s.1 as a physical or mental impairment having a substantial and adverse effect on a person's ability to carry out normal day-to-day activities. Disability includes a recognised mental illness, and progressive conditions such as cancer, muscular dystrophy and HIV, according to Schedule 1 of the Act. Discrimination is defined (ss. 4,5) as unjustifiable less favourable treatment provided by an employer, such as dismissal, worse terms of employment, or fewer opportunities for training.

Discrimination in the above Acts also covers the provision of goods, facilities and services, as well as of employment. In terms of disability discrimination (effective from 1997), service providers may *not* provide less favourable terms or standard of a service, without specifically defined justifications, including financial considerations (ss. 19,20). Organisations *may* however discriminate lawfully in certain instances, for example by providing specific services, training or employment under ss.7 and 48 of the Sex Discrimination Act 1975 and ss. 5 and 38 of the Race Relations Act 1976. The relevant sections could be used, for example, to recruit a black female counsellor to work in a hostel with young black adults.

Claims for discrimination in *employment* on the grounds of race, sex or disability are heard by an Industrial Tribunal. Complaints about discrimination in the provision of *services* are heard in the County Court, where proceedings must be started within six months of the occurrence of the discrimination (Grewal, 1988; 1990).

Developing good practice relating to discrimination   There is, as yet, no legislation prohibiting discrimination on the grounds of *age* or *sexual orientation* (Crane, 1982), but good practice would ensure that these are also included in the Equal Opportunities policy of any employer or agency providing therapy. Thus Ms Elmes, a transsexual probation officer, failed in an action against an employer, Insight Alcohol Services, for discrimination. The grounds for the case were that the employer had withdrawn Ms Elmes from work at Exeter prison on the basis of her 'sexual identity problems' (*Guardian*, 1 November 1995). However, a decision at the European Court of Justice has opened the door to protection of transsexuals from discrimination at work, on the basis of the EU Directive (76/207/EEC) on the right of men and women to Equal Treatment (*Guardian*, 15 December 1995; 1 May 1996).

Awareness of discrimination may be growing amongst therapists and related organisations, but there may still be practices which undermine good intentions in this area (Echiejile, 1995; Gordon, 1993). Some branches of psychoanalysis, for instance, have traditionally been considered to be reluctant to accept gay or lesbian therapists for training (Abram, 1992: 27; *Observer*, 18 June 1995). Gay clients and therapists have also criticised attempts by Church organisations which apparently offer therapy in order to 'reform' homosexuals (*Guardian*, 24 August 1995). Some forms of discrimination may be unintentional, but still need to be avoided. The widespread, and widely accepted, practice of 'networking' amongst therapist colleagues for work or employment may, in fact, actively disadvantage disabled people or members of ethnic minority groups, who are often on the outside of such established informal communication systems (DE, 1995).

The costs to employers of successful legal action against them for discrimination can be high. The previous £11,000 ceiling on compensation awards in cases of sex or racial discrimination has

Box 2.7

Guidelines for professional practice

Liability under tort and contract law

- review work practice for any potential areas of liability for therapists or students
- consider the use of clear contracts with clients
- look at protection of staff from harassment or abuse
- apply ethical standards in advertising and publicity

Communicating personal information

- monitor compliance with data protection requirements
- guard against breaches of copyright
- be cautious about making unprofessional or potentially defamatory comments about other therapists, clients or agencies

Employment and service provision

- clarify the standing of agency, staff and supervisers with regard to vicarious liability
- ensure that insurance cover adequately reflects such liability
- monitor health and safety requirements for staff
- clarify and apply relevant legal requirements concerning rehabilitation of offenders
- review practices for possible unlawful discrimination on the basis of race, gender and disability
- develop best practice concerning policies on harassment and avoiding discrimination on the basis of age and sexual orientation

now been lifted, with an award of £28,000 made to a black prison officer in 1995 for discrimination experienced at work (*Guardian*, 11 July 1995). As always, there is a cautionary, if perhaps exceptional, case from the USA to consider. An American executive fired because of his alcoholism, successfully sued his employer, Coca-Cola, for $300,000. He made his case on the grounds that alcoholism is considered a disability under US law, and that his employer had thus failed in its legal obligations towards him under the relevant disability legislation (*Guardian*, 4 July 1995).

Summary

The law in the UK contains significant differences between the legal systems of Scotland, Northern Ireland, and England and

Wales. The legal tradition in England and Wales is based on a combination of statute and common law, with a crucial division between civil and criminal law. For therapists, tort and contract within civil law have the most direct bearing on their practice. Tort rests on the concept of the therapist's duty of care to clients, exercised according to the appropriate standard for the profession. Use of contracts also offers protection and redress if necessary for clients. Problematic areas for practice include data protection, defamation and copyright.

There are important legal issues to consider with regard to employment or service provision, such as health and safety, and employer or superviser liability. Past criminal convictions are a further consideration for employers or service providers, in balancing the rights of past offenders with protection for vulnerable groups in society. Discrimination on the grounds of sex, race and disability is now covered under statute, but legal protection for other disadvantaged groups is still lacking.

Discussion points

1 What are the advantages and disadvantages of using formal contracts with clients? At what stage should they be introduced?

2 Tort case law suggests that the standard of care expected of a trainee professional is the same as that expected of a 'reasonably competent' practitioner. Is this fair to clients or trainees?

3 To what extent does your or your agency's practice conform to data protection principles? What changes would you consider need to be made in this area?

4 Should employers be held liable for stress-induced illness caused by work? Do therapists have a proactive role here which goes beyond that of responding to stress or distress in the workplace?

5 Identify the main ethical and legal principles in conflict in the case study taken from Stuart Sutherland's book, *Breakdown*. How might this outcome have been better managed or avoided altogether?

3

Professional Negligence

> 'As it happens', said Annette, 'I was out being indecently assaulted by a mad therapist'.
>
> 'There's a lot of it about,' said Ernie Gromback. 'Anyone can do a weekend course and set up in business. Or not even bother with the course.'

(Weldon, 1993: 63)

In her book *Affliction*, Fay Weldon launches a blistering attack on the destructive influences of two therapists on a long-standing, stable and apparently successful marriage. She has made it clear through interviews that her views on therapy as being both manipulative and beyond social or legal controls, are based on her own traumatic personal experiences (Weldon, 1994; Honigsbaum, 1995). This has raised an urgent question for others about the possibility of using the law to constrain bad therapists (Thompson, 1994).

'In these circumstances, the lack of cases involving counsellors in the courts, a desirable state of affairs from most viewpoints, creates uncertainty about the application of law to counselling in a legal system based on case law' (Bond, 1992b: 198–9). The nearest relative to case law on therapy in the UK is *medical* case law, and within that case law relating to *psychiatry*. There are obviously clear differences existing between therapy and psychiatry to be borne in mind, given that psychiatry comprises specific medical elements, such as diagnosis of illness, and the use of medication, electro-convulsive therapy and some surgical procedures. It is also part of a profession regulated by statute. However, the parallels between negligence by therapists and doctors or psychiatrists do indicate the form that the likely application of negligence principles to therapists would take. For this reason, this chapter explores some of the known features of **medical negligence case law**, particularly with regard to psychiatry, before moving on to examine some of the few but significant cases of **therapist negligence case law**, drawn both from the USA and the UK. Some of the main problematic areas such as defining the **therapist's duty of care**, advice-giving and third party claims are explored, before ending with a discussion of the services offered by **professional indemnity insurance schemes** and professional protection societies.

With regard to professional negligence, it is suggested that there are two main objectives of the law (Ham et al., 1988: 26):

- *deterring* professionals from acting negligently
- *compensating* people injured via negligence

The characteristics of professional negligence have been defined in Chapter 2, but will be briefly restated here: 'the ingredients of the tort of negligence are the existence of a duty of care, the breach of that duty and damage consequent on that breach' (Harrop-Griffiths and Bennington, 1985: 1).

Medical negligence case law

Discussion about medical negligence tends to be framed, implicitly or explicitly, by the apparent explosion of litigation in the USA, to the extent that whole fields of medical practice there are allegedly being abandoned by practitioners, or are now practised in a defensive and conservative manner, as in the case of obstetrics. Some writers have referred to such litigation in the USA as almost a form of therapy in itself, namely the 'therapy of tort liability' (Fleming, 1994: 167). It is implied that the USA shows us the future for medical litigation in the UK. This makes for a dramatic argument, but there are also strong counter factors making this somewhat less likely as a future for medical practitioners, or, indeed, for therapists, in the UK. Firstly, the actual claim rates of medical negligence are much lower in the UK than in the USA, for example eight claims per thousand of the population in the UK during the 1980s, compared with 30 per thousand of the population in the USA (Ham et al., 1988: 20). Besides having twice as many lawyers per head in the USA as the UK, the US is notoriously litigious as a society, as observers since De Tocqueville have been keen to point out (De Tocqueville, 1840/1956: 126). Overall, 'differences between the two countries in legal, health care and social insurance systems mean that it is highly unlikely that levels of litigation will reach those of the US' (Ham et al., 1988: 5). One such important difference concerns the high level of compensation awarded in US courts. These awards of damages are decided by *juries* in the USA, not by the judge, as in the UK. Partly as a result of this, 'compensation for pain and suffering is infinitely more generous in the USA than it is here' (Brazier, 1992: 117). High levels of compensation in the US may also reflect the higher personal or insurance cost of medical care otherwise currently provided free in the UK via the NHS.

In conclusion, despite increases in the cost of meeting medical negligence actions in the UK rising from £80 million in 1992–3, to an estimated £125 million in 1994–5, there is no real evidence yet of a 'malpractice crisis' in the UK (BMA, 1996a: 330). The introduction of new complaints systems for the NHS, arbitration schemes, and the exclusion of medical negligence from 'conditional fee' legal representation measures in the UK may still further inhibit the growth of a 'sue first, last and always' culture in the UK, at least where medical negligence is concerned.

Litigation against psychiatrists
Within the field of medical negligence, it is the area of legal action against *psychiatrists* that most closely compares to the situation of therapists, while acknowledging the crucial differences between the two groups. In the USA, psychiatrists are involved in less than 1% of legal cases against doctors, according to one study (Slawson and Guggenheim, 1984). However, a more recent report indicates that this had risen to a level of 5% by 1994, but without including a detailed analysis of claims made (Bowman and Mertz, 1996: 576, fn 165). In the UK, legal action against psychiatrists is rare, but the attendant costs in terms of time and expense are still high. 'Psychiatrists are among the greatest users of medico-legal advisory services of the medical defence organisations but they are not the heaviest users when it comes to claims. Some psychiatric claims

Table 3.1 *Comparison of grounds for negligence claims against psychiatrists in the UK and USA*

Basis of claim	UK	USA
Suicide/attempted suicide	25	26
Medication	16	8
Failure/delay in diagnosis	3	36
Use of ECT	1	13
Medical/surgical complications		11
Death		7
Inadequate physical examination		6
Miscellaneous	5	
Total	50	107

Sources: Bradley, 1989; Slawson and Guggenheim, 1984

are relatively expensive to settle, however' (Ingram and Roy, 1995: 620).

One study of negligence cases brought against psychiatrists in the UK indicates that half of the cases relate to suicide or attempted suicide. These negligence claims can be 'very expensive to settle, particularly when a patient has suffered head or spinal injury following a suicidal attempt' (Bradley, 1989: 165). In one such case, a young man aged 16 was awarded £500,000 for spinal injuries following such an attempt at suicide. The usual practice is that when psychiatric patients are admitted to hospital as being potentially suicidal, they are placed under 'special observation', or 'specialled' in nursing jargon. This means that they are placed under continuous observation on the ward by specific nurses, working on rotation, to monitor the patient closely, and prevent self-harm or suicide attempts. Bradley's study (1989) covered 50 cases dealt with by the Medical Protection Society. However, it should be noted that none of these actually reached trial, and as with most tort cases, the majority were dropped or settled out of court. Table 3.1 compares the basis of claims made in the US and UK surveys. It should be noted that the data are of descriptive value only, as Bradley's figures relate only to cases covered by the Medical Protection Society, rather than to *all* recorded cases in the UK. There is also no indication of the time period covered by his study.

Comparison is made difficult by the way that the data are presented in the original studies. Slawson refers to a total of 217 cases brought against US psychiatrists during the period 1974 to 1978, only 16 of which related specifically to psychotherapy. Most of the latter concerned breaches of confidentiality (Slawson and Guggenheim, 1984: 980).

Psychiatrists' duty of care   Bradley discusses a number of cases where negligence was alleged after hospitalised psychiatric patients caused themselves serious injury, such as partial paralysis or hemiplegia, by attempting suicide. In the USA, there seems to be a stronger duty on the part of psychiatrists to prevent harm to such patients by exercising reasonable care (Austin et al., 1990: 127–44). In the UK, the legal system seems to be much more protective towards psychiatrists, and inclined to give them the benefit of the doubt. In one case, Mr Justice Mustill declared that:

> the duty is not to prevent suicide but to take reasonable care to that end – and the word is 'reasonable', not 'perfect'. Thus there may well be cases in which the taking of no precautions is consistent with reasonable care. With hindsight such precautions can be seen to have been desirable, but there may have been nothing known at the time which would have led the doctors to suppose that precautions were needed. Moreover, precautions which were reasonable in all the circumstances might yet prove inadequate to forestall a really determined attempt. (Bradley, 1989: 166)

In a similar case in 1981, Lord Denning took the position that 'it should be the policy of the law to discourage such actions [against medical staff] whether the patient succeeds in his suicide or not' (Bradley, 1989: 167). The problems of bringing successful cases against medical and other professionals are built into the very nature of tort law, which offers a system of peer defence against patients or relative claims for negligent treatment. The well-known case of *Bolam v. Friern HMC* [1957] sets the benchmark for deciding the standard of care in negligence cases. Here, the patient was given electro-convulsive therapy (ECT) without anaesthetic or relaxant drugs, and suffered a spinal fracture during the treatment. An expert witness testified in court that this was accepted practice at the time, which provided a sufficient defence to clear the doctor concerned of negligence. Although medical practice has changed with regard to the use of anaesthetics during ECT, and in the use of ECT overall, the prevailing standard at the time provided justification for the medical practice then adopted.

The dangers of overlooking relevant physiological symptoms are also illustrated in one case described by Bradley. Here, a patient with what was seen as psychogenic or undiagnosable backache, was referred to a psychiatrist, who commented: 'He seemed to find it difficult to accept any psychological interpretation for his symptoms. Perhaps he is too naive to benefit from psychotherapy.' Two days later, the patient became paralysed from the waist down by an undetected spinal tumour (Bradley, 1989: 169).

Barriers to legal action against psychiatrists   In comparing rates of legal action against psychiatrists in the USA and UK, an important point to consider is that the Mental Health Act 1983 has acted as a substantial barrier to litigation. Bradley suggests two reasons for this, firstly because of the mechanisms for the thorough monitoring of the Act's operations by hospital managers, mental health review tribunals, and the Mental Health Act Commission. Secondly, there is the perhaps more significant role of s.139 of the Mental Health Act 1983, which specifically *restricts* the use of civil or criminal proceedings against staff. Under this part of the 1983 Act, medical practitioners, social workers, and other professionals, are protected 'unless the act was done in bad faith or without reasonable care', and only by permission of the High Court in the case of civil proceedings, or by the Director of Public Prosecutions in the case of criminal proceedings (Stanton, 1986: 106).

In terms of case law, a Miss Winch brought an unsuccessful case against a consultant psychiatrist and his employer, Clwyd Health Authority, for failure to consider her discharge before the expiry of a 12-month detention order under what was then the Mental Health Act 1959, having been diagnosed as suffering from paranoia (*Winch v. Jones* [1985]). There is also the case of *Ashingdane v. UK* (1985), which attempted to challenge this threshold clause in mental health legislation as contrary to Article 6(1) of the European Convention on Human Rights.

Psychiatrists in the UK are therefore subject to protection from legal action via the very nature of *tort law*, which requires the plaintiff to *prove* that the damage experienced was *caused* by the negligence of the professional concerned. They are also specifically defended against legal action by *statute*, which aims to limit the use of the courts by patients seeking redress for decisions made or treatment provided in the course of the exercise of professional judgement. The key question for therapists is whether they too will enjoy such a favourable position in the eyes of the law, assuming that their claim to professional status is fully recognised at some stage in the future.

Therapy case law

In the USA, interest relating to law and therapy has concentrated on malpractice (Thompson, 1983). Despite the greater volume of case law in the USA, psychiatric malpractice figures indicate a relatively low risk of litigation, in comparison with doctors, although both claims and awards are increasing (Slawson and Guggenheim, 1984). Significantly, 85–90% of such cases are settled out of court. 'Studies indicate that even cases that proceed to trial are generally won by therapists' (Meyer et al., 1988: 19). Data on actions against psychologists and psychotherapists suggest a similar relatively low risk of malpractice litigation. Thus the American Psychological Association (for clinical psychologists) had an average of less than 100 claims for the period 1976–86. Claims against social workers in the USA have shown an increase in the more recent period 1976–88. This may, however, possibly reflect their adoption of greater responsibilities under new legislation (Reamer, 1993).

In the UK, the number of cases involving professional negligence by therapists is still small, with two cases recorded in detail at Appeal Court level, namely *Werner v. Landau* (1961) (see below), and *R. v. Registrar General ex parte Smith* [1991] (see Chapter 5 for fuller discussion). Bond reports the existence of 12 cases known to insurance companies, none of which had come to court by 1993 (1993a: 55).

Case Study: Case of Werner v. Landau (1961)

This was a case brought by Miss Alice Landau against Dr Theodor Werner, aged 62, concerning 24 sessions of psychotherapy, which took place between March and August 1949, and during the resumption of treatment from March 1950 up until January 1951. In April 1951, she attempted suicide. During therapy, she had developed a strong emotional attachment to Dr Werner, and there was a period of social contact between them after the first part of treatment was ended, which included letters, discussion about a weekend away together, and visits by Dr Werner to her flat. She brought a successful case against him for £6,000 damages for personal injuries and pecuniary loss sustained by her as a result of wilful misconduct and/or negligence by him as her medical attendant. This was upheld at Appeal.

The judge divided the case into three phases: the first covering the course of treatment, the second, when social contact occurred, and the third when an unsuccessful attempt was made to continue and resolve the treatment. His criticism was of the second stage. 'Dr Werner, with the best intentions in the world, made a most tragic mistake by introducing social contact . . . this was negligence on the part of Dr Werner' (*Times Law Report*, 8 March 1961). The social contact could not be justified as part of the treatment, and had the unintended effect of encouraging Miss Landau's affections for him.

Dr Werner was defended by the Medical Protection Society. His defence was that the social contact was justified in the exceptional circumstances of the case, where a strong emotional attachment had been formed towards him by the patient. 'He feared that she might if she was removed from his influence have a relapse and go into the state of anxiety neurosis in which she had been when she started the treatment' (*TLR*, 8 March 1961). While demonstrating that he was aware of the unorthodoxy of this approach, he argued that it was still necessary to protect the client's wellbeing and promote a positive outcome to the treatment, or at least minimise the likelihood of a relapse.

Part of the plaintiff's case was that sexual impropriety had occurred on these social visits. Despite the evidence of the attachment in the form of letters, the court found the latter allegations unproven. The judge 'absolutely absolved Dr Werner of any such misconduct or any misconduct of any sexual kind to his patient' (*TLR*, 8 March 1961). The Doctor's professional reputation was, to this extent, protected by this aspect of the judgement.

Therapist's duty of care
The main principle confirmed here is that of the *breach* of the therapist's (here the psychiatrist's) *duty of care to the client or patient*. Thus, 'it was the duty of a doctor to exercise ordinary skill

and care according to the ordinary and reasonable standards of those who practised in the same field . . . The standard for the specialist was the standard of the specialists' (*TLR*, 23 November 1961). This standard essentially derives from medical precedent referred to elsewhere, such as the cases of *Bolam v. Friern HMC* [1957], and *Maynard v. West Midlands Regional Health Authority* [1985]. In the *Bolam* case, the judges set a standard for negligence as a failure to act 'in accordance with a practice of competent respected professional opinion' (at 121).

The evidence heard in the *Werner* case was that to introduce social contact, for whatever therapeutic purpose, could not be sustained as a viable form of treatment. From the expert witnesses heard, it was deduced that 'the evidence of the doctors was all one way in condemning social contacts' (*TLR*, 23 November 1961). Some variation of opinion here might have acted in favour of the defendant, as the more recent *Maynard* case has acknowledged that professional (here, *medical*) opinion is not necessarily unanimous in defining forms of treatment. Hence, in the *Maynard* case, 'it was not sufficient for the plaintiff to show there was a body of competent opinion which considered that the decision was wrong if there also existed a body of professional opinion, equally competent, which supported the decision as being reasonable in the circumstances' (at 635). At a stage where psychoanalysis may have been the dominant paradigm for therapy, there were no available competing schools of counselling to provide a contrary opinion to the view that social contact was likely to harm the client's well-being and future recovery.

The above action was brought under the scope of professional negligence law, which may possess two elements, that of action in *tort* (a civil wrong experienced by the plaintiff) or the separate grounds of *breach of contract*. Proving a case of negligence by establishing a tort is notoriously difficult to achieve, because of the difficulty in proving that the breach of the duty of care actually *caused* the injury suffered, rather than simply preceded it in time. This action via tort is distinct from an action brought for breach of contract, where the defendant may have failed to carry out specific undertakings set out in a contract, whether express or implied. One example of breaching express conditions of a contract might be a therapist failing to provide an agreed number of counselling sessions which had been paid for in advance by the client.

Problems of proving causation The difficulty for clients will often be in *proving* that the breach of the duty of care in therapy actually *caused* the damage alleged. In the case of *Werner v. Landau*, the judges were satisfied that the long-term emotional damage that the client suffered *was* due to the doctor's negligent behaviour, rather than being the result of some pre-existing condition, or being due to other external intervening factors. This degree of certainty about the relationship of cause and effect will often be absent from cases involving therapy, where it can be, by its very nature, problematic to specify its intended or actual outcomes in individual cases with any degree of precision. The *Werner* case is also unusual in the amount of documentary evidence, such as letters, which the plaintiff was able to produce in support of her case. Often, it seems, this kind of evidence suggesting professional negligence is simply not available to the aggrieved client.

The implication is that Dr Werner was working in private practice at this time, which determined his *personal* liability for damages. If he had been working as an employee of the National Health Service, then vicarious liability would have been borne by the relevant health authority, as established in the case of *Cassidy v. Ministry of Health* [1951].

Transference and negligence One of the most interesting aspects of the case is the weight given to a serious discussion of the concept of *transference* in a court of law. The reality of transference was accepted as a powerful and accepted part of analytic treatment. 'Describing the system of treatment known as "transference" his Lordship said that in the course of the process a great deal of past emotion became reactivated. A great deal of the emotion released could be attached or attracted to the doctor who had undertaken the treatment' (*TLR*, 8 March 1961). The criticism of the court was not of the adoption of transference as a method of working with the client, but in the doctor's failure to abide by accepted safeguards in its use. The necessary safeguards, as agreed by a wide body of informed professional opinion, included the avoidance of any planned social contact outside the consulting room (Gabbard, 1995).

The allegations of sexual contact between the doctor and his client were dismissed by the court as erotic fantasy on her part, perhaps reflecting the conservative social mores of the time.

Given more recent research into the widespread extent of sexual contact between therapists and clients, it seems possible that the client's case would perhaps be considered more sympathetically today, and not dismissed as easily as it appears to have been (Jehu et al., 1994; Masson, 1992; Russell, 1993: Rutter, 1991). Feldman and Ward provide a detailed critique of this case along with other malpractice cases, the remainder occurring in the USA (for examples, see Box 3.1 below). They are critical of the court's decision with respect to the finding regarding misconduct. 'The case is wrongly worded and internally inconsistent. If the doctor is "absolved of all professional misconduct", upon what is the liability based?' (1979: 93). In their view, the court's perception of professional liability is unnecessarily narrow. Their argument is for a greater reliance upon cases brought under breach of *contract*, rather than via tort, which they claim unfairly disadvantages clients in any legal proceedings, for the reasons given above. Similarly, Cohen suggests that, following this case, 'we are unlikely to see a dramatic increase in such cases because of the uncertain state of our knowledge about counselling and psychotherapy, and because of the general obstacles placed by the law in the path of any plaintiff in any negligence action' (1992: 11). Other commentators argue, on the other hand, that therapy constitutes 'a ripe environment for litigation', where malpractice is unchallenged only because of legal obstacles inhibiting client challenges to the profession (Otto and Schmidt, 1991: 319).

To summarise, the principles involved here relate to the application of a standard concerning the therapist's *duty of care*, based by analogy on the medical profession. The case was brought by Alice Landau under the law relating to the tort of negligence, which is arguably more difficult to establish than simple breach of contract. The standard of care which applies is based on the requirements for safe and competent practice of the method adopted by the practitioner. Simply because the method is one used only by a minority of practitioners does not necessarily mean that the therapist is negligent as such. Hence the sympathetic discussion in *Werner v. Landau* of the particular problems faced in working with transference issues. Finally, the values expressed by the court in summarily dismissing the claim of sexual contact are perhaps indicative of the unequal power relationships prevailing between male practitioners and female clients, and

Box 3.1

Cases of professional negligence in the USA

Anclote Manor Foundation v. Wilkinson (1972)   Husband sued after doctor encouraged his patient to divorce and marry him; she committed suicide one year after discharge/divorce

Doe v. Roe and Roe (1977)   A therapist couple were sued for publishing a book describing the therapy of the plaintiff and her late husband; $20,000 compensatory damages awarded

Hammer v. Rosen (1959)   Negligence via the use of 'direct analysis', regressing the patient to infancy, and then 're-parenting', using violent methods

Mazza v. Huffaker (1983)   Therapist had a relationship with the client's wife. Compensatory damages of $102,000 plus $500,000 punitive damages on grounds he 'reacted improperly to transference or countertransference' to a third party, the client's wife.

Nicholson v. Han (1968)   Counsellor had affair with wife of couple in marital counselling with him

Rowe v. Bennett (1986)   Client sued female therapist for negligent infliction of mental and emotional distress for continuing treatment after becoming involved with client's female partner

Roy v. Hartogs (1975)   Counsellor had affair with client as part of her therapy, allegedly to help her overcome her lesbianism. Client awarded $153,000 damages, reduced to $25,000 on appeal

Zipkin v. Freeman (1969)   Counsellor persuaded client to become involved in nude 'group swimming therapy', advised her to divorce husband and marry him, and lend him $14,000; client awarded $18,000 damages

(Sources: Feldman and Ward,1979; Kermani, 1989; Otto and Schmidt, 1991)

the way that the law approached issues of gender and power at that time.

Barriers to litigation via tort   The apparent uniqueness of the *Werner* case in UK case law perhaps illustrates some of the problems faced by clients in bringing actions for professional negligence against therapists under tort law. Various commentators have argued that this approach unduly favours the professional at the expense of the client. 'Establishing the causal link between the psychotherapist's breach and the injury is the most difficult burden of proof for the plaintiff' (Feldman and Ward, 1979: 68). They propose an alternative approach, where action for damages by a client would, instead, be based on breach of contract. 'In the contract approach the plaintiff need only show the existence of the contract, the breach of the fiduciary duty infused in the contract, and the injury' (1979: 80). By the 'fiduciary duty', they refer to the reposing of ultimate trust and confidence in the therapist.

The legal notion of fault at work in tort law is an *objective* standard, based on what is perceived by judges to be *reasonable* behaviour, and which is therefore distinct from the personal qualities of the practitioner. In several cases, courts have decided that trainee practitioners have to provide the same duty of care as their more experienced or senior colleagues. In the case of *Wilsher* [1988] concerning a junior doctor, 'argument by the defendants that staff concerned did the best in view of their inexperience was rejected. The law requires all medical staff in such a unit to meet the standard of competence and experience society expects from those fulfilling such demanding posts' (Brazier, 1992: 120). However, where a practitioner is represented as possessing *specialist* skills, they will be judged against the relevant *higher* standard to be expected of a specialist. 'The test is the standard of the ordinary skilled man exercising or professing to have special skill' (*Whitehouse v. Jordan* [1981], quoted in Reynolds and King, 1989: 35).

Deciding on the standard of care for therapists How are such standards to be set by the courts, who may be unfamiliar with many aspects of professional or therapeutic skill and practice? The answer is through hearing the testimony of expert witnesses, who can advise the court on the appropriate standards or procedures to be expected of the practitioner. However, simply calling one or more experts who can criticise the practice of another is not sufficient in itself to demonstrate that the first was negligent. The law recognises a degree of diversity in all forms of professional practice as healthy – to do otherwise would penalise new and innovative practice, which may, in turn, become the established benchmark of the future. Thus 'a doctor who departs from orthodox views is not automatically branded as negligent. But he will have to justify his course of action either by indicating features of the individual case which call for a different mode of treatment or by showing his novel method to be superior or at least equal to the general practice' (Brazier, 1992: 126). Lord Scarman put it more forcefully, as always, in the case of *Maynard v. West Midlands RHA* [1985] (at 638): 'In the realm of diagnosis and treatment, negligence is not established by preferring one respectable body of professional opinion to another.'

Case law therefore suggests several principles relevant to therapists:

- the standard of care expected of a trainee is *not* lower than that of a reasonably competent practitioner (*Nettleship v. Western* [1971]; *Wilsher v. Essex AHA* [1988])
- criticism of one style of practice by an opposing approach is not sufficient in itself to brand the first as negligent (*Maynard v. West Midland RHA* [1985])
- the standard required for specialist practitioners is that to be expected from a *specialist*, rather than from a less skilled practitioner (*Whitehouse v. Jordan* [1981])

The elements listed in Box 3.2 could provide the basis for suggesting the elements of a duty of care as applied to therapists.

Any set of statements such as those included in Box 3.2 are, no doubt, immediately open to criticism and challenge as being well-meaning, but rather vague. The list may also be incomplete, since it includes no reference to duties relating to recording, supervision or the role of third parties, for example. The reason for the choice of the above is to seek to define the boundaries of the therapist's duty of care more narrowly with regard to the *immediate client*, rather than to include all aspects of best professional practice. Ultimately, the precise set of standards for a therapist's duty of care has yet to be fully tested in the courts. Many of the above elements *were* involved in the *Werner* case discussed above. The full meaning of 'not engaging in exploitative or unethical conduct towards the client' will depend, in the final instance, on the decision of the court, assisted by the advice of expert witnesses. Until then, the above, or any established *Code of Ethics* for therapists, will orient therapists towards the likely standards they would have to meet (BAC, 1996; BASMT, 1991; BPS, 1995b; UKCP, 1995).

Box 3.2

Elements of a therapist's duty of care

- not engaging in exploitative or unethical conduct towards the client
- obtaining informed consent or agreeing a contract for therapeutic work with the client
- acting within limits of own training, expertise and competence
- providing selection and skilled use of methods appropriate to the client's situation
- not harming the client as a result of physical or psychological methods employed
- not giving inaccurate or damaging advice
- clarifying and maintaining agreed or agency limits to confidentiality
- making appropriate referral to another therapist or agency when required
- ending therapy in a way consistent with client's best interests

---

Negligent assessment and treatment

One element of professional negligence may be in terms of incorrect assessment and treatment. The very notion of diagnosis or assessment may itself be anathema to some schools of therapy, such as the person-centred approach, but it still remains as a potential area for therapeutic mishap to occur. Non-medical therapists in the USA seem much more likely than their UK counterparts to be well versed and comfortable in using the diagnostic categories of manuals such as the *DSM-IV* or *ICD-10*, which are routinely used by psychiatrists in the US and UK. This may reflect US therapists' greater dependence upon health insurance funding as a source of income, as classification via *DSM-IV* is generally a crucial criterion for such entitlement to therapy (APA, 1994; Fong, 1995; Hohensil, 1994; WHO, 1992).

The case of *Osheroff v. Chestnut Lodge* in the USA, discussed below, raises a number of key questions, both about the reliance upon such psychiatric categories for assessment and treatment, and also about the vulnerable status of psychotherapy in treating certain forms of mental illness. As described above, both in the USA and the UK, it is possible to defend against claims of negligence by establishing that the practice adopted was consistent with a body of informed opinion, even while not representing the current orthodoxy. In the USA, this is known as the 'respectable minority rule'. However, such a school 'must be grounded in sound scientific principles that are attested to by professional expert witnesses' (Packman et al., 1994: 178).

Case Study: Case of Osheroff v. Chestnut Lodge (1985)

In the USA, Dr Osheroff was hospitalised in 1979 for seven months at Chestnut Lodge, and was treated with individual psychotherapy four times a week. During this time, he lost 35 lbs in weight, experienced severe insomnia, and had marked symptoms of physical agitation. This was evident in his incessant pacing and was so extreme that his feet actually became swollen and blistered. He was discharged by his family, and then admitted to Silver Hill, where he was diagnosed as having a psychotic depressive reaction. Here he was treated with medication, started to improve within three weeks, and was discharged within three months, with a final diagnosis of manic-depressive illness, depressed type.

He then sued the private psychiatric facility, Chestnut Lodge, for negligence because the staff had incorrectly failed to prescribe medication and had instead treated him according to the psycho-dynamic model. The case was settled out of court for an undisclosed amount, and therefore has no value in terms of setting a legal precedent. The conflict was in part over the making of the correct diagnosis, biological depression, versus narcissistic personality disorder. The suit against Chestnut Lodge pointed out that their diagnosis (narcissistic personality disorder) did not appear in the then current edition of DSM-II (1968 version), and that negligence arose from not using a commonly agreed system of diagnosis. It also alleged failure to treat appropriately, claiming that the law should regard as negligence per se the treatment of serious mental disorders through psychotherapy alone. The defence case rested on the argument that the real cause of the patient's behaviour at both hospitals was due to negative transference.

(Source: Packman et al., 1994)

While the case sets no legal precedent for the USA, it does raise concern about the relative status of drug-based and psychotherapeutic methods of treating clients. Packman concludes from his discussion that 'given the current legal climate, negligent psychotherapy, negligent treatment and misdiagnosis of psychiatric conditions are likely to constitute a ripe area for future lawsuits against psychotherapists. Psychodynamic psychothera-pists may be particularly vulnerable to such lawsuits' (1994: 195). From another perspective, Bollas and Sundelson have expressed a parallel concern that psychotherapy may be marginalised as treatment for anxiety and depression, at least where the NHS in Scotland is concerned (1995: 142; CRAG, 1993; NMAC, 1994).

The tort system presents a number of difficult hurdles for clients wishing to establish that their therapist has been guilty of pro-fessional negligence. The very lack of case law, particularly in the UK, is more likely to point to the problems involved in *proving* damage caused by a therapist's failure to observe a duty of care, rather than the simple absence of cause for complaint by satisfied consumers. The flowering of rival schools of therapy, now numbered at 450, may also mean that a variety of approaches now have to be seen as consistent with professional practice, rather than the simple adoption of a single standard to judge all cases. The days of the *Werner* case in 1961, when the psychoanalytic school provided the dominant approach to therapy, have gone for good, and hundreds of competing schools now bloom. Without more case law, it is hard to say whether this will benefit therapist or client in defining the standard of care to apply in negligence cases.

Informed consent and contracting

One of the issues concerned in the US *Osheroff* case was that of the alleged failure to obtain the client's informed consent to treatment. The implication was that the client would not have agreed to psychotherapy if the proven benefits of medication had been properly made known to him. 'Consent, to be effective, must stem from a knowledgeable decision based on adequate information about the therapy, the available alternatives, and the collateral risks' (Bray et al., 1985: 53). Law in the USA has moved from a *relative* standard of disclosing risks of medical treatment to an *absolute* standard of disclosing *all* relevant information, even including a 1% outside chance of permanent damage from surgery (Kermani, 1989: 9). The more restrictive UK medical model of informed consent is based on the conservative model of the *Bolam* test, as applied in *Sidaway v. Bethlem Royal Hospital Governors* [1985]. This emphasises the doctor's *duty* to release *appropriate* information, rather than the US model of the patient's *right* to *all* relevant information, however limited the risk.

Part of the information needed for a client to give informed consent would be about the possible harmful effects of therapy, including, at least in the short-term, deterioration of mood, worsening of behavioural symptoms and potential adverse effects on family and other significant relationships. One therapist, working on this principle, refuses to counsel individuals without their current partner's knowledge and agreement, due to the risk of possible relationship break-up. Other well-established risks of therapy are described by a range of writers (Alexander, 1995; Grunebaum, 1986; Lambert et al., 1977; Masson, 1992; Striano, 1988). The effectiveness and relative benefits of different types of therapy obviously also need to be conveyed no less clearly to potential clients (Barkham, 1992; Bergin and Garfield, 1994; Bolger, 1991; Dryden and Feltham, 1992; McLeod, 1993; 1994).

The concept of informed consent raises a number of difficulties for non-medical therapists, not least that the outcomes of an interpersonal relationship cannot be specified in advance with any real precision, unlike the probable side-effects of medication or surgery. In addition, some aspects of the therapeutic relationship operate at other than a consciously understood level, for example, transference in psychoanalysis, and paradoxical injunction in family therapy (Holmes and Lindley, 1989). Holmes has argued that therapists in this situation cannot really offer their clients an informed choice between conscious and unconscious processes as alternatives, asking rhetorically 'can one give informed consent to transference?' (Holmes et al., 1994: 467).

One relevant factor here may be the concept of 'therapeutic paternalism' where the therapist balances the need for total disclosure with the need to preserve the client's well-being (Bray et al., 1985: 55). In medical terms, this is referred to in the *Sidaway* case in the UK as 'therapeutic privilege'. Here the doctor may decide *not* to disclose the full facts to a patient if it may cause the patient mental or physical harm or cause them to refuse necessary treatment (Chadwick and Ngwena, 1992).

In medical terms, informed consent depends upon two factors on the client's part, namely *capacity*, and *agreement* or consent to treatment (see Box 3.3).

For therapists, informed consent will usually refer to a current or imminent therapeutic relationship (see Box 3.4). The medical profession is increasingly looking at informed consent which *anticipates* a need for treatment at a stage in the future when the

Box 3.3

Requirements for informed consent

Capacity

An individual to have capacity must be able to:

- understand what medical treatment is and that somebody has said he needs it and why the treatment is being proposed
- understand in broad terms the nature of the proposed treatment
- understand its principal benefits and risks
- understand what will be the consequences of not receiving the proposed treatment
- possess the capacity to make a choice (Para 15.10)

Consent

'Consent' is the voluntary and continuing permission of the patient to receive a particular treatment, based on an adequate knowledge of the purpose, nature, likely effects and risks of that treatment including the likelihood of its successes and any alternative to it, Permission given under any unfair or undue pressure is not 'consent'. (Para 15.12)

A person with a mental disorder is not necessarily incapable of giving consent. (Para 15.11)

(Source: DoH/WO, 1993)

Box 3.4

Features of informed consent

- client's capacity to make a voluntary choice between alternatives
- client's understanding of costs, benefits and drawbacks of available alternatives
- client's voluntary and continuing permission for their involvement

---

patient's consent will be difficult to obtain, perhaps through the effect of trauma or dementia (BMA, 1995; PA, 1995; RCP, 1996). There are, however, limits to the medical analogy. Bond argues the case that counselling depends on the active and conscious participation of clients in therapy, rather than a passive acquiescence to clinical technique. His view is that a more explicit process of *contracting* is necessary so that the respective obligations of both parties are clearly understood (Bond, 1993a: 69–71;

1994b: 21). He suggests that contracting is a more appropriate method to use in therapy than informed consent, given that the client needs to be an *active* participant in the therapeutic process (Bond, 1993a: 70).

Some therapists, if using the informed consent approach, may tend to think of it as a one-off event, the signing of an agreement specifying the nature of the contact, and the risks and benefits involved. Packman argues against this approach, suggesting that informed consent really represents more of a *process of dialogue*, continuous updating and checking out with the client, rather than a once and for all event. 'Consent is an ongoing dialogue between the patient and mental health professional in which both parties exchange information, ask questions, and come to an agreement on the course of psychotherapy . . . Both parties must be active participants. A document cannot replace this important process. The emphasis is on communication, not the form' (Packman et al., 1994: 193).

Negligent advice

The benchmark for case law in terms of professionals offering negligent advice is that of *Hedley Byrne* [1964]. This concerned a faulty evaluation of a company's financial worth, but the basic principle will be held to apply to many fields well outside that of the commercial world. Professionals giving advice as a part of their activities need to be sure that the advice is accurate and well-founded. While adding a disclaimer to advice can reduce liability, it does not remove it entirely (Pannett, 1992: 29). A client could seek damages for pecuniary or financial loss caused by a therapist's faulty advice, as perhaps in the case of a client 'advised' by their stress counsellor to give up their highly demanding executive post.

Recent examples of negligent advice concern Lloyds Bank and mortgage lending, where this duty was again confirmed (*Guardian*, 5 September 1995; 17 January 1996). The principle has also been extended to explore the activities of debt counsellors working in Citizen's Advice Bureaux (CAB). Davies (1995) has suggested that such debt counsellors would carry liability together with the CAB for negligent advice, and cites the example of *Paskie v. Knightsbridge 165* [1985]. Here, a claim for unfair dismissal failed because the CAB concerned failed to lodge it within the required three-month time limit.

The BAC *Code of Ethics* explicitly says that 'Counsellors do not normally give advice' (1993a: Para 2.2.2). Most therapists would claim that they do not give advice because this approach runs directly counter to the ethical principle of promoting the client's right to autonomy. However, it may well be that the non-directive and nuanced style of therapy is unfamiliar to many clients, so that an invitation to reflect on conflict and feelings about a key relationship may instead become translated by the client in his or her mind into 'my therapist said I *must* end this relationship, because it is not meeting my needs'. Actually *proving* that a therapist gave advice of any kind may be somewhat difficult for the client to establish at a later stage. Two brief cases below illustrate some of the problematic issues involved in therapist advice-giving.

Case Study: Stuart Sutherland, on confessing to his analyst his wishes to beat up his wife's lover

He was a genuinely kind and considerate man, and although he used some Freudian interpretations he also used his common-sense. I told him that I was thinking of going up to London and beating hell out of 'the lout', whom I felt like murdering. To my surprise, he said: 'That would be a much more sensible thing to do than what you are doing at the moment – you would be better to take it out of him than to go on taking it out of yourself.' I said: 'I never expected an analyst to advise me to indulge in physical violence', and he replied: 'You would of course have to make the violence commensurate with the crime and be careful not to inflict any long-term injury.'

(Sutherland, 1977: 17)

No actual outcome is recorded to this therapeutic exchange. Assuming the accuracy of this account, the therapist is putting himself at risk here of encouraging his client to break the law.

Case Study: Advice or paradoxical injunction?

I first obtained Marvin's agreement to help Phyllis overcome her phobia by promising to follow any suggestions I gave him. I instructed him to say to her, punctually every two hours, phoning her if he were at work, these words precisely: 'Phyllis, please don't leave the house. I need to know you are there at all times to take care of me and prevent me from being frightened.'

. . . Phyllis, even though she knew Marvin was following my instructions, grew irritated with him for ordering her to stay at home. After a few days she went to the library alone, then shopping, and in the next few weeks ventured farther than she had for years.

(Yalom, 1991: 267–8)

Paradoxical injunction is a powerful therapeutic technique where the therapist relays advice to the client to do something, not necessarily intending that they will comply. The 'advice' actually highlights underlying needs and drives which have been hitherto unexplored or unresolved. In Yalom's example, the advice had the desired effect, and Phyllis, who was troubled by agoraphobia, quickly overcame it, perhaps as a consequence of this technique. If she had experienced a worsening of her condition, then she and her husband may have had legitimate cause for complaint or action against their therapist.

Third party liability
Professional negligence by therapists may harm third parties, rather than just affect the client who is receiving the service. Third parties, such as the client's partner or parents, are unable to sue for breach of contract, not having been part of the original agreement, and would need to take action under tort law. Here, the principle of establishing a causal link between negligence and harm becomes even more tenuous for clients to prove in court. However, a body of case law in the USA has been slowly growing which embodies this principle, extending the duty of care for therapists still wider in some exceptional cases (see Box 3.5 for examples).

Third party liability for UK professionals   UK law does not seem to be as extensive in relation to third party liability for professionals. For example, in a case which bears a similarity to some of the cases described above, Jayne Zito, widow of Jonathon Zito, has been unable to sue the relevant health authority for breach of their statutory duty of care. Christopher Clunis, a patient dis-

---

Box 3.5

Third party legal action against therapists in the USA

Brady et al. v. Hopper (1983)   President Reagan's former Press Secretary, seriously injured in an assassination attempt, brought an unsuccessful case against the attacker's therapist for failure to diagnose, treat or warn.

Currie v. US (1986)   Victim's widow sued Veterans' Association for failure to admit their patient for psychiatric treatment, in view of his deteriorating mental condition.

Lipari v. Sears (1980)   Out of court settlement for $20,000 by Sears company and Veterans' Association (VA) over case of ex-VA patient who bought a gun from the former and fatally wounded the plaintiff's husband, six weeks after terminating psychiatric treatment.

McIntosh v. Milano (1979)   Victim's parents sued a psychiatrist for failure to warn of the actual danger posed to her by his patient receiving therapy.

Peck v. Counseling Service of Addison County (1985)   A child's parents sued the agency for failure to warn them of his realistic threat to burn down their barn made during therapy.

Petersen v. Washington (1983)   The plaintiff sued the hospital team which had authorised the release from psychiatric treatment of a drug addict, who drove through a red light and injured her in a car crash.

Tarasoff v. Regents of the University of California (1974; 1976)   Victim's parents successfully sued the University concerning staff who counselled the assailant, for failing to warn their daughter of a realistic threat to her life.

(Source: Kermani, 1989)

---

charged from a psychiatric hospital, fatally stabbed her husband on an Underground station platform. However, the health authority's duty of care, under s.117 of the Mental Health Act 1983, was seen to extend only to the *patient*, and not to her as a third party. Her only option was to seek to sue Clunis *personally* for damages caused by assault and trespass to the person (*Guardian*, 16 December 1995). In another case, a psychiatrist who mistakenly identified a woman's cohabitee as the sexual abuser of the woman's child, was found *not* to be personally liable via a private law action brought by the mother for damages caused by social services' intervention, and by the court's subsequent decision to place the child in care. The psychiatrist's duty of care was seen by the court to lie *primarily* towards the health authority which authorised the interview process, rather than to the mother or the child herself (*M v. Newham Borough Council* [1994]).

However, there are some indications elsewhere that this legal perspective may be in the process of changing. An accountancy firm, Binder Hamlyn, was found liable for negligent estimation of a company's financial position to a third party intending to make a takeover (*Guardian*, 7 December 1995). In another case which widens the parameters of professional responsibility, *Spring v. Guardian Assurance plc* [1994], it was established that providers of references owe a duty of care not only to the recipient of the reference, but also to the *subject* of the reference. The trend of legal development seems therefore to be to widen the dimensions of the professional's duty of care to others in some cases, beyond that owing to the immediate client.

Liability of public sector professionals   For therapists working in the public sector, the question of their liability towards the immediate client seems to be somewhat inconsistent, according to recent case law (Rodger, 1995). The psychiatrist in the *Newham* [1995] case was judged to owe a duty of care to the *employing authority*, rather than to the mother and child being interviewed. However, under mental health law, the approved social worker and doctor each owe a duty of care to the individual *patient* being assessed (Dugdale, 1994: 396; Fennell, 1996: 395). In a case considered alongside the *Newham* case above, educational psychologists employed by an education authority were held to owe a duty of care to *parents and children* in providing advice and guidance (*E. v. Dorset C.C.* [1995]). In deciding the *Newham* case, the courts seemed reluctant to impose additional duties on professionals which might have a serious effect in undermining the complex child protection services in England and Wales. However, the result is that public sector professional liability towards the client currently appears to vary according to statute and setting.

Therapist liability for false memory   For therapists, the most dramatic and alarming development in terms of professional negligence law has been the growth of third party litigation in the

USA over the promotion of allegedly false memories of sexual abuse. Recent allegations that therapists have implanted or encouraged such memories of childhood sexual abuse have received a great deal of media publicity. In legal terms, action against therapists in the USA can take the form of third party actions by aggrieved parents alleged to be the abusers. Another variant, again in the USA, is for clients to make allegations of abuse against parents, retract, and then sue the therapist for encouraging the false memories, via what is termed 'retractor action'. The basis for such litigation would be on the grounds of professional negligence, normally an action rarely successful for clients to win. The best known case is that of *Ramona* (1994):

Case Study: The Ramona case: third party action in the USA for false memory

Holly Ramona, 24, claimed to recover memories of early childhood sexual abuse by her father during therapy for depression and bulimia. As a result of the allegations, Gary Ramona's wife, Stephanie, divorced him, his three daughters refused to speak to him, and he was dismissed from his $500,000 job in a wine company.

The therapists working with Holly were Marche Isabella, a licensed child, family and marriage counsellor, and Richard Rose, MD, a psychiatrist. In order to facilitate the recovery of her memories, the client had agreed to their suggestion to take sodium amytal, a drug used to produce abreaction.

Holly Ramona brought a lawsuit for $500,000 damages against her father, alleging abuse; he responded by bringing a case against Rose and Isabella for $8 million for malpractice, charging that they had implanted the abuse memories in his daughter. The case was unusual, as the first time there had been a third party action in the USA against therapists on these specific grounds. The plaintiff was successful, winning the case in May 1994, although being awarded the significantly lower sum of $475,000 in damages. Holly Ramona's subsequent case against her father was dismissed by the court, the judge declaring that the earlier case had demonstrated that no abuse had taken place.

(Sources: *Guardian*, 23 July 1994; 14 December 1994)

The *Ramona* case has been taken as the green light for a wave of litigation in the USA against therapists on the basis of encouraging false memories of abuse, including action by clients as well as by third parties (*New York Times*, 17 December 1994). Similar legal action has not taken place in the UK, although it seems to be widely feared by therapists. The *Ramona* case has undoubtedly received a large amount of media attention, but needs to be considered carefully. It does not demonstrate that therapist malpractice is widespread on the issue of encouraging unsound beliefs in sexual abuse. The question of malpractice may have been influenced by the therapists' use of sodium amytal, described as a 'truth serum' by the plaintiff, which can produce images and memories which are not reliable evidence for legal purposes (Perry and Jacobs, 1982; Putnam, 1992).

The *Ramona* case raises many important questions about the techniques used by therapists to explore complex and sensitive areas, where a client's current problems of self-esteem, anorexia, self-harming or depression, may originate in early unrecognised or unacknowledged childhood sexual abuse. The use of hypnosis, or related techniques, involving visualisation and regression, may lead to their client's evidence being dismissed by courts both in the UK and USA, in subsequent actions against alleged abusers. The conflict between the approaches of some branches of therapy, and the more exacting requirements of courts for admissible evidence, are graphically illustrated by the therapist Richard Rose's statement about the session using the drug sodium amytal.

> Rose and Isabella say they suggested nothing but asked Holly to talk about the memories she'd previously discussed. 'I was not grilling a witness. I was allowing a patient to speak', Rose said in a deposition. 'She could not see his face. She described a shadowy image of a person whom she thought was her father. She was afraid. She was believable. She felt some physical weight on top of her. She cried.' (Butler, 1994: 12)

The amount of damages awarded was significantly lower than the $8 million claimed. This suggests strongly that the jury, which sets damages under the US legal system, was not completely convinced of the strength of Gary Ramona's case. According to one report,

> . . . the jury verdict was ambiguous. Said jury foreman Thomas Dudum: 'We all got rather disturbed when Mr Ramona captured the

headlines by claiming a victory of sorts, when we knew the case did not prove that he did not do it. I want to make it clear that we did not believe, as Gary indicates, that these therapists gave Holly a wonder drug and implanted these memories. It was an uneasy decision and there were a lot of unanswered questions. (Butler, 1994: 7)

The unanswered questions remain, not least because the law seems to be such a blunt instrument in determining truth in such complex and unclear areas of human experience as recovering fragmented and elusive images of childhood trauma (Bowman and Mertz, 1996; Jenkins, 1997; Orr, 1996).

The reported litigation against therapists in the USA has raised concern in the UK amongst practitioners about the occurrence of similar legal action in the UK, and the need to establish boundaries of safe and competent practice. The probability of successful third party action in the UK against therapists for allegedly implanting false memories of abuse in clients' minds is currently limited. This is because tort law in England and Wales does not usually include third party action, as this is seen to be too remote from the original cause of action. The courts are also reluctant to keep progressively extending the boundaries of tort liability in an incremental fashion. By responding to each new cause for tort action, the courts would be in danger of creating whole new categories for civil action, with unintended consequences for the legal system and for society as a whole (*M v. Newham L.B.C.* [1995]).

There has been intense discussion about therapeutic practice and the development of allegedly false memories of abuse, which has clarified the merits of safe and competent practice methods for therapists (BPS, 1995a: 25; Dale, 1995: 47–51; Enns et al., 1995: 227–44; Yapko, 1994: 153–4). These are summarised in Box 3.6.

Other forms of liability
Besides third party liability, there are some other forms of liability which should be mentioned briefly. These include:

- *criminal liability*: where the degree of negligence amounts to a crime, as in the case of a doctor giving a fatal injection of sedative drugs for a routine operation
- *strict liability*: under EU and UK consumer protection law, damage, death or injury caused by faulty products remains the responsibility of the producer or retailer

---

Box 3.6

Guidelines for professional practice in working with recovered memories of childhood sexual abuse

- avoid using suggestion and leading questions
- be cautious about jumping to conclusions about abuse as *necessarily* being a causal factor, e.g. in eating disorders
- avoid *discounting* the possibility of abuse memories which are not conscious
- be aware of the danger of *imposing* views or information on the prevalence of childhood sexual abuse on to the client
- work at the client's level: recovered memories may be actual truth, or part of a wider therapeutic narrative
- evidence required for legal proceedings is weakened or invalidated by use of drugs or hypnosis
- strict criteria are applied in deciding whether material from a client is admissible as evidence in a court of law

---

- *public liability*: damage caused to a member of the public, for example injury to a client through tripping up on a carpet in the consulting room.

The tort system places clients and third parties at a severe disadvantage in trying to seek redress for damage caused by a therapist failing to exercise due care in their work. Litigation is expensive and uncertain of outcome. Legal aid may not be available, and the US system of 'conditional fee' charging, where lawyers make no charge but take a proportion of the final award, covers personal injury claims, but has yet to be introduced to this country for medical negligence work. The tort system has been described as a 'lottery', in comparison with 'no-fault' compensation schemes which operate in countries such as New Zealand (Ham et al., 1988: 5–6). The primary aim of such schemes is to separate out the element of *compensation* from *blame*. The tort system requires both the establishment of *fault*, and resultant *harm*. Against this, professionals operate a system of peer defence, where the standard of care is set by current norms of professional practice, rather than by best practice.

The Pearson Commission, reporting in 1978, was in favour of retaining the tort system as a check on medical malpractice, but the figures suggest that a strong series of filters operate to deflect most claims from ever reaching court. It recorded that 60% of such claims were abandoned, and 34% were settled out of court. Only 5% actually went to court. Of these, 80% were won by the defendants (Pearson Commission, 1978). Arguing a contrary case, Brazier comments, 'most of all the tort system is not fair . . . the difficulties and cost of litigation place enormous pressure on a claimant to settle for less than full compensation' (1992: 214). Some of the problems involved in taking legal action and making complaints are more fully explored in Chapter 6.

Indemnity insurance and professional protection societies

The increasing amount of litigation against professionals, from architects to doctors, and from veterinary surgeons to accountants, has pushed this issue to the forefront of current concerns of many therapists. Evidence of professional indemnity insurance is now required by some advertisers and even by some schemes for validating training courses. There are frequent references to the need for insurance cover, and to the dangers of inadequate or incorrect coverage, to which the media interest in false memory claims has given an added boost (Dobson, 1995; Litton, 1996). The therapist's fear of litigation may be greater than the actual risk, however. When the word 'sue' is mentioned, it is worth distinguishing between different levels of meaning. Suing may refer to:

- a dissatisfied client, who is *considering* action or complaint
- a similar client who has actually *engaged* a solicitor
- actual *receipt of a writ*, and the commencement of legal proceedings
- *settling* prior to, or out of, court
- *legal proceedings* in the Small Claims or County Court
- final resolution of the case, and *decision of the court* for or against the therapist or agency.

Only 5% of cases successfully proceed to court, and of these, most are won by the practitioner. This is not to deny the considerable stress involved, for all parties, but to put litigation in its proper context. In the medical field, there has been a rise in defence society subscriptions from £40 p.a. (1978) to £1,000 p.a. (1988).

The average time for settling such claims is about four years. One of the major defence societies, the Medical Protection Society, records an increase in the numbers of claims received from 1,000 in 1983 to 2,000 in 1987. Ham suggests that the most likely explanation for the rising number of claims is that they are due to 'claims consciousness, the awareness among victims of the possibility of legal redress and their readiness to pursue this route' (Ham et al., 1988: 9,15).

The spectre of medical litigation in the USA has led to a number of effects, such as the adoption of defensive medicine via the use of often unnecessary tests, and the withdrawal of doctors from practice in vulnerable areas like obstetrics. One extreme response has even been that of 'going bare', or practising without insurance on the basis that 'stones do not bleed'. All the practitioner's personal assets are at risk in this case, if successfully sued. It is also unfair to patients in cases of true liability, as no damages or compensation can be obtained, however valid the client's case (Hawkins, 1985: 251). One spectacular consequence has been the effect on the medical insurance system itself, which, it was claimed, almost collapsed under the weight of negligence claims in 1975. Many companies withdrew from the field, while others increased premiums by 750% (1985: 251).

Critique of indemnity insurance

In the UK, the issue of therapists obtaining indemnity insurance cover seems to have become fused with the wider question of their acquiring fully professional status. The main counter argument to the rush to insure has come from Mearns, writing from a person-centred perspective. His argument has a number of strands. Firstly, he points out that there has been no significant claim by a client in Great Britain to date. Secondly, the risks to clients are overstated, as therapy does not rest on physically intrusive measures, nor on the supply of potentially dangerous products. Thirdly, promoting publicity about insurance actually *increases* the risk of claims by clients. Finally, the development of an insurance mentality in therapy erodes the autonomy of clients, by emphasising their vulnerability and dependence. 'Indemnity insurance is a combatant defensive action to discourage possible challenge from clients' (Mearns, 1993: 164).

How widespread or influential Mearns' critique is seems unclear. The more mainstream position is that indemnity insurance is of benefit for therapists, and should be seriously considered by all practitioners. The arguments are that insurance can fund the legal advice necessary to protect the therapist, can pay the damages ordered against them in a successful claim, and are necessary in an ethical sense to recompense the client for injury or damage sustained by malpractice.

Forms of insurance cover and of liability

Some professional groups are covered against negligence claims via the nature of their employment; for example, doctors are partially covered by what is called NHS or 'Crown' indemnity. In addition, within the medical field, there are organisations such as the Medical Protection Society and the Medical Defence Union which offer additional support and legal advice on a wide range of issues beyond that of NHS liability.

Therapists may be covered in a similar way via the nature of their employment, on the principle of vicarious liability, whereby the employer must insure for acts carried out by employees in the course of their work. Syme makes the case that for those therapists working in independent practice, insurance coverage is both an ethical and a practical necessity (1994: 84). Domestic cover alone will not be sufficient for liability incurred while working at home (Kitching, 1995c; McMahon, 1994).

Different types of insurance cover to be considered include:

- professional indemnity insurance
- domestic insurance cover for home and car (if used in connection with work)
- product liability
- public liability
- libel and slander
- employer's liability

Professional indemnity policy is 'essentially an insurance which provides resources and funds required to *defend an allegation* of negligence' (Flaxman, 1989: 19). It embraces both *negligence* in the form of errors and omissions, for example, giving the wrong response, and *malpractice*, namely giving damaging forms of help. While less than 5% of claims actually go to court there can be a heavy cost of defending claims, in one case a cost of £53,000 was incurred to defend a claim of £12,000 in 1987 (Flaxman, 1989:

22). An employee will be covered by his employer's insurance, under the principle of vicarious liability, but it is argued that it is still prudent to have *independent* access to legal advice and representation, as the interests of the employer and the therapist need not always coincide. The employer, for example, may have less interest in contesting a case in order to defend the practitioner's reputation. It may seek to settle out of court when the therapist wishes, for various reasons, that the case be heard and brought to a successful conclusion.

Domestic insurance cover alone will not be sufficient for liability incurred while working at home; nor will it cover office equipment or other material used in such work. Working from home may also invalidate cover under contents or buildings policies (Kitching, 1995c).

Product liability covers the supply to clients of defective goods causing damage, for example, aromatherapy oils, candles, relaxation tapes, or biofeedback machines.

Public liability covers liability for death of or injury to persons other than employees or for damage to third party property, such as sustaining injury by tripping over a loose carpet.

Libel and slander, covering, for example, comments made about clients or third parties in reports to agencies, or to the courts. Litton (1996) gives an example where a relaxation tape made for a client also contained critical comments about them made in consultation with another professional colleague, which were potentially libellous.

Employer's liability insurance is necessary if the practitioner is employing others. If trading as a partnership or limited liability company, the company needs its own insurance cover, such as a 'firms' policy.

Joint and several liability: this is a collective form of liability held by *all* partners for the actions or negligence of their partners in the firm. For example, with a legal partnership of therapists, a claim for damages could be made by a client against *all* partners in the firm for the negligent or abusive therapy practised by one partner.

Legal representation

One of the major elements of indemnity insurance is for legal costs. 'Most of the claims against insured members have proved to be ill-founded, but not until after legal costs (and, in some cases, substantial legal costs) have been incurred on their behalf by the insurers' (BPS, 1995c: 82). Legal representation may be included for disciplinary proceedings such as the hearing of a complaint to the therapist's professional association. Legal costs are covered for the *successful* defence of an allegation of sexual impropriety with a client. An *unsuccessful* defence would not be covered, to avoid the problem of providing cover for a deliberate wrongful act by the therapist. The coverage is also reactive, rather than proactive, so that insurance companies will not undertake legal action to clear the therapist's good name. Companies will also usually provide a fully confidential legal helpline for those insured. While litigation will usually represent the genuine efforts of an aggrieved client to seek redress, there may also be other motives for the client pursuing a case beyond the stage of conciliation. Thus, 'a vindictive claimant may pursue a claim (not only) in the hope of generating financial reward but in the hope of generating the greatest degree of distress or the greatest amount of adverse publicity' (BPS, 1995c: 83).

Professional indemnity insurance rates in existence for 1996 were:

> £500,000 any one claim: £37.88
> £1,000,000 any one claim: £43.00
> £2,000,000 any one claim: £49.15
>
> (Litton, 1996)

(Details of insurance companies are given in the Resources section at the end of this book.)

When a claim is being made or is likely to be made, it is important to inform the insurers immediately. 'The policy contains clear instructions not to make any offers, promises, compromises, payments or admissions of liability' (Flaxman, 1989: 23).

The actual claim process is started when:

- the insured is served a writ, or
- the insured receives notice, either orally or in writing, of the intention of a third party to commence legal proceedings, or

---

Box 3.7

Action to take in the case of potential complaint or litigation by a client

- be alert to early signs of conflict, hostility or persistent misunderstanding with clients
- attempt to resolve these conflicts informally at an early stage wherever possible
- do _not_ make admissions of liability which may invalidate your insurance cover or weaken a later court case
- keep detailed records of contact (letters, phone calls, conversations) for later reference
- contact your professional indemnity insurance company or professional protection society at an early stage for advice

---

■ the insured becomes aware of circumstances which are likely to give rise to a claim

'Circumstances' are usually undefined, but could be indicated by persistent unresolved problems, acrimonious correspondence, the withholding of fees, or poor personal relationships with clients (Flaxman, 1989: 118–19). Systematic and regular record keeping may be one of the best ways for a practitioner to build a defence against a successful claim, according to one writer on indemnity insurance. 'In my insurance business we see many spurious claims simply disappear due to the rigorous attention to detail by the practitioner. Copious and detailed notes have been produced, while the client failed to produce solid evidence' (Balen, 1995: 15).

Protection by insurance can be either on a 'claims made' basis, or 'losses occurring' basis, for the current period of insurance cover. Under the first type of cover, the practitioner is protected for claims made against them while the insurance is in force, but not after it has ceased. It is important in this case, therefore, to acquire 'run-off' protection to cover a past period of practice, as there may be a delay of some years before a claim is actually made. Under a 'losses arising' approach, the insured is covered for the period to which the insurance relates, regardless of whether the claim is made at a much later date. Litton describes a policy for therapists offering both 'run-off' and 'retrospective cover' (1996). Past claims have been made against social workers, for example, for decisions made during their period of employment, despite the fact that they have since changed posts, or even left social work practice entirely. The British Psychological Society (BPS) has encouraged its 7,000 psychologists to take out indemnity insurance against the risk of claims. Endorsing a strong recommendation from its Professional Affairs Board, the BPS has stopped short of making this a mandatory requirement, but notes that such is the case for other chartered bodies (BPS, 1995c: 82).

Professional protection societies

It is sometimes assumed in the debate about malpractice protection, that the issue stops with a choice of professional indemnity insurance policy. It is worth remembering that there is another option, along the lines of the medical defence bodies which act to protect medical practitioners. These are not insurance companies, but operate on a different basis. The key difference is that between a 'mutual non-profit-making defence association and commercial insurance' (Hawkins, 1985: 38). 'Such a policy, rather than being a legal contract of indemnity, is actually a discretionary promise to pay for support, advice, protection and, if necessary, legal and defence costs and any damages awarded by the court, without specific amounts, preconditions or exclusions defined' (Balen, 1995: 15). A professional protection society does not increase subscriptions on the basis of the number of claims made by an individual, whereas renewal of a therapist's insurance cover could conceivably be refused by an insurance company because of the high level of claim(s) made previously. It may also be the case that an insurance company may sometimes settle out of court for financial reasons, irrespective of the merits of the particular case. A protection society will, it is argued, build up a degree of specialist experience in defence work for therapists which may be lacking in some commercial firms, which may not possess full sympathy with or understanding of the professional tasks involved.

The professional indemnity insurance model provides legal advice and representation via insurance policies. Organisations such as the Psychologists' Protection Society operate instead on a self-funding rather than an insured risk basis, similar to the medical protection societies mentioned above. The stated advantage here is that the access to legal assistance is more direct and immediate. Its proponents argue that the interests of the insurance companies and those of the insured therapist are not necessarily identical, and delays in legal representation can result until an assessment of the case's merits have been made (Murray, 1995: 6).

Any therapist needs to remember the potential, however remote, for a conflict of interest developing between him or herself, and their insured legal representation, however provided. One example of potential conflict of interest in a related field has been that of alleged pressure by one insurance firm to prevent publication of a report into long-standing abuse in children's homes in Clwyd County Council. A number of confidential internal reports have produced detailed evidence of abuse involving past members of staff. However, the Council's insurers have apparently warned officials *against* publishing the report, as this would provide material for claims by abused children against the Council. These claims for damages or compensation, if successful, would then have to be met by the insurance company concerned (*Independent*, 13 April 1996). This case relates to a *public* conflict of interest. There may be instances of conflicts of interest developing over professional issues. For example, from a professional point of view, there may be a need to appeal against a key court decision in a case of alleged false memory against a therapist in the UK, were one to occur. The commercial interest of the insurance companies may dictate otherwise, as appears to have happened in the USA, leaving the therapeutic community as a whole somewhat more vulnerable to litigation. This is admittedly still a hypothetical situation in the UK, but therapists need, nevertheless, to consider their own position very carefully with regard to legal protection.

There is another option which at present exists only in the USA. There, some professional associations also provide legal advice and assistance for therapists faced with legal action, as part of their overall remit. The American Counseling Association, for example, with 55,000 members, maintains a legal defence fund and provides an 'amicus curiae', or a friend of the court, to assist counsellors facing legal action (Hopkins and Anderson, 1990: 2). This may be an option for therapeutic organisations to follow in the UK at some stage in the future.

Whatever the relative merits of taking out professional indemnity insurance, or of joining an appropriate professional protection society, the therapist needs to be aware of the changing face of professional negligence action. Some of the practicalities of

---

Box 3.8

Guidelines for professional practice concerning professional negligence litigation

Review your current practice in the light of the therapist's 'duty to care', with regard to:

- provision of a safe working environment for clients and staff
- levels of your professional training and updating
- working within the limits of your competence
- appropriate selection and referral systems for clients
- maintaining professional boundaries in therapy with clients
- use of informed consent, contracting and review with clients
- avoidance of damaging forms of therapy, harmful 'advice' or risky 'homework' for clients
- use of properly negotiated endings for therapeutic contact
- compliance with an established *Code of Ethics*
- use of informed and up-to-date assessment methods where appropriate
- awareness of potential liability to third parties
- maintenance of adequate levels of insurance cover for all purposes needed
- membership of professional indemnity insurance scheme or professional protection society

---

responding to such legal action are covered in more detail in Chapter 6.

Summary

The lack of extensive UK case law on negligent therapy can be fleshed out by looking at the parallels with medical negligence principles. Fears of a 'malpractice crisis' of US proportions in medicine and therapy may be overstated, given the differences between the UK and US health and legal systems. Therapeutic case law is much more in evidence in the USA, and includes third party actions against practitioners, as in alleged false memory cases.

Therapeutic case law in England and Wales rests on the notion of the therapist's 'duty of care' to the client, as determined by expert witnesses in court. Therapists using a minority approach are *not* necessarily more vulnerable to legal action than those using more conventional methods. Both minority and majority approaches need to demonstrate the maintenance of appropriate professional standards, and of their duty to the client. Safe and competent practice would include the use of informed consent, contracting and the avoidance of unethical or damaging ways of working with clients. In reality, the system of tort liability has not succeeded in putting therapists massively at risk from legal action by litigious clients intent on claiming damages. Nevertheless, sensible insurance cover and access to expert professional and legal advice are sound precautions for therapists to take against the threat of legal action.

Discussion points

1   Is it fair to therapists and to their clients that the standard of care expected of a trainee could be that of a reasonably competent practitioner? How can trainee therapists best work with this requirement, but lessen their apparent vulnerability to legal challenge?

2   In the case of *Osheroff* in the USA, can the attempt to treat the patient with psychodynamic methods be properly described as negligence, in your view? If so, where does this leave psychodynamic approaches in terms of their vulnerability to litigation?

3   Is the tort system a just and effective means of identifying poor professional practice and compensating clients, or is it simply a 'lottery'? What changes should be made to the system to overcome its main shortcomings?

4   Should third parties, such as a client's parents or partner, be able to take legal action against a therapist for damages? What circumstances might justify a charge of negligence against a therapist by a person who was not directly involved in the therapeutic relationship?

5   Should all therapists be required to take out professional indemnity insurance, or to join a professional protection society, as a condition of practice? What view do you take of the argument that such insurance is unnecessary or counterproductive for therapists?

4

Confidentiality, Privilege and the Public Interest

Confidentiality is one of the areas where therapy and the legal world may potentially collide. Confidentiality is a central tenet of therapy, desirable both on pragmatic grounds, to enable the relationship of trust to develop, and on the ethical basis of promoting the client's autonomy and self-determination (Eastman, 1987). From a legal perspective, confidentiality is subsumed under another set of concepts, those of privilege and the public interest. Therapists may focus their attention on the idea of privilege, but without necessarily stopping to consider the over-riding principle of the public interest, which is of crucial significance in the world of the law.

This chapter explores the legal foundations of **confidentiality**, as an expectation or duty based on trust. The legal concept of **privilege** is defined. This provides a protected status for some forms of communication, albeit largely unavailable to therapists, except those working in marital counselling. The circumstances where therapists are obliged to **break client confidentiality** are described in detail. These can include breaking confidentiality under **contractual obligation**, or in the **public interest** to prevent harm to a third party, as in the cases of child abuse, potential suicide or suspected terrorism. Within these legal restrictions, some cautionary notes are finally added, covering the overall need to **maintain** confidentiality wherever possible, as an expression of the ethical value placed by therapists on promoting client autonomy and self-determination.

Confidentiality

The legal concept of confidentiality is based on the idea of equity, or fairness, in that a person who has received information in confidence should not take unfair advantage of it (Reid, 1986; *Seager v. Copydex* [1967]). Every therapist will have some under-standing of confidentiality, although it will not necessarily be one that other therapists would automatically accept. For many ther-apists, confidentiality is known to be limited, by reason of their professional code of practice or via their conditions of employ-ment. Reporting suspected child abuse, for many, will be a requirement of their daily practice, so that their perception of confidentiality is already *relative* to the material that the client brings to sessions. For other therapists, there are schools of counselling where the concept of confidentiality is held to be *absolute*; what goes on in the therapy session is not revealed to the outside world (cf. Langs, quoted in Phillips, 1991). What is often not clear are the legal *limits* to confidentiality in therapy. When, if ever, do therapists have to *break* confidentiality? When, if ever, can they *refuse* to do so?

In answering these questions, this chapter will consider some of the key aspects of confidentiality, such as the legal version of confidentiality called privilege. The related concept of the public interest, which lies both in maintaining confidentiality, but also in overriding it on occasion, is also explored. Situations where therapists can breach confidentiality inadvertently, for example through a lack of care in writing an article, or where they are required to do so, in order to warn or protect the client or others, are discussed with examples. The focus of this chapter is on the therapist as the custodian of sensitive personal information. *It is assumed that before making any breach of confidentiality, the therapist has taken every possible step to discuss the matter thoroughly with the client concerned, and has sought to obtain their permission to disclose the information in question.* In some extreme cases, this may not be practicable, perhaps for reasons of urgency, or because of the immediate nature of the action required. Breach of confidentiality therefore 'occurs if anyone deliberately or by accident gives information, which has been obtained in the course of professional practice, to a third party without the consent of the patient/client' (UKCC, 1987: 7). This chapter is based on the concept of the therapist as custodian, choosing to contain or disclose information. This is distinct from a discussion of the powers of other external bodies to *enforce* such disclosure. The powers of *other* parties, such as clients, the courts or the police, to gain access to this confidential information provide the subject of a separate analysis in Chapter 5.

Confidentiality as duty and trust

Given the tension between legal and therapeutic perceptions on confidentiality, it is worth restating that the law takes a benign and supportive view of the need for confidences, as part of the everyday working of the worlds of business, of the professions and of personal relationships generally. According to Lord Goff, 'a duty of confidence arises when confidential information comes to the knowledge of a person (the confidant) in circumstances where he has notice, or is held to have agreed, that the information is confidential, with the effect that it would be just in all the circumstances that he should be precluded from disclosing the information to others' (*A.-G. v. Guardian Newspapers (No. 2)* [1988] at 805).

Confidences arise due to the *special nature of the relationship*, where it would be expected that a *trust* would be kept. Therapy would qualify as one of these forms of relationship, along with others, such as a doctor–patient relationship, or even a friendship. If this is so, then surely confidentiality deserves some special form of protection? Such protection would prevent confidences being broken, and one party's interests perhaps being damaged as a result. However, the overall public interest in confidences being protected is not absolute; some confidential information is protected, but other confidences are not.

Privilege and confidentiality

The idea of privilege is perhaps an attractive one for certain therapists, as a way of seeking protection for client–therapist disclosures. In over half of the states in the USA, privilege is now held by a number of professional groups, such as psychiatrists, psychologists and social workers (Bollas and Sundelson, 1995: 11). Privileged information in these states is explicitly protected by law from action by the courts. For example, a Supreme Court ruling protects client–psychotherapist confidentiality from disclosure in federal trials (BMA, 1996b: 1629). In the UK, comments in Parliament are protected but these forms of privilege are rare. The main example is that of communications between lawyers and clients for the purposes of preparing legal action. The privilege is held by the *client*, rather than by the lawyer, who does not, therefore, have the right to waive it. The rationale is that this form of professional privilege, termed communication 'without prejudice', is necessary for the law to function; without it, giving and receiving legal advice would become almost impossible (*Anderson v. Bank of British Columbia* (1876)). Many other professional groups have an interest in similarly protecting their communication, whether with clients, patients, or parishioners. However, the lines of privilege are tightly drawn. They do not extend to priests, to doctors or even to close friends. The legal professional privilege held by lawyers, however, is not absolute. It may be over-ridden by the courts in extreme circumstances, such as the court requiring disclosure of information where a child's welfare is at risk.

Privilege in matrimonial cases

On the one hand, the public interest lies in the *protection* of confidences. On the other, it also lies in *over-riding* confidences when this is necessary for the wider social good. Areas where the law is reluctant to force such disclosure are rare. In matrimonial cases, there is a recognition that privilege should apply where the parties are seeking advice or guidance with a view to reconciliation or separation. In the case of *McTaggart v. McTaggart* [1949], Lord Justice Denning stated that 'negotiations which take place in the presence of the Probation Officer, with a view to reconciliation are on the understanding, in the ordinary way, by all concerned, that they are without prejudice to the rights of the parties. . . . The Probation Officer has no privilege of his own in respect of disclosure any more than a priest, or a medical man, or a banker' (at 97).

Another case further illustrates the principles at work here. This was a case of a probation officer giving evidence in court in support of the wife, based on what her husband had told the probation officer in a separate interview, regarding the cause of the break-up of the marriage. According to the probation officer, when giving evidence in court, the husband had made an admission of desertion, a so-called matrimonial crime at the time. According to Lord Merriman, the probation officer, working in his marriage guidance role at the time, 'certainly exceeded his authority in considering himself an agent to make vital admissions on the merits of the case' (at 806). The discussions with both parties were privileged from disclosure; it was not up to the probation officer to choose to break their confidences (*Smith v. Smith* [1957]).

The mention of probation officers in both examples should not be taken that somehow this form of privilege relates only to this official position. It simply refers to the probation service because matrimonial work has long been an acknowledged area of practice and expertise, as part of its work in conjunction with the civil courts. The privilege in matrimonial cases is actually held by the couples seeking advice or counselling with a view to reconciliation or separation – steps which have *legal* implications. Because of this feature, it comes under the umbrella of quasi-legal discussion, and is therefore protected by the notion of privilege, according to these judgements. For therapists working with couples in these circumstances, the implications are:

- couple counselling can be protected by privilege
- privilege, or protection from forced disclosure, is held by the *parties*, such as husband and wife, and *not* by the counsellor or therapist
- this privilege can be waived or given up only by the permission of the parties involved, namely husband and wife
- the counsellor does *not* have a right to waive this privilege, for example, to inform a court or a third party involved in legal proceedings of the content of the discussion or counselling, without the permission of both clients

Courts may sometimes have an interest in gaining access to privileged marital communication, for example when one party has apparently made serious threats against the other, of wanting to harm or even to kill the other party. The experience of Relate, the relationship counselling agency, in this respect, has been to argue the need to preserve its policy of confidentiality. However, the privilege rule concerning matrimonial communication, while usually recognised by the courts, seems to need to be re-established with every new case that is taken to court. It does not seem to hold the position of being a binding precedent (see Chapter 5). The need for clarifying legislation on the status of privilege in mediation is referred to in proposals for reform of the current divorce law (Lord Chancellor's Department, 1995: Para 7.34).

Communication within marriage is not absolutely protected. According to the Evidence Amendment Act 1853, husband and wife cannot be compelled to give evidence against each other. However, this exclusion has since been limited by the Civil Evidence Act 1968 to criminal proceedings only.

The limits of medical confidentiality

Medical confidentiality is often assumed to hold some sort of privileged or protected status, but this is far from being the complete truth. Doctors and medical personnel are required to maintain confidentiality, but they cannot claim exemption from a legal obligation to disclose information (Darley et al., 1994). In the case of *Hunter v. Mann* [1974], a doctor was fined on this basis. He was ruled unable to withhold confidential information from police investigating a car accident, under s. 168(2)(b) of the Road Traffic Act 1972. An even more stark example is provided in one case, where a psychiatrist was called to give evidence about consultations carried on with the wife and co-respondent in a divorce case.

> In the course of hearing a divorce suit, the husband subpoenaed as a witness a psychiatrist who had been consulted by the wife and the co-respondent. When examined-in-chief by the husband's counsel as to what the wife and the co-respondent had said to him, the psychiatrist protested against answering the questions on the grounds of professional confidence.
>
> Judge Edgedale said what a person said to a doctor in a professional consultation was not privileged, and the witness must either give the evidence or be committed to prison for contempt of court. The witness then gave the evidence. (*Nuttall v. Nuttall and Twyman* (1964: 605))

What was different about this case, compared with the two earlier matrimonial cases, was that the discussions between the psychiatrist, the wife and the co-respondent, were not principally about litigation; neither was a lawyer present. This contact was therefore described by the judge simply as a 'professional consultation'. It was not seen to be marital therapy for the purposes of reconciliation, separation or divorce. Medical confidentiality can thus be over-ridden by statute, or by the directions of the court, and the same applies to the confidentiality of the therapist.

Box 4.1

Confidentiality and privilege

- confidentiality arises where *trust* is expected in a relationship
- professional privilege (protection against compulsory disclosure of confidences) applies only to client–lawyer communications for legal advice
- marital negotiations for reconciliation or separation can be privileged from disclosure

---

One of the often repeated legal sayings in this context is that '"confidentiality" is not a separate head of privilege' (*Alfred Crompton Amusement Machines v. Customs and Excise* [1974] at 433). In other words, protection from disclosure is granted by the law as *privilege*; it cannot simply be claimed by a professional on the basis of it being a *confidential relationship*. Where there is a conflict here, the courts will decide. (See Box 4.1.)

Confidentiality and the public interest

The public interest, as defined by the courts, holds that confidences should be maintained and protected by law, rather than be broken without good cause (*A.-G. v. Guardian Newspapers (No. 2)* [1988]). Confidences need to be kept where there is an expectation that the relationship is one of trust. However, there are exceptions to the duty to keep confidences. These are where information is trivial; where it is already in the public domain; or where the public interest in preserving confidentiality 'may be outweighed by some other countervailing public interest which favours disclosure' (*X. v. Y.* [1988] at 807).

Public interest in requiring disclosure

In what circumstances does the public interest require disclosure? Broadly, it is accepted that there is an interest in preventing crime. Another legal saying has it that 'there could be no confidence in iniquity', meaning serious crime (*Gartside v. Outram* (1856)). Other judges have widened this principle to include 'antisocial' behaviour, however widely that might be defined (*Francome v. Mirror Group* [1984]; *Fraser v. Evans* [1969]).

Relating this to therapeutic practice at this point might seem somewhat abstract. However, the *Tarasoff* (1976) case in the USA (discussed below) has brought this principle directly into the heart of practice in many states in that country. Case law in the UK is less extensive, but the above principles should make it clear that therapists could use the 'iniquity' defence to break confidentiality. Obviously, this justification would be need to be carefully weighed against the potentially terminal damage to the therapist–client relationship, and the longer term public reputation both of the agency and of the individual therapist concerned. The most striking example of the use of a public interest defence to justify breach of confidentiality is that of the *Egdell* case described below.

Case Study: Breaking medical confidentiality in the public interest

'W.' was detained as a patient in a secure hospital without time limit as a potential danger to the public, after he had shot and killed five people and seriously wounded two more. In the belief that he was being persecuted by people living nearby, he shot five neighbours, and drove off in his car, throwing home-made bombs as he drove away. (He had a longstanding interest and expertise in bomb-making, and reported that he always carried some made-up explosives in his car.) Later he shot two more people, unconnected with the first incident. He was diagnosed as suffering from schizophrenia.

After ten years, he applied to the Mental Health Review Tribunal to begin the process of seeking his discharge. His solicitors instructed a consultant psychiatrist to prepare a report in support of his application. Dr Egdell strongly opposed his transfer, drawing attention to W.'s longstanding interest in firearms and explosives, and indicating a need for further tests and treatment. Dr Egdell sent the report to the solicitors, and W. withdrew his application, but without the Tribunal or the hospital being sent copies. Dr Egdell, on his own authority, then contacted the hospital director, and copies were sent to the Tribunal and to the Secretary of State. W. brought a legal action against Dr Egdell for damages for breach of confidence owed to him as part of the doctor–patient relationship.

In considering the case, the judge referred to the General Medical Council's 'Blue Book' regarding confidentiality, noting that the rules themselves do not have statutory authority, but that they were derived from the disciplinary function of the GMC under the Medical Act 1983.

W. v. Egdell [1990]

The case hinged on the question of defining the public interest. 'There is one consideration which in my judgement, as in that of judge, weights the public interest decisively in favour of disclosure' (at 852). This was not simply the fact of the patient's prior history of violence, but the need for any decision to release someone who had a history of multiple killings to be based on *informed judgement*. This need entitled the doctor to communicate the relevant facts on a restricted basis to the necessary authorities, even if the facts were obtained in the course of a confidential relationship.

Public interest in preventing disclosure

In other instances, the public interest may lie in the *prevention* of disclosure. In one case, the mother of a child aged 14 months brought a legal case to compel the NSPCC to reveal the identity of an informant. The latter had made unfounded allegations that the child was being maltreated. This had prompted a visit by a NSPCC (National Society for the Prevention of Cruelty to Children) Inspector, causing her a great deal of psychological distress (*D. v. NSPCC* [1978]).

The appeal supported the NSPCC, in that the public interest was maintained by finding *against* disclosure in this case. The public interest here was in supporting the work of an agency which was critically dependent upon its confidential links with the public. Confidentiality per se would *not* debar the ordering of disclosure. 'The sole touchstone is the public interest . . .' (Lord Edmund-Davies, 246 B). But, in situations where there is doubt about disclosure, disclosure should be ordered by the courts.

Defining what is in the public interest is not always straightforward. It has been said that what is of interest to the public, is not the same as being in the public interest, as the case of Doctors *X. v. Y.* illustrates. (See also *Lion Laboratories v. Evans* [1984].) In 1987, confidential information was supplied to newspaper reporters concerning two doctors continuing in general practice despite having contracted AIDS. Despite a restraining order, an article entitled 'Scandal of Docs with AIDS' was published. The doctors were to be identified in a planned second article. It was held by the court that the public interest in preserving confidentiality of hospital records under NHS Regulations (1974) outweighed the public interest in the freedom of the press to publish this information. The public interest here was in avoiding the likelihood of AIDS victims being deterred from going to hospital for treatment (*X. v. Y.* [1988]).

Statutory protection for confidentiality

There is some limited statutory protection for confidentiality in certain specific instances (Reid, 1986: 129). Examples include:

- journalists' sources: Contempt of Court Act 1981
- the customer in relation to his creditworthiness: Consumer Credit Act 1974
- the data subject: Data Protection Act 1984
- the offender: Rehabilitation of Offenders Act 1974

In other areas, protection of confidentiality is more uncertain. Bond (1993d) describes a situation in Further and Higher Education, where it was unclear whether Her Majesty's Inspectors (HMI) could actually insist on observing student counsellors at work in order to assess the quality of the overall service being provided. Clearly, clients could give their consent under the BAC *Code of Ethics*, but what if counsellors either did not agree, despite the client's agreement, or refused to seek that consent as it was not completely voluntary? The BAC obtained legal advice from John Friel, a barrister, who gave the legal opinion that the Inspectors had no established legal right to insist on observing counselling sessions, nor to insist on requesting the client's agreement against the counsellor's professional judgement. While such legal opinion does not possess the same authority as a court decision, it has been taken as encouraging that there are defences for therapeutic confidentiality, which carry some legal weight (Bond, 1993d: 177–8).

Confidentiality required by contract

For therapists, maintaining confidentiality may be a contractual obligation of employment, for example, while carrying out child

---

Box 4.2

Confidentiality and the public interest

- the public interest requires that confidences be maintained
- breaking confidence is possible if the information is
  - trivial
  - already in the public domain
  - in the public interest (as defined by the courts)
- legal opinion has supported the principle of confidentiality in student counselling against compulsory HMI scrutiny

---

protection duties, or working in a general practice, as well as being a professional obligation. In consequence, a therapist removing files from the office to work at home without first obtaining proper authorisation could well face disciplinary measures from his or her employing agency.

Confidentiality can be also reinforced by being specifically written into a private contract between client and therapist, although the nature of the relationship will itself provide an expectation that confidentiality will be maintained. Contracts can be used to maintain the secrecy of specific training or therapeutic techniques, which are not to be passed on to others. The agency or trainer could protect its investment in the technique by suing for breach of contract, subject to the necessary conditions for this action being met (see Chapter 2). This approach is not guaranteed to work in all circumstances, as the following case brought by the Church of Scientology indicates.

Case Study: Breach of confidentiality in the public interest: the Church of Scientology

This was a case brought against Cyril Vosper, a member of the Church of Scientology for 14 years, who wrote a book called The Mind Benders. *Lafayette Ronald Hubbard brought an action claiming infringement of copyright under s.6(2) of the Copyright Act 1956 for breach of confidence, and sought an interlocutory injunction restraining publication.*

Vosper had enrolled for £150 on an advanced, confidential course in Scientology, the Special Briefing Course at Saint Hill

Manor, where he had been required to sign an undertaking (a) to use the knowledge acquired for Scientology purposes only, and (b) to refrain from revealing the information to any non-Clear (non-Scientologist), namely those not entitled to receive it.

According to Vosper's later revelations in his book, insanity, severe illness and possible death were foretold for anyone who even glanced at the Solo-Audit or Clearing House worksheets without adequate preparation. He did not complete the course, and became disillusioned with Scientology; in response, he was declared by the cult to be a 'suppressive person', or someone acting to suppress or damage Scientology, and therefore to be an 'enemy'. As a result, he could be classified as 'fair game', under the 1968 version of 'Scientology Ethics' and had no right to 'self, possessions or position'. Any Scientologist could now take action against him with impunity.

Hubbard v. Vosper [1972]

Normally speaking, information obtained in confidence, such as a trade secret, is protected by the law of confidence. However, the courts felt this particular material to be sufficiently dangerous for it to made known to the general public in the public interest. Infringement of copyright depends on the question of 'fair dealing' for purposes of criticism, or review, assuming that the material is sufficiently acknowledged by the critic. Lord Denning dismissed the Scientologists' case, claiming, incidentally, that 'fair dealing' is 'impossible to define', and constitutes a question of degree. A therapist 'going public' to expose or reveal a therapeutic technique would therefore need to meet a public interest defence to avoid successful litigation by the owner or training agency.

This could put therapists in a difficult position if they were concerned about unethical practice, or about a new therapeutic technique which they felt was unsafe. For example, the employment of an abusive version of 'regression therapy' by Frank Beck with children in local authority care is referred to in Chapter 7. In Australia, the use of a 'deep sleep' technique similarly constituted a technique with dangerous implications for vulnerable psychiatric patients (Bromberger and Fife-Yeomans, 1991). However, the legal protection for therapists prepared to act as 'whistle-blowers' against their own agencies is uncertain and limited at present (Birley, 1994; 1996).

Maintaining confidentiality in research and publication

Research and publication are seen as a necessary part of the development of therapy as a professional activity. Care is needed to avoid inadvertent breaches of confidentiality, which could lead to legal action being taken against the author. One disturbing case was related by a woman who had paid £105 for a joint 50-minute session with her mother, with a nationally known therapist who wrote regularly for the quality press.

> Then one Saturday morning five weeks later a friend rang me to say I was in a column written by the therapist we had been to see. As I read I realised what I was reading was the session my mother and I had had with him, exactly as it had happened. He hadn't used names but he had put in the type of people we were, our ages, our relationship, so we easily recognised ourselves. In the article, he said 'While the daughter was speaking, the mother was behaving like a manipulative, demanding child.' He described things precisely as they had taken place.
>
> When my mother saw the article, she was terribly humiliated and upset. She kept saying 'He didn't like me.' She feels completely destroyed by it, and of course would never go near a therapist again. So this eminent, highly-paid man has not only undone any good he did but has ensured that I will never get my mother to see someone with me again. We are worse off than before we went.' (*Independent on Sunday*, 19 April 1992)

The client contacted the therapist to make a complaint by phone, but obtained little satisfaction other than to express her anger at what had happened. She could have decided to pursue the matter, either by making a formal complaint to the therapist's professional association, if known, or by taking legal action for breach of confidence. As in the case of Doctors *X. v. Y.* above, a first step could have been to obtain an interlocutory injunction, that is 'an injunction granted by the Court in advance of the trial as a freezing measure' (Reid, 1986: 165). Often, this is not practicable, because the offending article or book may already have been published. In this case, the plaintiff could have brought a legal action for damages, such as an injunction to restrain further breaches, and a case for damages to compensate the plaintiff for any harm caused by the defendant's acts. Therapists writing about their practice should obtain a prior release for publication from clients, and omit any identifying references to them. These steps will go a long way to protecting writers from falling into any legal difficulty.

Conversely, it could be the case that a client challenged the tradition of therapists writing about *their* clinical experience by revealing the practices of an identifiable *therapist*, without permission. This has occurred with the use of concealed video cameras to film therapists, with the camera operator posing as a client, perhaps anticipating therapist malpractice or an over-hasty diagnosis of childhood sexual abuse (BBC, 1994, 1996). If the material was defamatory and damaging, presumably the therapist could seek to restrain publication, or claim damages for libel, though the adverse publicity so engendered might ultimately prove to be more costly than the client's original breach of confidentiality. Litigation does not come cheap; an alternative might be to make a complaint to the Broadcasting Complaints Commission or to the relevant broadcasting authority (see Resources section for details).

Breaking confidentiality

While the law generally seeks to uphold client–therapist confidentiality, there are circumstances recognised or required by law where a therapist may seek, or be obliged, to break confidentiality. Again, it is repeated that it is expected therapists will usually first try to discuss this with the client concerned, rather than simply act on their own initiative, unless there are particularly urgent factors to consider. Therapists may be required to break confidentiality either via contract, or by statute. They may seek to break confidence in the wider public interest, as in the case of preventing or reporting serious crime. These situations are described in more detail below.

Legitimate breaches of confidentiality via contract
Apart from unintended breaches of confidentiality, there may be situations where a therapist is *required* to break confidentiality as part of their contractual obligation, for example, to their employer. Counsellors working for an employer such as the nuclear power industry or the police, amongst others, may be expected on occasion to reveal certain confidential information to the employer. An example would be where a client was seriously harming the employer's interests through fraud or incompetence,

or by presenting a risk to themselves or to the public. The counsellor's contract could specify that such information must be passed on to the employer. However, somewhat confusingly, this contractual obligation may *not* be a defence against action by the *employee* against the therapist for breach of confidence, unless the client has been specifically warned beforehand about the limitations to confidentiality. Bond describes this as a 'double bind' situation, where the therapist is caught between the professional and ethical duty to respect the client's confidences, and the contractual duty to reveal sensitive information to the employer (Bond, 1994b: 9; Law Commission, 1981: Para 4.56). The best protection here is for the therapist to obtain prior permission from the client to pass on any specific information required by an employer. This does not, unfortunately, remove the double-bind where such permission is refused. Any therapist facing this sort of situation should get expert legal advice from their indemnity insurance company or professional association.

The dilemma is not a new one. The medical press at the turn of the century debated the ethics of maintaining or breaking confidentiality in 'the case of the asthmatic signalman'. This was a situation where a doctor treated a railway signalman suffering from asthma, who was prone to falling to the floor, incapable of moving for up to an hour, and often being completely alone in the signal box. The signalman was refusing to tell his employers, or to allow the doctor to do so, for fear of dismissal or transfer to another lower paid job (BMA, 1906: 1753). The animated discussion this raised in the letters column does not indicate any outcome, but the principles outlined above suggest a public interest defence would justify disclosure here. As always, there is a risk for the person who breaks confidentiality, with no absolute guarantees as to how their action will be perceived by the courts. Clearly, the greater the risk to the public, the stronger is the public interest case for disclosing the perceived source of the danger. Therapists facing this difficult dilemma should first seek to explore the issue with their client, and try to explore avenues such as the client raising the problem him or herself with the relevant authority. If the client is in denial that there is a problem, as perhaps with an alcoholic airline pilot, then the therapist needs to weigh carefully the ethical commitment to the client against the wider duty to society and to potential victims. Careful recording, use of supervision and consultation are recommended precautions. The reality of the risk to others can be appreciable: an actual example of a similar airline pilot is discussed in Beauchamp and Childress (1989: 91).

Confidentiality in multi-disciplinary settings

Therapists working in multi-disciplinary settings, such as primary health care or social services, need to be clear about their agency's expectations regarding the agreed limits and exclusions to client confidentiality. Statutory agencies work on the basis of confidentiality meaning that client information may be shared within the clinical or therapeutic team where necessary. This may conflict with the more narrowly client-centred approach to confidentiality held by some therapists. Differing perceptions about the status of confidential client material, including records, need to be identified and resolved at an early stage, rather than experienced in the midst of a crisis. Statutory agencies will usually expect team members, including therapists, to pass on information concerning potential suicide by a client, credible threatened harm to a third party or alleged child abuse. It may also be expected that the therapist can recognise and report signs of a client's deteriorating mental health, with a view to facilitating an appropriate response by psychiatric or medical services. While expectations and practice may vary according to the nature of the setting and the therapist's actual role, limits to confidentiality need to be clearly communicated and agreed upon by all parties concerned (SDHA/DCC, 1996).

Box 4.3

Confidentiality and contract

- confidentiality is an expectation, whether specifically written into a contract or not, where trust arises
- contracts can be used to protect trade secrets
- therapists working for employers may be required by their employment contract to break confidentiality with employees; legal action by employees is possible here
- therapists working in multi-disciplinary or statutory settings should clarify agency limits to confidentiality
- confidentiality must be maintained in research and publication
- breach of confidence can be met by an injunction and action for damages by the client

Terrorism

Statutory restrictions on confidentiality are rare, but one particular example is the requirement for information on terrorist offences to be passed on to the police. Under s.18 of the Prevention of Terrorism (Temporary Provisions) Act 1989, it is an offence *not* to pass on information likely to prevent an act of terrorism, or lead to the arrest of another person connected with such acts. The directive nature of this piece of legislation is such that the Samaritans, well known as a befriending agency with strict rules about maintaining confidentiality, will pass on information about bomb threats to the authorities on this basis. This represents the sole exception to the Samaritans' otherwise strict policy on maintaining client confidentiality (Simon Armson, Chief Executive of the Samaritans, 1995). Bomb warnings, often with a code for recognition purposes, are passed on to the authorities immediately.

Many therapists will already be aware of this legal requirement through the BAC's *Code of Ethics and Practice for Counsellors* (1993a), but perhaps see a limited relevance to themselves. It is worth bearing in mind that not every application of this rule will meet the therapist's stereotype or expectations. In 1978, Anna Puttick was discovered teaching car mechanics on a government-funded job creation scheme in London. On arrest, her real name was revealed to be Astrid Proll, a former leading member of the Red Army Faction, an urban guerilla organisation in West Germany with a number of successful political assassinations and bombings behind it (*Daily Mail*, 16 September 1978). Whether she was in therapy at the time is unknown; while it is not a therapist's job to investigate crime, it is worth bearing in mind that not every situation will fit exactly one's own preconceptions about potential terrorists regarding accent, appearance and class. In the event of developing grave suspicions about a client, again the therapist would be advised to seek expert professional and legal advice.

Child protection

The most widely understood cause for breaking confidentiality is where child abuse is suspected. For many therapists working in a statutory setting, this will be a requirement of their employment, as well as a professional expectation. One example is in the case reported in the Court of Appeal (Criminal Division) in 1993, where a psychotherapist was counselling a woman for the results of the sexual abuse she had experienced as a child. During the year's therapy, she told the therapist that there might be another younger child in the family who was still being abused by the same abuser, the grandfather. The therapist informed the police, who interviewed the client and the other grandchildren. The man, then aged 79, was tried and sentenced to eight years imprisonment (*R. v. C.*, 14 January 1993).

The physical and emotional vulnerability of children provides a strong moral argument for breaking confidentiality, which has clear legal backing. According to Lord Justice Eveleigh, 'there is no law of confidentiality which would command silence when the welfare of the child is concerned' (*Gillick v. West Norfolk Area Health Authority* [1986] at 149H). This principle would also apply where therapists provide groupwork for sex offenders. According to Goring and Ward (1990), total confidentiality cannot realistically be offered to clients in this situation. The therapeutic needs of clients for disclosure and exploration of their activities are secondary to a wider need to protect the interests of the public, or more specifically, the interests of children or young people who may continue to be at risk of abuse. A client revealing violent paedophile fantasies in a therapeutic group setting could not, therefore, rely on a contract of confidentiality preventing the facilitators from passing this information on to the relevant authorities.

However, in some instances, breaking confidentiality in cases of child abuse may actually over-ride the wishes and feelings of the *child* concerned. Under the *Gillick* ruling, doctors have the right to provide confidential advice and treatment for 'mature minors' under the age of 16. This principle can be extended to providing therapy to children and young people under the age of 18 (see Chapter 7). In some cases, it may be that the young person him or herself does not wish confidentiality to be broken. Roche and Briggs (1990) present an argument that the rights of children and young people receiving counselling should be respected in this situation. Over-riding the child's wishes, and informing the authorities, may not always be in the child's best long-term interests, particularly if the investigation carried out into the suspected abuse is inconclusive (NCH, 1994). For some children and young people, the effect of a mishandled child protection investigation may be quite traumatic in itself. Alternatively, timely

---

Box 4.4

Reporting suspected child abuse

- during office hours: contact nearest Social Services Department Child Protection Team for your area
- in case of an emergency occurring out of hours: contact
  - Social Services Emergency Duty Team, or
  - National Society for Prevention of Cruelty to Children (0800-800500), or
  - the police
- the police have powers to remove and protect children at risk in emergency, under s. 17, Police and Criminal Evidence Act 1984
- child abuse can be reported in the case of children and young people under 18
- child's wishes should be considered, but may be over-ridden if necessary to avoid 'significant harm' occurring to him or her

---

and effective social work intervention may release the child from continuing abuse or exploitation.

In practical terms, suspected child abuse can be reported, anonymously if necessary, during office hours to the local authority social services department, and outside office hours, to the former's emergency duty team; or to the nearest branch of the National Society for the Prevention of Cruelty to Children. The police also have powers under s.17 of the Police and Criminal Evidence Act 1984 to remove and protect children at risk in a case of real emergency. Action on child abuse can be taken for young people below the age of 18, although policies may vary on the kind of response made in this regard by different local authorities regarding older teenagers (see Box 4.4).

Working with suspected child abuse can present difficult issues for therapists. An example might be where a counsellor is working with a single parent, who discloses increasing problems in controlling her 14-year-old son's outbursts, and who says that she has, on several occasions, lost her temper and 'leathered' him. Under the terms of the Children Act 1989 and the guidance document *Working Together* (Home Office/DoH, 1991), the therapist would be justified in breaking confidentiality. However, there may be countervailing factors to consider, such as the fact that there is a social worker already involved with the family, and the age of the child as a teenager, with a possibly reduced consequent risk of 'significant harm'. On the other hand, teenagers are also at risk of serious harm, or of added dangers should they try to escape violence at home by running away. One option is for the counsellor simply to say that the *adult* is the client; and that the violent restraint is an expression of past abuse which is currently being worked on successfully in the therapy. The question remains, however, of how far the *child* has to bear the risk of abuse continuing or escalating in the meantime. Faced with acute dilemmas like this, the counsellor needs to carefully consider the cases for and against breaking confidentiality, should the client not wish to seek specific help on this issue herself. Seeking out consultation with a supervisor who has some knowledge and expertise in this area of practice could be a first step, prior to seeking advice from a professional association on how to proceed.

Policy perspectives on reporting suspected child abuse Many therapists assume that reporting child abuse is mandatory in the UK, as it is in the US (Ebert, 1992; Hopkins and Anderson, 1990). In reality, the situation is more complex than this. The counsellor's obligation to report suspected child abuse depends upon whether or not they are *required* to do so by reason of their position, for example as a therapist working for the health authority or social services. Therapists working independently, or for voluntary organisations with no policy obliging them to report all abuse, are under no *absolute* duty to report child abuse; whether they do so will depend upon their professional judgement as to the benefits for their client, or for the child concerned, in doing so.

The legal situation is that under s.47 of the Children Act 1989, the local authority is required to investigate cases where it is suspected that a child in their area is suffering or is likely to suffer 'significant harm'. Certain agencies, such as the local education authority, housing and health authority are required to assist with enquiries, 'in particular by providing relevant information and advice'. However, apart from those specified or authorised by the Secretary of State, this part of the Act 'does not oblige any person to assist a local authority where doing so would be unreasonable in all the circumstances of the case'. Put more plainly, this means that a therapist has a *choice* in whether or not to report suspected child abuse, *assuming* that they are not required to do so by their terms of employment, or by their own professional code of practice.

This choice can put therapists in a difficult position, perhaps in working with older teenagers who are at risk of abuse, but who have no wish for an investigation of the family to be started in motion. The British Association for Counselling has recognised this dilemma, and has suggested that local Area Child Protection Committees, who are responsible for coordinating child protection arrangements, include accredited and registered therapists within their liaison remit (BAC, 1995a: 95–8; Home Office/DoH, 1991: 109). This would mean that *all* accredited or registered therapists, whether working under the local authority guidelines on child protection or working independently, would be party to arrangements for helping the local authority with enquiries. This would clarify the current distinction between therapists required to report child abuse and those not so required.

Views of parents and families on confidentiality
The strong commitment to confidentiality within therapy can present an unhelpful and frustrating face to the parents and families of young people. In the case of Further and Higher Education, parents may be unwilling to recognise that their young people are not in the position of being '*in loco parentis*', and that key decisions may be made in which they have no say, or even no knowledge (Civil, 1992: 671–677; Earwaker, 1992: 68–77). In reality, the protection for confidentiality begins at a much younger age, given that, according to the *Gillick* principle, young people may be receiving completely confidential counselling under the age of 16, without parents needing to be informed or to give their consent.

One parent has written powerfully about her feelings concerning her daughter at university, where she was excluded from a whole series of decisions of major importance.

When we visited my sick daughter, it slowly emerged that the college had been concerned about her for weeks. She had lost a lot of weight, they feared anorexia, she was emotionally unstable and had threatened suicide. She had concealed her problems from us and the college had felt it had no right to inform us. If she hadn't caught flu, we might have gone on thinking that all was well until it was too late. As my daughter was too ill to be moved, we told her we would come and fetch her home as soon as it was safe. However, the college decided they couldn't cope with a sick and by now seriously depressed girl, and had her admitted to a psychiatric hospital. We were not informed. [A] family friend went to visit and found her gone. He bullied information about her whereabouts out of the unwilling authorities and called us. We had no legal right to know where she was. (Dalton, 1993)

The writer is correct in saying that she had no absolute legal right to know where her daughter was; it could have been the daughter's express *wish* that her parents *not* be told. The therapist's first commitment here would clearly be to the student as client; it is worth remembering that other interested parties such as family, parents and close friends, will not necessarily see the legal and ethical issues in the same light. Therapists need to be clear on the legal issues involved, and to cope with the emotional responses of those excluded from the process of therapy. Being clear about the client's right to confidentiality provides a firmer basis for prioritising this above the requests from other interested parties for information.

Breach of confidentiality: risk to third party

Initial discussions about confidentiality on training courses for therapists tend, almost inevitably, to bring up the situation where the client is a potential or actual murderer as the acid test of the therapist's commitment to client confidentiality. Discussion may assume that this is a hypothetical situation, but this is not necessarily the case. Laing describes a case related to him by another psychotherapist, about his patient, a consultant anaesthetist.

This patient had led him to suppose (had told him directly, in so many words) that he had killed three people in the last year, while he had been in therapy, by unobtrusively curtailing their oxygen in the course of long, complex, surgical operations. He kept his overall statistics normal, so that he had no more statistically significant anaesthetic deaths than the average for his sort of job. Anyway, he had had a good run for the last three months so was now about to kill the next victim. He would choose someone with a bad heart, poor lungs, or what not, so that their death would not raise any eyebrows. (Laing, 1985: 126)

The patient was not responding to therapy, and showed no indication of ceasing his murderous pastime. No decision or outcome is recorded in Laing's account. As said above, there is a longstanding principle in law that there is no confidence in

---

Box 4.5

Legitimate breaches of confidentiality

- therapists are *required* to pass on information on terrorist offences
- therapists *may* be required to report suspected child abuse by their contract of employment or professional code of practice
- the child's own views *may* be considered in deciding to report suspected child abuse, but may also be over-ridden
- therapists *may* break confidentiality to report serious crime, including drug trafficking offences

---

iniquity or serious crime, or even in anti-social behaviour, which clearly has a much wider remit. Either therapist would have been justified in breaking confidentiality on the basis of the threat to a third party, on the basis of the public interest in the prevention of crime, assuming that their action was taken in good faith.

Of course, it may be possible that the client is convinced that he or she has caused harm to another person, but without good cause. This may be an expression of an obsessive preoccupation, rather than an accurate reflection of reality, as in Freud's case-history of the 'Rat Man' (Freud, 1909/1991: 113–14). Supervision with a more experienced therapist may help the trainee therapist to clarify the actual degree of threat, if any, posed to other parties, without the therapist assuming that the instances disclosed by the client are necessarily real in every case.

A specific example of the therapist's statutory right to break confidentiality is with reference to drug trafficking. In the possibility that a therapist is working with a client involved in making or selling drugs, the therapist is empowered, under s.52 of the Drug Trafficking Act 1994, to pass this information on, without fear of action for breach of contract or breach of confidence (Bond, 1996) (see Box 4.5).

Duty to warn third parties: the Tarasoff case in the USA The *Tarasoff* case is widely recognised and is frequently used on training courses to illustrate the issue of the therapist's apparent 'duty to warn' (McLeod, 1993: 166–7). It is perhaps not always fully appreciated that its legal significance for therapists does not, as yet, extend to the UK.

Case Study: Therapist's duty to warn: the Tarasoff Case

Prosenjit Poddar was an Indian national studying at the University of California in 1969. While he was receiving therapy from Dr Moore, he made threats against an unnamed girl, who was identifiable as Tatiana Tarasoff. Dr Moore then took steps to have Poddar placed under observation in a psychiatric hospital, and notified the Berkeley campus police.

Poddar gave an undertaking to the police that he would stay away from Tarasoff, and he was released. He later went to her flat and killed her. Dr Moore's superior, Dr Powelson, asked the police to return Dr Moore's letter, ordered the destruction of all records and correspondence on the therapy, and finally ordered 'no action' on the decision to place Poddar under psychiatric observation.

Tatiana Tarasoff's parents brought a case against Dr Moore, the campus police and the University of California. The case was lost, but subsequently won on appeal, on the basis that the therapist had a duty of care, in this case to warn the intended victim of any threats, where there was a foreseeable danger.

According to the court: 'public policy favouring protection of the confidential character of the patient-psychotherapist relationship must yield in instances in which disclosure is essential to avert danger to others; the protective privilege ends where the public peril begins.'

(Source: Kermani, 1989; Van Hoose and Kottler, 1985: *Tarasoff v. Board of Regents of the University of California* (1976))

The *Tarasoff* case has had an appreciable impact in the USA on extending the legal liability of therapists for clients' actions. In California, a law was later passed requiring a therapist to break confidentiality and warn another person where there was 'a serious threat of physical violence against a reasonably identifiable victim or victims' (Kermani, 1989: 34). In the ensuing period, a further 14 states enacted legislation on similar lines (Meyer et al., 1988: 47). The *Tarasoff* ruling is capable of different interpretations regarding the therapist's precise duties. Austin et al. distinguish between laws based on the '*Tarasoff* 1 rule', which dictates that it is the therapist's duty to warn the *intended victim*, and the '*Tarasoff* 2 rule', whereby the therapist is responsible for assessing foreseeable harm, and for exercising a duty to protect *foreseeable* victims (Austin et al., 1990: 120). The latter places a much wider responsibility on therapists where the danger presented may be to persons as yet unknown. Assessing 'dangerousness' is in itself a complex and imprecise task, which many therapists would feel lies outside their professional remit (Campbell, 1995).

One view on the *Tarasoff* case, however, suggests that US therapists' anxiety about their apparently increased liability is unnecessary. The legislation following *Tarasoff* applies unevenly within a limited number of US states, rather than deriving from a federal requirement, such as the requirement to report suspected child abuse, under the US Child Abuse Prevention and Treatment Act 1974. Confusion about the exact import of the *Tarasoff* ruling perhaps derives from the fact that the case was, unusually, taken to court twice, being re-heard in 1976. Whereas the first ruling in 1974 required warning the client's potential *victim(s)*, the second ruling in 1976 actually sets a lesser standard, of the therapist simply exercising '*reasonable care* to protect the intended victim against danger'. This could include consulting a superviser, and informing the relevant authorities, rather than necessarily contacting the intended victim. As with any negligence case, the appropriate standard of care would depend crucially upon what was judged to be normal and acceptable practice for a substantial proportion of the professional group in question (see Chapter 3). The main effect of *Tarasoff* is perhaps seen in the doubling of the number of cases where psychiatrists have contacted the police with regard to clients making threats (Mangalmurti, 1994: 391). Otherwise, the effect of *Tarasoff* has not substantially increased therapists' liability in *real* terms, as measured by successful court cases won against therapists on this issue. 'Twenty years after *Tarasoff*, plaintiffs win few court battles against psychotherapists. Therapists themselves pay little heed to *Tarasoff*, and the practice of psychotherapy thrives' (Mangalmurti, 1994: 404–5).

Some US courts have been realistic in recognising that therapists are not in a position to predict future client behaviour with any scientific accuracy. Following the attempted assassination of President Ronald Reagan, his former press secretary, seriously wounded in the incident, brought a lawsuit against the psychiatrist who had treated John Hinckley, Junior, the attempted assassin (*Brady et al. v. Hopper* (1983)). His case was that

Hinckley had been inadequately diagnosed and treated, being given Valium and biofeedback treatment, rather than having been correctly diagnosed as a schizophrenic, who was, incidentally, dangerously obsessed with the film star Jodie Foster from the film *Taxi Driver*. However, the case was dismissed because no *identifiable* intended victim could be recognised via his therapy. Other cases have failed on a similar basis (Kermani, 1989: 35–6).

Developments in the USA since Tarasoff The pattern of findings in US courts regarding the therapist's duty to warn varies significantly from state to state. Another important case which extended this duty was that of *Peck v. Counseling Service of Addison County* (1985). Here, the plaintiff's son was in therapy, where he claimed that he wanted to burn down his father's barn to get back at him. The therapist extracted a promise from him not to do so, but did not warn the boy's parents of the threat, which was later carried out. The boy's parents then successfully sued the counselling service for negligence, in failing to warn them of the intended threat. This case extended the *Tarasoff* principles to include threats to *property*, as well as to persons; to *all* mental health professionals; and underlined the principle of vicarious liability, that *organisations* bore liability for the actions of their employees (Kermani, 1989: 45). The agency was judged to be at fault in not having established consultation procedures for responding to clients posing a serious threat to life or property.

The outcome of all this for therapists in the USA is that systems for their liability vary from state to state. The *Tarasoff* ruling appears to be about the justification for *breaching* a professional duty of confidentiality, but this overlooks the fact that the therapist, Dr Moore, had *already* broken confidentiality by approaching the campus police about the threats posed by his client. As Thompson puts it, 'more closely read, the issue is more that of *failure to follow through an already executed breach of confidentiality*, than that of making the breach in the first place' (Thompson, 1983: 84, emphasis added).

Therapists in the UK: a duty to warn? For therapists in the UK, the implications of *Tarasoff* and subsequent cases indicate one possible line of development, but a hypothetical one at that. The price that therapists in the USA have had to pay for a limited form of statutory recognition has been a much more extensive form of regulation and liability to litigation. Therapists in the UK are left with the skeleton framework of legal principles outlined above; therapeutic confidentiality is partially recognised, but not protected by the law. Breaking confidentiality in the public interest would be an acceptable defence, provided that the court accepted the definition of the public interest and that it was done in good faith. The professional group which comes closest to holding a *Tarasoff* type position on responding to threats to third parties is that of forensic psychiatrists, who on anecdotal evidence are expected to respond to a client's threat towards a 'named person' (RCP, 1990: 104). The lack of extensive therapeutic case law in the UK compared with the USA leaves us with the example of the *Egdell* case (*W. v. Egdell* [1990]). Here, the public interest was seen to be served by the doctor's actions in breaking confidentiality with his patient.

Discussion of a therapist's apparent 'duty to warn' reveals major problems with this approach held by some schools of therapy. The need for absolute confidentiality is stressed particularly by psychoanalytic approaches to therapy, which rest on the 'freedom to free associate' (Bollas and Sundelson, 1995: 59). These authors describe the example of a client who regularly fantasised stalking and attacking female victims, but who, apparently, successfully worked through and resolved these violent fantasies by means of intensive psychotherapy. Other therapists may instead have judged the danger posed to these women sufficiently great to take steps to warn either them or the authorities of the threat posed by the client.

This example illustrates the definition employed for breaches of confidentiality as a *voluntary* disclosure of sensitive personal information by the therapist. Without this disclosure, the information, whether of stalking, intended harm or child abuse, would be unknown to anyone except the therapist or client. This is in contrast with the *involuntary* disclosure of information required by a third party, such as by a court or by the police, which suspects that the therapist may hold certain information, or wishes to have that information confirmed. Deciding whether or not to breach confidentiality on such a voluntary basis places professional and personal responsibility squarely on the therapist.

AIDS and HIV   One situation where a therapist may be faced with the potential need for breaking confidentiality might be where a client is HIV positive, or has the AIDS virus, and is apparently placing a sexual partner at risk of infection. This has been a topic that has been extensively discussed in the counselling press in the USA, usually attempting to devise a therapist's duty to warn on the basis of extending the *Tarasoff* principle (Cohen, 1990; Erickson, 1990; Gray and Harding, 1988; Harding et al., 1993; Stanard and Hazler, 1995). No firm conclusion has been reached, although there seems to be growing support amongst US counsellors for breaching confidentiality, to prevent probable harm to the third party concerned, and also to minimise their own legal liability. One client's partner has, in fact, filed a lawsuit against a counsellor for failure to warn of their client's AIDS illness. They have also lodged a complaint with the counsellor's professional body, the American Counseling Association's Ethics Committee, which is still pending (Costa and Altekreuse, 1994: 346; ACA, 1995).

The current law in the UK would *not* seem to support a therapist who broke confidentiality to warn a third party of the risk they faced from a sexual partner with HIV or AIDS. In the case of a Birmingham man alleged to be deliberately infecting women with the virus, the then Home Secretary, Kenneth Clarke, ruled out the use of the law in such cases. 'It is very difficult to prove that someone knew that they were HIV positive at the time they had sexual intercourse with the person who was infected . . . I don't think there is any advantage in using the law in cases like this' (*Guardian*, 31 July 1995). The medical profession has some powers to seek authorisation for compulsory treatment of AIDS patients under s. 38 of the Public Health Act 1984, which is apparently rarely used (Brazier, 1992: 107–8). In addition, GMC guidelines permit a doctor to breach confidentiality in the case of a patient's partner who is at risk: 'where such consent is withheld, the doctor may consider it a duty to seek to ensure that any sexual partner is informed, in order to safeguard such persons from infection' (GMC, 1995b: 9).

A therapist taking such action, however, might well be placing him or herself at risk of legal action for breach of confidentiality, libel or slander. However, this does not seem to have prevented the counselling service of one Further Education College from taking such action to inform one student's partner, who was also a student at the same college (Civil, 1992: 675).

Box 4.6

A duty to warn?

- therapists in the UK are *not* under a specific obligation to warn third parties as may apply under the *Tarasoff* principle in the USA
- therapists may *not* break confidentiality to warn third parties of a client's AIDS/HIV status
- therapists *may* break confidentiality to report or seek help for an attempted suicide
- it is illegal to assist another person to commit suicide

Suicidal clients

Under the Suicide Act 1961, suicide ceased to be a crime. However, under s.2(1) of the Act, 'a person who aids, abets, counsels or procures the suicide of another, or an attempt by another to commit suicide, shall be liable on conviction on indictment to imprisonment for a term not exceeding fourteen years'. Proceedings require the consent of the Director of Public Prosecutions.

Views about suicide as a conscious act vary amongst therapists; one therapist may decide to break confidentiality to warn a third party, for example, a GP or psychiatrist, about a client who is seriously depressed and contemplating suicide. Another therapist, perhaps working from a person-centred perspective, might see this more in terms of the client's right to choose to terminate their life according to principles which it is not up to the therapist to deny or seek to change. Where the therapist has a relationship which is perceived by others to be influential, then the aftermath of a successful suicide may be for the therapist to be called as a witness in the Coroner's Court. The attitude of the deceased person's relatives and of their legal representatives may not be sympathetic to the counsellor's professional stance (Bond, 1991). Short of actually *assisting* the client to commit suicide, perhaps via euthanasia for a terminally ill client, the therapist is not liable for failing to prevent its occurrence, or for failing to warn third parties of the client's intentions. However, to break confidentiality in order to prevent or reduce the risk of suicide would also not necessarily put the therapist in jeopardy.

From the perspective of the law, suicide needs to be based on evidence of *intention* on the part of the deceased. This is described as 'the essential legal ingredient' for suicide, which would, for example, be explored at a Coroner's Court (*Halsbury's Laws of England*, 1974: 680). For the therapist, part of the professional problem in responding to this issue is trying to distinguish between clients where the risk is of repeated suicide attempts, and those where the intention is to kill him or herself. According to Eldrid, 'the object of actual suicide is to solve a problem whereas the object of parasuicide is to reduce tension and evoke a response' (1988: 151). Distinguishing between the two is obviously of critical importance. Suggested predictors of parasuicide, or what is more usually known now as *deliberate self-harm*, include:

- history of psychiatric treatment
- previous deliberate self-harm
- sociopathic or criminal behaviour
- alcohol problems or drug dependence
- low socio-economic status or unemployment
- single status

(Daly, 1993: 31)

Suggested factors in assessing a client's *suicide risk* include:

- level of intent to die (such as constant preoccupation)
- lethality of chosen means (such as antidepressant tablets)
- access to and knowledge of those means (e.g. possession of a shotgun)
- presence or absence of a protective individual (partner, parent)
- purpose of the attempt (suicide or self-harm)
- degree of control over the desire to die
- presence of deterrents (such as dependent children)

(Weishaar and Beck, 1990: 68)

From this cognitive perspective, *hopelessness* is a key factor for therapists to look out for, as it is more closely related to suicide intent than depression as such (1990: 74). A therapist known to be closely involved in working with a client who succeeds in a suicide attempt may well be called as witness to the Coroner's Court (see Chapter 6). Complaints and legal action by family and relatives against psychiatrists after a successful suicide may also follow on (Bradley, 1989).

Box 4.7

Guidelines for professional practice regarding confidentiality

- carry out an audit of confidentiality within your own practice, and that of your agency, if appropriate
- identify strengths and weaknesses
- devise an action plan for changes to be made
- write and update a policy statement on confidentiality, taking account of statute and case law, such as the Children Act 1989
- discuss this statement with all interested parties
  - employing agency, or managing committee of voluntary agency
  - counsellors and therapists
  - administrative and reception staff
- provide clients with information on your policy on confidentiality
  - a brief verbal explanation at first interview
  - a leaflet summarising main aspects of your approach
  - access to more detailed policy statement for inspection or photocopy if required
- negotiate provision within your policy statement for legitimate professional limitations on confidentiality
  - consultation and supervision
  - requirements for outline information on client user population by employing or funding agency
  - research and publication
- discuss scenarios and develop clear staff understanding on best responses to public interest conflicts with therapeutic confidentiality
  - criminal activity by clients
  - HIV/AIDS risk to third party
  - physical threat to third party
  - terrorism
  - child abuse
  - suicidal clients

For the therapist, action intended to reduce the client's potential risk of suicide might include:

- explicitly acknowledging and exploring any suicidal ideas
- giving information on out-of-hours help, such as the Samaritans (0345-909090)
- referral to the client's GP or local community mental health team for medication or possible admission to psychiatric hospital

The previous discussion has indicated some of the main areas where a therapist may consider breaching client confidentiality. The guidelines in Box 4.7 are not all-embracing, but may provide a starting-point for therapists to consider their practice in order to take account of the law, and minimise the risk of complaint or possible future legal action.

Public interest defence for breaking confidentiality

One final note of caution needs to be sounded with regard to therapists seeking to use a public interest defence for breaking confidentiality with a client, for example, to report a credible threat towards a third party. It is crucial that any intended breaches of confidentiality must be carried out in a thoroughly professional manner, otherwise the public interest defence is invalidated. Thus the therapist should:

- act in accordance with relevant *Codes of Practice* and agency guidelines, including any requirements to seek professional consultation or supervision on the issue
- restrict disclosure to matters which are *directly* relevant to the reasons claimed for the disclosure (for instance, a client's intended threat of harm may be relevant to disclose; their sexual orientation may not be relevant)
- restrict disclosure to those persons best able to act in the public interest (for example, by informing the police, rather than the local press).

Again, it is assumed that, wherever possible, the therapist has sought to discuss the matter with the client concerned. This last point is a matter of professional ethics, rather than strictly being a legal requirement for claiming a valid public interest defence for breach of client confidentiality. (For a more detailed discussion, see Bond/BAC, 1994a: 2–7; BAC, 1993a.)

The emphasis in this chapter has necessarily been on restrictions to therapist–client confidentiality. Hopefully, for most therapists, the need to break confidentiality will be a rare occurrence, but, nevertheless, one for which they are adequately informed and prepared. Confidentiality provides a cornerstone for effective therapeutic practice, both as a pragmatic measure to build trust and rapport, and as an expression of ethical principles supporting the client's right to autonomy and self-determination. This right to

---

Box 4.8

Therapists and confidentiality

Summary

- therapists do not possess privilege for client communications, except for some aspects of marital counselling
- therapists are required to maintain confidences obtained via their work, e.g. a client's AIDS/HIV status
- breach of confidence can be met by
  - disciplinary action by an employer
  - legal action by clients for damages
- therapists *may* break confidence
  - to prevent crime
  - to report suspected child abuse
  - to prevent suicide
  - to report professional misconduct
- therapists *must* break confidence
  - to prevent terrorism
- therapists in the UK are *not* under an obligation to warn threatened third parties on the US *Tarasoff* model

---

confidence is understood and respected by the law, except where the wider public interest requires that it be limited for the benefit of society as a whole.

Discussion points

1 Should therapists be afforded 'privilege' to protect the confidentiality of their sessions with clients? What advantages or disadvantages might this present for therapists?

2 How well are therapists prepared by their agency or by their previous training to understand the legal limits of confidentiality? How, in practical terms, might this be improved?

3 Should therapists in the UK have 'a public duty to warn' on the US *Tarasoff* model? How can the rights of clients, therapists, and vulnerable third parties best be balanced here?

4 When, if ever, have you broken confidentiality without the client's consent? In the light of the information presented in this chapter, would you now revise your past decision or practice in this respect?

5   How might client confidentiality in your own practice best be
    preserved in order to be consistent with the public interest?
    What practical steps could be taken to meet the complaint of a
    client who felt that their confidentiality had been broken
    without due cause?

5

Access to Records and Disclosure of Information

The concepts of confidentiality and access to information may appear to cover the same ground, to the extent that it might seem that little is gained by separating these aspects into different chapters. The difference between confidentiality and access to information suggested here is that, in Chapter 4, the focus is on the *therapist* as the 'active agent', releasing information either inadvertently, or under legal obligation. The focus in this chapter is on the *client or external agencies* as the 'active agents', in seeking and *obtaining access* to information. Both the therapist *releasing* information and the client or other party *obtaining* such access may infringe confidentiality, but the processes involved are often quite distinct. While this not a distinction rooted in the law, it is suggested here as a way for therapists to be clear about the different processes and responses involved for them as practitioners.

This chapter considers the processes involved in external bodies obtaining **access to records of therapy**. Persons with a statutory right of access to personal records include **clients**, both in specialist settings such as social services, health and education, and all clients who are covered by data access legislation. Demands for **disclosure of information** can be made by agencies such as the police and courts, under statute or by the authority of the courts. The legal process of 'discovery' can involve the therapist in attending court, and being required to answer the court's questions in the witness box. The role of the therapist as witness in court is considered more fully in Chapter 6, but this chapter sets out the wider legal constraints on therapists subject to the processes of the law with regard to access and disclosure.

Access to records

In exploring the concept of access to information, there are distinctions to be made between:

■   access to therapist's actual *practice* with the client
■   access to the therapist's *files*, such as manual or computerised records
■   access to therapist's *personal experience* of practice with the client

The first may seem a rather remote possibility. However, this has been discussed in the context of Her Majesty's Inspectorate (HMI) seeking to observe *directly* student counsellors at work, under their statutory powers to inspect schools, colleges and universities. The legal opinion obtained by BAC was that the HMIs appeared to have no statutory authority to *insist* on a right to observation against the objections of the client (Bond, 1993d: 177–8). It should be borne in mind that access to a therapist's actual *practice* with a client could also be obtained via access to audio or video tapes of their work. While these latter methods have decided advantages as recording techniques, the client is also more easily identifiable, especially via video recordings. Other interested parties may thus gain access to the therapist's actual work with the client via this means. Audio and video material could also be copied easily, and made accessible to others well beyond the original intended professional audience.

Therapists providing a service for an employer are usually expected to pass on, at minimum, summary information about their workloads and outline client information (EAPA, 1995: 22–3; Ratigan, 1991: 161). They may also be under a direct contractual obligation to reveal to employers those client disclosures which directly damage the employer's interests. One example would be that of a client being counselled by a therapist from an Employee Assistance Programme, where the client admitted to stealing from an employer, such as a bank. The interest in employer's access to counselling records has apparently been heightened after the case of Beverly Allitt, a nurse convicted after the deaths of several children in her care (Clothier, 1994). Employers may require information where staff being counselled present a risk to the public. An example here would be of the airline pilot who revealed information to a therapist under hypnosis about his responsibility for the crash of a commercial plane. He later crashed a second plane on a transatlantic flight, causing loss of life (Beauchamp and Childress, 1989: 338). According to the Law Commission, therapists under such a contractual obligation to *employers* should clarify the limits to confidentiality with prospective clients to reduce their parallel liability to the *client* for possible breach of confidence (Bond, 1992d; Bond/BAC, 1994a; Law Commission, 1981: 52). While the above examples strictly relate to the boundaries of *confidentiality*, therapists providing a service for employers also need to determine the exact limits of employer access to files. This might, for example, concern the kinds of summary data or information that will be expected by the employer to evaluate the effectiveness of the service being provided, or for audit purposes in the NHS.

Access to records by clients

Access to records, in the form of access to personal files, is usually seen primarily as access by *clients*. The crucial development accelerating client access to files was brought about by the case of Graham Gaskin. Gaskin, born in 1959, spent almost the whole of his life in the care of Liverpool Social Services Department, with frequent moves and disruptions up until leaving care in 1974. He applied to see his case file, intending to bring an action against the local authority for negligence, and was refused access on the grounds of previous court rulings protecting such records by social workers, medical practitioners and teachers as confidential. Liverpool City Council took steps to release some but not all of the documents, depending upon whether the original authors of the reports would give their permission (Gomien, 1991: 64–5).

Gaskin's formal application was instrumental in opening up client access to files. He applied under s.31 of the Administration of Justice Act 1970 for an Order requiring disclosure of records by Liverpool City Council to assist in his claim for damages experienced by his treatment in care (*Gaskin v. Liverpool C.C.* [1980]). He lost the case, but Liverpool City Council then responded by developing a plan for *all* clients to have access to files holding personal information – this spurred the then Department of Health and Social Security (DHSS) to produce a consultative document in 1983, which was then followed by a government circular ((LAC(83)14); Parsloe, 1988: 29).

Graham Gaskin later took his case to the European Court of Human Rights, and this applied some additional pressure for changes in the legislation. A series of Acts followed, opening up a wider degree of client access to files. After the Access to Personal Files Act 1987, the Access to Personal Files (Social Services) Regulations 1989 came into force, permitting limited access to social work files prior to the date of its effect, and more extensive access to files made subsequently (but excluding full access to adoption records). Gaskin later won compensation of £5,000 for breach of Article 10 of the European Convention on Human Rights, concerning his right to receive and impart information, but not, significantly, for the alleged violation of Article 10, i.e. the right to respect for his private and family life (Gomien, 1991: 86; *Gaskin v. UK* (1988) [1990]).

Access to social work records has been increased by legislation following on from the case brought by Graham Gaskin. This also applies to access to school records, under the Education (School Records) Regulations Act 1989. Usually, there is provision for *refusing* access to health, education or social work records where there is a risk of 'serious harm' being caused to the individual. However, the Department of Social Security and the Department of Health have made it clear in their guidance that data will be withheld only in 'exceptional circumstances'.

Clients' access to computerised data   Access to social work files may affect relatively few clients of therapists. More widely applicable, and also better known, are the rights of clients to *computerised* data held on them by therapists (Bradbury, 1993). The therapist or agency is known as the *data user*; the client is referred to as the *data subject*, with a corresponding right of *data access*. 'The Data Protection Act 1984 gives not a *general* right to information, but a right of subject access' (Pearce, 1988: 2). Under s.21 of the Data Protection Act 1984, individuals have the right to be informed by any data user of information about them held by the data user, and to be supplied with a copy of that information, on payment of a fee.

Individuals can apply to have access to computerised data held on them, and to have the data corrected or deleted where appropriate. The data held should be adequate, relevant and not excessive for the purposes required. A potential example of excessive recording of data relates to the concern expressed by the Terrence Higgins Trust about practice by the police; the HIV status of individuals is routinely recorded on the Police National Computer, when the Trust felt that this may not be strictly necessary or justifiable (Hamilton, 1995: 21–3).

Individuals or, properly speaking, *data subjects* can claim compensation through the courts if, after 11 September 1984, damage has been caused by the loss, unauthorised destruction or unauthorised disclosure of their personal data. If the damage is proven, the court may also order compensation for any associated distress caused. Data subjects may also seek compensation through the courts for damage caused after 10 May 1986 by inaccurate data, with similar provision for distress if damage is proven (DPR, 1992a: 12). The first step for a client attempting to exercise his or her rights to have access to computerised data would be to phone the Data Protection Registrar, and check that the therapist or agency was registered as a data user (details in Resources section).

The right of subject access is not restricted by age. 'All individuals, including children, have the right of subject access. However, a child will not always be able to make his or her own request' (DPR, 1992b: 17). In England, Wales and Northern Ireland, requests for data access by children are first evaluated to see if the child understands the nature of the request being made. Access can be given directly to the child, *or* to the child's parent or guardian, if the request has been properly authorised by the child. Parents or guardians should only make such requests in the child's interests, and not simply in pursuit of their *own* interests. In Scotland, individuals of or over the age of 16 are entitled to make their own subject access requests. For a child under the age of 16 the subject access right will be exercised by the child's guardian – usually the parent.

Access to *manual* records is covered by an European Community (EC) Directive due to come into effect in 1998 (95/46/EC). Legislation to implement this is under consideration. This will widen the rights of clients to files still further, and has, for example, implications for employee access to personnel or counselling files, many of which are often hand-written rather than computerised (IPD, 1995).

It needs to be remembered that the legislation does have teeth. The Data Protection Registrar takes legal action for breaches of the law on a regular basis. In 1994–5, for example, it took court action in 61 cases, winning in 75% of them. Fines ranged from £100 to £2,500 (DPR, 1995: 37). According to the office of the Data Protection Registrar, as of 1996, there had been no substantive cases concerning client access to therapeutic records.

Clients' access to health records Clients may have access to medical reports prepared for insurance or employment purposes under the Access to Medical Reports Act 1988. They also have access to health records, which may include therapeutic files, as governed by the Access to Health Records Act 1990. Health records are defined as any record 'consisting of information relating to the physical or mental health of an individual who can be identified from that information, or from that and other information in possession of the holder of the record' and 'that has been made by or on behalf of the health professional in connection with the care of that individual' (Panting and Palmer, 1992: 9). Under s.2 of the 1990 Act, 'health professional' includes clinical psychologists and child psychotherapists as well as psychiatrists. A common belief amongst therapists is that there are 'official records', available for access by clients, and 'therapeutic records' which can be held back for the therapist's personal use in training, supervision, and professional development. This distinction is not recognised in the legislation. 'Reports and correspondence headed "private and confidential" cannot be withheld from the patient merely because they bear that heading. There is no point in maintaining a second "private" set of notes as the patient would also be entitled to access to these' (Panting and Palmer, 1992: 9).

Clients' access to records of therapy These requirements for disclosure of health records highlight a more general dilemma for therapists, trainers and supervisers. The practice of holding a second set of therapeutic notes may be unknown to clients, but their existence will increasingly be appreciated by other interested professionals such as solicitors. These 'informal' sets of therapeutic records could be required for disclosure under 'discovery' rules applying to legal proceedings. Refusal to surrender required documents could then constitute contempt of court.

The development of client rights of access to health records has posed particular problems for psychiatric files, which, according to the Royal College of Psychiatrists, differ 'markedly from other medical records', given the sensitive nature of the information contained, and the potential damage caused by disclosure (RCP, 1990: 97). The widespread use of team work with the patient has also broadened the numbers of professionals with access to records. 'Psychiatric case notes nowadays may have only limited confidentiality, particularly with multidisciplinary team work' (1990: 98). In one health authority, no less than 26 categories of staff were identified who needed access to case notes when dealing with patients (1990: 103).

Some of the limitations of the value of client access to therapeutic records are suggested by comments made by the Royal College of Psychiatrists. Their description of the individual and subjective nature of much therapeutic recording will probably be recognised by other professionals. Case notes are:

> compiled principally as an aide-memoire to the doctor who makes the entries and can only be interpreted accurately by that doctor. . . . These records have never been produced to be seen by the patient or relatives and are not in a form that would in any way be suitable to be seen. Much of the treatment of a patient takes place at the verbal and not the written level and in the end is negotiated between patient and therapist in the course of their direct relationship. This is the best safeguard of confidentiality. There should be a record, however brief, of all treatment. (RCP, 1990: 103)

While clients have a right of access to health records, the data held may well need to be interpreted by another competent professional to have much meaning. As with social work records, the client's right of access is *qualified* and *conditional*, rather than absolute. This point is shown by the court's decision refusing access to health files requested by one patient with a history of depression and psychological problems (*R. v. Mid-Glamorgan FHSA* [1993]). Access can be withheld on the grounds that it may cause 'serious harm' to the individual's physical or mental health, for example, in disclosing a diagnosis of paranoid personality disorder. Data may also identify third parties, such as family members, who have given information, perhaps concerning an individual's past aggressive behaviour. Disclosure may then put

---

Box 5.1

Clients' right of access to personal records

- Adoption Act 1976
- Data Protection Act 1984
- Access to Personal Files Act 1987; Access to Personal Files (Social Services) Regulations 1989
- Access to Medical Reports Act 1988
- Education (School Records) Regulations Act 1989
- Access to Health Records Act 1990
- EU Directive (95/46/EC) (effective from October 1998)

---

the third parties at risk, should the client have unrestricted access to the data held.

Unauthorised access to client records The increasing numbers of professionals with access to patient data users widens the possibility for *unauthorised* access or disclosure. The widespread use of computer technology for data retention and transfer also opens up new possibilities for intercepting data and gaining access to data storage systems. This concern is currently centred on proposals to establish an NHS computer system, on the grounds of improving efficiency in handling patient information. There are concerns expressed by the British Medical Association, amongst others, that the proposed NHS computer system for carrying confidential medical records, with up to 180,000 users, is not sufficiently secure (*Guardian*, 13 October 1995; *Observer*, 3 March 1996). The main criticisms concern the lack of an agreed common security policy, and the ethical objection that the networking system makes patient information potentially available to much larger numbers of people who are not directly involved in patient care (Anderson, 1996; DoH, 1996).

As computer technology becomes increasingly international, so the possibilities for its misuse also expand on a global scale. Details of the late President Mitterand's health and medical treatment, published in France and then restrained by the courts, have been discovered posted on the Internet. Other personal medical information has been circulated on the Internet. In the case of Zhu Ling, a 21-year-old Chinese student, her medical records were posted on the Internet by her parents with their daughter's permission, seeking information on possible diagnoses. These were confirmed by international responses as thallium poisoning (Craft, 1996). Further inroads into patient or client confidentiality through international data exchange may well arise in the future.

Not all access to client records is legitimate or authorised. At the most basic level, a client or other interested party might simply break into a therapist's house or office, and steal or damage files. Adequate security of files is therefore an obvious requirement. Other forms of unauthorised access may well be less easy to prevent. In a recent decision, the House of Lords ruled that 'browsing' through restricted information on a computer screen did *not* amount to misuse of information under the Data Protection Act 1984. According to critics, this decision removes one of the major defences against unauthorised access and misuse of computer information (*Observer*, 18 February 1996).

Unauthorised access to information may be obtained by a number of means. In the health service, some of the main problems identified in this area have included carelessness about answering telephone enquiries or in sending information by fax. Private investigators have been known to seek information, perhaps about celebrities, over the telephone, by posing as a doctor in a hospital casualty department. They may be seeking access to or confirmation of particularly sensitive information, known in many instances to therapists as well as to medical personnel, for example, concerning a client's or patient's HIV status, details of their contraceptive or psychiatric history, drug or alcohol dependency, or medication. A regular cause of loss of potentially damaging information can be via the theft of computers and hard disks, or through damage caused by a computer virus (Anderson, 1996: 109–11). Transfer of information via computer systems or even by telephone may be less frequent amongst therapists, particularly if working alone or in private practice. The growing possibilities of unauthorised access to damaging client data nevertheless need to be seriously considered by therapists.

Conflict of legal duties in granting access to clients' records   In some cases, clients possess a clear statutory right of access to information held on them. Under the Adoption Act 1976, individuals can apply for information about their original adoption. Counselling is provided as the first step in the process of gaining access to information, which may lead to their ability to trace their birth parents. This right of data access is not absolute, as was made clear in one of the few cases involving therapy to be heard at Appeal Court level.

Case Study: Client's right of access to adoption records denied

This case concerns the correct interpretation of a statutory duty to provide counselling and information to an applicant concerning their adoptive parent. Under s.51 of the Adoption Act 1976, counselling is provided for persons who have been adopted and who wish to obtain information about their birth records.

In this particular case, the request for information was from R., a psychiatric patient at Broadmoor Hospital, who had a history of extreme aggression, and who had expressed violent feelings towards the birth mother who had placed him for adoption at the age of nine weeks. His request for information could have revealed his mother's identity. This request was refused by the Registrar General, after first obtaining medical reports. The applicant then requested a judicial review of this administrative decision, but his case was dismissed by the Court of Appeal.

R. v. Registrar General ex parte Smith [1991]

The clash here was between the rights of the individual under statute to information, where the original law had not specified any advance limits to its disclosure, and the rights to privacy and safety of the birth mother. When this request was refused, the client was able to challenge this decision by applying for a judicial review, to clarify the grounds for this administrative decision. Greater priority, however, was given to the protection required by his birth mother. It was decided that to release the information would have been to place her in substantial threat of attack, based on the client's past behaviour, as interpreted by expert medical witnesses. This calls to mind the *Tarasoff* case in the USA, which established a duty for therapists to exercise a duty of care regarding third parties who were threatened by clients (see Chapter 4 for further discussion).

The Court of Appeal's decision confirmed the correctness of the Registrar General's decision to deny access to the information. It also provided, incidentally, a degree of protection for the counselling staff who would have had to respond directly to R.'s request for the information, and who themselves may have been at some degree of personal risk in doing so. The court's decision set a clear path through a tangle of conflicting legal principles, concerning the rights of the individual on the one hand, and the need to prevent serious breaches of the law on the other. Its conclusion was that 'the performance of the statutory duty would not be enforced, even when framed in absolute terms, if to do so would enable someone to cause serious harm to others in the future' (at 255). The right of the individual to personal information is therefore subject to wider considerations of the public good.

Conflicts within adoption counselling

For therapists, this case is a reminder that their work is not carried on in a social vacuum. Activities which are by their nature highly intimate and private can be charged with a wider social responsibility, as demonstrated here, albeit with rather an extreme example. The case also underlines some of the special problems associated with adoption records counselling, and the ambiguous position that this can be seen to occupy. It was originally welcomed as the first statutory recognition of the value of counselling as a service, and of its provision by agencies and local authorities. It introduced the concept of 'compulsory counselling' for those adopted before 12 November 1975, and voluntary counselling for those adopted after this date. The counselling was intended to help individuals explore the meaning of the information they sought, and the possible consequences of receiving it for themselves and all the parties concerned. The provision of counselling seems to underline the ambiguity inherent in the process of opening up access to birth record information. The information is available by right to applicants, but it is almost implied in the framing of the legislation that to use it might somehow be unwise (Hodgkins, 1991: 7).

In addition, adoption records counselling places a strain on the therapist's usual primary allegiance to the *client* as the recipient of their service. As illustrated in this example, a threat of violence to a third party existed. There is a need here for the interests of other interested parties, besides the client, to be fully explored in each situation. 'The counsellor does have a responsibility to represent to the adopted person the interests of other people involved . . .', which is not necessarily standard practice with all schools of therapy. However, 'this should always be done on the basis of researched facts and not assumptions' (Hodgkins, 1991: 14).

To summarise, the judgement established a point of law about the subordination of a statutory duty to a wider principle of preventing serious crime. It raises the issue for therapists of their responsibilities to third parties not present in the consulting room, and of the added pressures that this expectation places upon adoption records counsellors as part of their work.

Access to information by the police and courts

Access to client information may be obtained by external agencies such as the police and the courts. Under the Police and Criminal Evidence Act 1984, the police can be authorised to search premises and remove material as evidence if there are reasonable grounds that 'a serious arrestable offence' has been committed. A serious arrestable offence here could include: murder, manslaughter, rape, other sexual offences, firearms or explosives offences, terrorist offences or causing death by reckless driving. The Act specifically excludes from police powers what are termed 'personal records'. Under s.12 of the Act, this refers to:

> documentary or other records concerning an individual (whether living or dead) who can be identified from them and relating –
>
> (a) to his physical or mental health;
> (b) to spiritual counselling or assistance given or to be given to him; or
> (c) to counselling or assistance given or to be given to him, for the purposes of his personal welfare, by any voluntary organisation or by any individual who –
>   (i) by reason of his office or occupation has responsibilities for his personal welfare; or
>   (ii) by reason of an order of a court has responsibilities for his supervision.

The protection afforded to therapeutic records here is both specific and extensive. Authorisation for seizure of such 'excluded material' can only be obtained by the police applying to a Circuit Judge, not simply to a Magistrate ('excluded' here means excluded from the powers of the Magistrate) (Feldman, 1985: 26). The warrant needs to refer to *specified premises*, to be executed *within one month* of having been authorised, and to apply to *one search only* (excluding an overnight interruption to observe normal business hours). The advice to practitioners faced with such a search is to get a complete list of all such files or documents removed, to assist in their eventual return.

Other types of client information may also be specifically protected by statute. Under the Human Fertilisation and Embryology Act 1990, confidentiality of *medical* information was initially absolute. This presented problems, in that medical personnel were unable to release possibly crucial information even for treatment in an emergency (McHale, 1993a). Later legislation amended this absolute requirement for medical confidentiality. Under the statutory *Code of Practice* produced by the Human Fertilisation and Embryology Authority (HFEA), counselling records occupy a protected status, under para 6.25: 'All information obtained in the course of counselling should be kept confidential, subject to paragraph 3.27, above' (HFEA, 1993: 33). Para 3.27 reads:

> If a member of the team receives information which is of such gravity that confidentiality *cannot* be maintained, he or she should use his or her own discretion, based on good professional practice, in deciding in what circumstances it should be discussed with the rest of the team. (HFEA, 1993: 16).

Other information may also be protected by statute. Under the Rehabilitation of Offenders Act 1974, employers cannot require the disclosure of 'spent' convictions from applicants, except in specified circumstances (see Chapter 2). Unauthorised disclosure of such information by an employer or other party could constitute an offence.

The various, often overlapping, routes for clients to pursue rejected claims for access to information are outlined in Box 5.2.

Access to information by the courts

'Discovery' is the legal term used to describe the process of sharing information between the opposing sides in court proceedings. Discovery in criminal cases is a fairly recent procedure, introduced after the miscarriage of justice concerning Judith Ward. Ward was convicted for an IRA coach bombing on the M62 on the basis of false confessions, and imprisoned. This was in spite of psychiatric reports made at the time of her arrest which questioned her ability to distinguish fantasy from reality, which were not released to her defence solicitors. Judith Ward was subsequently

---

Box 5.2

Client remedies for refusal of access to information, failure to comply with data protection requirements, or unauthorised disclosure of information

- complaint to therapist's professional body or employer
- complaint to Data Protection Registrar
- application for compensation under Data Protection Act 1984
- application to relevant Secretary of State, for Health or Education and Employment
- application for judicial review if access refused by a public body
- civil suit for negligence or breach of confidentiality against therapist or agency
- application to European Court for Breach of European Convention on Human Rights

---

released from prison after a long and public successful campaign against her conviction. The High Court ruled that all relevant prosecution material must in future be disclosed to the defence (Rozenberg, 1994: 316–17; 341–4). Recent controversial legislation by the Government limits disclosure in criminal cases to what is decided by the police as 'relevant', under the Criminal Procedure and Investigations Act 1996. This is on the grounds that the release of information can hamper the prosecution case, and lead to delays caused by having to process a huge volume of often irrelevant documentation.

Discovery is a well-established procedure under civil law. Under ss. 33 and 34 of the Supreme Court Act 1981, the High Court has the power to order production of relevant documents in legal proceedings for personal injuries or in respect of a person's death, with regard to litigation or proposed litigation. 'Ownership of notes per se is not a relevant consideration . . . If a court order for disclosure is made it lies against the person who has *possession, custody or power of the documents*. In the case of NHS patients the Secretary of State is the legal owner of the records and his or her legal rights are vested in the health authorities' (Panting and Palmer, 1992: 2; emphasis added). In private practice, notes are within the 'power, possession or custody' of the individual practitioner.

One of the concerns about the process of discovery in legal proceedings is its potential misuse as a 'fishing expedition' for

Box 5.3

Access to confidential therapy records by police or courts

- by order of the courts in civil or criminal proceedings, as under ss. 33, 34, Supreme Court Act 1981; s.31 Administration of Justice Act 1970; s.20, Criminal Procedure and Investigations Act 1996
- 'private' or second sets of therapeutic notes may still be subject to 'discovery', i.e. surrendered in legal processes
- access by police by warrant authorised by Circuit Judge under s.12 Police and Criminal Evidence Act 1984
- defence against discovery of confidential documents possible on grounds of 'public interest immunity'
- public interest in disclosure as decided by court will over-ride a private or personal interest in confidentiality
- refusal to surrender documents or to give evidence in legal proceedings can be treated as contempt of court
- original case notes taken into the witness box may be examined by the court

material damaging to the opposing side. In one case, a man was found not guilty of charges of rape, incest and indecent assault of his adult daughter at Teesside Crown Court in March 1995, after the prosecution failed to offer evidence in court. The father's barrister had obtained the daughter's psychiatric records of treatment and therapy under a court order. The outcome illustrates not only that therapeutic records may be obtained for court proceedings, as shown here in a criminal case, but that records of a psychiatric or therapeutic nature may convey a particular meaning to the court. Given that clients who have experienced assault or sexual abuse often need psychiatric treatment or therapy to help them to overcome these past experiences, the existence of the relevant records may be used to undermine their very attempts to obtain justice against their alleged abusers. It would appear from this and other instances that records of psychiatric or therapeutic treatment may well be used to undermine the credibility of the client as a future witness in legal proceedings (*Guardian*, 29 March 1995).

Court access to records of therapy via discovery   The question of court access to therapists' notes continues to raise concern amongst practitioners (Dyer, 1994). What therapists need to understand is that professional confidentiality is over-ridden by the notion of the 'public interest' as determined by the courts. In the absence of any professional privilege, therapists are necessarily *obliged* to provide access to information when required by the courts. Stephen Jakobi, of the Psychologists' Protection Society, has described a case where the status of therapeutic case notes was central to the process of litigation. Here, the therapist's client had given birth to a child who was disabled, and had started proceedings for medical negligence concerning the child's birth. Two years on from starting the proceedings, the client began therapy to explore her feelings about the child and the birth. Three years into the therapy, the client's lawyer requested a report from the therapist as an expert witness on the client's mental condition. The report was written up, using session notes from the therapy, and was disclosed to the lawyers for the defendants in the normal way. These lawyers then requested access to the *original* notes of the therapy sessions, rather than just to the summary and conclusions which made up the therapist's report.

As a solicitor with a close personal involvement in the case, Stephen Jakobi has clarified that the therapist's notes had no privileged status, and would be liable to be given up to the court if required. In the event, this did not happen, but this seemed to have had more to do with the judge's somewhat dismissive perceptions of the role of therapy, rather than on account of any judicial concern to preserve the confidentiality of therapeutic sessions (Jakobi and Pratt, 1992).

The process of discovery may also lead to new candidates being drawn into, and even becoming the subject of, legal proceedings. In the case of *M. v. Newham L.B.C.* [1995], a woman brought proceedings against the local authority for taking her child into care. The local authority's action crucially relied on the incorrect information that the girl had been abused by the woman's current cohabitee. At a later stage of the legal proceedings, the mother had access to a transcript of the original video recording of her daughter being interviewed by the social worker and psychiatrist. In this video interview, the alleged abuser was mistakenly identified as her cohabitee; in fact, the alleged abuser was another person, with the same name, who lived elsewhere. On the basis of this new information, she then brought an (unsuccessful) private law action seeking to sue the psychiatrist and social worker who had conducted the interview. The purpose of the action was to obtain compensation for the damage caused by taking the child into local authority care.

In a similar process, confidential records may cross-refer, and provide a bonus of additional, unexpected information beyond that which was originally sought. In one case, a client obtained access to his file under the Access to Health Records Act 1990, in pursuit of a claim for medical negligence caused by an operation. He found a reference in the medical notes to the difficult circumstances in which his child had been taken into care by social workers some 15 years earlier. He thus gained indirect access to social work records, and took steps to gain access to the original social work records to follow up this new line of enquiry. His purpose was now to explore any possible challenge that the defence team might try to make against him as an 'unfit parent', which might damage his integrity and credibility in bringing the medical negligence case.

Protection of client records under public interest immunity   In certain cases, access to records may be denied on the decision of the court, on the basis of their protected status, if granted 'public interest immunity'.

Case Study: Access to information: 'public interest immunity' defence

Joyce Campbell, a teacher, was seriously assaulted by an 11-year-old boy in her class. She suffered severe injuries as a result, was off work for seven months, and had to take early retirement. To support her legal action against the local authority for negligence, she applied for an order for disclosure for all relevant documents, including reports on the pupil made by teachers, psychologists and psychiatrists. This material included a dossier describing previous assaults by the boy in school. A 'green form' was apparently used for making reports on the boy's behaviour, before being passed on to the head teacher. The school log had also been used for the purposes of recording incidents, and in addition there were previous reports on his behaviour from a special school he had attended.

Disclosure was applied for under s.31 of the Administration of Justice Act 1970. A case for negligence was brought against the local authority on the grounds that it was already known that the boy was likely to be violent against members of staff, and inadequate steps had been taken to warn and protect the staff involved. There were three documents which were especially relevant to her case: the head teacher's request for advice, the assessments of the boy's behaviour made by other teachers and the report and recommendations produced by an educational psychologist.

The request for access to records was defended by the authorities on the basis of 'public interest immunity'. This requested that the documents be protected from discovery on the grounds that, if released, this would adversely affect the 'candour' of future recordings. In other words, if these professional recordings were made public, then the willingness of professionals to keep full and accurate recordings in future would be undermined by the threat of their use in possible litigation. The Local Authority's case was overruled, however, and access to the records was ordered by the judge as being in the public interest.

Campbell v. Tameside Council [1982]

The local authority's case in seeking protection for the records was based on the 'candour doctrine', in other words that access would undermine the keeping of full and accurate recordings by professionals. This argument was said by the court to no longer be persuasive, following more recent rulings, as it referred to a *private interest* which must subject to the greater *public interest* in disclosure. Protection in these circumstances can be sought on the basis of either a 'class' or 'contents' argument. In the first, it is claimed that the documents belong to a particular *class*, in this case statutory records, requiring protection from disclosure. In the second situation, immunity is sought on the basis of the *contents* of a particular document. This was considered as a 'class' action to restrict access to recordings made under statutory authority, in carrying out the duties of the local education authority, with a claim by the defendants to 'public interest immunity'. (This is the same principle referred to in the Scott Report on the 'Arms to Iraq' Inquiry, where Public Interest Immunity Certificates were authorised by the Attorney General.)

According to Lord Justice Ackner, '(t)he private promise of confidentiality must yield to the general public interest, in that in the administration of justice truth will out, unless by reason of the character of the information or the relationship of the recipient of the information to the informant a more important public interest is served by protecting the information or identity of the informant from disclosure in a court of law' (at 1075). Whether immunity is sought on a class or contents basis, in both cases the courts weigh the balance between justice and the immunity of the nation or public service, and may inspect the documents and order disclosure. Public interest immunity is normally held to apply to a very narrow range of records, such as child care cases, and to police informer cases.

Access to client information in the courtroom   Access to information may be obtained by the courts requiring a therapist to act as a witness in proceedings concerning their client. In this way, the courts gain access not just to written records or documents, but also to the therapist's *experience* of working with the client. While the Samaritans see themselves as a befriending agency rather than as one providing therapy as such, their experience in this area is interesting. Simon Armson, Chief Executive of the Samaritans, clarified the response usually made by the organisation to requests for volunteers to attend court as witnesses.

> whenever this happens (which is very infrequent) we are always careful to ensure that we attend court as a result of a requirement to do so by Court Order (subpoena). We feel that this is important so as to be able to demonstrate that it is only in order to comply with the law that we would cooperate in this way and that we would never voluntarily attend to give evidence about a contact that was made with us by a caller. We generally manage to succeed in gaining the court's cooperation in maintaining the anonymity of the Samaritan volunteer. To do this we usually write to the Crown Prosecution Service and, if appropriate, the defence solicitors seeking their assistance in this matter and to the Clerk of the Court asking for the necessary request to be made to the Judge. (Armson, 1995)

Normally, it seems, courts will respect this arrangement, given that it is based on the need to maintain public confidence in the Samaritans' professionalism and their strict policy of client confidentiality.

Relate (formerly Marriage Guidance Council) have a different experience of handling requests for therapists to appear as witnesses in court. This is based on the degree of privilege which, unusually, can be claimed for marital or relationship counselling where legal proceedings such as divorce or legal separation may be considered. Derek Hill, Head of Counselling at Relate, refers to

> situations in which subpoenas, witness orders and less official pressures are applied to Relate counsellors in an effort to get them to disclose information acquired during counselling. In the former cases we have used a barrister several times to argue that privacy and confidentiality outweigh the public interest in securing a disclosure. We have been successful – but not in securing a reasoned judgement, so each time we start anew. (Hill, 1995)

The limited case law on privilege concerning marital counselling does not appear to carry the full status of legal precedent, which would require courts to recognise therapist privilege in this field. (For a fuller discussion of these issues, see Chapter 4.)

The case for therapist evidential privilege   The lack of therapist privilege in the UK is not surprising, considering that doctors also do not hold such rights. This is unlike the situation in the US, where medical and therapist privilege is recognised by many states (Bollas and Sundelson, 1995: 11). The term used to describe this situation is 'evidential privilege', namely the right *not* to have to give evidence in court concerning a patient or client. The most widely cited example of a therapist seeking to obtain evidential privilege is that relating to the case of Dr Anne Hayman outlined below.

Case Study: Therapists and the arguments for evidential privilege: the Hayman case

Dr Anne Hayman was subpoenaed to give evidence in the High Court about one of her patients, thus being faced with a difficult personal and professional dilemma, described originally in an anonymous article in The Lancet.

> *I had to decide whether to obey the Law or to abide by the rules of professional conduct. I complied with the subpoena by attending Court, but I decided I could not answer any questions about the 'patient', and I made all the arrangements, including having a barrister to plead in mitigation of sentence, for the possibility that I should be sent to prison for contempt of court. In the event, although my silence probably did constitute a contempt, the judge declared he would not sentence me, saying it was obviously a matter of conscience. (Hayman, 1965: 785)*

Part of the strength of Hayman's argument lay in the particular stress placed by her on transference *as a therapeutic tool, and how this professional commitment precluded breaking confidentiality.*

> *To the judge's query whether I would still object if 'the patient' gave permission, I answered with an example: suppose a patient had been in treatment for some time and was going through a temporary phase of admiring and depending on me; he might therefore feel it necessary to sacrifice himself and give permission, but it might not be proper for me to act on this. (Hayman, 1965: 786)*

(Source: Bond, 1993a; Hayman, 1965)

In this particular instance, Dr Hayman's approach was successful, and she was able to convince the judge that justice would not be best served by requiring her to give evidence. The example does not set a legal precedent for others to claim, however. Refusal to give evidence on the grounds that this infringes client–therapist confidentiality is likely to be treated as contempt of court. In another case, a psychiatrist was threatened with contempt for refusing to give evidence, and promptly complied with the judge's instructions (*Nuttall v. Nuttall and Twyman* (1964)). In the USA, a Californian psychiatrist, George Romero, was imprisoned in 1977 for three days for refusing to testify about a patient he had seen (Van Hoose and Kottler, 1985: 52).

A therapist cannot simply *claim* confidentiality as a reason for not providing the court with information, except at the risk of being held to be in contempt of court. However, they might request that sensitive information about a client be disclosed firstly to the judge, in order to restrict disclosure of information in open court to that which is strictly relevant to the needs of the proceedings in question. This may be more likely to gain a favourable response from the court than a therapist's simple refusal to discuss client material in court. The experience of professional organisations such as BAC indicates that a therapist may be well advised to obtain their own separate legal representation if called to give evidence in these circumstances (Bond, 1996).

The courts and other parties in legal proceedings may gain access to information through reports prepared for the court. It is worth bearing in mind that when preparing reports for the court,

Box 5.4

Guidelines for professional practice regarding access to records

- review arrangements for the physical security of *all* recordings of therapy, including
  - official or agency records
  - computerised records
  - 'private' or personal notes
  - videos and tape recordings
- share policy on access to records via a brief leaflet given to clients, backed up by a more detailed document
- follow good practice concerning the focus and content of client records. Avoid comments which are trivialising, unjustifiable or defamatory
- check arrangements for storage and destruction of client records after expiry (normally six years)
- consider your own responses to the unexpected, such as
  - request by a former client for surrender of records
  - witness summons to appear in court
- in the case of police or court demands for client records or attendance in court as a witness, seek immediate expert legal and professional advice

the final report in effect becomes a public document. Once the report leaves the possession of the therapist, he or she has no control over its future use or distribution, and it may even possibly be read out in open court. The potential readership and impact of very sensitive client information should be carefully considered before inclusion in such reports (RCP, 1990: 105). In addition, therapists acting as witnesses should avoid at all costs taking their original case notes with them into the witness box. This might make it easier to refer to notes made at the time, or to check significant dates, but this can be as easily achieved by making a summary of relevant information. The court has a right to inspect the original case notes if taken with the witness into the witness box, thus gaining access to the most direct form of information about the therapeutic process short of a video recording. Acting as a witness may present another way in which the therapist comes into direct contact with the legal system as a result of his or her practice. This is discussed more fully in the following chapter.

Summary

Access to records describes the rights and powers of parties such as clients, the police and the courts to gain access to otherwise confidential information. Client rights have been significantly enhanced by recent laws following the *Gaskin* case. In certain situations, access may be denied to clients, either to prevent harm to others or to the clients themselves.

The police may have access to client files only with specific judicial authority. The courts have wider powers of access, even to the therapist's 'private' notes, under the process of 'discovery', or the disclosure of evidence to the other side in legal proceedings. A therapist may request the court's permission to restrict disclosure to material essential for the legal proceedings in hand. However, refusal by a therapist to surrender files, or to give evidence when required by the court under subpoena or witness summons, can be punished as contempt of court. Some counselling organisations seek to underline their commitment to client confidentiality by requiring that their counsellors only attend court as witnesses when formally summoned, and not on a voluntary basis. In the final analysis, therapeutic confidentiality is subject to the needs of the wider public interest. In the case of conflict or dispute, the courts will provide the final authority on what constitutes the public interest regarding confidentiality or the disclosure of client material.

Discussion points

1 On what grounds could therapists justify *not* disclosing therapeutic records to their clients? What types of information might be legitimately withheld from clients as potentially damaging?
2 What are the implications of full client access to computerised and manual records by therapists? How might therapists record information about their personal responses to client material, such as transference and counter-transference issues, or material intended for use in supervision?
3 Should therapists seek to acquire 'evidential privilege', as held by some licensed therapists in the USA? What advantages or disadvantages would this entail?

4   How would you respond if required to attend court as a witness in court proceedings concerning your client? How might you prepare yourself for such a role?

5   Does the process of 'discovery' concerning records of therapy disadvantage clients, or ensure fairness, by bringing all relevant material into consideration by the court? How might therapists counter assumptions that a client who has received psychiatric treatment or therapy is less reliable as a witness in a court of law?

6

Courts and the Legal System

There are a number of ways in which therapists may find a shift in perspective necessary to adapt to the world of the legal system. Fishwick has described some of the factors which may amount to a culture shock for social workers and other caring professionals working in the courts (1988: 175–90). Some of these factors, slightly adapted, are relevant to understanding possible conflicts or misunderstandings between therapists and the court system. Some of the major contrasts relate to:

- a potential clash of values, perhaps regarding therapeutic confidentiality versus the concept of 'the public interest'
- precision in the use of language versus 'greyness' and ambiguity
- public versus private practice: therapy is usually a private activity, whereas court is a public arena
- formal versus informal practice: the court's appearance and functioning are heavily bound by rules and tradition
- adversarial rather than cooperative approach to establishing the meaning of communication between parties

The legal system in England and Wales is based on adversarial proceedings, unlike the French system, which operates via inquisitorial proceedings in criminal law. Under an adversarial system, the judge appears to play little active role during the proceedings. The case is heard as a contest between two versions of events, with the judge acting as an umpire, and with advocates playing a partisan role in marshalling witnesses and in presenting the case. The burden of proof rests with the party bringing the case, which needs to be proven beyond reasonable doubt in the case of criminal courts, or on the balance of probabilities in civil cases. A high value is placed on evidence given *orally*, particularly in criminal trials, and on the manner in which it is presented. 'Hearsay' or second-hand evidence not directly observed by a witness is normally excluded. Giving evidence is usually done by witnesses via a process of 'examination-in-chief' followed by cross examination by the advocates for the opposing side (Jackson, 1995). The legal system is usually open to the public, except in the case of child care proceedings. Involvement by the public in the form of attendance on juries is an important aspect of the system of justice in England and Wales (McEwan, 1995). Juries are widely used in hearing criminal cases, including fraud trials such as the Guinness trial, but are less frequently used in civil cases, except for libel, as in the Jeffrey Archer case, and in cases of false imprisonment.

The system of justice in England and Wales is based on a fundamental division between criminal law, or offences against the rule of law, and civil law, where the courts are used to resolve disputes between individuals or corporate bodies. The legal system operates as a ladder of courts, extending from Magistrates' Courts at the local level, to the House of Lords at the highest level. Decisions made at the higher levels of the court system are then binding on courts deliberating at lower levels. In most cases, therapists are probably more likely to come into contact with the lower levels of the court hierarchy, such as the Coroner's Court, in dealing with suicide, or the Magistrates' Court, in supporting a client bringing a court case against an abusing parent, or the County Court, in initiating or responding to litigation. For many therapists, involvement with the courts may never extend beyond the mundane level of taking action over unpaid fees by a client. However, some therapists may be involved as witnesses of fact, or possibly as expert witnesses in proceedings which are heard at different levels of the judicial system.

Faced with the different language, structure and values of the legal system, therapists without experience of legal proceedings may be tempted on the one hand to 'deskill' themselves, or on the other hand to dismiss the legal system as unfeeling and archaic. It is important for therapists to avoid falling into either of these responses, and to find ways in which their expertise and professionalism will be of value to the courts when required. This chapter attempts to help therapists by focusing on three key aspects of the court system. It provides an outline of **current developments in the legal system**, and explores areas of possible **involvement by therapists**, such as acting as a witness in court. It also considers some of the issues raised by the **system of damages**, particularly for psychiatric illness, which have a bearing on the concerns of therapists. Although much of this information is probably more detailed than most therapists will require for their day-to-day work, a basic knowledge of the court system may be helpful, should the need arise in the future concerning a particular case.

Current developments within the legal system

The legal system as a whole is currently experiencing major problems in certain areas. Focusing on the civil justice system, there are key difficulties such as cost, delay, uncertainty over outcome, unavailability of legal advice, and the overall complexity of the system. The Woolf Report describes the dimensions of the current crisis in the civil legal system, and notes the growing consensus on the need for radical reform (1995).

Costs Solicitors' charges will vary regionally, but are currently about £90 per hour. The cost of legal representation at the top end of the scale can be a major deterrent for those involved in court action. For example, an initial 'brief fee' for a barrister can cost tens of thousands of pounds, plus £1,500–£2,000 in 'refreshers'. Legal Aid pays Queen's Counsels (QCs) £300 per hour for reading papers in a civil case. Consultations in chambers can cost a minimum of £200. Criminal barristers can cost £500–£750 per day in refreshers for 'heavy cases' plus a brief fee (*Guardian*, 18 April 1995). Criticism has focused on cases where the eventual cost of legal charges has outweighed the actual value of the property or compensation at issue.

Delays Delays can occur in the amount of time taken from the initial claim to final hearing; in the time taken to reach a final settlement; in obtaining a date for a hearing; and in the time taken by the hearing itself (Woolf, 1995: 13). General cases can take six months to be heard, while specialist cases, such as medical negligence, can take up to three years to be resolved.

Uncertainty Litigation is in many ways a gamble, given that many cases are settled out of court at the last minute. One observer notes that 'there is frequently a stage in personal injury cases – generally a few days or hours before the hearing – when the defendant will be offered a sum of money to settle the case. The plaintiff has to decide whether to accept the offer, which he will probably think too small, or go ahead and fight the case in court. If he fights and loses he will end up with nothing' (Rozenberg, 1994: 186). Generally speaking, the loser pays the legal costs for the winning side.

Access to legal advice In most cases, legal representation is a necessity for going to court, although this is not the case for bringing small claims actions or for some other civil actions (Rudinger, 1985). There are, exceptionally, examples of defendants successfully mounting their own defence in a criminal trial (Randle, 1995). The skill and experience of a lawyer can be a crucial factor in deciding whether the case is won or lost. 'As in criminal trials, many cases are won and lost on tactics and advocacy rather than on where the truth lies' (Berlin and Dyer, 1990: 145). While numbers of 'litigants in person', i.e. without lawyers, are bringing their cases to the Appeal Courts, only an estimated 4% are successful (*Guardian*, 7 July 1995). Flexibility with regard to legal representation has increased to some degree. Solicitors have lost their monopoly on conveyancing, and barristers now have to share their rights of audience, or representation of clients, at the higher levels of the court system. However, it is still necessary to go through a solicitor to have access to a barrister, and the attendance of juniors together with barristers in court can significantly inflate the legal costs to litigants.

Access to Legal Aid The Legal Aid scheme was set up in 1949 to provide access to justice for people of 'small and moderate means'. The total cost of the Legal Aid budget was £1.4 billion in 1995. When it was first introduced in 1950, nearly 80% of households qualified; the figure is now nearer 47% (*Guardian*, 10 January 1995). Criminal Legal Aid is widely available, but civil Legal Aid is restricted to those on low incomes. There are currently proposals to cap the Legal Aid budget, and franchise Legal Aid work to legal firms, who bid on a contract basis to cover a fixed number of cases for a fixed price. Legal Aid will no longer be free, and may only be granted on the strength of the case being proposed. Even applicants on benefit may be required to make some contribution, such as £10 or £20 (Lord Chancellor's Department, 1996). The concern is that this will limit the numbers with access to Legal Aid in the future.

Complexity of the system   There has been an explosion of litigation which has doubled to almost three million cases per year over the last 15 years, causing the legal system to overload and slow down drastically in its workings (*Guardian*, 20 May 1995). The shift to litigation may partly be due to the loss of conveyancing as a dependable source of income for solicitors. The difficulties facing inexperienced litigants are numerous and substantial. Lord Alexander, QC, is quoted as saying of the civil justice system:

> whilst everyone operates it fairly and conscientiously within the rules, the rules are not satisfactory for resolving disputes. They are particularly unsatisfactory where individuals are involved as, for example, in personal injury litigation, where individuals are, as claimants, suing companies . . . I think only people who've been involved in it can realise the uncertainty, the emotional energy and the anxiety that go into litigation. (Berlin and Dyer, 1990: 150)

There are a number of reforms under consideration, designed to make the civil justice system more responsive and effective. In part, this includes the proposed reform of the Legal Aid system referred to above, namely a cap on overall spending, and a franchise system to law firms undertaking this work. In addition, there are developments such as:

'No win, no fee'   This is also called a conditional or contingency fee arrangement. Under this scheme, the lawyer takes on the case, and takes a 'mark-up' on their ordinary fee if they win the case, but receives nothing if they lose. Those currently ineligible for Legal Aid can insure with the Law Society for £100 against having to pay the winning side's legal costs, should they lose the case. Initially, only personal injury, insolvency and human rights cases are covered by the scheme. No insurance is currently available for medical negligence, pharmaceutical or tobacco-related litigation (*Guardian*, 16 May 1995).

Reform of legal processes and systems   Lord Woolf has proposed reforms of the structure and procedures used by civil justice (1995):

- expansion of small claims procedures for claims up to £3,000
- 'fast track' for straightforward claims less than £10,000 with a fixed timetable of six months and fixed costs (e.g. for example, in defamation and negligence cases)
- 'multi-track' system for larger cases over £10,000 with strict controls over costs, timetables, and the volume of paperwork, and provision for the appointment of expert witnesses by the court.

Use of alternative means of resolving civil disputes   There are also measures designed to divert some forms of dispute resolution out of the court system, and into more appropriate areas of the judicial system or elsewhere. Alternatives to litigation are suggested, such as:

- *conciliation*   This can include referral to a counselling service, for example for couples undergoing relationship problems, as in the service provided by Relate and other agencies. Conciliation may help couples to resolve issues concerning contact and custody of children from the marriage.
- *mediation*   This service helps couples to sort out financial and property disputes whilst going through a divorce. Mediation is a voluntary process to which both parties must agree, under the Family Law Act 1996 (Lord Chancellor's Department, 1995: Para 5.28). Mediation also has a role to play in other fields: a pilot mediation scheme is providing redress in disputes over medical care in certain parts of the NHS.
- *arbitration*   The Small Claims Court, a branch of the County Court, deals with small claims of up to £3,000. This is an informal private hearing, with a less strict observance of the usual rules of evidence, where the Registrar may adopt a more active, inquisitorial role than is usually the case in other legal proceedings. More complex cases can be referred back to the County Court if necessary. Usually, the unsuccessful party is not required to pay the costs of the winning side, although the successful party can recover some limited costs and expenses.

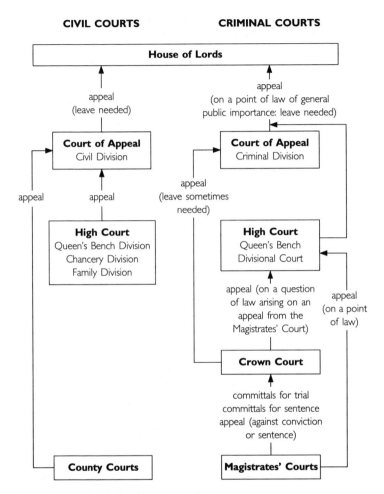

Figure 6.1 *Simplified diagram of the English Courts*
(*Source*: Rozenberg, 1994: 124. Reproduced with permission)

Structure of the court system
The structure of the legal system in England and Wales is briefly
outlined above. (See Figure 6.1.)

Industrial Tribunals These deal with employment protection,
equal pay cases, and discrimination on the grounds of sex, race or

disability. They are described as being informal, but the growing complexity of case law and increasing use of legal representation mean that this appearance of informality may sometimes be misleading.

Coroner's Courts   Inquests into sudden or suspicious deaths are held on an inquisitorial basis, where the coroner investigates the circumstances, sometimes with the assistance of a jury. (Further detail is given in the discussion below.)

Magistrates' Courts   These deal with 98% of all criminal cases, excepting those where the defendant opts for jury trial at Crown Court. It also deals with a wide range of civil matters including child care proceedings in the role of the Family Proceedings Court.

Crown Courts   In Crown Court, cases are heard by a jury, and by a judge from the High Court, or by a Circuit Judge or Recorder. The rate of acquittals by juries is much higher in the Crown Court than in Magistrates' Courts for similar offences, as is the proportion of cases where the defendant changes their plea from not guilty to guilty at the trial.

County Courts   These deal with most civil cases, such as payment of money, debt, compensation, claims concerning matrimonial property, maintenance, domestic violence, custody, and undefended divorces. Most consumer cases will be dealt with by the County Court. Claims under £3,000 are dealt with in a less formal manner via the Small Claims Court referred to above.

High Courts and Court of Appeal   There is a complex system of appealing from lower courts to higher ones, in order to challenge verdicts. This can extend to the House of Lords, which only hears cases involving points of law of major public importance.

The law in England and Wales is increasingly affected by the decisions of European Courts, for example concerning access to information. The two main courts are:

Court of Justice of the European Communities, at Luxembourg
This is the main legislative body of the European Union (EU). The

European Community became the European Union following the Treaty of Maastricht, which came into force in November 1993. European Law consists of Treaties, which are primary legislation. In other words, they are directly enforceable in the UK, without any further need for legislation. Secondary legislation consists of Regulations made by Brussels, which have immediate effect, whereas Directives usually need to be incorporated into domestic legislation.

European Court of Human Rights, at Strasbourg   This deals with violations of the European Convention on Human Rights. Cases need to be made first to the European Commission on Human Rights (ECHR). Since 1966, the UK has allowed individuals right of petition to the ECHR. Up to 1996, the UK government had lost 38 out of 79 cases referred to it, with a further 14 cases still pending. When the UK government loses, it is required to amend UK law accordingly. Obtaining a decision by the ECHR can take up to five to six years (*Guardian*, 28 September 1995).

Therapists' involvement with the courts

In most cases, therapists are unlikely to come into contact with the courts, apart from in exceptional circumstances. Yet these may occur from time to time, and could include:

- attending Coroner's Court following the suicide of a client
- taking legal action in the Small Claims Court over non-payment of fees by a client
- supporting a client taking legal action against alleged abusers, either via prosecution or in a case for damages
- being called as a witness or expert witness in legal proceedings
- being sued in the County Court by a client for breach of contract or for professional negligence
- being the subject of criminal prosecution for rape, assault, fraud or other serious offence.

(The latter two situations are not dealt with in detail here. Action against therapists for professional negligence is described in Chapter 3.)

Sources of legal advice

Problems for individuals in gaining access to information about the law, or to legal representation have been identified as a major problem of the civil justice system at present. For therapists or clients seeking legal advice or representation, the following avenues should be considered. Legal advice can be obtained from a wide variety of organisations and sources:

■ Citizens' Advice Bureaux may have a solicitor's surgery
■ Law Centres can advise on housing, employment, juvenile crime and child care cases
■ The Consumers' Association have a personal advice service, available by subscription only
■ Initial legal advice and information can be obtained from Employee Assistance Programmes
■ Trade unions, professional associations and pressure groups such as MIND (National Association for Mental Health) and the Children's Legal Centre will have expertise in particular areas of the law. The Equal Opportunities Commission and Commission for Racial Equality can also give information on case law and legislation.
■ Solicitors sometimes provide fixed fee advice, or offer a free first session. Under the Green Form scheme operated by the Law Society, legal advice is based on financial eligibility. There is a *Regional Directory of Solicitors* published by the Law Society, which includes panels of specialist lawyers, such as those in child care law and mental health.
■ Professional indemnity insurance companies and professional protection societies will usually provide telephone advice and legal representation for those insured.

(See Resources for relevant addresses and telephone numbers.) In the USA, most therapists obtain information about the law and get legal advice from their professional associations – a role that may be taken up more by similar associations in the UK (Bowman and Mertz, 1996: 595).

First steps in obtaining legal advice

When looking for legal advice, it is worth trying to find a solicitor who specialises in the required area to deal with the case, whether this is to do with professional negligence, personal injury or child care law. On first meeting, assuming a decision to proceed with the case and with this representative, the following points need to be checked out verbally before finishing discussion, and then confirmed in writing afterwards. The National Consumer Council (1993) suggest that key points to confirm would include:

- estimated costs, or *ceilings* to costs, likely to be incurred
- probable time the case will take to resolve
- the name of the solicitor dealing with your case
- establishing agreement on the basic facts of the case
- details of any further information required
- who to complain to if necessary about quality of service
- the next step to be taken in any legal action

(Addresses and phone numbers for complaints about legal representation are in the Resources section.)

Taking action via the Small Claims Court

The most common form of involvement by therapists in the courts is likely to be taking action to reclaim unpaid fees by clients. Claims of this kind can be dealt with in a very straightforward way by using the Small Claims Court, which is a branch of the County Court. Legal representation by a solicitor is not usually necessary or to be recommended, as the purpose of the Small Claims procedure is to provide a quick and informal way of resolving civil disputes. Resolving the dispute may follow the following sequence, starting with a formal letter to the other person (Applebey, 1994: 29).

First stage: writing a letter to the client or company concerning the problem

- set out the main facts at issue, presenting points to support your claim
- explain the steps already taken to resolve the dispute
- remember that the letter may later be used in court (heading the letter 'Without prejudice' prevents this from happening)
- remain polite, and avoid becoming aggressive in tone, as this may be counter-productive in the long run

- be cautious about offering to accept less than the full amount at issue, as this may count against you later in court
- indicate that you intend to start legal proceedings in the County Court within 14 days unless the matter is settled

Second stage: taking legal action to recover a debt

- contact the local Small Claims Court (this is a branch of the local County Court)
- obtain and complete the relevant forms to start the action
- issue a 'default summons', using forms N1 or N2, retaining a second copy for your records, and a third copy for the court
- claim proceeds automatically if the defendant does not respond within 21 days

There are a number of practical guides to help plaintiffs considering taking legal action via the Small Claims Court, but who are unused to the procedures or terms involved (Matthews, 1995; Whimster, 1995). Applebey (1994), for example, gives detailed advice on completing the necessary forms. Further practical advice to consumers is given in *Small claims in the County Court* and *How to sue and defend action without a solicitor*, available from Citizens' Advice Bureaux; and the leaflet *A buyer's guide*, available from the Office of Fair Trading (1994).

The expansion of the Small Claims system is some indication of its success, given that it now handles 88,000 cases per year. However, recent findings are that fully a third of those winning their cases recover no money at all, and that there are still weaknesses to be overcome with this approach (*Guardian*, 13 March 1996). As with all legal action, there is no certainty of outcome, however apparently straightforward the procedures involved.

Appearing in court as a witness
Most material on the subject of appearing in court seems to be geared to the needs of professionals such as social workers or probation officers, who appear in court on a regular basis. There seems to be very little information published for other professionals such as therapists, who may also have to appear in court for similar reasons. The following section offers some pointers for those unfamiliar with the procedures involved in attending court to give evidence for the first time.

Advice to witnesses has been described succinctly in the past as: 'Dress up, stand up, speak up and shut up!' (Knight and Palmer, 1992: 14).

The purpose of the witness appearing is to put their evidence before the court. This may be done through giving evidence verbally, or also via a written report or statement. It is a mistake to assume that the court already knows the details of the evidence to be given. Unless the evidence is given clearly and carefully, it may be that certain important facts are 'lost' to the court in the process.

Preparation   Some points to consider before going to court:

- dress, appearance, and overall level of confidence will all have some impact on the overall impression made on the court
- there may be a Witness Support Programme to explain the court layout and procedure beforehand, plus a separate waiting room may be available
- know the evidence to be given. The solicitor or barrister will make contact briefly in court on the day to quickly go over the statement before the case starts
- on arrival, witnesses need to give the usher their name and whereabouts while waiting to be called, which may take some time

In court   Witnesses wait outside the court itself until called, while the case is going on.

Taking the witness stand:

- enter the witness box as directed by the usher
- stand up, take the oath on the Bible or affirm to tell the truth
- state your name and occupation when asked

Order of proceedings for witnesses giving evidence

- introduction (as immediately above)
- examination-in-chief by the solicitor calling you as a witness
- cross-examination by the solicitor for the opposing party
- re-examination by the first solicitor
- release from giving evidence by the court

Style of giving evidence

- address answers to the judge(s), not to the solicitor who is actually asking the questions
- take your time and consider your responses carefully
- be clear and definite in your answers
- if you don't know or can't remember, say so
- project your voice clearly so that you can be heard properly in the court
- you can, with the court's permission, refer to notes made at the time of the events you are being asked about, but the solicitor may ask to see them personally during re-examination
- magistrates are addressed as 'Your Worship'; Crown Court judges as 'Your Honour'; High Court judges as 'My Lord' or 'My Lady'
- when the court has finished with hearing your evidence, you may stay in court, as directed by the usher, to hear the rest of the case

Expenses   You should be able to claim for travelling expenses, meals, and lost wages arising from your court appearance, by contacting the solicitor who has called you to give evidence.

Carson (1990) has devised self-assessment exercises for potential witnesses, and a training video for expert witnesses, which provide a greater level of detail about preparation for court work (BPS, 1995d).

Status of professional Codes of Practice   A key issue for therapists appearing in court as a witness may well be the professional rationale for their actions. It is easy to assume that the correctness of a particular course of action can be established simply by the therapist referring to their professional *Code of Practice* as justification for making certain decisions, or for having acted in a certain way with their client. However, professional *Codes of Practice* do not necessarily carry authority in a court of law. Bond (1991) gives a telling example from a Coroner's Court. In this case, a counsellor working for a college's student services appeared in the Coroner's Court following the suicide of her client. She referred to the existing BAC *Code* in order to legitimate her work. 'After some discussion it was established that professional codes do not have any legal standing' (1991: 285). (This particular case is discussed in more detail below.)

The *Codes of Practice* which do carry some weight in courts are those which have a statutory basis. Thus, in the *Egdell* case, discussed in Chapter 4, the judge referred to the General Medical Council's 'Blue Book' on *Fitness to practise* in reaching his decision. He noted that the rules themselves do not have statutory authority, but that they were derived from the disciplinary function of the GMC under the Medical Act 1983 (*W. v. Egdell*, [1990], at 843).

Similarly, the Mental Health Act *Code of Practice* carries authority because of its statutory basis. 'The Mental Health Act 1983 does not impose a legal duty to comply with the *Code* but failure to follow the *Code* could be referred to in evidence in legal proceedings' (DoH and Welsh Office, 1993: s. 1.1). However, the courts are not bound to respect slavishly any existing guidelines in reaching a decision about the rightness of a course of action. Guidelines or Codes may be overruled by the court as in deciding the case of 'W.', an anorexic girl of 16, in 1992. Lord Donaldson indicated that the Department of Health *Guidelines for Ethics Committees* (1991) were not, in his view, consistent with the law on consent to treatment.

Normally, where there are statutory *Codes of Practice*, compliance with their provisions will provide some defence. In other cases, guidelines may indicate 'best practice' within the profession, but it should not be assumed that they automatically provide a defence for a particular line of action in legal proceedings (Hurwitz, 1995).

Courts and clients
Therapists would not normally come into contact with the legal system as such unless there were overriding circumstances which made this advisable or necessary. In some cases, a client may *request* their involvement, as, for example, when a distressed client is brought into police custody. The client may then be seen by the police to be a 'vulnerable adult', requiring the presence of an appropriate adult. This situation is briefly described below. In other situations, a client may be involved in legal processes where an understanding of the procedures will be helpful to the therapist working with them. In the case of clients who have experienced traumatic bereavement, acquiring fuller knowledge of the

circumstances of the death via an inquest may have an important part to play in coming to terms with their loss; failure to do so may delay or further complicate the grieving process (Lendrum and Syme, 1992: 42). In the case of clients who allege that they have been abused in childhood, taking court proceedings, either criminal or civil in nature, can represent a search for justice and reparation. At another level, it may express needs for validation and acknowledgement, which are important in coming to terms with the abuse and in starting to build a new life (Bass and Davis, 1991: 307–10). These two situations are explored in more detail below, with reference to case examples.

Under the Police and Criminal Evidence Act 1984, and the relevant *Code of Practice* (Home Office, 1991), the police are required to identify 'vulnerable groups' of those brought into custody. This includes juveniles under 17, and persons with a mental disorder or mental handicap. The police are then required to inform an 'appropriate adult'. Often this will be a social worker. The role of the appropriate adult (Home Office, 1991: 77–9) is to:

- *advise* the person concerned
- *observe* that the interview is conducted fairly
- *facilitate* communication between that person and the police
- *safeguard* the rights of the person concerned

Without proper experience and training, this is not a role that a therapist would normally wish to take on, but it could be the case that a client might request their attendance, without the therapist being fully aware of what was entailed in the role (Littlechild, 1994; Sheppard, 1995).

Coroner's Court
Therapists may be more likely to come into contact with the courts at the lower levels of the system, for example, by attending a Coroner's Court to establish the cause of death of a client. It may also be that clients are directly affected by the processes and outcomes of courts in making decisions, for example in deciding the cause of death of a close relative or partner. An inquest is, therefore, 'often a key factor in assisting the family to come to terms with the bereavement' (Grealis and Coles, 1994: 321). This is shown in the case of one parent, who was bitterly critical of the Coroner's conduct in the hearing about the death of her two-year-

old son in hospital: 'I don't think we are going to come to terms with it. We don't accept it and you can't come to terms with something you can't accept' (*Guardian*, 5 May 1996).

The main purpose of inquests is to establish the causes of sudden or unnatural deaths, where there are no criminal proceedings, or where a death occurs in police custody or in prison. In fact, 'the inquest is the only formal state tribunal whose exclusive concern is death' (Wells, 1994: 213). There are certain unusual features of the Coroner's Court which can surprise and distress parties not used to the format of this court. It is informal and inquisitorial, rather than adversarial. This places more discretionary powers in the hands of the Coroner, regarding the procedures adopted in court, and in calling witnesses. Juries can be called, for example, where there is a concern for public health or safety, or concerning a death in prison or custody. Legal aid for representation is not available, and there is no right to have advance disclosure of documents, as applies in other civil and criminal proceedings. The verdicts available to the court include: death by natural causes; unlawful killing; accident; misadventure; suicide and open verdict, where there is insufficient evidence to justify any definite verdict (Inquest, nd).

Concern has been expressed at the unsatisfactory nature of the inquest system in dealing with the needs of families and relatives, in particular after the Hillsborough stadium and *Marchioness* disasters (*Guardian*, 14 November 1995). For families and relatives, a primary need is often to establish the *truth*, rather than necessarily to make out a case for financial compensation.

Case Study: One family's experience of the Coroner's Court

He was our son. He was dead. We were worried, anxious, angry and frustrated . . . the atmosphere of the court was alien to us. Why should the prison authorities be represented by barristers and solicitors if they were hiding nothing? We felt intimidated and contrite, cowed and oppressed. The coroner would not call our witnesses; we had to intercede in his summing up. What was the purpose of our son's inquest? To determine the cause of death, or to bury forever the flaws in the system that killed him? The system failed him, the system failed us. (Brinkley, 1993)

This experience is not intended to be representative of all families or relatives, but highlights some of the strong emotions which can be aroused by attending a Coroner's Court. The campaign group Inquest has identified a particular weakness of the legal system in responding to the needs and distress of the bereaved, for example in failing to provide a private waiting space before going into court. According to Inquest,

> there is no specific professional emotional support or counselling available for families facing inquests. Counselling agencies, be they generic or specific bereavement projects, rarely have the knowledge to understand the additional strain on the bereaved of having to deal with both the inquest system and the secrecy of many of the institutions in which people die. . . . The available literature on bereavement does not address the particular needs of this client group. (Inquest, 1995: 2)

Inquest are currently developing training and other materials useful to therapists working with bereaved clients who come into contact with the Coroner's Courts. Therapists need to be aware of the specific features of the inquest system which distinguish it from other types of court, and how this may affect the clients' bereavement process.

Supporting clients taking legal action
Therapists may well prefer to avoid involvement in legal pro-cesses, unless there are strong reasons for becoming involved. In some cases, it may be that the therapist takes on the role of supporting a client in taking legal action, perhaps where there is no other source of support for the client. One form this can take is as an informal supporter, actually alongside the client in the courtroom, as a '*McKenzie*'. This term was first used where a party in a divorce case was assisted informally by a barrister as an aid and supporter. According to this principle, 'any person, whether he be a professional man or not, may attend as a friend of either party, may take notes, may quietly make suggestions, and give advice; but no one can demand to take part in the proceedings as an advocate' (*McKenzie v. McKenzie* [1970]).

For most therapists, their activity will probably be much more limited to providing emotional support rather than active advice and encouragement. In the following case, one therapist worked with her female client for a lengthy period in exploring the context and effects of the sexual abuse she had experienced in her childhood from male family members. Ultimately, the client decided to confront them and inform the police, with the result that the alleged perpetrators were prosecuted. The therapist provided support for the client throughout the court case, extending to accompanying her to court. For legal reasons, the process of the client giving her evidence in court became very complex and involved, as part of a lengthy and drawn-out legal process lasting two and a half years. One defendant was eventually found guilty on one of the more minor charges. The other cases were still continuing at the time of the interview.

Case Study: A therapist's experience of supporting a client in court

The therapist summed up her experience in court as:

An incredible feeling of helplessness. Initially, I thought it was brilliant that this could happen, because I've often wanted to say to her 'but all this is all being paid for, somebody's behind you, somebody believes you. The police have pushed it, the Crown Prosecution have taken it on board. They wouldn't do all this if there wasn't enough evidence'. But because the legal system took over, and the explanation for what happened wasn't really sound, there is a frustration and a feeling of . . . You have it taken away from you, when you were being offered something that was really good, and it's just been snatched away from you.

What would have been more helpful to therapist and client?

Somebody to explain how it all works. [Witness Support] did try to look after us. I guess knowing more about the system and not being very naive in not . . . what was going to happen. There's a sense when you go to court, it will all just go through. It's a whole other world. I was just naive about all that. My over-riding feeling now is that I've got another client, she can't take it to court, because her family won't support her, and my sense is, you're not really missing much, because, who knows? Who knows? It's a whole other set of issues that it brings up, on top of the ones you've already got, and sometimes it might work, and you might get a good . . . It might go well, and other times it can be just as damaging. That's the key thing, without me, I don't know how she would have survived.

If I had to go to court again, I would be able to be much clearer with her about [how] this is going to be a very difficult procedure, and you have to understand that it isn't just you standing up and saying what you want to say, because there are other people working in there

*that can take it out of your hands, and you have to be very, very clear
that that is what you want to do. Now I know that it can be long,
gruelling, complicated, and you won't necessarily get the result that
you want, even though it's quite clear that you should. (Interview)*

The legal process introduced a new and unfamiliar set of technical
procedures into what had started out as the resolution of a
therapeutic activity, that is, of achieving justice for the abuse
experienced by the client. The process had included delays both
within and before the court hearing, adjournments, a change of
judges and major reversals of direction for the way in which the
case would be heard. Support was provided to the client by the
police and by the Witness Support programme, in what was
otherwise felt to be an intimidating and unfamiliar environment.

In the court situation, the client's previous mental health history
was available to the defence, and there was a concern that her
history of receiving therapy and even the presence of the therapist
were weakening factors in her credibility in giving evidence.

The therapist as the client's supporter in court was not acting in
any formal sense as a *McKenzie* as such, but was still unprepared
for the professional and personal demands being made on her.
The therapeutic principle of the abused client seeking acknowledgement for her experiences is one that is strongly voiced by
feminist schools of therapy and by the abuse survivors' self-help
movement (Bass and Davis, 1991: 307–10). The conflict here is
between the need of the individual to tell their story and obtain
redress, and the more stringent requirements of bringing a
prosecution in a court of law, where the accused is innocent until
proven guilty, and the standard of proof in criminal proceedings is
that of being 'beyond reasonable doubt'.

What was also disturbing for the therapist was that her supportive activity may itself have been perceived by the court as
undermining the case being brought, in suggesting either that the
client was unstable, was being manipulated by the therapist to
bring the action, or was otherwise in an undesirable, dependent
relationship with the therapist.

A further consideration is that compensation is available to the
client in this case, via the Criminal Injuries Compensation Scheme,
where the applicant has sustained 'personal injury directly attributable to a crime of violence'. This is also available to the victims
of child or sexual abuse, with the restriction that compensation is

not payable where the incident occurred before 1 October 1979 and the victim and offender were living together as members of the same family, as this is governed by the terms of an earlier scheme (CICA, 1994; Plotnikoff, 1990). Therapists working with abuse survivors may be contacted by the Criminal Injuries Compensation Board to provide a report on a client applying for compensation. As always, confidentiality should be maintained, and the proposed content of any report needs to be carefully checked out with the client before being released to the Board.

According to the therapist concerned in the above case, 'the over-riding feeling when you're in court is that you're at their mercy. You feel so helpless.' Ultimately, the therapist reached the point where she was no longer able to continue attending court, given the amount of time it was taking, and the demands of the rest of her work load. She saw her role primarily as support for the client, 'so that she knew there was somebody in court that was there for her'. The therapist had no prior experience of this process, and had previously seen the law as being a neutral or benign force. 'The issue in taking it to court is that you want the world to hear in some sort of forum what really happened. It isn't that important what happens afterwards.' The therapist described her client as feeling angry and upset because she had not been able to say her piece in the way that she felt she needed to, but had to conform to the restrictions imposed by a court of law, and the principles concerning the admissibility of evidence.

Standard of evidence in court   An important consideration here is that therapists are not normally prepared for attendance in court as a part of their role, unlike comparable professionals such as social workers (Brayne and Martin, 1995). A therapist's involvement in court proceedings could take the form of supporting a client, as in the above case, or acting as a *McKenzie* or informal supporter in court. Other forms of involvement may be via giving evidence, or acting as an expert witness. Whilst these activities are probably rare or exceptional occurrences for most therapists, they still may arise in some circumstances, and will be described more fully below.

Evidence obtained by drugs or hypnosis   The debate over 'false memories' of abuse, allegedly implanted by over-zealous therapists, has highlighted the differences between material that has *therapeutic value and resonance,* and that which has *evidential material* for legal purposes. The problems in using children's testimony in proving charges of child sexual abuse has brought this issue to the fore. The focus on strict protocols for interviewing children on video to avoid contaminating their evidence through the use of leading questions illustrates the differences between evidential and therapeutic style of interviewing (Home Office/ Department of Health, 1992). It may be that therapists are required to attend court to give evidence concerning their practice, or their contact with a client. The basic rule which applies here is that such evidence must rely on what has been directly perceived by the therapist, supplemented, with the court's permission, by reference to notes or records made at the time. Refusing to give evidence concerning a client may be accepted in exceptional circumstances, as in the *Hayman* case, but is as likely to be treated as contempt of court, as in the *Nuttall* case (see Chapters 4 and 5). In some situations, agency policy may require that the therapist be subpoenaed by the court in order to make clear that client confidentiality is a principle which is not lightly discarded.

Certain forms of therapeutic technique, such as the use of hypnosis or drugs, may invalidate the testimony of therapists or clients. Barbiturate drugs such as sodium amytal have been used with varying degrees of effectiveness and popularity since the time of Freud, to assist the process of abreaction, and aid the cathartic release of traumatic memories (Bazire, 1995: 63). This technique has tended to wane in popularity during peace-time periods, to be revived by the military as an effective short-term measure during war-time, for example during the Second World War, in the post-Vietnam period, and in Israel during periods of conflict with neighbouring Arab states (Perry and Jacobs, 1982). It has also been used to assist in the recovery of memories of childhood sexual abuse, for example in the *Ramona* (1994) case, or to help in the retrieval of other unconscious material (Brown and Pedder, 1979: 73–5). However, while abreaction may be useful as a therapeutic measure, its value for producing convincing evidence for a court of law is much more doubtful. According to Putnam, 'therapists should be cautious about initiating legal allegations based solely on memories recovered during abreactive therapy'. Hence, 'abreaction is as likely to contaminate the process as it is to reveal the truth' (1992: 62).

Neither the vivid nature of the memories retrieved, nor the force of the emotions released, provide guarantees of the accuracy of the memory for evidential purposes in a court of law.

The therapeutic use of hypnosis has similarly gone through changes in the way that it is perceived in legal circles as a valid tool for producing evidence. Cases in the USA have emphasised the unreliability of memories retrieved under hypnosis, and limited the value of the witnesses' testimony as a result (Munday, 1987). This view is confirmed by a Home Office circular on the use of hypnosis in criminal proceedings in England and Wales:

> The view of the Home Secretary is that, as hypnosis may be a fallible and limited instrument for obtaining reliable evidence; as evidence so obtained is likely to be inadmissible; and as it carries a risk of longer term harm to the subject, its use should be discouraged. (HOC 66/88)

The circular stresses the danger of 'confabulation', namely of the subject incorporating inaccurate material into otherwise authentic memories. The potential for suggestibility and lying as well as for the retrieval of accurate material is noted. Under s.76 of the Police and Criminal Evidence Act 1984, the court is unable to accept evidence which may have been obtained via an unreliable method. Under s.78, the court has discretion to exclude evidence unfairly obtained, since hypnotically obtained evidence can not be properly cross-examined. The final decision to use hypnosis rests with the chief officer of the police force involved. In the so-called 'M50 murder trial', the evidence of a key witness was disallowed when it was revealed that hypnosis had been involved, and the guilty verdict was overturned by the court (*Guardian*, 20 May 1994). Therapists may respond to this discussion that they do not use drugs, and do not use hypnosis in any formal sense with clients. However, it has been pointed out that the dividing line between hypnosis and therapeutic techniques such as regression, visualisation and guided imagery may be a difficult one to draw with certainty. Client material retrieved in these ways may be more useful for therapeutic purposes, than for establishing the actual historic truth of events in an earlier part of the client's life (Yapko, 1994: 121).

Therapist's role as witness of fact

There are two types of witness in a court of law. Firstly, a therapist may be called simply as a witness to facts, on the grounds that any person can give evidence about something they have witnessed. This would exclude a person who has severe learning disabilities, who may be deemed not to be 'a competent witness' (Gunn, 1989; Sinason, 1995: 298–316; Williams, 1995). Under s.53 of the Criminal Justice Act 1991, children are now deemed to be competent witnesses in giving evidence in court. Evidence of fact must be limited to the facts, and must not include inference or opinion. Thus, 'witnesses should give as much factual evidence as is possible and pay particular attention to its quality, credibility, authority and presentation' (Carson, 1990: 18). There is a danger in witnesses assuming that the court has some prior knowledge or understanding of the facts they are about to deliver. In fact, the outcome of the case may depend on their evidence. The clear and confident manner in which it is delivered can be a crucial factor in its acceptance. 'The goal for the witness should be to describe and explain his or her evidence in a way which will be clear, memorable and authoritative to the judge and any jury' (Carson, 1990: 28).

Therapist's role as expert witness   The second kind of witness role that a therapist might assume is that of an *expert witness*. Only expert witnesses can give evidence of fact *and opinions*. 'The courts decide who they will recognise as an expert. It does not depend upon having special professional qualifications. Extensive practical experience could suffice. The distinguishing feature of an expert witness is the right to give *opinion* in court' (Carson, 1990: 2). Expert witnesses are experts in their particular field and, it should be stressed, need to be more than just enthusiastic amateurs (Nijboer, 1995).

Psychologists and therapists, using both terms in a broad sense, have been involved in contributing their expertise to the courts since the time of Freud (1906/1971; 1931/1971). The use of psychologists and psychiatrists has been more marked in the USA, but it seems that the reluctance to use their expertise in England and Wales is now diminishing (Lloyd-Bostock, 1988: 137–57). Part of the resistance to the use of expert witnesses in courts in England and Wales has been the legal view that matters of emotions and behaviour are largely ones which will be within the commonsense and life experience of judges and juries, rather than ones which are the preserve of possibly tendentious experts. Some critics in the USA have also pointed to the research weaknesses of much expert evidence given by psychologists and psychiatrists (Faust and Ziskin, 1988).

Helena Kennedy, a noted Queen's Counsel, makes the point that some expert witnesses seem unprepared to adapt their language to the more exacting requirements of the courts: 'expert witnesses at times complain of their treatment as either patronising or dismissive. Psychiatrists, psychologists and sociologists have a particularly rough ride. They come like lambs to the slaughter if their reports are full of references to "cycles of deprivation" or "cognitive dissonance"' (Kennedy, 1992: 15).

Expert witnesses normally enjoy immunity from litigation, for example for negligence (Hervey, 1985). Following recent court decisions in the USA and the UK, courts are now more open to hearing expert evidence on a wide range of psychological issues. In the USA, the long-established *Frye* test has been overruled by a decision in *Daubert v. Merell Dow Pharmaceuticals* (1993) to allow *any* relevant evidence to be admitted. In the *Emery* case (1993) in the UK, Helena Kennedy, QC called for two expert witnesses' evidence to be heard by the court on the effects of post traumatic stress disorder, namely 'learned helplessness' and the 'battered woman syndrome'. The purpose was to explain to the court the reasons for the defendant's failure to protect her child from abuse by her partner. According to the experts, 'prolonged violence and abuse of a woman by her partner can induce a flat hopelessness, an inability to stand up to the abuser, a feeling of dependence on the abuser, and an inability to withdraw from the situation' (Colman and Mackay, 1995: 264). The woman was still found guilty of not protecting the child, but the Court of Appeal endorsed the judge's decision to hear the controversial expert testimony. 'The effect of the *Emery* judgement therefore appears to open the door to psychological evidence in a far wider range of areas than has hitherto been the case' (Colman and Mackay, 1995: 264).

This opens up an opportunity for therapists to develop a role in widening the courts' understanding of the extremes of human emotions and behaviour, a field in which they have some expertise through their clinical practice. The real value of therapists in giving expert evidence is precisely in order to challenge commonsense perceptions of what is normal or predictable behaviour. For instance, the concept of post-traumatic stress disorder is now accepted by the courts, following testimony given by a psychiatrist at hearings about the Zeebrugge ferry disaster (Pugh and Trimble, 1993). Another example is indicated by the work of Sandra Horley, director of the battered women's aid organisation, Refuge. She is a social psychologist who has worked with battered women for 16 years, and who has acted as an expert witness since 1992.

> The effects of prolonged battering are complex and can lead to contradictory behaviour in the victim, she says. A battered woman will suffer low self esteem, feelings of helplessness and 'an impaired ability to make decisions'. All these factors may make it impossible for her to respond 'normally' to an event (such as her child being brutalised). . . . Some women are effectively immobilised because they are suffering post-traumatic stress disorder as a result of the violence.

> One difficulty the defence faces is that battered women often don't conform to jurors' expectations of what a victim should be like. The numbing effects of the violence can mean women don't appear distraught and desperate, but cool and detached. (Bawdon, 1994: 20)

A third example is given in the case of Dr Eric Shepher, a forensic psychologist, who gave evidence at Crown Court suggesting that two juveniles, who had confessed to a robbery, had been manipulated into making false confessions. The Police and Criminal Evidence Act 1984 guidelines had been adhered to, but this had not prevented unsound confessions being obtained by the police. Dr Shepher focused on the clients' suggestibility, compliance and intellectual/social functioning, as evident in the suspects' performance during the police interview. In the case of the two juveniles, 'the officer constantly "upgraded" their responses – distorting and exaggerating what they said to fit his view of what happened. "I gave evidence of five or six examples of upgrading, where they didn't come back and object when anyone in their right mind would have done", he says' (Bawdon, 1994: 20; Evans, 1993).

The demand for expert witnesses seems to have increased in recent years, although often this has been in relatively specialised areas of work associated with children and families (CAAC, 1993; DECP/BPS, 1985; Foster and Preston-Shoot, 1995). Advice on the preparation and presentation of reports for the court is also much more evident with regard to this area of work (Biggs and Robson, 1992; Black et al., 1991: 12–17; Plotnikoff and Woolfson, 1996).

Some of the qualities required of an expert witness are outlined in Box 6.1.

Box 6.1

Qualities of an expert witness

- working to a higher standard of care than the average practitioner
- an ability to analyse and make reasoned judgements
- skills in research and concise reporting
- personal qualities: patience, tact, ability to stay calm under pressure, negotiating skills
- relevant experience and professional credibility
- thorough knowledge of the subject in hand including recognition of the merits of alternative approaches

(Adapted from Reynolds and King, 1989: 22–3)

The presentation of evidence by an expert goes through a number of stages:

- preparation of the preliminary report, which is privileged in a legal sense
- presentation of the report to court
- examination and cross-examination in court

A more extended role for the expert may involve evaluating the evidence from the opposing party, and advising on negotiations for any possible settlement (Reynolds and King, 1989). Increasing concern has been expressed about the highly partisan role played by expert witnesses and the resultant delays in litigation that this can produce. In the USA, one expert witness was alleged to be acting as a 'hired gun', ready and willing to appear for high fees to any parents subject to allegations in 'false memory' cases (*Underwager v. Salter* (1994)). Lord Woolf's proposed reforms of litigation envisage a system where the expert witness is appointed by the *court* to assist it in decision-making, rather than for the expert simply to provide ammunition to the solicitor who engages them (Woolf, 1995: 181–93). To improve access to choosing appropriate experts, the Law Society has now produced its own *Directory of Expert Witnesses*.

Guidelines for good practice by expert witnesses in civil cases were suggested by the Honourable Mr Justice Cresswell following a complex insurance case (*The Ikarian Reefer* [1993]) (see Box 6.2).

Box 6.2

Role of the expert witness

An expert witness should:

- be independent and not influenced by the requirements of litigation
- provide independent, unbiased opinion in relation to matters within their area of expertise, and should not assume the role of advocate
- state the facts or assumptions on which the opinion is based, without omitting material facts which contradict this view
- make it clear when a particular question or issue falls outside his or her expertise
- should state where necessary that the opinion is no more than a provisional one, requiring further research
- promptly acknowledge to the court any change in opinion following an exchange of reports
- share relevant documentation with other parties

The Ikarian Reefer [1993] at 69

Cross-examination of witnesses   A crucial aspect of giving evidence, either as a witness of fact, or as an expert witness, is the process of cross-examination by the solicitor for the opposing party. This follows the presentation of evidence as the 'examination-in-chief', where the solicitor who has called the witness takes them through their evidence. Cross-examination can be a sobering and anxiety-provoking experience for the uninitiated. In the following case, a student counsellor was cross-examined in the Coroner's Court about the suicide of a client. The counsellor defended her course of action by referring to the BAC *Code of Ethics and Practice for Counsellors*.

Case Study: Cross-examination of a counsellor in the Coroner's Court

. . . one lawyer started to consider other provisions in the code to explore whether these had been implemented with equal vigour. He turned his attention to, 'Counsellors must take account of the limitations of their competence and make an appropriate referral when necessary' . . . After the section was read out to the court, the counsellor was cross-examined about her training in the assessment and treatment of suicidal clients, to determine whether she was working within her competence. The clear

*implication of this line of questioning was that if she had not
been adequately trained, she was therefore working outside her
level of competence, then she ought to have sought specialist help
for her client. (Bond, 1991: 285)*

This line of questioning was not successful in discrediting the
counsellor involved here, but underlines the importance of
recognising the direction that a certain line of questioning is likely
to take, and preparing oneself adequately in advance to meet it if
possible. Simply basing one's professional stance on a *Code of
Practice* does not meet all possible objections to be mounted by a
hostile lawyer, but rather sets out the terrain on which the debate
may take place. Any inconsistency between the therapist's
practice and the *Code*, or between one section of the *Code* and
another, will be used to undermine the overall value of the
evidence given by that witness. Carson (1990) describes some of
the more common techniques used by lawyers in carrying out
cross-examination:

■ 'pinning out': a sequence of apparently innocuous questions
  which actually fix the witness as if to a board, before the
  critical question is fired at them
■ 'leading witnesses up the garden path': inviting a witness to
  stretch their evidence by degrees to absurd or unlikely conclusions, based on their previous answers, which has the
  intended effect of discrediting their whole position

Some of his suggested responses include:

■ 'riding the bumps', i.e. remaining calm, seeking to clarify any
  possible misconceptions arising from the evidence or replies
  given
■ using opening comments to regain communication with the
  judge, and to correct or rephrase the information being given,
  e.g. 'With respect, neither term would be appropriate. It would
  be much more accurate to say . . .' (Carson, 1990: 47).

The sequence of the lawyer's questions, and the answers they
engender, effectively control the process of communication in
court. A problem for therapists may be that the nuanced and

sensitive language used to describe emotional processes and states of feeling or behaviour does not easily lend itself to the harsher, more dichotomous judgements required by the court (Carson, 1990: 62). To refer, for example, to a client as being 'borderline depressed', will probably prompt an inquiry from the cross-examining lawyer as to the medical qualifications possessed which can justify making such a diagnosis. This might well then be followed up by inviting the therapist to make clear to the court, in the therapist's view, *was* the client clinically depressed *or not?* Treading a path through the dangers of exceeding one's expertise, or overstating the case, is not easy for the witness to achieve. As a result, expert witnesses 'often feel that the questions misrepresent what they have to say or it does not give them an opportunity to isolate what they believe is important and want to communicate in court' (Carson, 1990: 64). One important failing is when a witness begins to weaken their case through becoming hesitant and doubtful about views which were previously stated with some conviction. This is 'an exasperating habit called by lawyers "failing to come up to proof"' (Knight and Palmer, 1992: 13). Another technique used by lawyers to disorient witnesses is telling the witness they must answer yes or no to their questions. Simeon Maskrey, QC, claims 'that witnesses are not bound to give such a concise reply. "Be firm and courteous but stick to the point", he says. "Tell the judge, 'I am not prepared to give a yes or no answer because it would not be complete'"' (Ward, 1995: 22). On the other hand, witnesses also need to avoid appearing unreasonable and inflexible in ways that seem to undermine the value of their evidence (Cohen, 1995: 105).

One example of the potential clash of values between therapy and the legal process may arise in the way that therapy itself is perceived. Rather than being a positive and enhancing experience, it may be assumed by the court that the client's need for therapy points to some underlying instability, which undermines their credibility in the proceedings. Helena Kennedy, QC suggests that there is a gender issue operating here, given that stereotypes of the neurotic or hysterical female may be subtly or not so subtly conjured up by hostile lawyers.

> Suggestions of instability cling to women much more readily than to men, and even a mention of going to psychotherapy in search of self-enlightenment is confused with mental illness. There are no dividing lines for many people: 'Psycho' means mad, and barristers know the

mileage that can be made with juries at the merest hint of any problem. (Kennedy, 1992: 116)

A further problem for expert witnesses can lie in predicting a client's *future* behaviour based on past experience. 'Expert witnesses, particularly those such as social workers and psychiatrists giving evidence about people with problems in living, should be much more willing to refuse to answer certain questions that misrepresent what they have to say' (Carson, 1990: 66; Campbell, 1995).

Providing reports on clients

Therapists may be approached to write reports on clients in a number of situations. This may include a request for a report from an organisation such as the Criminal Injuries Compensation Authority, from an insurance company paying for therapy, or from a lawyer pursuing legal action on behalf of a client. Agreement to write a report can open the doors to a series of situations, each of which potentially impinges on client–therapist confidentiality. At the simplest level, a report may be requested to confirm the nature and extent of contact with a client. Assuming client agreement, then a brief factual report may be sufficient. In some instances, lawyers have requested reports from therapists seeking to substantiate a particular psychological condition, such as post-traumatic stress disorder, in order to support the client's legal case for damages. It is important here that the therapist does not presume to hold a level of training or expertise which may be more properly associated with that of a qualified doctor, psychiatrist or psychologist. It may even be true that the solicitor is looking for a free opinion on their client from a therapist, when the advisable course of action would be to pay an expert medical witness for a formal psychiatric assessment (Eastman, 1995).

Reports for the court need to be concise, relevant, and should distinguish between established facts and the writer's own professional opinions (Bluglass, 1995). A frontsheet should set out the author's qualifications, experience and current post held. The sources of information on which the report is based need to be described, such as via interview, a series of counselling sessions, or through the use of psychological tests. Professional jargon tends to undermine the impact of a report, unless it is essential to the point being made. Any expressions which are unclear or 'woolly' will be picked up in cross-examination, should the case come to court. The best rule is never to state facts or express opinions in a report that may be later regretted when having to defend them in court.

Therapists may initially agree to prepare a report on a client in order to help him or her in some legal difficulty, or under the assumption that they are somehow required to do so on grounds of professional responsibility, as perhaps following on from taking part in a child protection case conference. However, report writing may have unintended consequences, as the report can become evidence in a wider legal arena, over which the therapist has effectively relinquished control. *Authorship* of a report in this sense is not the same as *ownership or control*, once legal proceedings begin. If the therapist agrees to prepare a report, with the client's agreement, then this may be in the capacity of an expert witness. Reports of this kind are initially protected by legal privilege, but may then be requested by the legal representatives of the opposing party, under the process of discovery prior to going to court. It may be that receipt of the report then leads to a further request for the *original* notes on which the report was based, which would presumably be the notes of the actual therapy sessions with the client. The original notes are *not* subject to privilege. The therapist may then be required to present a level of detail in court about their client which was never their intention (Jakobi and Pratt, 1992). Alternatively, while being careful to avoid being found in contempt of court, the therapist may seek to persuade the court that full disclosure of the records would not be strictly pertinent to the matter considered. A further concern to therapists may be that their description of therapeutic work with a client may actually be used to undermine the latter's credibility as a witness. This has occurred in the case of some abuse survivors who have undergone extensive psychological treatment on account of their experiences.

Another response by therapists to involvement in legal proceedings may be to emphasise the *confidential* nature of the relationship with the client. Thus, when approched by a third party for information, clearly even to acknowledge that the individual is a current or former client may constitute an inadvertent breach of confidentiality. A solicitor seeking to pressurise the therapist for access to records, or to present a report, has less power than may seem to be the case at first sight. Responding immediately to telephone requests may be unwise, rather than insisting that only written correspondence can be considered, in line with agency policy or individual practice. The next step may be a warning that the therapist can be required to attend court under a subpoena or witness summons, if they do not assist the solicitor voluntarily. However, some agencies, such as the Samaritans, make it their policy to only attend as witness when under a court order, precisely to underline the point that their commitment to client confidentiality is not lightly broken. Therapists without training or expertise in court work need to be cautious that their efforts to support or assist their clients do not work in the longer run to the latter's disadvantage.

Seeking damages via the courts

The main purpose in taking civil legal action under tort or for breach of contract is usually to claim damages, in order to compensate the innocent party in monetary terms as far as possible. This is designed to put the claimant in the same position as he or she would have been if the contract had been duly performed, or had the tort not been committed (Pannett, 1992: 91). Legal views seem to vary according to whether plaintiffs should seek to recover damages *both* for breach of contract *and* for tort where both are an option (Leder and Shears, 1991: 61; Pannett, 1992: 5).

There are a number of different time limits which apply to claims for damages, under the Limitation Act 1980, the Latent Damage Act 1986 and the Defamation Act 1996 (Applebey, 1994: 46; Pannett, 1992: 264).

Time limits for bringing legal actions

- libel or slander: within one year of incident
- personal injury: within three years of *incident*, or within three years of *knowledge of effect*, whichever is later (can be extended by court)
- consumer protection: within three years
- breach of contract or tort action: within six years, or within three years of *knowledge of effect*, whichever is later
- over-riding time limit of 15 years for actions for damages

The confusing array of time limits for bringing civil legal action has worked to the disadvantage of some clients, such as survivors of sexual abuse. Damages have been refused to women claiming for abuse experienced prior to 1979, when compensation first became payable to victims living in the same household as the abuser. In one case, a woman who was 'out of time' for suing her father for past abuse, won a ruling by the Appeal Court permitting her to sue her mother instead for negligently failing to protect her from the abuse (*Guardian*, 2 December 1994). A test case for extending the six-year time limit beyond the age of 24 in the case of abused children for bringing actions for damages against alleged abusers has since been rejected by the European Court of Human Rights (*Guardian*, 23 October 1996). The time limits for taking legal action are currently under review by the Law Commission, with a report expected after 1996, so it is possible that future legislation on this topic will be enacted.

Types of compensation
The purpose of damages is to provide compensation for loss or injury suffered. Damages can be awarded for:

- loss of earnings
- other financial loss or expenses
- loss of amenity or enjoyment of life
- pain and suffering

(Applebey, 1994: 112)

Damages may be *special*, that is a precise sum estimated or calculated, or *general*, as a round sum, to be calculated by the judge. In personal injury cases, pecuniary damages refer to loss of earnings and the cost of medical expenses and of the care required. An individual can also be compensated for pain and distress and physical incapacity, or what is referred to as 'pain and suffering and loss of amenity'. The latter are usually lumped together by judges as a global figure. Damages are paid based on a system of case law established in the early 1960s, which has led to the development of a flexible tariff of compensation. 'Pain' refers to the physical discomfort of medical treatment. 'Suffering' relates to mental or emotional distress. 'Amenity' means the capacity to do things previously enjoyed before the accident, or to participate in the normal activities of life. Loss of amenity can still apply, even though the plaintiff may not be *conscious* of the loss they have endured, for example as a result of incurring a brain injury. In Scotland, the relevant terms are 'solatium', referring to 'pain, suffering and amenity', while 'patrimonial' refers to pecuniary loss (Law Commission, 1995b).

Claims for damages could obviously be made against therapists for causing loss to a client. The *Ramona* case (1994) in the USA brought an award of third party damages totalling $475,000. Case law regarding successful claims against therapists in England and Wales is much more limited. In the *Landau* case (*Werner v. Landau*, 1961), discussed in detail in Chapter 3, the judge commented on the difficulty in assessing damages to be awarded to the client. In the event, £6,000 was awarded to Miss Landau for personal injuries, including an attempted suicide, and for pecuniary loss, given that she had been unable to earn a living following her negligently handled therapy. This would amount to approximately £60,000 at current values.

A recent Law Commission report opposes the option of transferring assessment of compensatory damages for personal injury cases to juries for deciding, because of their lack of knowledge of the scale of values and the resultant problems in achieving a fair and uniform system. There is also a concern that juries tend to make comparatively high and rather unrealistic awards in defamation cases, where the damage done is to an individual's *reputation* (Law Commission, 1995b).

Damages for psychological injury

The concept of damages payable for psychological injury is one of particular interest to therapists, given that this is, by definition, closely related to their area of work. However, this is undoubtedly a confusing aspect of law, with many inconsistencies remaining to be ironed out. As one authoritative legal survey of the topic states: 'Broken minds have always been greeted with a scepticism which contrasts sharply with the sympathy generated by broken bones' (Mullaney and Handford, 1993: 1).

The starting point for discussion is that under the law there are no damages payable for the normal human feelings of grief, anxiety and depression (Mullis and Oliphant, 1993: 23). This is as opposed to *compensation*, for example, for the death of a child, loss of an eye through assault, and so on, fixed rates for which are set. Damages may be payable for psychological injury where they follow on from physical injury, for example, in the case of depression following amputation of a limb.

However, the crucial point is that no damages are normally allowable for psychological injury which falls short of being a recognised psychiatric illness. Thus in the case of *Nicholls v. Rushton* (1992), the individual's damages for a severe shock and a bad shaking up caused in a car crash were disallowed, because they did not amount to a psychiatric illness as such. This line of reasoning may seem unfair or limited to some therapists, such as those who prefer to stress the interconnections between physiological states and mental well-being, and who take a broadly holistic approach to their work.

The more narrow legal view is framed by a number of factors, such as the problems of establishing *proof* of causation, where emotional states, feelings and distress are concerned. There is a greater degree of speculation in assessing psychiatric damages, due to

- differing medical or expert opinions on the subject
- the fact that the effects of psychiatric illness vary from one individual to another
- psychiatric illness may be attributable to a wide range of factors which need to be separated out for the purpose of deciding damages (Law Commission, 1995a: 36)

Even where defining a 'recognised psychiatric illness' is concerned, this can become somewhat problematic, as psychiatrists do not always agree on their diagnosis. Most famously, this occurred in the case of conflict over the diagnosis of schizophrenia at the trial of Peter Sutcliffe, the 'Yorkshire Ripper'. There is also the 'floodgates argument' which is often invoked as a reason for not widening the criteria for claims for damages to non-psychiatric emotional distress. The fear is that conceding a general principle capable of wide application to a massive number of situations will provoke a flood of litigation of American proportions, which would then overwhelm and disable the court system. It could also be said that fear of opening the floodgates is a very effective argument for restricting the wider public's access to justice.

Box 6.3

Damages for non-physical injury

- damages available for pain and suffering, and loss of previous abilities
- no damages solely for normal human emotions of grief, anxiety, distress
- damages for emotional distress require evidence of a positive psychiatric illness
- damages for psychiatric illness require plaintiff to be a direct victim of the event
- damages for psychiatric illness not payable to persons less directly involved in the event, subject to narrow criteria
- damages for psychiatric illness now available for professional rescuers

Nevertheless, psychiatric categories do adapt and change over time, as evidenced by the successive editions of the psychiatric diagnostic manuals such as the *Diagnostic and Statistical Manual* (APA, 1994), and *International Classification of Diseases* (WHO, 1992). The most obvious example of this has been in the addition of post-traumatic stress disorder (PTSD). The 1980 edition of the *DSM-3* introduced PTSD in terms of psychiatric symptoms and eligibility for compensation by the courts (Pugh and Trimble, 1993: 425). It was added to the legally accepted range of psychiatric illness, following the cases of the *Herald of Free Enterprise* sinking at Zeebrugge, the fire at King's Cross underground station, and the death of 95 football fans at Hillsborough stadium.

The categories of psychiatric illness accepted in the past have included 'anxiety neurosis', 'reactive depression', 'PTSD', and 'pathological grief' (Law Commission, 1995a: 10). Others listed in a range of cases include 'recognised psychiatric illness', 'all relevant forms of mental illness, neurosis and personality change', and 'positive psychiatric illness' (Pugh and Trimble, 1993: 425).

Persons eligible for psychiatric damages A further important factor is that there is a limited range of persons eligible for psychiatric damages. These are normally restricted to what are called 'primary victims', rather than to 'secondary victims', however badly affected the latter might be as a result of their trauma. Primary victims are those considered to be *directly* affected by the incident or event, *via their immediate, personal involvement.* The claims of secondary victims such as bystanders or witnesses are subject to special scrutiny, along the lines of:

- a 'proximity test', in terms of eyesight, earshot, or immediate aftermath, i.e. within an 'hour or so' of the event
- or a 'relationship test', requiring a closeness of relationship, such as a spouse, parent or child, or one of 'loving care and affection' with the victim

Thus, for example, most claims by *relatives* claiming damages for the Hillsborough disaster were rejected because they witnessed the events on TV, which was not held to be sufficiently direct to meet the test required. Damages to professional helpers used to be limited to *physical* injury until the award to police officers who experienced PTSD following the Hillsborough disaster (*Guardian*, 4 June 1996). One review has highlighted the seemingly arbitrary nature of compensation in this regard: 'The law is plainly a lottery in which some bystanders are spattered with blood and others with money' (Pugh and Trimble, 1993: 429).

In all, the law's approach to awarding damages for psychiatric illness or injury seems to be locked into the ideas of the last century. It is based on the Victorian concept of nervous shock being caused by a *single* horrific incident, rather than by repeated strain or long-term stress, for example, caring for a dying child. Thus it requires 'a sudden assault on the nervous system' or 'the sudden appreciation . . . of a horrifying event which violently agitates the mind' (*Alcock*, [1992] at 400, per Lord Ackner). This is clearly unlike the situation concerning *physical* injuries, where compensation is allowable for repetitive movement, gradual onset of deafness, and industrial diseases such as asbestosis. There is a grain of ambiguity here, however, in the comments of one judge regarding an unsuccessful case against a psychiatrist's faulty assessment, which may be a pointer for future cases (*M. v. Newham L.B.C.* [1994]).

Scottish law on negligently inflicted psychiatric illness is broadly similar to English law in this field, and it has been similarly reluctant to extend the boundaries of recovery. The Law Commission has argued a need for a reform of the law on negligently inflicted psychiatric illness (Law Commission, 1995a: 88). It is therefore possible that the current boundaries of case law on damages for psychiatric illness may well be redrawn in the future.

Given some of the anomalies described above, the somewhat rigid legal distinction between physical and psychiatric illness proves increasingly hard to maintain in practice. Several pointers in this direction include the recognition of the psychological effects on victims caused by stalking (Home Office, 1996b), and the acknowledgement of the *interplay* of physical and emotional factors in the development of chronic fatigue syndrome (Straus, 1996).

Assessing psychiatric damages The purpose in awarding psychiatric damages is the same as for non-psychiatric cases: 'on the principle that the plaintiff is to be put into the position he or she would have been if the wrong had not occurred, damages will be awarded to cover both the plaintiff's pecuniary loss (such as the cost of psychiatric treatment and the loss of earnings if ability to work is impaired) and non-pecuniary loss (that is, for any pain, suffering and loss of amenity)' (Law Commission, 1995a: 35).

The lines are narrowly drawn in deciding compensation. Lord Denning MR declared in *Heinz v. Berry* [1970]:

> the court has to draw a line between sorrow and grief for which damages are not recoverable, and nervous shock and psychiatric illness for which damages are recoverable. The way to do this is to estimate how much [the plaintiff] would have suffered if, for instance, her husband had been killed in an accident when she was 500 miles away: and compare it with what she is now, having suffered all the shock due to being present at the accident (at 43).

It also needs to be reasonably *foreseeable* that the plaintiff might suffer a psychiatric illness as a result of the defendant's negligence. In the case of *Page v. Smith* [1994] the plaintiff successfully claimed for shock-induced psychiatric illness, namely recurrence of myalgic encephalomyelitis (ME), brought on by the impact of the car crash. The underlying ambiguity of whether this was a case primarily of a *physical* or a *psychiatric* injury somehow seems to have been left unresolved (Fennell, 1996: 368).

In applying the reasonable foreseeability test, the plaintiff is assumed to be a person 'of normal disposition and phlegm, or reasonable fortitude'. The judge will decide what is reasonably foreseeable. However, the defendant must also take the plaintiff's injuries as he finds them, and is therefore responsible for any additional injuries caused, for example, by the plaintiff's exceptionally 'thin skull', or any predisposition to psychiatric illness (Mullaney and Handford, 1993: 229–30; 273). This is despite the fact that these features might well not have been known to the defendant at the time of causation.

Guidelines for assessing damages, including for post-traumatic stress disorder, are now set out for reference by the judiciary (JSB, 1994). These indicate the factors to be taken into account when deciding the level of award and include:

- plaintiff's ability to cope with life and particularly with work
- effect on relationships with family
- extent to which treatment would be successful
- future vulnerability
- prognosis
- the extent and/or nature of any associated physical injuries
- whether medical help has been sought

The scale of damages is set out in the form of a tariff, which ranges from minor psychiatric damage (£500–£1,500) to severe psychiatric damage (£22,500–£45,000). In exceptional circumstances, the scale of a loss incurred will result in a proportionately higher amount of damages being awarded. The highest recorded amount of damages for psychiatric illness was made in 1995 to a father who witnessed his family car plunge into a river, causing his two daughters to drown, together with the daughter of a neighbour. According to the judges, witnessing the accident was 'not the sole cause, but it was an initiating cause of an uneven but perceptible sequence of mental deterioration and personality collapse in an already vulnerable individual' (*Guardian*, 31 January 1995). The combination of shock, grief and post-traumatic stress disorder contributed to the break-up of his marriage, and meant that he was incapable of continuing to work other than in sheltered employment. However, the award of £1.178 million was reduced to £622,000 on appeal (*Guardian*, 30 March 1996). The award and its subsequent reversal perhaps illustrate some of the problems inherent in trying to put a financial value to psychological distress. Whether therapists have an easier task in trying to work with the human consequences of such loss, rather than trying to put a figure on its financial worth in the courts, would seem to be an open question.

Summary

The civil justice system is undergoing major changes, designed to remedy the strains evident in its manner of working. A knowledge of the basic structure of the legal system will be useful to therapists, as will being aware of how to gain access to legal advice if required. Therapists may become involved in legal proceedings at a number of different levels, for example in acting as an informal aide to an otherwise unsupported client, in acting as a witness of fact, or as an expert witness. Preparation for such roles is advisable, in order to assist the court as effectively as possible in its decision-making. Finally, the system for awarding damages has implications both for clients and for therapists, in terms of the limited recognition afforded for emotional injury and distress.

Discussion points

1   In what circumstances might a therapist become involved in legal action? How might therapists prepare themselves more effectively for such involvement?
2   What points of conflict or contrast can you identify concerning therapy and the law? What points of similarity and overlap are there? How might mutual understanding be promoted?
3   Is there a role for therapists in bringing their experience and expertise into the courts? What are the advantages and disadvantages of therapists taking on a role of expert witness with greater frequency?
4   Discuss the case history of the therapist involved in supporting her client taking legal proceedings for abuse. Should therapists take on this active role, in the absence of other support systems for their clients? What effects, if any, might this have on the therapeutic relationship?
5   Should the legal system award damages for normal human emotions, such as grief, anxiety or distress, rather than simply for psychiatric illness? How might the current system of damages be made fairer from the point of view of clients and therapists?

7

Counselling and Therapy for Children and Young People

The starting point for this chapter is the view that there is a close relationship between the *rights of children* and their rights as *clients* in counselling and therapy. (Children are defined here as being under the age of 18 years, as per the Children Act 1989). The complexity of the law relating to children mirrors the differing perceptions that adults have of children and of young people's abilities to take an active responsibility for their own lives. For therapists working with children and young people, there is often a degree of urgency in confronting day-to-day issues, such as whether to inform their parents, problems of maintaining confidentiality, and trying to assess the level of responsible decision-making held by the young person. These issues are matched by the confusing variety of therapeutic approaches, from the traditional and adult-centred typified by writers such as Campion (1991) to the more child-centred approach of Crompton (1992). The therapist's decision-making is not helped by the lack of a clear picture of the legal responsibilities of those working in this field.

This chapter links changes in the law relating to therapy for children to corresponding changes in **children's rights**. **Key issues within therapeutic work with children**, such as confidentiality, child protection, access to files and rights to compensation are explored. As will be noted, the legal position of therapists working with children and young people is closely determined according to the **setting** in which they work, whether this is in the field of education, health, social work, psychiatry or in private practice. This will mean that the chapter necessarily explores some material which may seem unrelated at first to the specific needs of therapists who work *outside* these settings. However, this broader discussion of the issues is needed to provide a more complete picture of the range of possible responses open to therapists. It is also necessary to illustrate the legal anomalies and complexities which are inherent in therapeutic work with children and young people. Finally, some disturbing instances of abusive therapy inflicted upon children are described, together with discussion of children's legal rights over complaint and compensation.

Children's rights

The right of children to be treated as independent beings, rather than as the possessions of parents and adult caretakers has been a major development in society in the last two decades (Jenkins, 1993a). As the landmark Cleveland Report expressed it, 'the child is a person and not an object of concern' (Butler-Sloss, 1988: 245). A wide body of legislative and case law, culminating in the *Gillick* decision, has increasingly emphasised the rights of children to become active decision-makers where their own futures are being decided by the courts and by other authorities. Their right to consideration as an independent party in therapy, rather than simply as a dependent member of the wider family group is now clearly acknowledged by the law and in statutory *Codes of Practice*.

The impact of the Gillick decision

The development of the right to *confidentiality* has been a central aspect of this shift in perspective. The right of children and young people to a confidential therapeutic relationship can be traced to the watershed *Gillick* decision, which recognised that those under 16 are capable of making some decisions for themselves, without requiring parental knowledge or consent. In the original case, Victoria Gillick, the mother of five daughters under the age of 16, sought assurances from her local area health authority that none of them would receive contraceptive advice or treatment from a doctor without her knowledge. This challenged the existing DHSS advice given to doctors that this was a clinical matter solely for the doctor to decide. The action she then brought against the health authority was based on the grounds that such advice was unlawful, amounting to doctors committing an offence by encouraging unlawful sexual intercourse by a girl under the age of consent. In addition, the action alleged that it constituted a serious infringement of the rights of the parent. The legal action was refused in the High Court, and was then heard in the House of Lords in 1986. By a majority of three to two, it was held by the Law Lords that children of 'mature understanding' *were* entitled to confidential medical treatment by a doctor, *depending* upon the doctor's assessment of their degree of maturity and level of understanding (De Cruz, 1987).

If the *Gillick* principle opens the way to a child-centred therapeutic relationship, a crucial difficulty still remains for therapists and counsellors in deciding *how* to assess whether the child is of 'mature understanding'. Some of the main factors relative to deciding medical treatment are discussed by Pearce (1994). These are adapted and extended in Table 7.1 to identify some of the critical factors that a therapist would need to consider in deciding whether the child or young person was sufficiently competent for a confidential therapeutic relationship to ensue.

The guidelines for responding to 'immediate issues' are based on the reasoning contained in the *Gillick* decision, such as by Lord Scarman: 'Emergency, parental neglect, abandonment of the child or inability to find the parent are examples of exceptional situations justifying the doctor to treat the child without parental knowledge or consent;' (at 424), and Lord Fraser at 413. The guidelines for short- and longer-term issues extend this approach to include other relevant factors that therapists may need to consider carefully.

These factors obviously do not provide ready-made answers for the therapist trying to decide how best to respond to a child or young person seeking help, but they may indicate some of the main issues to bear in mind. The version of the *Gillick* test above is based on the comments of Lord Scarman and Lord Fraser in the House of Lords decision, and will give therapists a basic framework for deciding whether or not to proceed without parental involvement.

Child's right to confidential counselling after Gillick   The *Gillick* decision lays the basis for working independently with the child

Table 7.1 *Assessing competence to consent by children and young people*

Factors to consider	Checklist for questions
Immediate issues:	
Child's age:	How old is the child or young person?
'Gillick' test:	Does the child or young person *understand* the counselling or advice?
	Are they *refusing* to allow their parents to be informed?
	Do their *best interests* require that the advice or counselling be given without parental consent?
Short-term issues	
Nature of contact:	Is the *contact* with the counsellor or therapist controlled entirely by the child or young person? (e.g. emergency phone call, drop-in centre)
Support systems:	What *support* does the child or young person have access to alongside or in the place of counselling or therapy, should contact be broken or withdrawn?
Nature of the immediate issue or problem:	What is the *degree of risk*, if any, posed by the child to him or herself or to others (e.g. drugs, abuse, suicide, arson)?
	Is the risk significant, immediate or longer term?
Child protection responsibilities:	Is the counsellor or therapist required by their conditions of employment, or agency policy to report *all suspected child abuse* to social services?
Child or young person's legal status and right to confidentiality:	Is the child currently under any *legal authority* which limits their ability to make decisions for themselves? (e.g. wardship, care order, youth custody)
Longer term issues	
Stage of cognitive and emotional development:	Does the child or young person *understand*
	• the nature of the issue or problem?
	• their own needs and the needs of others?
	• the risks and benefits of counselling or therapy?
	Does the child or young person have
	• a sense of their own identity?
	• a sense of time, past, present and future?
Relationship of the child or young person to parent or other adult care-taker:	Is this a *supportive relationship?*
	Does the parent or other adult recognise that the child or young person may have *distinct and separate needs* from the adults caring for them? (e.g. children of alcoholic parents)
Relationship with counsellor or therapist:	Is there a 'good enough' *therapeutic alliance* for continuing work to take place?

continued overleaf

Table 7.1 (*cont.*)

Factors to consider	Checklist for questions
Views of significant others:	What are the views and attitudes to contact with the therapist held by *others*? (e.g. teacher, youth worker, friends, siblings, other significant family members)
Risks and benefits of counselling or therapy being ended:	What risks or benefits might ensue if *contact* with the child or young person were to be *broken* by him or her, or to be *ended* by other parties? (e.g. continuation of current abuse)
Consultation and supervision:	To what extent can the counsellor or therapist make decisions about continuing contact on their own? What degree, if any, of *consultation* with an agency manager, supervisor or colleagues is necessary or advisable?
Risks to the counsellor or therapist:	What *risks* might the *counsellor or therapist* incur by continuing contact with the child or young person? (e.g. disciplinary action, threats by third parties, withdrawal of funding for agency)

or young person as the client, particularly where there is any degree of conflict regarding parental involvement or oversight of the therapeutic relationship. According to Lord Scarman, 'parental right yields to the child's right to make his own decisions when he reaches a sufficient understanding and intelligence to be capable of making up his own mind on the matter requiring decision' (*Gillick* [1986]). The Children's Legal Centre have deduced from this that 'mature children have the right to seek independent advice and counselling' (*Childright*, 1989b: 12). This marks a significant step forward for children, and for those who provide a child-centred counselling service. However, it still remains the case that the crucial decision as to whether a child is of mature understanding rests with the doctor or therapist. The latter must, in all cases, try to persuade the child to allow their parents to be consulted, unless the child has refused, or where there is a risk of child abuse. The adult needs to be satisfied that the young person understands the implications of the help they are seeking. Even where the child is judged not to be of mature understanding, advice and counselling can be given in the case of emergency, parental neglect, abandonment of the child, or inability to find the parent (*Childright*, 1989b: 13).

Box 7.1

Children's independent rights to counselling and therapy

- *Gillick* decision in House of Lords, 1986
- Article 12, UN Convention on the Rights of the Child 1989
- s.22, Children Act 1989

The value of the *Gillick* decision lies in helping the therapist to decide on whether to work with the child or young person where there is an apparent *conflict of interest* between them and their parent(s). For example, a 15-year-old boy may wish to come for counselling, but without his alcoholic parents being informed of this, in order to discuss his feelings about difficult family relationships. For the parents even to be informed of the fact that he was seeking counselling would perhaps bring pressure on him to disclose what he was discussing, and why he felt the need to go outside the family for help. The therapist here could work with the young person, without needing to inform the parents, if the *Gillick* criteria were met, namely the boy *understanding* the counselling, *refusing* to let his parents be informed, and the counselling meeting his *best interests*.

Counselling and the Children Act 1989

The earlier child-centred principles of the Butler-Sloss Report and the *Gillick* decision have been further strengthened by the Children Act 1989. The Act provided the response to a mounting public and media concern about the exercise of social workers' powers during the preceding two decades. Based on a comprehensive review of child care law, the Act brought together clear and consistent principles about the welfare of children, the related responsibilities of parents, and the duties of local authorities. It integrated *private law* relating to children, as for example with divorce, parental responsibility and contact, with *public law*, which detailed the responsibilities of the local authority in looking after children. Promoting the welfare of 'children in need' is to be based on the principles of partnership and support for families, and in avoiding the need for statutory interventions into family life wherever possible.

The Children Act 1989 makes specific reference to counselling as a service for children and families, and to the independent

Box 7.2

UN Convention 1989

Article 12: States Parties shall assure to the child who is capable of forming his or her own views the right to express those views freely in all matters affecting the child, the views of the child being given due weight in accordance with the age and maturity of the child. (UNICEF, 1989: 6)

rights of children and young people in decision-making (Jenkins, 1993a). Under s.22 of the Act, it states that 'before making any decision with respect to a child whom they are looking after, or proposing to look after, a local authority shall, so far as is reasonably practicable, ascertain the wishes and feelings of . . . the child'. Building on the welfare principle from earlier legislation such as the Children Act 1975, children are assured some degree of say in the decisions being made about their lives by concerned professionals. This principle is further underlined by the United Nations Convention on the Rights of the Child 1989, ratified by the UK Government in 1991 (Jenkins, 1995a).

Key issues in therapeutic work with children

Based on the legal framework for counselling children provided by the *Gillick* decision and the Children Act 1989, therapists may confront certain issues of key importance in their work with children. These include the crucial area of confidentiality and its limits, work in relation to child protection and the reporting of potential or actual child abuse. Children may also hold rights of access to their personal files, and to compensation for past physical or sexual abuse.

Confidentiality
Confidentiality is widely taken to be a central component of the therapeutic relationship, and this is particularly relevant in the case of working with children and young people. Many agencies will have policies with regard to the confidentiality of counselling children and young people which have been influenced by the *Gillick* decision. However, the overall picture with regard to actual practice by agencies is somewhat mixed. A survey of 63

children's and young people's advice and counselling organisations carried out by the Children's Legal Centre in 1988 found wide
variations in practice. Twenty-two agencies indicated that they
offered a guarantee of absolute confidentiality. Seven guaranteed
confidentiality, but in fact revealed that there were limits to this in
practice, for example, concerning clients who were felt to be at
risk, or who presented a risk to others. A further 13 indicated that
they had defined exceptions to absolute confidentiality within their
codes of practice (*Childright*, 1989a).

Childline, as a prominent national telephone helpline for children (0800–1111), has provided counselling to some 300,000
children (Harrison, 1994). It offers a policy of qualified rather than
unrestricted confidentiality. Material is confidential unless 'the child
is recognised to be in a situation that would lead to the child being
in imminent danger of injury or death or a danger to themselves'
(*Childright*, 1989c: 19). One such situation is described below:

Case Study: Childline's response to a potentially suicidal young person

*. . . a child rang the line after taking an overdose. For three
hours, a single counsellor kept talking to the child, who was
fading in and out of consciousness. They did not know where the
child was ringing from; all the child would tell them was the
name of his/her school.*

*While the counsellor kept talking, other staff tried to trace the
school. Eventually they found it, and the headteacher searched
the school records for the child's address. With the child still
talking on the phone to the counsellor, an ambulance arrived.*

(Eaton, 1990: 20; Crompton, 1992: 208–17)

This child-centred approach to confidentiality is subject to certain restrictions, however. The Butler-Sloss Report which analysed
the taking into care of 121 children in Cleveland in 1987 made this
point clear (1988: 245). A child or young person should not be
promised confidentiality where the promise could not be sustained, being over-ridden, for example, by the need to pass
information on to the authorities, or to the courts (Law Report,
Guardian, 5 December 1994).

A further set of grounds for over-riding confidentiality may lie in
the powers held by the courts. Under s.1 of the Children Act 1989,

the welfare of the child is held to be of *paramount* importance. This gives the courts wide powers of access to information which may have a bearing on deciding issues about a child's future. This can include ordering or preventing disclosure of confidential medical reports, therapeutic records or video recordings, if so decided by the court. The power of the court overturns the professional privilege which normally protects solicitors' material from disclosure, if the court decides that it is warranted in the interests of the child.

Child protection
In the last two decades, much therapeutic work with children, whether by statutory agencies or by other therapists, has been heavily overshadowed by the issue of child abuse. The reporting of suspected child abuse is mandatory in the USA, an obligation which has led to concern that this inflates the number of reported cases of abuse. It may also place professionals with more dis-criminating criteria of abuse at risk of negligence claims against them, and may fail to substantially reduce the numbers of those abused (Ebert, 1992; Levine and Doueck, 1995). Reporting child abuse is *not* mandatory in England and Wales, but most pro-fessionals will be obliged to act on suspected abuse under their terms of employment or professional codes of ethics. Under s.47(1) of the Children Act 1989, the local authority is required to investigate cases where it is suspected that a child in their area is suffering or is likely to suffer 'significant harm', which is a key phrase. Certain agencies, such as the local authority, education authority, health authority and housing, are *required* to assist the local authority with their enquiries, 'in particular by providing relevant information and advice'. However, apart from those specified, or those authorised by the Secretary of State, this part of the Act 'does not oblige any person to assist a local authority where doing so would be unreasonable in all the circumstances of the case'. Some therapists are not bound by agency policy or professional codes of practice to report suspected child abuse. Their position is more complex. In effect, they will have to exercise their professional judgement in deciding whether or not to report child abuse. It also needs to be borne in mind that, according to the key document *Working Together*, child protection procedures cover teenagers up to the age of 18, rather than solely being concerned with younger children (Home Office/DoH, 1991).

In some cases, concern about the welfare of children may be raised when working with an *adult*. In one case, a young woman began counselling with a psychotherapist to explore the abuse that she had undergone from her grandfather. She received counselling for about a year, and informed the therapist that she thought that another of the grandchildren might still be the subject of abuse. The psychotherapist reported the matter to the police, who brought a prosecution against the grandfather. Although aged 79, he received sentences totalling eight years imprisonment for offences against his grandchildren committed over a period of 15 years, ending 10 years before his trial (*R. v. C.*, (1993)). Whether, or to what extent, the psychotherapist discussed this course of action with the *client* is unclear. What is important is that such a breach of client confidentiality will be seen to be justified by the over-riding need to protect a potentially vulnerable child from abuse.

This urgent need to protect children from physical or sexual abuse can be taken as over-riding the *child's* own right to confidentiality within the therapeutic relationship. Lord Justice Eveleigh asserted this principle at an earlier stage of the *Gillick* hearing: 'there is no law of confidentiality which would command silence when the welfare of the child is concerned' (*Gillick* [1986], quoted in *A Child in Mind*, 1987: 17). However, a counter argument has been put that even relatively young children from the age of eight need to be able to make their own decisions, for example about whether an allegation of abuse is actually reported to the authorities (Roche and Briggs, 1990). This approach may be difficult for some therapists to accept. However, the continuing discussion around the problems of assessing children's competence to consent to *medical* treatment may be relevant here. One view is that children may be competent to give or refuse consent to medical treatment from as young as five years, unless there are sound reasons for overruling this. This is based on the experience of children as young as five or six years quite competently handling their own analgesia or pain relief systems when under-going medical treatment (Alderson and Montgomery, 1996). Other research into children's decision-making regarding competence and consent to non-critical medical treatment found a rough consensus of children putting the appropriate age at 14 years, with parents deciding on 13.9 years, and health professionals opting for 10.3 years (Shield and Baum, 1994: 1183). None of this is conclusive, but it suggests that there is a wide variation of professional opinion on what remains a difficult issue to decide. Whatever their basis for assessing the child or young person's competence to consent, the therapist's rationale for the decision needs to be clearly worked out, in order to be presented to a court, if necessary.

Access to files

Another area where children's rights may have implications for therapists is that of access to files. Children's right of access to counselling or therapeutic files has been greatly increased since the *Gaskin* decision by the European Court of Human Rights. Graham Gaskin, who spent a large part of his life in local authority care, brought an action against Liverpool Social Services Department in order to see his social work file. Refused on the grounds of confidentiality, he was eventually successful in winning his case on the basis of violation of Article 8 of the European Convention of Human Rights (*Gaskin* (1988); Gomien, 1991: 64–5). He was awarded £5,000 damages on the grounds that the procedures followed by Liverpool Social Services while he was in their care failed to secure respect for his private and family life, as required by this part of the Convention. (The case for a breach of Article 10, relating to freedom of expression and the right to information, was not found to apply by the court.)

In other settings, a person aged 16 or over can apply for access to a health record, by inspecting it or taking a copy of it. Access may be refused in certain circumstances, for example, where the record holder considers that the information would be likely to cause serious harm to any person's mental or physical health (Access to Health Records Act 1990). Similarly, children over 16 are entitled to see their personal school files, but only for material recorded after September 1989. Access may again be denied if the school considers that it would cause 'serious harm' (Education (School Records) Regulations Act 1989). Under s.1 of the Access to Personal Files Act 1987, a child, namely a person under the age of 18, can request access to their personal social work files and records (excluding adoption records), subject to the authority's being satisfied of their capacity to make an informed request. If the person considers any information to be inaccurate, they can apply to have it corrected or erased. The risk of 'serious harm' grounds can again be used to deny access to the individual.

Box 7.3

Children's right of access to files

- s.21, Data Protection Act 1984
- Access to Personal Files Act 1987
- *Gaskin* decision by European Court in 1989
- Education (School Records) Regulations Act 1989
- Access to Health Records Act 1990

Finally, a child of any age has a right of access to computerised records being kept on them, under s.21 of the Data Protection Act 1984 (excluding material made for the purpose of an assessment under the Education Act 1981). Therapists need to bear in mind that children's rights of access to files are extensive, and are backed by statute (see Box 7.3).

Compensation for child abuse

A growing area for many counsellors is that of working with survivors of child sexual abuse, which may involve assisting the client with information about their rights to compensation. Since 1964, it has been possible for individuals to claim compensation for criminal violence. To qualify for an award, an applicant must have sustained 'personal injury directly attributable to a crime of violence'. There is no legal definition of the term 'crime of violence', but it can include physical assault, rape, incest, buggery and indecent assault. 'Personal injury' means injury of a physical or mental nature, including shock or psychological disturbance, which is directly attributable to the crime of violence. The injury needs to be one for which a civil court would be able to make a compensation award of not less than £1,000, otherwise no award can be made under the scheme.

Normally, claims need to be made within three years of the incident giving rise to the injury, but more latitude has been shown when claims are made on behalf of children, or by children themselves when made within a reasonable time of reaching full age. Where claims are made on the basis of incidents which occurred before 1 October 1979, no compensation is payable where the victim and offender were living together as members of the same household, as the scheme is bound by the regulations of the system in force up to this date. In the case of injuries experienced as a result of child abuse, criminal prosecution of the offender is not essential as a prerequisite for a claim, as would normally be the case.

For children and young people under 18, the claim can be made by a parent, person with parental responsibility, a local authority if they are in care, or the Official Solicitor for England and Wales (CICA, 1994; Plotnikoff, 1990). Some of the anomalies of the current system of claiming for compensation are discussed further in Chapter 6. While it may not be appropriate for the therapist to work through this process of making a claim with the child or young person, unless that is an agreed part of their role, it is advisable that the therapist knows of the potential rights that might apply to their client in this respect.

Settings for counselling children

Children's rights regarding counselling and therapy vary significantly according to the context in which the service is offered, whether in private practice, or in an education, health, social work or psychiatric setting (Malek, 1991, 1993).

Private practice

A therapist working in private practice will be governed by the law of contract, subject to the usual legal redress for any breach of confidence, or for professional negligence (see Chapters 2 and 3). They are not *required* to report child abuse under the Children Act 1989, but may *choose* whether or not to do so, unless they are bound to report it by their agency policy, conditions of employment, or professional *Code of Practice*. The law does not require private citizens as such to report child abuse, and, according to judicial comment, they 'may see a child in need but pass by on the other side' (*M. v. Newham L.B.C.*, [1995] at 581). However, it is *also* the case that a therapist, as a private citizen, *may* safely break confidentiality in order to report child abuse, since it is clearly in the public interest to protect children from 'significant harm'.

The key issue for the therapist to decide is *who* the contract is with, the child or young person, or the parents who may be paying for the therapy. Any contract drawn up needs to specify what rights to information, if any, the parents have regarding the progress or content of the therapeutic work. The danger will be that, if refused information, the parents may end the therapy and withdraw the child. If therapeutic confidentiality is set out in the original contract, it will be harder for parents to insist later on knowing what is happening in each session.

School

Children's independent rights within the school setting have been gradually eclipsed by the educational reforms of the 1980s (Jeffs, 1995). This legislation stresses that *parents* rather than pupils are the consumers of education, despite the contrary values inherent within the Children Act 1989 and the UN Convention (Harris, 1993: 1). Hence complaints procedures refer to *parents* rather than children, in the Department for Education guidance on s.23 of the Education Reform Act 1988 (DES, *Circular 1/89*).

Within the school setting, children's rights have been set by the concept of *'in loco parentis'*, or the school as substitute parent (*Williams v. Eady*, (1893)). 'The concept of in *loco parentis* has always been acknowledged and accepted by teachers – and most parents and other adults – during the hours that pupils have attended school' (Davis, 1993: 14). The more child-centred values of the Children Act 1989 have been explicitly held *not* to apply within schools (*Hansard*, 1993a; 1993b). This sets up a potential conflict between schools, counsellors, school children and parents, over the issue of confidentiality (Bond, 1992a).

For example, a counsellor working in a state school was approached by a 13-year-old boy, who discussed his concerns that he might be gay. He said that his father was very hostile to 'poufs' as he called them, and saw homosexual relationships as being completely unnatural. This made it almost impossible for the boy to talk over his feelings with his father. In this situation, the counsellor had worked out a clear policy of client confidentiality with the Head Teacher, and enjoyed the later's full support. He was able to work with the boy in a confidential manner, without feeling under pressure to pass on his concerns to the Head. The counsellor did take the step of informing the boy that, while he may feel that he might be gay, he was under the age of consent for any active relationship (now set at 18).

So does the counsellor or therapist working in a school setting follow the *Gillick* principle of treating the child or young person as the client, or work to the 'school as substitute parent' approach, where confidentiality can be more easily broken? Either approach could currently be justified by appealing to the law. Concern has also been increased by recent settlements out of court by local authorities over claims for bullying, which appear to endorse a widening of school authorities' duty of care for pupils' welfare (*Guardian*, 16 November 1996). Until this situation is resolved by further case law or by legislation, therapists working in schools need to make clear to children, parents and the school authorities what their policy on confidentiality consists of (Casemore, 1995). Clear contracting with the school authorities and with the child as client are essential here to avoid any future misunderstandings about the limits of confidentiality that apply.

Local Government Act 1988   One area where the rights of children in school have been redefined over the last decade has been in relation to obtaining information on sexuality. Section 28 of the Local Government Act 1988 bans the intentional 'promotion' of homosexuality by local authorities, following concern about material on gay lifestyles adversely influencing children and young people. Initially, there was great concern in some quarters about the adverse effect that this might have on counselling young people about their sexual orientation (Manning, 1988). The Association of London Authorities commissioned a legal opinion on this subject, which 'found that there was a duty of equal treatment owed by the education authorities to pupils'. This opinion states that 'to promote homosexuality involves active advocacy directed by the local authorities towards individuals in order to persuade them to become homosexual, or to experiment with homosexual relationships' (NALGO, 1992: 14). Provided that therapists are not taking the somewhat unlikely step of actively pressurising young people to experiment with gay or lesbian sexual relationships, section 28 should not impede therapeutic work within local authority settings.

Section 28 was not originally directed specifically at voluntary organisations, but it does have implications for work done by voluntary organisations which is local authority grant-funded. It is claimed that some local authorities now demand of lesbian and gay groups that they sign declarations that they will not intentionally promote homosexuality via their work or activities. Liberty/NCCL point out that s.28 can only relate to the *local authority* funded elements of their work, assuming funding distinctions are strictly

---

Box 7.4

Counselling children in educational settings

- Doctrine of '*in loco parentis*' (*Williams v. Eady* (1893))
- *Gillick* principle [1986]
- s.28, Local Government Act 1988
- s.20, DoE *Circular 12/88*

---

maintained, and that voluntary organisations as such are not affected by s.28. Despite the sound and fury surrounding the issue, a later Department of the Environment *Circular* states that s.28 'will not prevent the objective discussion of homosexuality in the classroom, nor the counselling of pupils concerned about their sexuality' (s.20, DoE *Circular 12/88*). This statement should reassure therapists and counsellors working with young people that sexuality is not a taboo subject, despite the intense scrutiny of government policy and media publicity on this issue in the late 1980s.

The continuing uncertainty for teachers and counsellors working with issues of sexuality has prompted guidance from one of the main teaching unions, the National Union of Teachers. Referring to counselling agencies, on the issue of working with pupils regarding their sexual orientation, it suggests:

> It is not for teachers to give general counselling to gay and lesbian pupils outside the educational context but teachers who have pastoral responsibilities can benefit from maintaining contact with these agencies. Where appropriate if a teacher has gained a professional confidence in an outside agency it would not be unreasonable to draw a pupil's attention to its existence and to the counselling service it provides. (NUT, 1991: 5)

Contraceptive advice

In some areas of work with young people, counselling skills may be used as part of a wider role, in giving information on options for contraception. In 1993–4, some 37,000 girls aged under 16 attended family planning clinics in England, for example (Stuart-Smith, 1996). Given the crucial significance of the *Gillick* decision, it seems ironic that a Family Planning Association Report in 1993 found some GPs were unhappy or unclear about their responsibilities in the area of counselling and contraceptive advice for

---

Box 7.5

After *Gillick*: young people and consent to medical treatment

- Any competent young person, regardless of age, can independently seek medical advice and give valid consent to medical treatment
- Competency is understood in terms of the patient's ability to understand the choices and their consequences, including the nature, purpose and possible risk of any treatment (or non-treatment)
- Parental consent to that treatment is not necessary.

(BMA et al., 1993: 3)

---

young people. One GP said bluntly that 'I usually send them away with a flea in their ear and ask them to bring their parents' (*Guardian*, 26 August 1993).

The confusion revealed by the report prompted the issuing of clearer guidance to those working in this area, summarised in Box 7.5.

Counselling is seen in the guidance as valuable for promoting a sense of personal worth and of decision-making skills on the part of the young person faced with dilemmas about sexual activity and contraception. This is consistent with the Government's own target of halving the teenage pregnancy rate in under-16s by the year 2000 as set out in *The Health of the Nation* (DoH, 1992). The guidance acknowledges that breaches of confidentiality may be necessary in order to protect the vulnerable or to protect other children in a family at risk of abuse. However, 'in any situation where confidentiality is breached, the doctor must be prepared to justify his or her decision to the General Medical Council' (BMA et al., 1993: 4). The statements in the box above provide a very clear expression of the *Gillick* principle, which could be adopted by other counsellors and therapists as the basis for their work.

Social work
Social work is one of the main providers of counselling for children and young people. Counselling or, more accurately, the use of counselling *skills*, is clearly identified as an important element of the social worker's overall professional role (*Barclay Report*, 1982: 41). Counselling is highlighted in the Children Act 1989 as a service provided by the local authority for children in

need while living with their families. This service is particularly linked to the provision of Family Centres in s.9 of the Children Act 1989 (Jenkins, 1993b).

Family Centres

Family Centres are described in the *Guidance* accompanying the Act as being of three main types, in having a community, a self-help or a therapeutic orientation. 'In these, skilled workers carry out intensive casework with families experiencing severe difficulties with the aim of improving the ability to function as a family and relationships between parents and children or between siblings' (DoH, 1991a: Para 3.20). More generally, the *Guidance* to the Children Act argues that 'local authorities should have an agreed policy about the provision of counselling for parents, those with parental responsibility or looking after a child and workers, and should ensure that information about this is available. It need not be provided by the local authority but all concerned should know how to gain access to the service' (DoH, 1991a: Para 3.28).

Accommodation and residential care

Family Centres are intended to provide a supportive service to reduce the numbers of children coming into local authority residential care. Where children are placed in care by the courts, or are accommodated in residential care, counselling is increasingly recognised as being of key importance for many of them.

> Some young people may need considerable counselling before they come to accept themselves. Young people who have been rejected by their parents may need a lot of help before they can accept, emotionally, that this is no reflection on their own worth. Young people with disabilities may also require a lot of counselling to enable them to accept themselves and to develop a sense of self-esteem. Gay young men and women may require very sympathetic carers to enable them to accept their sexuality and to develop their own self-esteem. And young people from ethnic minorities may need help – preferably from someone from the same background – to enable them to take a pride in their racial, cultural, linguistic background. (DoH, 1991b: Para 9.50)

The irony is that the staff in most day-to-day contact with children in residential care may be the ones least trained or skilled in providing counselling. Caution is sounded by the *Guidance* to the Children Act about untrained staff attempting to provide complex and demanding interventions beyond their capabilities, such as family therapy, for example (DoH, 1991c: 7). This point is also made in a recent report by the outgoing head of the Social Services Inspectorate, referring to:

> the gap between the therapeutic aspirations of homes in this respect and the lack of adequate competence and skills on the part of the staff of the home. The term 'counselling' was frequently used by staff to describe talking and listening to children privately. This activity is an essential part of looking after any child and to invest it with therapeutic significance is to isolate it from the basic craft of child care. (Utting, 1991: 35)

Sir William Utting's point is that counselling is a skilled and complex activity, which needs to be recognised and preserved as such, rather than being subsumed and lost under a host of other day-to-day activities in the residential care setting. While it would be more accurate to describe social workers as using counselling skills as part of a wide role, this official recognition of the value of counselling is worth noting.

Interviewing in sexual abuse cases

One major example of the potential conflict between therapy and the law is in the case of video-recorded interviews for children subjected to alleged sexual abuse. Under the Criminal Justice Act 1991, video recordings of interviews made by police and social workers may supplement the oral testimony of children in subsequent court proceedings. The format of the interviews is closely defined by detailed guidance from the Home Office, in what is usually referred to as the *Memorandum of Good Practice* (Home Office/Department of Health, 1992).

As the *Memorandum* makes clear, 'therapy is not the primary aim of these interviews', but rather the presentation of children's evidence in a way which will reduce the traumatic impact of their appearing in court, which is still consistent with the principles of justice. The weakness of the procedure is that the child's need for therapy may conflict with the requirements of their giving evidence against the alleged perpetrators (Bull, 1995; Ryan and Wilson, 1995).

> Once the video recorded interview is complete, it should be possible for appropriate counselling and therapy to take place. It should

become standard practice to inform the police and the Crown Prosecution Service about the nature of any such therapy in each case. The defence may justifiably wish to know about both the nature and content of the therapy that has taken place before the child gives evidence in cross-examination. (Home Office/DoH, 1992: Para 3.44)

The policy and practice which flow from the Home Office *Memorandum* have been sharply criticised for the effects on children, whose urgent need for therapy is subordinated to the slow turning of the wheels of justice. In one survey, 81 children who had experienced child sexual abuse were interviewed by researchers from the National Children's Home to explore their perceptions of the treatment they had received from courts, police, social workers and therapists. The children's evaluations of the therapeutic help they had received, whether individual, group or family therapy, was broadly positive, with higher ratings for the two former types of therapy. Where therapy was perceived in negative or critical terms, this was sometimes because they had experienced the process as one which seemed to repeatedly encourage them to talk about the actual abuse itself.

Case Study: Children's responses to therapy following sexual abuse

Child D: *Well she didn't go on about the abuse. The panic attacks stopped. She helped me with symptoms of stress, got me to be a lot calmer and with a lot of school problems and things like that. I don't know really, I just told her about things and that was it sort of thing. Just talking. I never really talked to her about all that happened (abuse). They just stopped. I don't know why, I just stopped panicking.*

Child G: *When I thought about it the first time before I told anyone, I used to cry just thinking about it. After talking to someone and knowing that someone's sharing my feelings, I never wanted to cry as much. Like the first time I could have cried a bucketful then only just a little cupful. But I can't talk about it loads of times because I want to forget it. It doesn't get easier. Like the first time I knew I was on my own, second time I knew someone was sharing my feelings, but I'm still crying cupfuls, its not getting any less or it's not getting any bigger. I know I'm not on my own. (NCH, 1994: 40)*

The overall conviction rate for the alleged abusers was low, in the region of one quarter of the cases interviewed. The main criticisms of the current procedures relate to the unwieldy process, where children are interviewed on video about suspected abuse. Very few of the recordings are actually used in court proceedings. Over an 18-month period in 1992–93, almost 15,000 taped interviews with children were made, of which over three and a half thousand were sent to the Crown Prosecution Service. Yet, in the first six months of 1993, only 44 were used in court (*Daily Telegraph*, 29 November 1993).

What has been seen as a 'ban' on therapy pending court proceedings is more properly defined as a Crown Prosecution Service restriction for legal reasons.

> Defence counsel may well use the provision of therapy to undermine the child's testimony, suggesting that their evidence is tainted and 'coached'. Group therapy cannot be offered, since the possibility that children will confuse their own experience with that of others in the group will be suggested by the defence. In fact, the children interviewed favoured group therapy. Some therapy may be given, but in so doing it may jeopardise the case. This itself may be therapeutically detrimental to the child. (NCH, 1994: 45)

The dilemma faced by professionals and therapists working with children is an acute one, as one worker comments:

> As a child psychologist I consider it unethical to deprive a child who is traumatised of treatment pending legal proceedings going forward. If a child, as a consequence of non-accidental injury, had a broken leg, I don't think anybody in this country would propose that the broken leg should go untreated until the prosecution was brought, and psychologically it's exactly the same. (NCH, 1994: 45)

The situation is described as a 'disaster' by one counsellor who has extensive experience of *Memorandum* interviewing and court work involving children. From the point of view of the impact on therapeutic work of pending court proceedings and cross-examination, she says that:

> the whole time, we're walking a tightrope about whether we're coaching the children, putting words in their mouth . . . The difficulty is that, sometimes, once children have disclosed, they just want to talk about it all the time . . . I have to be really mindful, whether I'm doing *Memorandum* [interviewing], all the time, there's part of my brain,

although I try to be there 95% for the child, there's 5% that's thinking 'Oh my God! Am I going to be ripped to pieces about what I've just said?' (Interview with counsellor)

This illustrates some of the conflicts which can occur between therapy and the law, which are further discussed in Chapter 6. The Crown Prosecution Service has indicated that there is no 'ban' as such on therapeutic work being undertaken with children after they have made videos of evidence for court purposes. However, it does show some of the conflict inherent in the process of promoting abused children's need for therapy and their right to justice.

Abusive therapy in residential care: Pindown

The experience of abusive therapy is not limited to adult clients. Some of the most closely documented cases have occurred in the case of local authority care, as in the case of the Pindown and Beck Reports. This is not to suggest that abuse is unknown in private settings. The so-called 'Pindown' regime affected 132 children between 1983 and 1989, in children's homes in Staffordshire Social Services. Pindown was the name for a punitive type of residential care which affected children labelled by the residential system as hard to control. Under this approach, medicine and hot food were considered to be privileges, as were conversation with staff, reading, contact with parents and day-time clothing (Levy and Kahan, 1991: 40–2). It was described in the official report as 'a regime intrinsically dependent on elements of isolation, humiliation and confrontation' (1991: 124).

The authors of Pindown within the local authority care system were not mavericks, but provided a residential service which was an essential part of the overall framework of care while it lasted. Based on crude principles of behaviour modification, it adapted in time to incorporate a revised version of 'negative behaviour modification', with the injunction to staff regarding one particular girl in care, 'be nasty to her' (1991:60). The clear intention was that 'care is presented as a totally negative experience' (1991: 68).

The effects on the young people who experienced this regime were powerful and long-lasting, including a generalised loss of trust in adults, and distressing flashbacks of their harsh treatment in care. As Michael, one of the young people affected by Pindown put it, the care system 'has totally messed up my life' (1991: 111).

Following the report's findings, the local authority was faced with a barrage of claims for damages from young people who had experienced the Pindown regime, on the grounds of breach of its statutory duties under the Education Act 1944, and its common law duty of acting *in loco parentis*, as the legal parent of the children in its care.

The official report into Pindown described the system as 'intrinsically unethical, unprofessional and unacceptable' (Levy and Kahan, 1991: 127). It pointed out that it was 'likely to have stemmed initially from an ill-digested understanding of behavioural psychology; the regime had no theoretical framework and no safeguards' (1991: 167). What is crucial is that the regime was justified as a *therapeutic* process for those who experienced it, rather than simply existing as a measure of control in its own right. 'Pindown provides a salutary example of the dressing up of oppressive control in the rhetorical garb of therapy, and of the capacity of that rhetoric to convince those running the regime that what they were doing was in the best interests of the children' (Fennell, 1992: 312).

The Pindown experience may represent to some simply an aberration of the social work system for young people in care. However, it is important to consider how control can sometimes be exercised over vulnerable groups in the guise of therapy. It also raises questions about therapists who may be working alongside such regimes, or who have knowledge of such activities. Legal protection for 'whistle blowers' is limited, and those trying to publicise unethical or unsafe practice can themselves become victimised in turn. Sue Machin, a senior social worker at Ashworth Special Hospital, helped to reveal bad practice there, but was then dismissed and had to take her case to an industrial tribunal to gain compensation (Sone, 1995). The defence of 'qualified privilege', or citing a public interest in disclosure are two options open to therapists concerned about bad practice, where raising the issue with management has produced no effective response (see Chapter 2). A Public Interest Disclosure Bill was put before Parliament as a Private Members Bill in 1996, to protect those who bring these issues into the open, on the lines of similar legislation in the USA, but this failed to reach the statute books. There is a pressure group, Freedom to Care, which also offers advice and support to professionals in this position (see Resources section for details).

Case Study: Abusive therapy and the law: the Beck Report

One of the most alarming and best-documented cases of abusive therapy inflicted upon children can be found in the report on the activities of Frank Beck, who ran a number of local authority children's homes in Leicestershire between 1973 and 1986. A qualified and charismatic social worker, Beck ran a regime staffed by junior and untrained workers, with a personal blend of techniques designed to break down and remodel the behaviours of children in care via 'reparenting' them. This technique also acted as a cover for the systematic harassment, humiliation and sexual abuse of children entrusted to his care. At his trial in 1991, he was found guilty on 17 counts including sexual and physical assault, for which he was sentenced to life imprisonment.

As with the Pindown regime (Levy and Kahan, 1991), the pattern of abusive control was dignified with a therapeutic label, in this case that of 'regression therapy'. This 'treatment cocktail' included the 'apparently bizarre use of the paraphernalia of babyhood in the treatment of adolescent boys and girls'. The Report into Beck's activities noted that '"regression therapy" does not stand in professional circles as a distinct and credible therapy', which is not to deny the value of the concept of regression in psychotherapy more generally (Kirkwood, 1993: 56). (Appendix 6 of the Report consists of a paper on 'Psychotherapy and Regression' by Peter Wilson, Director of Young Minds (presently National Association for Child and Family Mental Health) (Kirkwood, 1993: 343–8).)

With no formal training in specialist therapeutic methods, there were two main sources for Beck's approach: 'his largely untutored reading of psychoanalytical works about child development and regression', including Bruno Bettelheim's book, Love is not Enough; *and his personal understanding of the documentary film* Warrendale *(Kirkwood, 1993: 61). This was a film made in Canada in the 1950s and 60s, showing confrontational methods used in a children's home. This film was regularly shown by Beck to his largely untrained staff. The film has a powerful emotional impact, illustrating methods of confrontation and restraint by staff with children, to remove a child's defences and enable them to regress to an earlier emotional stage of development, from which they can learn more adaptive behaviours. As the Report notes, 'this film must be regarded as a very dangerous model and* training aid indeed', principally because of the absence of commentary and analysis to identify good and bad practice (Kirkwood, 1993: 61). Beck used the film as a training device to legitimate his own methods from a credible and authoritative external source.

Other management and professional safeguards were either missing or ineffective. There was little outside supervision of practice by external specialists such as psychiatrists. Consequently, 'supervision and counselling were contained within the home and carried out by staff with no training or experience to do it. It was abused by Mr Beck' (Kirkwood, 1993: 62).

The young people in residential care 'found the treatment to which they were subjected in the name of therapy abusive in itself' (Kirkwood, 1993: 62). The Report includes an account by AB, a 14-year-old boy who was at the Poplars when Mr Beck arrived.

> Over a period of time I was subjected to the so-called regression treatment by Frank Beck mainly. He stated that I was a sad person and tried to make me cry. Later he wanted me to become angry, and would pin me down to make me angry to release my emotions. He tried to make me go back in time to babyhood and at times I suffered humiliation as a result of this. For example, I remember one day when I was in a sleeping bag with a large pink fluffy elephant, when the other children came in from school with friends outside the home I was very embarrassed. (Kirkwood, 1993: 62)

Some of the most striking descriptions of Beck's methods in practice came from the evidence of Mrs Brenda Biamonti, a social work student on placement at the time. She told the enquiry that she 'saw children being systematically tormented and humiliated, verbally and physically'. In practice, 'children were systematically targeted for this breaking down process which was orchestrated by Frank Beck and from what I saw, carried out largely by his junior staff' (Kirkwood, 1993: 63). She continued:

> The worker was following the child around, pushing him hard in the back and verbally abusing him in the manner described above. This continued to my knowledge for a good half hour. . . . another child had regressed. A sort of nest had been built in the corner of a room or corridor. It was hung around with curtains to create a dark and womb-like atmosphere and there was a mattress or cushions on the floor. I was told that the child slept there and spent part of the day

> *there too, that he was bottle-fed and wore nappies. All of this was
> explained within the framework of the treatment and as such did not
> appear to be secret. (Kirkwood, 1993: 63)*

*Following investigation of complaints into Beck's activities, which
had lasted for a total of 13 years, Beck was successfully prosecuted for serious offences against children. Eighty-six children
placed claims for compensation totalling one million pounds
against Leicestershire County Council (Independent, 9 February
1993). Frank Beck, who was then serving five life sentences plus
24 years for sexual and physical assault, died in prison of a heart
attack while preparing his appeal (Guardian, 2 June 1994). Two
women who were abused under the Beck regime were awarded a
total of £225,000 damages (Guardian, 3 April 1996).*

Psychiatric treatment

Each year several thousand young people are admitted to
psychiatric hospitals for treatment under the Mental Health Act
1983 – almost 9,000 aged up to 19 during 1991/92 (DoH, 1995a:
50; Malek, 1991, 1993). Therapeutic work represents one of the
treatments on offer. In this relatively specialised area of
psychiatric care for young people, the *Gillick* decision has had
a major influence in recognising their independent rights as
patients (CLC, 1994). In relation to the crucial issue of their
consent to treatment, Alderson comments that 'legal views of
children's competence to consent are changing in many countries
from an emphasis on a stated *age* of consent to interest in
individual *ability or competence*' (1993: 44). The *Gillick* decision
is in line with this trend towards acknowledging the rights and
abilities of children to make complex decisions under certain
circumstances, rather than on their acquisition of this power by
achieving the age of 16 or 18 years. The outcome of recent cases
has complicated a situation where the notion of competence,
recognised by legislation such as the Children Act 1989 in s.43(8),
has been qualified and redefined, as discussed below. Doctors are
now left in some uncertainty as to which principle to follow in
reaching decisions about obtaining children's consent to treatment
(Shield and Baum, 1994: 1182–3).

Voluntary psychiatric treatment Provision for psychiatric treatment of young people under 18 is set out in the *Code of Practice*

for the Mental Health Act 1983. (The Act does not impose a legal duty to follow the *Code*, but it is noted that failure to do so 'could be referred to in evidence in legal proceedings' (DoH/WO, 1993: Para 1.1.) There is no minimum age set for admission to hospital under the Act. Fennell (1992) identifies three principles for the operation of the Act in relation to young people: that they should be kept fully informed about their care and treatment; that they should generally be regarded as being able to make their own decisions with certain provisos; and that any intervention in the life of a young person should be 'the least restrictive possible', in accordance with the overall philosophy of the Act. The legal situation regarding the treatment of young people under the age of 18, and under 16 in particular, is complex and affected by recent case law decisions, and by the principles of the Children Act 1989.

Parents or guardians of young people may agree to the admission of a young person under the age of 16 as an informal patient. Following *Gillick*, 'where a doctor concludes that a child under the age of 16 has the capacity to make such a decision for himself, there is no right to admit him to hospital informally or to keep him there on an informal basis against his will' (DoH/WO, 1993: Para 30.5). With young people aged 16–17, anyone in this age group capable of expressing his or her own wishes can decide for themselves about admission or discharge, regardless of parental wishes.

Psychiatric assessment for a child may be ordered by the courts, under s.38 of the Children Act 1989, as part of an Interim Care Order. These Orders normally last eight weeks, but can be extended by the court. However, the assessment is subject to the agreement of the child, assuming that they are deemed to be 'Gillick-competent'.

Under the Mental Health Act 1983, medical treatment is taken to include physical treatment, such as the administration of drugs and electro-convulsive therapy, and psychotherapy. Attention is drawn in the *Code* to the possible drawbacks of using psychological treatments, such as group therapy, individual psychotherapy and behaviour modification. The issue of *consent* is stressed in relation to the use of behaviour modification programmes in particular. 'Psychological treatments should be conducted under the supervision of those properly trained in the use of the specific methods employed' (DoH/WO, 1993: Para 19.1).

The complexity of the law relating to the therapeutic treatment of young people in psychiatric systems is explored in detail by Fennell (1992). He concludes that 'the current multiplicity of legal frameworks creates a climate of legal uncertainty where it is little wonder that staff are unsure about the limits of their authority and the extent of the legal and ethical entitlements of the children in their care' (1992: 332). In one case, the discovery that a private health company was using high levels of sedation, and solitary confinement, without a proper complaints procedure, led to its closure, following a critical report by the Social Services Inspectorate (*Guardian*, 26 June 1991).

Compulsory psychiatric treament A range of powers exist for authorising compulsory psychiatric assessment or treatment of children where these measures are thought to be needed. Children may receive compulsory psychiatric treatment under ss. 2, 3 and 4 of the Mental Health Act 1983 (see Chapter 1 for details of this Act). Under the Children Act 1989, a s.8 'specific issue' order may be sought by the local authority, with the parents' consent, to authorise the use of a particular regime in a specialist unit, or for the emergency use of medication. Via wardship proceedings under s.100 of the same Act, the High Court has authorised medical or psychiatric treatment in extreme cases, based on its own powers of inherent jurisdiction.

Impact of medical case law after Gillick Several recent cases have appeared to qualify the impact of the *Gillick* decision regarding the rights of mature minors to make decisions regarding their medical care. In the case referred to as *Re R.* in 1991, a local authority sought legal powers to administer anti-psychotic drugs to a 15-year-old girl with a history of severe behaviour problems. The Court of Appeal dismissed the girl's case that she did not consent to the treatment, on the grounds that parents or the courts could over-ride her refusal. Using the analogy of the consent as a 'key' to unlock a door, Lord Donaldson argued that a competent minor could lock the door, or refuse consent, but that other keyholders, such as parents or the courts, could unlock it and over-ride the child's wishes (Urwin, 1992). The effect of the decision is to undermine the effect of *Gillick*. Taking the lock analogy a step further, it has been aptly pointed out that 'if the child is inside and has turned the key in the lock, the doctor and a parent may jointly break the door in' (Fennell, 1992: 326).

The relevance of this case to therapists is that it *appears* to limit the impact of the *Gillick* decision, and creates an air of uncertainty for therapists working with children. This effect is even more evident in a second key legal case, referred to as *Re W.* in 1992, to protect the child's anonymity. In this case, a 16-year-old girl, suffering from anorexia nervosa, was to be moved against her will to a unit specialising in the treatment of this disorder. This move also entailed a break in the psychotherapy she was receiving, as the local authority seeking her removal preferred the more behaviourally based form of treatment available at the specialist unit. Under s.8 of the Family Law Reform Act 1969, minors of 16 or over can consent to surgical, medical or dental treatment. In this case, the issue was whether the right of 16-year-olds to consent to treatment meant that they could also *veto* treatment by *withholding* their agreement. Rejecting her appeal, the court found against her, claiming that neither the 1969 Act nor the *Gillick* decision meant that the rights of young people were absolute with regard to consent to treatment and in fact that W.'s views 'were of no weight' in the court's decision (Mulholland, 1993). Alderson, among others, has pointed out that both cases 'could have been discussed within provisions made by the Mental Health Act 1983 . . . without needing to refer to *Gillick*' (Alderson, 1993: 49). In other words, both girls could have been treated on a compulsory basis under the Mental Health Act 1983, without needing to take the issues to court.

This second case, *Re W.*, is important because it sets some limits on the right of young people aged 16–17 years to decide their own medical or psychotherapeutic treatment in life-threatening circumstances. However, the *Gillick* principle still holds good for the vast majority of children and young people of 'mature understanding' who seek counselling or therapy. It is therefore important that therapists know enough about the conflicting case law as outlined above to refute any mistaken claims that *Gillick* has now been overturned or no longer applies with its previous relevance to therapy.

The increasing complexity of the law here is shown by the example of a 14-year-girl, who sought counselling from an eating disorders clinic, with the full knowledge and permission of her worried parents. While the therapists at the clinic were able to

---

Box 7.6

Medical and psychiatric treatment of children

- s.8, Family Law Reform Act 1969
- ss. 2, 3, 4, Mental Health Act 1983
- *Gillick* decision by House of Lords [1986]
- ss. 8, 38, 100, Children Act 1989
- Case of *Re R.* [1991]
- Case of *Re W.* [1992]
- Mental Health Act *Code of Practice* 1993

---

work productively with the girl as the client under *Gillick*, there was also the knowledge that the parents had the option of seeking her admission to a local psychiatric unit for young people, should the clinic's therapy not produce the desired results. Being aware of both options provided a basis of information for trying to establish a therapeutic alliance with the girl, acknowledged and supported by her parents, which would provide the time and space for effective therapeutic work to take place. The law provides an uneasy blend of voluntary and coercive elements concerning therapeutic work with children and young people, which therapists need to consider, but without permitting this to side-track them from carrying out their work.

Complaints systems
If children are to have a valid and effective counselling and therapy service, they also need to be able to make complaints if their needs are not met, or if they are actually abused, as in the cases described above relating to Pindown and the Beck regime. Their statutory rights to complaints procedures are patchy, reflecting the lack of consistency within the law. The clearest expression of their right to an independent complaints procedure is under s.26 of the Children Act 1989, although criticisms have been voiced of the effectiveness of the system and of the problems experienced by young people in making their voices heard (Lindsay, 1991). The right to complain about education is held by *parents* as consumers rather than children, under s.23 of the Education Reform Act 1988, and DES *Circular 1/89*. Complaints can be made concerning community care provision under s.50 of the NHS and Community Care Act 1990. Children admitted as informal patients under the Mental

---

Box 7.7

Children and statutory complaints procedures

- Mental Health Act 1983
- s.23, Education Reform Act 1988
- DES *Circular 1/89*
- s.26, Children Act 1989
- s.50, NHS and Community Care Act 1990
- Complaint to local Ombudsman for maladministration

Health Act 1983 do not receive the same degree of protection of their rights as adults, despite the incorporation of the *Gillick* principle into the revised *Code of Practice* for the Act. Complaints against a local authority for maladministration can be made by the young person to the local Ombudsman if this is appropriate. In the case of private treatment, then a person under the age of 18 could seek to sue the therapist via 'a next friend' or parent.

Limitations on right to sue councils

The Pindown case represented the first example of a mass claim for damages by young people against a local authority, followed by further action by young people affected by the abusive Beck regime in Leicestershire County Council. In the case of Pindown, 140 of its victims were later awarded compensation totalling £2 million (*Independent*, 20 April 1996). However, the right of individuals to sue local authorities in the courts is not automatic or straightforward. The House of Lords has ruled that an individual cannot sue or bring a private law action against a local authority for breaches of its statutory duties under the Children Act 1989, and of other relevant legislation which determines its child protection responsibilities. In this case it was claimed, unsuccessfully, that a local authority had failed to take five siblings into care, despite repeated reports of alleged abuse. The House of Lords also held that a second council was *not* liable under a common law duty of care for negligence in the welfare of children, in this case for wrongly diagnosing sexual abuse, and for then removing the child from her mother (*M. v. Newham L.B.C.* [1995].

The apparent complexity and unfamiliarity of the law relating to therapy with children and young people may seem daunting at first sight. Some basic guidelines are suggested in Box 7.8 to help

---

Box 7.8

Guidelines for professional practice in therapeutic work with children and young people

- be clear about your helping role and its boundaries, as counsellor, therapist, befriender, or advocate
- find out about the statute or case law which governs your particular area of work with children, such as the Children Act 1989, *Gillick*, etc.
- be sure of your agency policy or your own key personal principles in working with children and young people
- be clear about *who* is the main client you are working with – the child/young person, or the family unit as a whole
- set and communicate the limits to keeping confidentiality which apply to your work
- negotiate and work to a contract with the child or young person as far as possible, covering:
  - risk issues
  - child protection procedures
  - recording and access to files
  - complaints systems
- be clear about your own working arrangements for:
  - professional supervision
  - personal and agency accountability
  - personal or vicarious liability in the case of legal action
  - obtaining legal advice as required
  - advice from your professional association
  - membership of professional protection society or coverage by indemnity insurance policy

---

therapists who are unsure of how best to base their practice on sound principles.

Summary

The position of children as clients in the therapeutic relationship is closely linked to their rights as set out in law. The right of children and young people to an independent counselling relationship is acknowledged by the *Gillick* decision, and by the Children Act and UN Convention on the Rights of the Child of 1989. It follows from the *Gillick* decision that children have a right to confidentiality, depending upon their level of maturity and understanding as perceived by the adult therapist, independently of the wishes of the parents. Children enjoy rights of access to their files in many situations, to claim damages or compensation for child abuse, and to make complaints about their treatment, according to the setting in which it was provided. Children under the age of 16 may receive information about contraception, and may determine their own medical and psychiatric treatment, given a doctor's assessment that they are of 'mature understanding'.

Children's rights are heavily qualified by the setting in which the counselling or therapy service is provided. Schools are governed by the doctrine of '*in loco parentis*', and attempts have been made in law to proscribe the advocating of homosexuality by teachers. This has resulted in some uncertainty for teachers and counsellors in a school environment about counselling young people about their sexual orientation.

The *Gillick* decision underscored the right of young people to make choices about medical treatment. More recent case law has challenged this in extreme circumstances where the young person exhibits serious behaviour problems, or faces a life-threatening illness. However, the principle is still intact for the vast majority of children outside of the school setting.

The duties of therapists in counselling children are perhaps more complex than for adults. Confidentiality can be broken in order to report suspected child abuse, but this is discretionary rather than mandatory for therapists not explicitly bound to do so by their agency policy or by their own professional *Codes of Practice*. Therapists have a responsibility to *know* the appropriate law, and to work within it – not an easy task in this area. Crucially, they need to decide *who* is their client, child or parent, and to make this explicit in any contract which is drawn up. The problem of determining whether a child is of 'mature understanding' for the therapist remains a difficult appraisal where official guidelines can only complement rather than replace the exercise of professional judgement.

Discussion points

1   What do you understand by the *Gillick* principle? How would you go about establishing that a child or young person could show 'mature understanding' of what was on offer in a counselling or therapeutic relationship?

2   What policy, if any, does your agency have on counselling children and young people? In what ways does the service differ from that provided for adult clients, and why?

3   How should counsellors and therapists working in schools best meet their professional responsibilities to children, parents and the education authorities? How should the balance be drawn between the principles of the *Gillick* decision and the idea of the 'school as parent' where counselling is concerned?

4   Should *all* therapists be legally obliged to report child abuse, as in the USA? When should the child's right to confidentiality be respected, even if it means that child abuse is not reported?

5   Has the concept of children's rights applied to counselling and therapy gone too far? In what circumstances should the therapist seek to work with the child as the client, rather than including parents, or working with the family as a whole?

8

Complaints System

This chapter is addressed both to clients and to their therapists, given that the boundaries between membership of the two groups are fluid and ever-changing. Many clients first develop an interest in becoming a therapist as a result of their experience of being the subject of a therapeutic relationship; many therapists are also clients on an intermittent or regular basis, either as part of their training, or as a necessary part of their continuing professional and personal self-development. In either case, the experience of unsatisfactory therapy will be a crucial one, shaping future attitudes about the core elements of respect, trust and high standards of practice which should be embodied in the therapeutic alliance. Awareness of shortcomings in professional practice may alert therapists to the need to practise at the highest standards possible. It may also sensitise them to the rights of those clients who feel that their therapy has fallen short of such standards.

From a legal perspective, there is another rationale for including this topic in a book on law and therapy. This concerns the potentially close relationship existing between complaints and litigation. An unsuccessful complaint may be pursued to its resolution via the courts. Alternatively, a fair and effective complaints procedure may mean that this threat of legal action against therapists or their employing organisations is correspondingly reduced. Discussion of complaints procedures currently takes place against a backdrop of government initiatives on promoting consumer rights and implementing accessible complaints systems through the network of Citizens' Charters (HMG, 1991). The growth of a market philosophy in the service sectors of the economy, such as in health and social services, has registered the forceful impact of these changes. Another significant factor here has been the introduction of 'conditional fee' cases for lawyers acting on behalf of aggrieved clients. Initially, this will apply only to personal injury cases, insolvency and human rights cases, rather than to negligence as such, but the longer term effect of this development may mean that legal assistance will be more easily available to complainants seeking redress in a wide range of situations.

This chapter explores the growing attention paid to complaints within a culture of **consumer rights** in the personal services. Some of the possible sources of client dissatisfaction are considered, together with a **comparison of complaints and litigation** as a means for clients to achieve redress. Existing **professional complaints systems** are discussed, as are current complaints systems operated by a range of **therapists' organisations**, and comparisons drawn with the features of a **model complaints system**.

Consumer rights and complaints

The growth of a market approach and of the concept of consumer rights relating to personal services is clearly illustrated by the rising number of complaints within the National Health Service. This has been the focus of a major report by the Wilson Committee (DoH, 1994). The complaints procedures in the NHS have been roundly criticised in the past as being cumbersome and bureaucratic. Despite this, there has been an increase in the number of complaints within the Family Health Service in England and Wales from 1,590 in 1984 to 2,125 in 1992. Hospital complaints increased from 23,335 to 47,057 in the same period (DoH, 1994: 103). The increase in the number of complaints has been attributed by the then Secretary of State, Virginia Bottomley, to rising consumer expectations, rather than to any decline in standards.

Complaints against therapists

If recent years have heralded the development of a consumer culture, then the number of actual complaints against therapists still remains low at present. The British Association for Counselling (BAC), for instance, recorded 20 complaints received in one year, out of an individual membership which then stood at 10,000 with an organisational membership of 500 (Baron, 1993: 10; Jones, 1993: 14). The majority of complaints are about boundary an~' training issues, with around a quarter relating to indiv~

counsellors and their clients (Palmer-Barnes, 1993: 84). Fiona
Palmer-Barnes, Chair of the BAC's Complaints Sub-Committee, has
expressed the hope that there will be fewer complaints about
counsellors in the future, while nevertheless acknowledging that
complaints are linked to a general rise in consumer awareness and
to the overall struggle to raise standards of professional practice
(Palmer-Barnes, 1995: 39).

What causes clients to make complaints, or to feel dissatisfied
with their experience of therapy? Some clues are suggested by the
cases of clients who have recorded their lack of satisfaction with
therapists in newspaper articles. One survey included the
following examples:

■ a male therapist who expressed his attraction for a female
  client, and kissed her on the lips
■ a therapist who ended a client's therapy abruptly and without
  explanation
■ a therapist who wrote about a counselling session in an article,
  enabling the client to be identified by her friends
■ a psychodynamic counsellor working for a GP, who refused to
  explore any aspects of the client's *physical* symptoms, such as
  panic attacks
■ a therapist who 'refereed marital counselling like a boxing
  match'
■ a counselling service where the therapists were changed
  without notice between sessions, were remote and full of
  jargon (*Independent on Sunday*, 19 April 1992)

Each of these situations could have led to a formal complaint
being lodged by the client concerned. The first three examples
describe what appear to be clear breaches of ethical standards.
However, the other accounts do not include the alternative point
of view of the therapists involved. It may well be that there were
very valid reasons for the therapists adopting a certain style, or
approach, which may not have matched the clients' expectations,
but were justifiable, nevertheless. This illustrates some of the
difficulty involved in investigating complaints about therapy,
where there may be very little in the way of solid evidence to
support the complainant, and little agreement between client and
therapist as to what actually happened that was the cause of the
complaint.

Complaints and litigation

One of the principal reasons advanced for therapists' organisations to possess an effective complaints procedure is to offer clients a realistic alternative to potentially expensive litigation procedures (Bond, 1993a: 50). However, the relationship between complaints and litigation is not necessarily a case of clear-cut alternatives. Clients may not wish to bring a case in court against their therapist, preferring to try and sort out complex interpersonal issues in a more informal and confidential atmosphere. Alternatively, a successful complaint may produce sanctions against an erring therapist, but will not produce financial compensation for the client, which may perhaps be needed to pay for additional therapy to resolve their original concerns. The Wilson Committee on the NHS makes the point that, according to their research, 'the vast majority of cases of litigation in hospitals do not start out as complaints' (DoH, 1994: 13). In some cases, taking legal action may not be possible: for example, a patient or their family need to have suffered reasonably direct *damage* in order to be able to sue the doctor or health service concerned (Harpwood, 1994). Furthermore, financial compensation is not always the primary goal of those taking legal action (DoH, 1994: 17). The relationship between making a complaint and taking legal action is not always clear, although it makes sense that an open, accessible and effective complaints system might reduce the numbers of clients taking action through the courts. In the last analysis, *cost* may be a deciding factor for clients in choosing whether to make a complaint or to take legal action. Jehu et al. (1994: 177–94) list the options open to dissatisfied clients. These include:

- civil suit to sue the therapist for damages
- criminal prosecution, via the Crown Prosecution Service, or through initiating a private prosecution
- complaint to employer, leading to disciplinary action
- complaint to professional association, initiating professional misconduct proceedings

The options available will vary according to the nature of the complaint, and the circumstances of the therapist, in terms of whether they are a member of a professional association, and whether they are employed or work in private practice. Certain complaints procedures, such as the BAC's, *preclude* taking legal

Table 8.1 *Comparison of potential outcomes of complaints to professional bodies with legal action*

Complaint	Legal action
Apology from therapist	
Public acknowledgement	Public acknowledgement
	Establishment of legal precedent (if applicable)
Changes in practice/policy by organisation	
	Sanctioning of therapist, i.e. fine/payment of damages
	Compensation to client
Monitoring of therapist performance	
Supervision/retraining of therapist	
Suspension from professional membership	
Removal from Register (if applicable)	

action at the same time (1994a); others, such as the BPS, do not restrict complainants in this way (1995b). Deciding on the best course of action may itself be a difficult starting-point for a dissatisfied client. Some of the relative outcomes of a successful complaint versus legal action are suggested in Table 8.1.

The relationship between making a complaint and taking legal action is clearly a complex one. It may well follow that establishing a legal precedent, such as the principle of third party liability for fostering false memories of abuse in clients, may then in turn have a marked effect on the policy and practice of therapeutic practitioners and organisations, as has occurred in the USA. A successful criminal prosecution or civil action against a therapist could also lead to their suspension from membership of the relevant professional organisations. However, without statutory regulation of therapists, this would not necessarily remove their licence to practice. Where statutory regulation does apply, as in the case of therapists who are doctors or psychiatrists, the General Medical Council has recently moved to adopt a model of monitoring and supervision of doctors performing at unacceptable levels. This incorporates some of the features included under the Complaints section of the diagram above, but with statutory backing in the form of legislation, as the Medical (Professional Performance) Act 1995.

This chapter now concentrates on the role of complaints about therapists made to their professional associations. Legal action against therapists under civil law is discussed in more detail in Chapters 2, 3 and 6.

Comparison of professional complaints systems

Complaints procedures need to offer clients reassurance that their concerns will be taken seriously, investigated thoroughly, and will have some effect. The underlying concern of clients may well be that complaints procedures are operated by professionals simply as a public relations exercise, more to appease the public, rather than to monitor therapists effectively or to sanction bad practice by their members. Practitioners, for their part, may well be concerned that complaints procedures do not entertain spurious or malicious complaints by aggrieved clients, and that principles of fairness and natural justice are held to by the investigating body. In exploring appropriate complaints systems for therapists, it is useful to draw on the experience of other complaints procedures for professionals. The two main models which exist for comparison are those operated by the Law Society for solicitors, and by the General Medical Council for doctors.

Complaints against solicitors

The Solicitors' Complaints Bureau (SCB) was established in 1986 to separate investigation of complaints from the general running of the Law Society, which acts as the professional body for solicitors. It deals with complaints about professional misconduct and poor quality work. It can order a solicitor to waive a bill, refund money and correct mistakes, award compensation of up to £1,000, under s.93 of the Courts and Legal Services Act 1990, and take disciplinary action. Clients can appeal from the SCB to the Legal Services Ombudsman.

The Law Society complaints procedure is based on an *investigative model*. However, the Bureau has been consistently criticised by the Legal Services Ombudsman, and even described as a 'bureaucratic nightmare' by the National Consumer Council (Hansen, 1994). It receives 20,000 complaints per year, and costs £11 million per year to operate. Proposals have been made for its replacement by a Supervision of Solicitors Agency, with 'distinguished lay people' playing a key role.

The National Consumer Council (NCC) survey criticised the Bureau on the grounds that it was

- inaccessible and confusing for complainants
- procedural barriers made it difficult for the client to complain about their own solicitor
- conciliation was often used as a routine measure without the client having given consent to this
- some complaints were wrongly categorised as complaints over cost rather than about the poor service received
- delays of up to two years could occur in the resolution of disputes
- the overall scheme was not seen to be sufficiently independent of the solicitor's own professional body, the Law Society.

These criticisms appear to be borne out by the Law Society's own consumer research, which indicated low levels of satisfaction with the existing system (Law Society, 1990). The National Consumer Council recommendations for radical reform propose an Independent Legal Services Complaints Council, containing a majority of non-lawyers appointed by the Lord Chancellor, and chaired by a non-lawyer. This would fulfil the roles of both the current SCB and of the Legal Services Ombudsman, and would be able to award compensation of up to £5,000. In fact, following much criticism, the Solicitors' Complaints Bureau has been wound up and replaced by a new body, the Office for the Supervision of Solicitors (see Resources section for details). The key points arising from the research, concerning the need for accessibility, accurate information, avoidance of delay and independence from professional interest will have some direct relevance to any proposed complaints procedures for therapists.

Complaints against doctors
The General Medical Council (GMC) follows a *protectionist model*. Professional standards for doctors are set out in the GMC Code based on powers set out by the Medical Act 1858 (GMC, 1992, 1995a). The disciplinary powers of the GMC regarding criminal offences or serious professional misconduct are governed by the Medical Act 1983 (Smith, 1995). The GMC operates a three-stage

process for investigating complaints, moving from initial consideration, to referral to the Preliminary Proceedings Committee, and finally to public inquiry by the Professional Conduct Committee for hearing individual cases. The following sanctions can be imposed, ranging from admonition, imposing of conditions on registration for up to three years, to suspension of registration for up to one year, to erasure from the Medical Register. The number of complaints considered by the GMC increased from 1,104 in 1989 to 1,626 in 1994 (GMC, 1994). The biggest single category of complaints relate to failure to provide a proper standard of professional care, while others relate to abuses of professional trust, dishonesty, indecent or improper behaviour towards patients and irresponsible prescribing. (Charges of negligence as such are usually brought in the form of legal proceedings by the patient, rather than referred to the GMC.) Forty doctors were removed from the Register in 1994, for a variety of reasons, including dishonesty, fraud, deception, indecency and disregard of professional responsibilities to patients. Legislation has been enacted to close a gap in the GMC's powers, where it has been unable to intervene in the past on the grounds of poor professional performance, such as 'persistently inappropriate' behaviour.

The criticism has been voiced that the primary role of the GMC is, in fact, to preserve the hierarchical power of the medical profession, rather than to act as an effective self-regulatory body. Stacey refers to 'the failure of the GMC hitherto to consider any except the grossest cases of incompetence as "serious professional misconduct"' (1994: 120). Thus doctors can only be struck off the Medical Register for 'serious professional misconduct', whereas nurses can be similarly disciplined simply for 'misconduct', arguably a lower threshold for disciplinary action to be taken. Another example of a statutory protectionist model is provided in the case of nurses, recently revised by statute under the Nurses, Midwives and Health Visitors Act 1992 (Bailey, 1988; Fletcher, 1992). This has been the subject of criticism regarding problems of delay of up to three years in hearing and resolving complaints against practitioners, of poor drafting of regulations and of alleged breaches of natural justice. However, a more sympathetic view is advanced by Sumerling, who proposes the statutory protectionist model as an appropriate one for the regulation of the emerging complementary therapies (1994).

Complaints against therapists
Within the therapeutic community, one of the clearest complaints procedures is that held by the BAC (1992b; 1994a). This operates an investigative procedure, following a three-stage process. This includes:

■ investigation and conciliation
■ adjudication
■ application of sanctions, if appropriate

The main features of the procedure include the following:

■ complaint is not part of current or intended legal action
■ three-year time limit for bringing complaints
■ provision for the presence of a 'friend' for both parties before the Adjudication Panel
■ continuation of complaint process despite any lapse in membership of the subject of complaint
■ complaints can be against organisational members of the BAC as well as individual members

The current BAC procedure contains no provision for making third party complaints, for example by the partner or parent of a client receiving therapy. This provision has been removed, as these have proved problematic in the past (Jones, 1993: 14). The over-riding problem of confidentiality is cited as one of the main factors for this decision (Palmer-Barnes, 1993: 85). The alternative way of dealing with these issues raised could be via referral to Article 5 of the BAC Constitution, concerning serious matters relating to members, clients and counselling in general which would bring the Association into disrepute (Palmer-Barnes, 1993: 85).

The therapists' professional organisations are increasingly aware of the need to have effective and credible complaints systems in place. The United Kingdom Council for Psychotherapy (UKCP) is an umbrella organisation, arising out of meetings held from 1982 onwards, and which was then inaugurated in 1989 as the UK Standing Conference on Psychotherapy (UKSCP). Under its Ethical Guidelines, each member organisation of the UKCP must have a published *Code of Ethics*, covering ten points of professional practice, for example, qualifications, research, confidentiality, and professional competence. All psychotherapists on the UKCP Register must adhere to the relevant *Code of Practice* for their own member organisation, which in turn is based on the *Code of Ethics* (UKCP, 1995).

Complaints are initially heard by the member organisation. Appeals, unresolved issues, or instances where it is not appropriate for the Section of UKCP to hear the complaint can be referred to the Governing Board of the UKCP. In terms of sanctions, psychotherapists suspended or expelled from a member organisation are automatically deleted from the UKCP Register. Psychotherapists are required to inform their member organisation if a complaint is successfully heard against them in another member organisation, or if they are convicted of a notifiable criminal offence, or if they are the subject of successful civil action against them concerning their work as a psychotherapist. Lapsed membership is not a bar to being the subject of a complaint, providing that the alleged offence took place during the period of their membership. Complaints procedures for the federal sections of the UKCP are in the process of finalisation.

For the British Confederation of Psychotherapists, another major umbrella organisation of psychotherapists, complaints need to be addressed to the constituent organisations, such as the British Association of Psychotherapists, or the British Psycho-Analytical Society. Finally, the Independent Practitioners' Network operates an unusual system of peer review, where groups of therapists are responsible for each others' practice. A complaint against a single practitioner is treated as a complaint against the collective group to which that therapist belongs, and needs to be collectively resolved.

Complaints against psychologists

The British Psychological Society (BPS), holding Chartered status by order of the Privy Council, has a two-stage investigatory model for complaints, based on breaches of its *Code of Conduct* for Psychologists (BPS, 1995b). Complaints by any party are first looked at by an Investigatory Committee, to establish whether there has been a prima facie or obvious breach of the Code. Should this be the case, the complaint is then formally heard by the Disciplinary Committee, with legal representation available to the parties concerned. An individual found guilty of professional misconduct may be reprimanded; required to give an undertaking to refrain from the offending conduct; suspended for up to two years; expelled and/or removed from the Register of Chartered Psychologists.

One example of a potential complaint was in the case of the person cleared of the murder of Rachel Nickell on Wimbledon Common in 1994. The suspect's lawyer subsequently sought to bring a complaint against the psychologist involved in the case. The psychologist had worked closely with the police in devising an undercover operation to elicit details of the individual's violent fantasies about women which appeared to correspond closely to the known circumstances of the murder (*Guardian*, 24 September 1994).

Other complaints about psychologists received by one of the main professional indemnity insurance companies have included the following (Dobson, 1995):

- a claim by one company that the advice of an occupational psychologist in hiring a top executive had turned out to be faulty
- allegations of sexual impropriety, including one by a boy, where the case was thrown out after the psychologist in question was found to be impotent
- a complaint by parents against a psychologist that false memories of abuse had been fostered in their daughter.

Subjects of complaints

Problems concerning *contracts* figure largely amongst complaints issues. As a result of the experience of handling complaints, Fiona Palmer-Barnes has argued the case for a better and clearer understanding of the use of contracts by counsellors (Palmer-Barnes, 1995: 36, 38–9). A range of model contracts have been suggested for use by therapists (Kitching, 1995a; Syme, 1994). Any valid contract will be deemed to include protection for consumer rights under the Supply of Goods and Services Act 1982, even where these are not directly specified (McAllister, 1995). Mowbray has suggested a need for the contract, and the therapeutic relationship which it proposes, to be based on the principle of full disclosure by the therapist, and of wide access to information by the client, without which informed consumer choice becomes impossible (1995: 204). At minimum, contracts can spell out the respective expectations of client and therapist, and reduce the likelihood of later complaint (MIND, 1995; Palmer and Szymanska, 1994). (For a fuller discussion of contracts, see Chapter 2.)

One of the other problematic areas subject to complaints is that of training. Again, Fiona Palmer-Barnes has referred to complaints by students that goal-posts have been moved by courses while the course is still in progress, for example regarding assessment requirements. There are issues of the expense and time invested by students in their training, which raise corresponding expectations about the quality of the training that they are entitled to receive (1995: 36). Within organisations which offer training, complaints procedures regarding academic assessment, professional assessment and the overall quality of training and facilities available need to be clearly distinguished, and communicated to students. Solicitors have suggested that contracts and clear course documentation may be useful for staff and courses facing complaints, in order to clarify what are often complex and confusing issues to resolve (Jakobi, 1995; Murray, 1995). For example, students may complain that the status of the counselling qualification has been changed from Certificate to Diploma for internal academic reasons, while the course was still in progress. The cause for complaint here could be that not all students would have the option of achieving the Diploma, which would depend upon having a first degree or professional quali-fication. Some changes or modifications to a programme are unavoidable, but major changes may appear to students to over-look or ignore their interests. The rights of students on courses in Higher and Further Education are now emphasised by colleges and universities under various students' charters (DfEE, 1993a, 1993b), giving further need for course organisers to carefully consider the rights of students and provide clear, effective com-plaints and appeals procedures.

Third party complaints

As referred to above, complaints may not necessarily be made solely by clients or ex-clients, but by third parties affected by the therapy, as in the case of alleged false memory cases (Jenkins, in press). In the medical field, most complaints against psychiatrists, for example, are made by relatives and advocates rather than by the patients themselves (Ingram and Roy, 1995: 621). Another third party situation may arise where a male partner is attending anger management therapy, but where his partner continues to feel at risk. The male client is apparently compliant within the therapy, but still acts in a physically aggressive manner towards his partner or children, a situation frequently reported by London Women's Aid (*Guardian*, 3 April 1995).

Complaints procedures vary considerably in terms of whether they will hear third party complaints, with the problem of confidentiality frequently being cited as a major reason for not considering them. An individual who considers making a third party complaint will need to check carefully that this is covered by the therapist's relevant professional *Code of Practice*. The following example describes a true case, but with the identities of all participating individuals and organisations disguised to preserve confidentiality.

Case Study: Complaint by client's partner against a counselling agency

This was a third party complaint brought against a well-established counselling agency by the partner of a client who was receiving therapy. The complaint was that the client receiving therapy continued to harass the partner, and that the counselling agency took no effective steps to prevent this from happening. 'During this time my daughter and I were subjected by [the client] to verbal, emotional, physical and physically threatening abuse, due specifically to the counselling process that he was undergoing.' After initial enquiries, the relevant professional association made a decision not to formally pursue the complaint through their Complaints Committee. Following an approach to the president of the organisation, the complaint was re-opened and heard, with adjudication by an independent therapist, which outlined the issues at stake, and the respective positions of complainant, client and agency. The case was then formally heard by the Complaints Committee, which found that none of the alleged breaches of the relevant Code of Ethics *were held to be substantiated.*

The case illustrates the limited potential of complaints systems to consider the interests of third parties who are not directly involved in the counselling process. The client himself was not directly involved or represented in the complaint procedure, but his interests were considered in so far as access to the confidential records of his therapy were denied to the complainant on the grounds of confidentiality. The agency concerned which had provided the therapy was able to represent its view, as its methods of working and of supervision were directly criticised in the complaint. Finally, the interest of the professional organisation with a responsibility to monitor and uphold the reputation of counselling members and agencies was exercised through the complaints process, via its willingness to reconsider an initial decision not to hear the original complaint.

The decision of the Complaints Committee was that specific breaches of the *Code of Ethics* concerning inadequate supervision, and the therapist's failure to break confidentiality in order to prevent harm to others, were not substantiated. It was extremely difficult to *prove* that the therapy received by the client necessarily contributed to or prolonged the abuse experienced by his partner and child, although this was clearly the complainant's perception. She queried whether the professional association and the agency believed that 'high levels of abuse to third parties are an inevitable but regrettable part of the counselling process'. Given the element of doubt, it appears that the professional association was unwilling to establish a wider principle of counsellor liability, in the absence of major and proven breaches of the *Code of Ethics*. Again, the *Tarasoff* case in the USA is relevant here, in underlining the absence of any specific statutory duty in current UK law for counsellors to warn or protect third parties threatened in the counselling process, with the specific exception of terrorist offences. It is also clear from the operation of the complaints procedure that confidentiality of counselling records will be preserved as a general rule, even when they are requested by a complainant as evidence in their case, should the client or agency refuse access to them, as happened here. In a court case, such protection for confidential records would not be absolute. Indeed, it may have been to the complainant's advantage to bring a civil case rather than a complaint. Under the process of 'discovery' in civil proceedings, she may then have had access to the confidential records she felt she needed to prove her case.

Given the outcome, the complaints process was perceived in this instance by the complainant as a professional association, therapist and counselling agency, all protecting their own interests, with the complainant being put at a major disadvantage in trying to prove her case. At the adjudication stage, an investigating therapist seemed to have discovered common ground for a satisfactory resolution, including an apology by the agency to the complainant, but this did not materialise for reasons that are not clear.

A crucial point that needs to be made concerns the *emotional* cost of entering into a complaints process, for all parties involved. Certainly, from the point of view of the complainant, this was a very emotionally testing and unsatisfactory experience, with a strong sense of injustice and grievance which still remains. Regarding the agency in question, the complainant wrote that it 'has caused me immense pain, grief, suffering and distress over a three-year period. They still continue to cause me distress by their appalling insensitivity to my feelings.' She felt that it was primarily the threat of taking the case to her MP and to the Secretary of State for Health which prompted the re-opening of the complaint, but that this could not overcome the bias of the system towards protecting organisational interests at the expense of the individual making the complaint. She describes it, finally, as 'a drama of farce and tragedy. The experience has left an indelible impression on my memory. I wish I could wake up and discover that this nightmare was in fact not real. The horror is that this is a true story.'

Complaints about abuse within therapy

One potential source of complaints about therapists is from fellow professionals. However, the apparent reluctance of therapists to report their colleagues has been noted in recent research (Jehu et al., 1994: 40). This may relate to the problematic issue of therapist abuse, including sexual contact between therapist and client, which has recently become a cause of concern within the therapeutic community (Gartrell, 1994; Masson, 1992; Rutter, 1991). One piece of research suggests that therapist attitudes which permit therapist–client sexual contact are the best predictor of such contact actually occurring; however, it is not clear whether the attitudes *promote* the occurrence of sexual contact, or simply serve to *rationalise* it after it has happened (Thoreson et al., 1993). Advising practitioners who have encountered counsellor malpractice involving sex with clients, Tim Bond has argued strongly that 'the priority of your concerns should be the client, professional issues and the counsellor in that order' (Bond, 1993c: 111).

Some forms of therapist–client sexual contact may be clearly illegal under the Sexual Offences Act 1956, for example, in the case of counselling children and young people in schools. In one reported case, the 28-year-old head of religious education in a secondary school was jailed for a year for having sex with a 15-year-old girl who came for counselling sessions with him (*Guardian*, 9 April 1994). A male having sex with a girl aged under 13 years commits an *absolute* offence, for which there is no defence. If the girl is aged over 13 and under 16, there are several possible defences. These include believing himself to be married to the girl, with reasonable cause; believing the girl to be aged 16 or over; or if he is aged under 24 years, and has not been charged previously with a similar offence (Gunn, 1991: 22). Other legislation also provides protection for vulnerable clients. Section 128 of the earlier Mental Health Act 1959 proscribes sex by male staff with female patients, whether in- or out-patients. This section has not been repealed, unlike most parts of the 1959 Act, which have been incorporated into the 1983 Act. This would apply in cases such as those describing sexual abuse of patients by community psychiatric nurses in the *Public Eye* TV documentary, and in the MIND Report on abuse occurring within therapy (BBC, 1992; Wood, 1993). Sexual contact between therapists and adults with learning difficulties is similarly proscribed by law (Gunn, 1991). Whereas the law often only refers to male staff, legal action may also be taken against female staff for ill-treatment of vulnerable patients or clients. As a more general point, apart from this specific legisation, Jehu et al. have indicated that a male therapist who persuades a female client that sex is a part of the therapy being provided may be guilty of rape, given that her consent to sexual intercourse has been fraudulently obtained (1994: 182).

Sexual contact with current clients not covered by these legal categories is nevertheless widely proscribed by professional codes of ethics for therapists. However, the question of defining the status of 'client' is not straightforward. The BAC adopted a rule in 1992 prohibiting sexual contact with former clients for a 12-week period after the termination of therapy (BAC, 1992a; Bond, 1993b: 103–7). This interim measure was replaced in 1993 by a section in the *Code* stressing the counsellor's personal and professional accountability regarding all forms of relationship with former clients, whether they were social, sexual or business ones (BAC, 1993a).

For some practitioners, restrictions on socialising with clients seem unnecessarily prescriptive, when the actual therapeutic contact may be concerned with resolving specific behavioural problems, such as smoking, through the use of hypnosis over a short time period. A therapist working from a person-centred perspective might also challenge the assumption of inevitable development of transference within the therapeutic relationship, and the denial of client and therapist autonomy contained within blanket prohibitions on future client–therapist social or sexual contact (Wilkins, 1994).

Some therapists, such as Lazarus, would disagree with the view that socialising with clients is necessarily unethical or counter-productive in therapeutic terms (Dryden, 1991: 62). However, there is a clear potential for role conflicts to emerge in situations where a therapist takes on additional responsibilities on behalf of the client. An extreme case, drawn from the USA, is that of a therapist using his own high-dependency '24-hour therapy' with Brian Wilson of the Beach Boys. Advocating 'complete patient dependency on the therapist and total control of the patient's life', the therapist came to be listed as co-writer of lyrics, co-producer of music, a business partner, and chief beneficiary of Brian Wilson's will, all in addition to acting as his personal therapist. Charges of professional negligence in maintaining multiple relationships with his client led to the withdrawal of the therapist's state licence to practise in 1992 (White, 1996: 307).

Defining therapist sexual abuse of clients

Therapist abuse has been defined as 'behaviour or experience where one person in a position of power over another, abuses this position without the informed consent of the other party, for their own sexual gratification' (Russell, 1993: 2). This definition is based on qualitative research with 40 former clients who claimed to have experienced therapist abuse. While this approach emphasises the sexual aspect of exploitation, rather than other elements such as financial exploitation, or the promotion of long-term emotional dependency on the therapist, it recognises the major problem of actually defining what is meant by the term 'sexual'. Hence 'proscriptions to sexual relationships within ethical codes are limited by their inability to clarify what is sexual' (1993: 59). For example, one piece of unorthodox therapy was described by its practitioner, a well-respected person-centred therapist, as culminating in a nude embrace with his female client. He later emphatically denied that this constituted sexual activity as such, given the spiritual underpinning and rationale for its adoption (see debate about 'Sally' in Thorne, 1987; Thorne, 1993: 113–17). This unusual practice preceded the revision to the BAC *Code of Ethics and Practice* of 1984 which proscribed sexual activity between counsellors and clients. For some practitioners Thorne's discussion leaves unresolved the safe and ethical limits to the therapeutic uses of touch, massage or close physical contact with clients.

The apparent dangers of being sued for libel when making allegations against a former therapist may be an inhibiting factor for a client considering making a complaint about abuse. One client said 'I knew he would deny it all and that I would have to be able to prove it in court' (Russell, 1993: 26). Conversely, for therapists reporting a colleague's alleged malpractice, it should be possible to claim qualified privilege as a defence against an action for libel or slander, in reporting them without malice to a responsible body (see Chapter 2).

Russell's research into therapist abuse carries with it clear implications for developing fair and effective complaints procedures for clients to make their voice heard by professionals.

> . . . it seems crucial and logical that there should be some system of arbitration within ethical committees. However well-intentioned particular individuals or groups are, while organisations are purely self-disciplinary they will carry their blind spots. My preference would be that clients who complain are allowed someone of their choosing to be with them to offer support where necessary, and that at least one independent arbitrator be involved in any complaint procedure. I have no doubt that this would provoke conflicting responses and that there might be difficulties mechanically, but this issue needs serious attention. What needs to be looked at is the mechanisms for making the process meaningful and fair for the client. (1993: 149)

These views have a particular relevance to the following case of a client whose experience of therapy, and of her general treatment by therapists, proved to be highly unsatisfactory in several respects.

Case Study: Experiencing abuse within therapy

This client received counselling over a period of nine months for anxiety and relationship difficulties with men, from an eminent male therapist in private practice. The counselling she received involved degrees of physical familiarity, such as a kiss on the cheek, and massage, that she found uncomfortable. In addition, there was also an element of role reversal, with the therapist often talking about his own issues, which was confusing to her. However, despite her misgivings, she accepted both aspects as part of the therapy, principally because she valued the relationship for the real support that it provided for her. At one point, she contacted a consultant psychiatrist to discuss aspects of the therapy about which she felt concerned. The consultant appeared to dismiss her anxieties as a manifestation of her underlying problems in relationships and of her general status as a 'very needy person'. No action was taken against the original therapist, after his having been identified to the consultant, and he continued to practise.

The client did not perceive her experiences as being abusive until seven years later when watching a documentary on this issue, when she had a powerful emotional response to hearing others recount stories similar to her own.

From the point of view of consumer rights, the protection offered to this client was minimal, both within the original therapeutic relationship, and from the consultant she approached for a second opinion on what was happening in therapy. In fact, it seems more that the second therapist was protecting the first by failing to report the allegations made, and by seeking to pathologise the complainant's behaviour. Principally, the client's protection derives from the therapist's claimed commitment to ethical and non-exploitative behaviour, from peer supervision, *and* from their own support via client self-help groups, such as those for abuse survivors. It is difficult for the client to protect their own interests when, despite their concerns, they perceive the therapeutic relationship as being mainly professional and helpful, and the therapist as being a benign and empathic person.

Sexual activity between therapist and client is widely seen as exploitative and unethical. (See, for example, the *Code of Practice* for the British Association for Sexual and Marital Therapy, 1991.) However, defining sexual contact may itself be problematic, when there may be no overt physical contact between counsellor and client, but when the client is still left with an enduring sense of unease, and that personal, emotional boundaries have been violated for the satisfaction of the counsellor (Russell, 1993: 7).

Problems for clients in seeking redress

A major factor in the reporting of therapist abuse is the client's *perception* of the experience as being exploitative or damaging. Initially, it may not be experienced as abusive, until placed in a different context. In this situation, the client did not fully perceive the behaviour as abusive until some seven years afterwards. Even then, there can be no automatic presumption that the client wishes to make a complaint or seek legal redress. Certain complaints procedures, such as the BAC's, have a three-year time limit for bringing complaints, which would have precluded the client's taking action in this case, assuming that she was aware which professional association, if any, he belonged to. In addition, fear of a libel action brought by the therapist may also have been an inhibiting factor for the client (Russell, 1993: 26).

The client may seek to sue the counsellor for malpractice, with the problem of substantiating a case in court without, in many cases, a great deal of supporting evidence. The anticipated cost of legal action may be a deterrent, unless the complainant qualifies for Legal Aid. (The problems in bringing a successful legal case are discussed more fully in Chapter 3.)

In the view of one self-help organisation for clients who have experienced therapist abuse, the Prevention of Professional Abuse Network (POPAN), the remedy sought by the client may simply be at the level of receiving *recognition* of their complaint. Thus all that was required was 'if somebody had had their story heard and been listened to and some sort of mediation had taken place that meant something to that person, which is very often an apology and not necessarily always a great deal more' (Fasal, 1994).

In the previous case study, the client's perception about the therapy received had changed markedly over time. Her view now was that it had clearly been an unequal relationship in terms of power and emotional gratification. 'I felt in the end that his needs were being met by the counselling situation.' However, the complexity and intensity of her feelings about the relationship with her therapist made this a very difficult issue to explore or resolve, rather than one where she immediately wanted to make a complaint.

I couldn't do that because I wasn't sure of what to do, and because of my feelings of guilt. I felt very much like a criminal. I felt very much that if I opened this, I'd come out a loser, that was the way it had been in the relationship with my husband. Anyway, I felt the risk was too great. But also, I didn't think I knew what to do anyway . . . no hate, no anger. I couldn't do it to hurt him.

Her feelings of powerlessness were compounded by the unfavourable response she got from the consultant she then went to see. 'So what I felt I received from Dr Y. was abuse on top of abuse. Maybe it wasn't. Maybe that was my interpretation because I was feeling . . . but I am still feeling very angry.'

Power issues in the making of complaints

The above example highlights some of the power issues implicit in the therapeutic relationship, which may act to inhibit the client from making a complaint. This is specifically mentioned as one of a range of barriers to consumers making complaints, as identified by the National Consumer Council in its evidence to the Wilson Committee (DoH, 1994: 21):

- gratitude
- powerlessness
- medical language
- the erosion of a sense of entitlement
- lack of information on procedures, standards, and outcomes

The report also acknowledges the particular problems faced by complainants who cannot write or cannot speak English. Powerlessness is acknowledged as a crucial factor by Tim Bond, referring to 'the relative powerlessness of the individual making the complaint to an organisation of people sharing similar background and interests' (1994b: 23). This is borne out by the example of a Burnley psychiatrist jailed in 1994 for indecent assaults on patients under the guise of 'therapy' (NHS NW, 1994). The assaults were made over a period of 20 years on the young male drug addicts under his care, providing a graphic and disturbing illustration of the forces at work within abusive therapy. When asked why he hadn't raised his concerns as a client with the authorities, one drug user vehemently replied to the radio interviewer:

> I *did* complain. I *did* complain. I complained to my own doctor, I complained to nurses. I will be campaigning very, very vigorously to try and find out exactly why our complaints were never ever taken. Looking back, I needed help. I would have taken help from anybody. (Radio Lancashire, 1994).

The seriousness of the complaint may be associated with the status of the complainant. It follows that the most stigmatised and least powerful clients may find it hard to get their voices heard by the very systems which are meant to protect their interests.

Barriers to clients making complaints against therapists

Another part of the problem may lie in tracing the primary accountability and responsibility for the therapist's practice, and achieving redress. One dissatisfied client wrote:

> In my own case, although the Health Authority and other professional bodies agreed that the behaviour of 'my' ex-psychiatrist/therapist was unethical, not the GMC, the UKCP, the SIP, the Guild of Therapists, the Ethical Committee of the College of Psychiatrists nor the BMA did anything – apart from sympathise and change procedures in some instances. The offender was not disciplined. Many others have suffered terrible abuse with no redress whatsoever, and will continue to do so while the professional organisations 'police' themselves. (*Guardian*, 26 March 1994)

The therapist involved may have multiple affiliations and membership of a number of relevant professional associations or employing bodies. It may be hard, therefore, for the client to determine which is the key one to hold official responsibility for monitoring their behaviour (see Box 8.1, below).

Elements of a model complaints system

Devising and operating a model complaints system for clients is not simply a question of producing impressive guidelines and procedures. Questions of clients' perceptions of professional defensiveness and a persistent power imbalance may undermine the credibility of the best-intentioned systems for redress. Some of the key elements to be considered by those running complaints systems include issues of advocacy, lay representation, the role of natural justice and overall responsiveness to clients' needs.

Box 8.1

Useful questions for a client considering making a complaint against a therapist

- does the therapist work for an organisation or work privately?
- what is the nature of the post and of the professional qualification held by the therapist?
- is the therapist fully qualified or in training?
- which professional associations does the therapist belong to?
- which code of ethics and practice is the therapist required to follow?
- which specific breaches of the code(s) are relevant?
- is the therapist receiving supervision?
- should a complaint be directed to the employer (if applicable) or to the therapist's professional body?

Advocacy and lay representation
A discussion of the relative powerlessness of some clients points up the need for support from professional bodies to be available to them when making a complaint about their treatment. This view is confirmed by a growing range of organisations. MIND, the National Association for Mental Health, stresses the need for advocacy and user-involvement in complaints systems (Wood, 1993: 26). The Wilson Report on the NHS has also pointed to the potential role for advocacy in supporting complainants, and for the provision of independent professional advice in the case of clinical complaints (DoH, 1994: 44, 61). The proposals for a new legal complaints body made by the National Consumer Council further suggest that the Ombudsman's role would be to 'act for' complainants in a supportive capacity (Hansen, 1994: 108). Having access to established systems of skilled and experienced advocates would help to support clients who felt disadvantaged in bringing a complaint against an official and seemingly powerful organisation or individual. Advocacy groups who may be approached could include mental health survivor organisations, such as UKAN and 'Survivors Speak Out', POPAN and consumer rights organisations. In the case of children and young people, organisations such as ASC and IRCHIN specialise in advocacy and representation for this group (see Resources section for addresses).

Developing advocacy and support networks for complainants is also linked with the issue of increasing the amount of lay representation on complaints committees, to ensure an element of public accountability, to introduce a wider non-professional perspective on complaints, and to avoid charges that professionals are merely going through the motions of keeping their own house in order. An element of lay representation on disciplinary committees is provided for in the regulations of the British Psychological Society, for instance (1995b). The Sieghart Report on psychotherapy similarly recommended a substantial lay membership of the Council overseeing statutory registration (Sieghart, 1978: ix).

The introduction of an outside viewpoint may appear unnecessary or even threatening to the professionals concerned, who may feel that a lay person will not appreciate the issues at stake in the same way as an 'insider' would. However, the opposite may also be true, in that a lay person can bring a fresh perspective, or an awareness of the wider implications for consumer protection that a professional body may miss. Jenny Fasal of POPAN refers to one complaint, which, in the client's view, was very successfully handled in terms of the process and outcome.

> The complaints panel brought in somebody from the Citizens' Advice Bureau, and the local council offices, and the director of the particular services involved, and someone from the Consumers' Association. All these people sat down together with the other people involved in the complaint. The complainant felt that it was because those sensible outsiders were there that the complaint was dealt with in the way that she wanted. (Fasal, 1994)

However, there remain the admitted dangers of lay persons not fully appreciating the complex professional issues involved, or alternatively, of being subtly co-opted by the professionals to the point where they lose their 'external' perspective. Informal mediation may also be a valuable element of the process of resolving a complaint, according to the experience of POPAN: 'if things could be sorted out between the therapist and their client informally and early on, where this is the case most people it seems would prefer to do that, rather than embark much later on, on these horrendous complaints procedures'. Furthermore, 'what we hear people asking for nearly always seems entirely reasonable and usually rather moderate. If things had been dealt with in the way that made sense and met them adequately enough people would not have felt impelled to push and push in their search for redress to the point of the last and final option, the complaints procedure'

(Fasal, 1994). This emphasis on mediation or alternative dispute resolution is a key feature of current reforms of the civil justice system (Woolf, 1995).

Natural justice

Complaints procedures are needed to protect consumers, but also to investigate issues in a spirit of fairness to all concerned, including, not least, the therapist or the organisation against whom a complaint is brought. The principles of natural justice require that:

- the accused person should be informed of the complaint, and be permitted to respond in person
- that no person with a direct involvement in the offence should sit in judgement on the case
- that the alleged offender and the person bringing the complaint should both be able to have their say
- that all parties should have access to material relevant to the case, such as policy documents and records.

(Jakobi, 1995)

Complaints sytems which ignore such fundamental principles of natural justice are liable to legal challenge in the courts. Solicitors have argued for a greater 'legalisation' of complaints procedures, in order to ensure fairness prevails. The counter-argument is that greater involvement of solicitors does not necessarily produce more effective dispensing of justice, and may undermine the very informality of proceedings which are complex and delicate in their nature. There is a difficult balance to be struck here between preserving a degree of informality which may make client access and resolution of disputes easier to achieve, while retaining sufficient formality of procedure to protect the rights of all concerned to a fair hearing.

Responsiveness of complaints systems

According to the Wilson Report on complaints systems in the NHS, much of the current initiative for improved and more responsive complaints procedures has come from the private sector, where complaints may be seen less as a cause for alarm,

> **Box 8.2**
>
> **Recommended principles of complaints procedure**
>
> - responsiveness
> - cost effectiveness
> - impartiality
> - speed
> - accountability
> - quality enhancement
> - accessibility
> - simplicity
> - confidentiality
>
> (Source: Wilson Report (DoH, 1994: 37))

than as a useful source of feedback from consumers. For a commercial organisation, the importance of customer retention as a major aim in complaint handling is often stressed. This may be less significant for an individual therapist or for an organisation providing therapy, but the overall need to retain the client's goodwill no doubt remains valid. The basic principles suggested include (DoH, 1994: 30):

- offering an apology, without necessarily accepting responsibility in law for the cause of the complaint
- making a speedy acknowledgement and response to a complaint
- offering the client reassurance that the matter is being taken seriously, to avoid it happening again

The main recommendations of the Wilson Committee (see Box 8.2) were substantially accepted and implemented by the Government. As one direct result, GPs are required to establish practice-based complaints procedures, with immediate implications for therapists based in general practice (*General Practice*, 24 March 1995). All GP practices and NHS Trusts will have their own complaints procedures in place from April 1996, with a designated complaints manager. In GP practices, the complaints procedures are to be practice-based and practice-owned, with publicity to make patients aware of their rights. The system of time limits adopted under the scheme requires that complaints be acknowledged within two working days, and receive an explanation within ten working days. For the patient or client's part, complaints need to be made within six months of the date of the incident, or within six months of discovering the cause of the complaint, provided that it is still within a year of the original incident. The basic principles of the complaints procedure are that the system should be:

- simple and responsive
- accessible and well-publicised
- confidential
- understood by all practice staff, so they can advise patients on how to use it

The complaints procedure is distinct from disciplinary measures affecting staff. It provides a ladder of complaint responses, beginning with the practice complaints procedure, and, if necessary, progressing up through a process of Independent Review, to consideration by the Health Service Ombudsman, and ultimately, in exceptional cases, to the European Court of Human Rights (NHS Executive, 1996). Counsellors and therapists working in GP practice or within NHS Trusts will be directly affected by these measures, as a system of complaints directed at *employers*, rather than at the relevant professional association.

The original Wilson Report's findings have a number of implications for designing complaints procedures for therapists and their organisations. For instance, the overall picture presented by the report was one of a plethora of complaints procedures across the National Health Service, relating to different institutions, issues or professional groups, which made little sense to consumers. There was a pressing need for one common complaints procedure across different aspects of the service.

On the question of time limits, the report had recommended that complaints receive a speedy acknowledgement, but 'provided the complainant is informed of the practical difficulties involved, there seems no reason in principle why time limits are necessary' for the making of a complaint (DoH, 1994: 46). Removing time limits for complaints about therapists would, at the very least, have direct implications for retaining records, but would enable clients to pursue claims which are currently ineligible, as in the case described above.

Future developments for therapists' complaints systems
There may be some other points to be drawn from the Wilson Report, without losing sight of the fact that therapists and agencies

providing therapy do not necessarily possess the scale, complexity or, it must be said, a fraction of the resources of the National Health Service. Overall, the report stressed the advantage of complaints procedures over litigation in most cases, 'in terms of ease of access, informality, speed and costs' (DoH, 1994: 14). In terms of access, the principle of a unified complaints procedure across different therapeutic specialisms is one worth considering, according to the former Chair of the BAC, Tim Bond. Thus it 'may be advantageous for several organisations to co-operate in sponsoring an independent complaints procedure or ombudsman. This is likely to have greater credibility than any in-house complaints procedure as well as develop the expertise for this difficult area of work' (Bond, 1994b: 23).

Some useful lessons could also be learned from the chequered experience of the Law Society in operating its own complaints systems. Any complaints procedure, whether unified or not, needs to be widely publicised and available to clients, in spelling out their rights, and the steps needed to be taken to voice a complaint. This is not always the case, even when specifically required. One Law Society survey found that 80% of clients were not told about complaints procedures, despite this being compulsory under Practice Rule 15, which came into effect in 1991 (Dyer, 1995; Hansen, 1994: 42).

Marlene Winfield of the National Consumer Council has made a further point with wider implications, regarding the close relationship between the then Solicitors' Complaints Bureau, and the actual professional body it was meant to monitor, the Law Society. The task has been made that much more difficult for the Law Society, she argues, 'given its dual role as regulator and solicitors' trade union' (Dyer, 1995). Paralleling this, there is perhaps a need to separate out the different functions of counselling and psychotherapy organisations much more clearly. According to POPAN, within the therapeutic community 'there is a confusion of role between a professional interest body and a body which is there to set standards, in the sense that there's a distinction between the Royal College of Nursing and the UKCC' (Fasal, 1994). However, for counselling and therapy associations to reach the stage of distinguishing between their activities as a lobby for promoting professional interests, such as the British Medical Association, and their role in safeguarding recognised standards of practice, on the lines of the General Medical Council, it is likely that full statutory

Box 8.2

Guidelines for professional practice regarding complaints

Preparation
- ensure clients or students have adequate information about
  - the nature of the counselling, therapeutic or training service provided
  - codes of ethics and practice which are relevant
  - complaints systems, both informal and formal
- review arrangements for getting feedback on the service, whether practice or training, from clients and students, as a source of information
- pick out potential or actual problem areas, and respond to these promptly
- review and update documentation such as handbooks for students on courses

Responding to a potential complaint
- acknowledge the legitimacy of the complaint and of the feelings involved wherever possible
- avoid defensive reactions to criticism and complaint
- react speedily to set up informal channels to explore problems and negotiate solutions
- seek expert advice from professional organisations at an early stage
- identify personal support systems: undergoing a complaint can be personally challenging and draining
- record all significant contact with clients or students where a pattern of conflict, misunderstanding or complaint emerges, including phone contact, copies of letters, minutes of meetings

Responding to an actual complaint
- identify areas of practice or organisation needing change as a result of a complaint; put these into effect sooner rather than later
- de-personalise the complaint: try to separate out aspects which are about practice, the service provided or the organisation from any personal feelings of being attacked
- distinguish carefully between an expression of concern and any admission of liability, which may weaken a future defence in court
- for key meetings, encourage the client or student to bring a supporter; also bring an independent person to chair or minute the meeting
- record and promptly document agreed outcomes; send a letter immediately to those attending recording any decisions made
- identify potential conflicts of interest between yourself, the client and the organisation, if relevant; consider your own separate need for independent legal representation or advice

recognition as a profession will be required. This topic will be explored in the following final chapter.

Summary

Complaints systems may reflect a process of empowerment for clients, and the growth of a culture of consumer rights in the service and training sectors. Complaints to professional associations about therapists may be one option for dissatisfied clients, compared with the uncertainty and expense involved in taking legal proceedings. Complaints systems for therapists vary according to the nature of the professional association concerned, with a range of criteria and procedures which apply. Complaints may be concerned with the effect of therapy on third parties, such as the client's partner, about abusive therapy or simply about mismatched expectations of the type of therapy involved. Clients may require the support of an advocate. Complaints systems should be designed to follow the principles of natural justice, and, where appropriate, involve lay members of the public to provide an external perspective on complex professional issues. As with the review of complaints systems in the NHS, there may be value in developing a complaints system which operates *across* the currently divided membership of different therapeutic traditions and associations.

Discussion points

1 Would you ever consider making a formal complaint about any aspect of counselling or therapy that you have received as a client? What factors would influence your decision on whether or not to proceed with such a complaint?

2 What explains the apparent reluctance of therapists to report malpractice by their colleagues? Should the responsibility for making complaints be left to dissatisfied clients, or be taken on equally by practitioners?

3 Should complaints by third parties be allowed under complaints procedures? What benefits and drawbacks for therapeutic practice would result?

4 How might an advocacy system for clients operate, when making complaints about therapy, or seeking redress? Should this be a role for therapists or for non-therapists to take on?

5 Discuss the ethical and legal issues raised by either of the two case studies in this chapter. What changes in current complaints procedures might have contributed to a more positive outcome in either case?

9

Statutory Regulation of Therapists

It transpires that . . . has just begun advertising her services as a psychotherapist. Asked about her qualifications, she replies, her neck shaking: 'I've experienced *everything*. I've been institutionalised in an African mental institution. I saw a man having his ear bitten off. I managed to get out. I came from a family of nine people. It was like being born an alien. I couldn't relate to any of them. I thought it was my fault. It is experience, everything in life. I could advise on every subject. I don't need to take a degree on it.' (Mitchison, 1992)

The major remaining area where therapy and the law interact is in terms of professional status. The drive for statutory recognition of psychotherapy and counselling is underway, a declared part of the therapeutic community's agenda for the next decade. The process is often presented as a series of measures or steps that organised groups of therapists need to take in order both to obtain full recognition for their work, and to protect the public against untrained or incompetent practitioners. This approach is heavily influenced by what is described as the 'trait' model of professionalisation, namely that professional groups are distinguished by possession of key characteristics or traits (Baron, 1996). The acquisition of the full range of traits signals that the process of professionalisation is complete. According to Johnson (1972: 23), professional status according to the trait model includes most of the following characteristics:

- skill based on theoretical knowledge
- provision of training and education
- testing the competence of members
- organisation of members

- adherence to a professional code of conduct
- altruistic service
- complaints and disciplinary procedures
- statutory recognition

This chapter describes the main aspects of **statutory regulation of therapists** in the USA and UK, and notes **developments towards regulation**. The **Foster** and **Seighart Reports** were significant milestones along this path, as has been the adoption of measures of voluntary registration. The European dimension to statutory regulation is explored, together with the growing critique of moves towards statutory regulation of therapy.

Statutory regulation of therapists

Statutory recognition would entail the use of legal sanctions concerning the authorised use of a specific *title*, or possessing the right to *practise*. Disciplinary measures could entail the removal of the individual's right to use the title or to practice the profession, as in the case of doctors disciplined by the General Medical Council.

Statutory regulation in the USA

The experience of counsellor licensure in the USA is often seen as a guide or example to follow (Bloom et al., 1990; Lee and Six, 1992). There are the usual distinctions between different levels of therapist practitioners, each of which may be regulated via different codes or legal machinery. Counselling is regulated by more than half of all states (Alberding et al., 1993). The latter identified five potentially negative and five potentially positive consequences of regulation.

Table 9.1 lists many of the arguments for and against statutory regulation currently rehearsed with regard to therapy in the UK. In the USA, regulation at state level entails the right for counsellors of *privileged communication*, which is not applicable to therapists in the UK. Under this privilege, counsellors in the USA are not required to disclose information to the courts, or to act as a witness concerning a client. There is an added importance for US counsellors in achieving legal regulation, in that this status can provide access to funding by insurance companies for therapy or mental

Table 9.1 *Potential positive and negative consequences of counsellor regulation in the USA*

Positive consequences	Negative consequences
• Protects public from incompetent practitioners	• Discriminates against some competent practitioners
• Profession increases power and prestige	• Public may lose some power and control
• Counsellors more likely to receive third party insurance payments for providing service	• Cost of service to consumers may rise
• Right of privileged communication acquired by law	• Regulation may lead to a stagnating profession
• Protects right of counsellors to practise from encroachment by potential competitors in mental health field	• Regulation lulls consumers into unwary and vulnerable state

Source: Alberding et al., 1993: 35

health care as a reliable source of income. This is an issue of major concern to counsellors in the USA, where public provision of therapy or mental health care is limited compared with the UK.

Statutory regulation in the UK

Attempts to achieve statutory regulation of therapy in the UK have been underway for some years. In the field of complementary medicine, statutory regulation of osteopaths and chiropractors was achieved via Private Member's Bills in 1993. In 1981, a Private Member's Bill to regulate psychotherapy was proposed by Graham Bright MP, but it was talked out at its second reading in the House of Commons (Syme, 1994: 114). Short of introducing fresh legislation, the most likely route for statutory recognition of psychotherapy would be via the use of the Professions Supplementary to Medicine Act 1960 (see Box 9.1). In response to a parliamentary question by Lord Stallard, Baroness Cumberledge has indicated that this legislative framework is currently under review (*Hansard*, 1995). The focus of this review is to identify problems in protecting the use of titles covered by the Act, and to update a form of regulatory framework that is felt to be increasingly unmanageable. For example, striking a practitioner off the relevant Register requires evidence of 'infamous conduct'. There is also inadequate provision for requiring professional

---

Box 9.1

Professions Supplementary to Medicine Act 1960

s.1   The Act set up a Council to supervise and coordinate activities of the various councils established under this Act. There are Boards set up for specific professions, such as medical laboratory technicians, occupational therapists, physiotherapists, and radiographers, to oversee operation of the Act

s.2   establishment and maintenance of registers of practitioners

s.3   qualifications for registration

s.4   approval of courses, qualifications and institutions

s.5   supervision of the former

s.6   use of titles

s.7   penalty for false representations to obtain registration (liable on summary conviction to a fine)

s.8   investigating and disciplinary committees

s.9   removal of name from register for:
    (1)(a) 'criminal offence, which, in the opinion of the disciplinary committee set up by the board, renders him unfit to be registered';
    (1)(b) 'judged by the disciplinary committee to be guilty of infamous conduct in any professional respect', or
    (1)(c) name fraudulently entered on register

s.10 Power of the Board to extend the Act to 'a profession which appears to the Council to be supplementary to medicine and is not mentioned in section one of this Act'; or to withdraw or alter recognition to professions already recognised. Council to make recommendations to Privy Council, which would then place a draft of the proposed order before both Houses of Parliament. Overall power held by the Privy Council in overseeing operation of this legislation, via the use of Statutory Instrument.

---

updating from a practitioner who has been out of practice for a number of years (J.M. Consulting Ltd, 1996).

The terminology can quickly become confusing in any discussion about achieving professional status. For example, counselling students and clients frequently confuse the *recognition of courses* by the BAC with the *accreditation of individual practitioners*, a process that is related but separate and distinct. Mowbray (1995: 8) suggests a form of terminology adopted from Hogan (1979). This distinguishes between key terms (see Box 9.2).

The BAC, for example, use the above terms differently, so that Hogan's term *Certification* of individual practitioner standards is

---

Box 9.2

Levels of professional regulation

Practice Acts	These regulate the provision of licences to *practise*, and the monitoring of standards of professional competence
Title Acts	These place restrictions on the use of professional *titles*, for example, psychologist or psychotherapist
Certification	This relates to the operation of professional standards set by *organisations*, such as the BAC, BCP, UKCP
Accreditation	This refers to the recognition of training and professional *organisations*, rather than of *individuals*

---

called *Accreditation*, while courses are *Recognised* by the BAC, rather than Accredited.

The purpose of therapists achieving statutory regulation is twofold. Firstly, there is seen to be a need to protect the public and other consumers from incompetent or fraudulent practitioners. Secondly, regulation provides a degree of formal recognition of the status and value of the profession's contribution to society (Sieghart, 1978: iv). Thus, it follows that, under regulation, an individual's ability to practise would be tied to their having to follow a stringent code of ethics. Breach of the code could result in removal from a list of qualified practitioners, which would debar the erring individual from future practice (Wood, 1993: 28).

Developments towards achieving professional status

Out of the range of therapists' professional organisations, only the British Psychological Society currently possesses statutory recognition, in the form of Chartered Status. Chartered Status can be awarded to psychologists with six years training, made up of three years of study at degree level, plus three years postgraduate training and professional supervision. They are also subject to a *Code of Ethics*, where the ultimate decision-makers about breaches of the code and disciplinary measures include non-psychologists (BPS, 1995b).

The BPS has been a Chartered Body since its incorporation by Royal Charter in 1965. It has been authorised to maintain a Register of Chartered Psychologists since 1987, a step achieved through an order of the Privy Council rather than via primary

---

Box 9.3

Developments in self-regulation by therapists

1971:   Foster Report on Scientology
1978:   Sieghart Report on the statutory regulation of psychotherapy
1982:   Rugby conference of psychotherapy groups, under BAC auspices
1989:   UK Standing Conference for Psychotherapy set up (Later to become the UKCP)
1993:   Voluntary Register of UKCP psychotherapists
1995:   Voluntary Register of BCP psychotherapists
1996:   Voluntary Register of BAC/COSCA counsellors

---

legislation such as a Bill placed before Parliament. The 1995 BPS conference sought to restrict the use of the term 'psychologist' to authorised members of the BPS, thus moving from control via a *Practice Act* to added control via use of a *Title Act*, using the definitions suggested above (Mowbray, 1995: 18–19).

Statutory recognition is thus available for Chartered Psychologists via membership of the BPS, and for medically qualified psychotherapists via their status as medical practitioners regulated by the General Medical Council. For non-medical (or lay) therapists, the search for full professional recognition has been a long process. Landmarks in this drive for recognition have included those listed in Box 9.3.

The policy adopted by therapists' organisations in seeking government approval for statutory recognition has been a gradualist one. The Foster Report in 1971 broached the issue of regulating 'psychological medicine' or therapeutic treatment, as a consequence of its investigation of the Church of Scientology. The Sieghart Report in 1978 represented the response made to this encouraging signal by a wide range of professional organisations. However, the latter failed to provide a united response, and the Government then took more of a 'wait and see' approach towards implementing legislation: 'the DHSS stated that legislation would not be possible until a coherent picture of the psychotherapy profession could be presented' (Abram, 1992: 14). The policy adopted by the therapeutic community has since sought to operate in a number of ways. The movement towards regulation has focused on achieving greater coherence and unity within the different sectors of the therapy community, for example, under the broad umbrella of the UKCP. This has been evident in the widening participation of psychotherapy organisations at the Rugby conferences, rising from 30 in 1982 to 70 by 1989 (Holmes and Lindley, 1989: 207). However, the underlying split between psychotherapy and counselling has yet to be resolved. There have been moves to establish *voluntary* registers of competent practitioners, which will indicate a high degree of professional commitment to self regulation, and demonstrate an ability to identify and maintain standards of good practice. The next stage would be for this process to be crowned by formal *statutory* recognition. As Syme suggests, 'with a register of psychotherapists in place, the UKSCP will then be in a position to press for legislation' (1994: 16). This could take the form of a Practice Act or a Title Act, either restricting the practice of therapy, or the use of specified terms such as 'counsellor', 'therapist', or 'psychotherapist'.

The Foster Report
The Foster Report represented a landmark in the process of acquiring statutory recognition. Its terms of reference were announced in 1969 by Richard Crossman as being 'to enquire into the practice and effects of scientology' (Foster, 1971: v). This followed growing public concern about the secretive practices allegedly used by the Church of Scientology, and its use of psychological measures to recruit, retain and control its membership (see the case discussed in Chapter 4). Moving from its original focus on scientology, the Report went on to explore the benefits of regulating psychological treatments in a more general form.

Amongst its principal recommendations was the following statement:

> (a) that psychotherapy (in the general sense of the treatment, for fee or reward, of illnesses, complaints by psychological means) should be organised as a restricted profession open only to those who undergo an appropriate training and are willing to adhere to a proper code of ethics, and that the necessary legislation should be drafted and presented to Parliament as soon as possible. (Foster, 1971: v)

Chapter 9 of the Report provided a detailed case for the regulation of 'psychological medicine' (1971: 176–81). The author's conclusion was that 'the intervention of Parliament has become necessary' (1971: 17). Intervention and regulation were justified on the grounds of therapy's capacity to cause *harm*: 'the danger in anything other than the most skilled hands is great and, what is worse, the possibilities of abuse by the unscrupulous are immense' (Foster, 1971: 177).

The conclusion was that:

> it is high time that the practice of psychotherapy for reward should be restricted to members of a profession properly qualified in its techniques and trained – as all organised professions are trained – to use the patient's dependence which flows from the inherent inequality of the relationship only for the good of the patient himself, and never for the exploitation of his weakness to the therapist's profit. (1971: 179)

However, the Report betrays a marked degree of confusion about the distinctions to be drawn between different psychological therapies. It founders on a recurrent problem, that of producing *definitions* of the types of therapy which are *acceptable* to the professionals concerned, and *understandable* by the wider public. Foster thus tried to differentiate between psychiatry, psychology, counselling and psychotherapy. 'Psychiatry' dealt with emotional or mental problems, 'psychology' mainly with problems of the intellect (1971: 176). 'Counselling' was widely practised in everyday life, as was 'psychotherapy without a fee'. There was, therefore, no compelling case for restricting the practice of either counselling or psychology as such. Given that almost everyone practised some form of psychotherapy on others in terms of personal relationships, the Report concluded that *only psychotherapy which was based on a fee or reward in cash or in kind should be subject to statutory control* (1971: 180, emphasis added). The problem of definition may have proved intractable, but the overall message to the relevant professions was clear: steps towards the formal regulation of psychotherapy would now be favourably received by the authorities.

The Sieghart Report

The next development was in the form of the Sieghart Report (1978), the product of a two-year working party, following the recommendations of the Foster Report on Scientology. The working party grew out of discussions between the DHSS, the British Psycho-Analytical Society and six other practitioner organisations in the field of psychotherapy (Mowbray, 1995: 42). The Report limited itself to the law relating to England and Wales. It picked up, but failed to resolve, the problem of definition bequeathed to it by the Foster Report. Thus, the Report commented:

> we have serious doubts whether psychotherapy as a function could be defined precisely enough by statutory language to prevent evasion, without at the same time casting the net so wide as to catch many people who are outside the mischief which the statute is designed to meet. We have in mind here professions as diverse as general medical practitioners, applied psychologists, clergymen, counsellors and educators who do not present themselves as specialised psychotherapists, but many of whom use interpersonal techniques in the course of their ordinary work which could be interpreted as falling within the definition of 'psychotherapy' if that definition were made sufficiently wide to prevent evasion by the unscrupulous. (Sieghart, 1978: 6)

A further problem was acknowledged in that there were other professional groups, such as social workers, who were not necessarily psychotherapists as such, but who might possess and use some similar skills. The role of the proposed Council was accordingly 'to encourage continued variety and innovation, rather than attempt to impose any kind of uniformity' (1978: 8).

The Report came up with an elegant organisational solution to the problem of controlling a profession which resisted easy or comprehensive definition. This was in the form of a preference for regulation by means of a *Title Act*, rather than a Practice Act. The working party described the use of a Title Act as 'indicative registration', and a Practice Act as 'functional registration'.

> we were driven to the conclusion that functional regulation was not feasible in our case, because there is simply no way of defining the practice of psychotherapy with enough certainty to make it possible for, say, a Magistrates' Court to decide whether someone has been practising it or not . . . only 'indicative' regulation would be feasible. (1978: vi)

A crucial role in operating statutory regulation would be performed by the adoption of a *Code of Ethics*. It was envisaged that there would be a single *Code* to cover all registered practitioners, which would specify the kinds of professional misconduct requiring disciplinary action, such as the following examples:

- breach of professional confidence
- sexual or financial exploitation of a patient
- commercial advertising

- 'fee-splitting', or the making of any payments for the referral of patients
- failure to obtain the patient's informed consent to treatment
- conviction of a crime rendering the practitioner unfit to remain on the register
- dishonestly claiming possession of qualifications in psychotherapy, or of specialised skills, for example in behavioural techniques

The Report was based on the model of the Professions Supplementary to Medicine Act 1960, with the exception that the relevant powers would be held by one Council rather than by a series of separate Boards. In view of comments elsewhere (see Chapter 8), the Report makes a number of observations on the need for lay involvement, which are in line with current thinking such as the Wilson Report on the NHS. It 'recommended a substantial "lay" membership for the Council'. 'Ideally, there should be someone who can represent the interests of the profession's patients, but we have not been able to suggest how such a representation could be easily identified' (Sieghart, 1978: ix–x). Any appeal against erasure from the register would be made to the Privy Council, 'a wholly independent body within the British Constitution which has wide experience in exercising ultimate supervision over bodies of this kind' (1978: x.)

Differences betweeen therapists' organisations
However, the problems in achieving statutory recognition were brought to a head by the expression of unresolved differences within the field of therapy. An interesting (and ultimately persuasive) note of dissent to the otherwise unanimous Sieghart Report was sounded by the British Association for Behavioural Psychotherapy. This presented an argument for treatments to be evaluated on the basis of their proven *effectiveness*, rather than on the basis of their practitioners simply having completed a recognised form of *training*. Hence, it claimed that 'registration in the main report is suggested on the basis of training which is largely of unproven value at the present time' (1978: 18). This reflected more than just the well-known tension between psychoanalytic and behavioural methods within therapeutic circles (see the relevant debate in Dryden and Feltham, 1992). It actually goes to the very heart of the stated rationale for professional organisation.

Professional organisation contains conflicting pressures towards, on the one hand, protecting the interests of members as a guild or quasi-monopoly, and, on the other, defending the interests of the public or consumer in receiving a service of proven effectiveness. This note of dissent revealed the existence of continuing differences in the camp of psychotherapy, which have taken two decades of work to overcome, and which, to a certain extent, may still remain.

At yet another level, the underlying structural divide between counselling and psychotherapy remains unbridged (Thorne, 1992). While the UKCP has made major strides towards establishing itself as an umbrella organisation for self-monitoring and regulation, tendencies towards differentiation between different brands of therapy continue to make themselves felt. For example, the British Confederation of Psychotherapists (BCP) has been established to maintain standards that were felt to be threatened by moves towards greater homogenisation. The BCP is particularly critical of the UKCP's decision to join in government initiatives on the mapping of competencies for National Vocational Qualifications (NVQs), which it describes as a 'highly inappropriate' form of qualification for psychoanalytic psychotherapy (BCP, 1994: 2).

Voluntary registration

Movement towards professional status has included a regrouping of therapist organisations and the development of voluntary registers of qualified practitioners. 'It is clear that the future must bring first a voluntary and then a government recognized National Register if clients are to be protected and counsellors respected' (Syme, 1994: 127). The major initiatives with regard to voluntary registration are described in more detail below.

UKCP The UKCP national register was announced at the House of Lords in May 1993. 'The launch of this register is not just about making the profession accountable and giving the public better access to its services, it is also about making the profession full stop . . . We hope to be able to move towards a position where we can take full responsibility for our profession Europe-wide, by becoming the designated authority' (Wood, 1993: 26). The UKCP has a federal structure, based on member organisations grouped in sections. It requires a post-graduate membership, with a minimum three years part-time training.

BCP   The British Confederation of Psychotherapists is a separate organisation from the UKCP, and includes within its membership psychoanalysts, analytical psychologists, psychoanalytical psychotherapists and child psychotherapists. Its register of 1,200 therapists was published in 1995.

BAC   A United Kingdom Register of Counsellors is planned for 1996, arising from the work of the BAC and the Confederation of Scottish Counselling Agencies. This will cover both sponsoring agencies and individual accredited practitioners, in order to 'indicate as far as possible safe and competent practice in the setting in which it is delivered' (BAC, 1994b). The BAC accreditation procedure requires counsellor training and a minimum of 450 hours supervised practice (Foss, 1986; Frankland, 1995).

Access to the above registers, or to the parallel BPS register of Chartered Psychologists, by clients or other interested parties, is straightforward (see relevant phone numbers in Resources section).

Registration is held to be both a necessary protection measure for clients, and a crucial step towards achieving full statutory recognition. However, this persuasive view is not shared by all consumer organisations. Jenny Fasal, formerly of POPAN (Prevention of Professional Abuse Network), describes herself as being not so much opposed to registration as such, but rather as holding no illusions about its real efficacy. 'Registration will mean that people will have a body to whom they can complain. It's not going to guarantee higher standards of practice. The fact that therapists are registered as having undergone a certain training can't guarantee their competency, integrity or sense of responsibility. It just means that they can damage with more registered knowledge' (Fasal, 1994). Her views carry some weight, given POPAN's experience of the resistance in practice shown by many professional organisations to tackling the issue of therapist abuse of clients. Another critic, Mowbray, quotes Carl Rogers to the effect that 'there are as many certified charlatans and exploiters of people as there are uncertified' (1995: 113). It seems that for critics such as Fasal and Mowbray, the key to higher standards of therapeutic practice lies in the development of a more assertive consumer movement in the field of therapy, rather than through reliance on defensive self-organisation by the professionals concerned.

The extent to which professional self-regulation would reduce bad or incompetent practice remains to be seen. Current concerns in the media in the USA and UK over the apparent retrieval of 'false memories' of early childhood sexual abuse are, for example, levelled at trained and highly qualified therapists rather than simply at the unregulated fringe (Lindsay and Read, 1994). Given the evident difficulties in controlling the practice of therapy, it may well be that any attempt to control the use of titles will simply displace the problem of unethical or incompetent practice to other unregulated levels. Practitioners unable to call themselves 'counsellor', 'psychologist', or 'psychotherapist' will, accordingly, perhaps advertise themselves as 'psychological helpers', 'befrienders' or 'therapists'. There is, in addition, an argument that voluntary registration, rather than being a step *towards* statutory recognition, is in reality a step *away* from it, and actually makes its achievement less likely in the near future. This outcome is strongly suggested in the sub-text of the speech delivered by the then Under-Secretary of State for Health, John Bowis MP, at the 1995 launch of the BCP register. 'The voluntary register of the British Confederation of Psychotherapists, and those established or being drawn up by other organisations are likely to remain the main method of regulating the psychotherapy profession for some considerable time' (BCP, 1995a). There is no discernible commitment here to making rapid progress towards a full statutory form of regulation. The current government position is that voluntary registration, while encouraged, is a long-term measure. Indeed, if it can be demonstrated that voluntary registration can *resolve* the problem of defining practice boundaries and policing standards, then, from a government perspective, it may actually *reduce* rather than increase any perceived need for legislation.

The European Challenge

One of the main pressures towards professional regulation of therapists in the UK has come about by referring to the European dimension. The 1957 Treaty of Rome aimed to open up the European market by ensuring mutual recognition of professional qualifications in the member states, thus aiding the free movement of professionals across national boundaries. To date, this has enabled some 6,000 UK professionals to live and work in other EU states; the vast majority of these have been teachers or lawyers (*Week in Europe*, 22 February 1996). The European Commission, the main executive body of the European Union (EU), has sought to define professions by the following criteria:

- a high level of training
- adherence to an ethical code of practice
- independence from outside influences
- personal liability for professional actions
- professional secrecy that exists between the professional adviser and his client

(Devine, 1989: 186)

However, the reference to Europe in terms of professionalisation often conflates two separate issues. Mowbray argues for making a necessary distinction between the role of the European Commission in regulating the movement of professionals *between* member states, and the regulation of UK therapists *practising* in the UK (1995: 20). In terms of establishing uniform standards, the early approach adopted by the EC proved to be both cumbersome and time-consuming, for example taking no less than 17 years to produce results in the case of architects, and 16 in the case of pharmacists (Devine, 1989: 187). This earlier, centralising approach has been replaced by the automatic mutual recognition of professional qualifications of three years duration within the member states (Higher Educational Diplomas Directive of 1988 (89/48/EEC), effective from 1991). Thus, 'UK professionals falling within the scope of the Directive will enjoy the right to become a member of their equivalent professional body in other member states, without having to requalify' (Devine, 1989: 187).

Where the length of training required in the host country is greater than that applying in the professional's home country, professionals seeking to transfer their employment from one state to another are required to show their competence to practise by demonstrating evidence of their relevant practical experience. Professionals thus affected (excluding lawyers and accountants) can choose whether to undergo either an 'aptitude test', or up to three years supervised practice, in order to achieve the professional standard required by the host state. Interestingly, the BPS is the only 'regulated profession' referred to specifically in the document on three-year Diplomas. A second Directive (92/51/EEC) governing a complementary system of mutual recognition for Diplomas of less than three years at Higher Education or similar level has now been agreed. This shift by the European Union towards a flexible system of mutual recognition of professional qualifications by member states means that centralised EC legislation on regulationg therapy is increasingly unlikely. The need sometimes referred to in the UK for achieving statutory regulation of therapy because of probable legislation by the EC is therefore unfounded. According to the 1993 EC discussion document *Psychotherapy in the European Communities (Outline)*:

> B.3 Recognition of psychotherapy as practised by a non-medical doctor, depending on the level of training, is provided for by Council Directive 89/84/EEC (as of December 1988).
>
> C.2 *The Commission does not plan to make specific proposals for psychotherapists regarding their activities in general* or their access to social security systems in particular. (EC, 1993: 1–2, emphasis added)

The majority of EU states currently have *no* statutory recognition of psychotherapy as a distinct profession. The paragraphs quoted above would seem to confirm that the EC is *not* attempting to harmonise or regulate the training of any profession, particularly psychotherapy, partly because of the continuing problem of definition ('A government source', 1990; Mowbray, 1995: 25).

The use of the European dimension as a lever for promoting statutory regulation of therapy in the UK also has another strand to the argument (van Deurzen-Smith, 1991). While centralised EU legislation is unlikely, there is space for professional associations such as the BAC or UKCP to achieve the status of 'competent authorities', which would then oversee professional activity and training (Lefébure, 1996). However, achieving such status to act as a European power-broker for UK therapists still requires a degree of formal recognition from the UK Government which remains extremely elusive. As the history of the Foster and Sieghart Reports demonstrates, government resistance to statutory regulation of therapists can continue as long as the major divisions between the various branches of therapy persist.

Critiques of the professionalisation of therapy

The desirability and even *inevitability* of making progress towards statutory regulation of therapy now seems to be part of the received wisdom of the therapeutic community. The main critique of the movement towards professionalisation has been provided by Mowbray. 'In my view, proposals for the accreditation and registration of psychotherapy are most usefully addressed as part of a political process concerned with power and control' (1995: 2). His critique of the case for statutory regulation of therapy is based on three main arguments. In the first place, proponents of regulation are guilty of a misreading of the current state of the law, and of its probable future development. Secondly, professionalisation amounts to the establishment of a legal *monopoly* of service provision, which removes wider choice from the consumer. Finally, the case for statutory regulation overlooks the existence of adequate and effective remedies available to the consumer under the common law, a view also broadly held by Stone and Matthews in looking at the related field of complementary medicine (1996).

Given the importance of the issue of statutory regulation of therapy, these arguments will be explored in more detail below. In the first place, in arguing that much of the case for regulation is based on a clear misreading of the law and of future legal developments, Mowbray closely documents the case that EU regulation of UK therapists is unlikely, and is certainly not currently being planned. There is also no likelihood of any government initiative in terms of legislation, voluntary registers or no, given that the UK government agenda is quite pointedly for the *deregulation* of existing professions, rather than encouraging the creation of new ones (Mowbray, 1995: 27).

He notes, incidentally, in the Foster Report a curious absence of substantive evidence for its sweeping conclusions about the need for regulating psychotherapy, except for some material drawn from Australia. The Report 'in effect says there isn't law, there could be abuse, therefore there should be a law as there is elsewhere' (Mowbray, 1995: 41). He further notes the irony that the proposed statutory regulation of psychotherapy in the UK took its first step with an inquiry into the activities of a group, Scientology, 'which does not use the term "psychotherapy", is organised as a religion and is therefore unlikely to be much affected by any legislative restrictions that may arise' (Mowbray, 1995: 45).

A second theme of the argument relates to the nature of professionalisation as a legalised occupational monopoly, which seeks to outlaw legitimate competition. Based on Hogan's earlier comprehensive work on regulation of therapy in the USA, he argues that the establishment of a Title Act employing a broad definition of professional practice progressively leads to the control of practice by degrees. Regulation need not always be friendly to the professions concerned, namely designed or approved by them with their professional criteria and interests in mind. It may well be based on the hostile intent of rival professional groups, with the purpose of constraining the right to practise of legitimate professional groups, rather than being promoted for the purpose of protecting the vulnerable consumer. Attempts at hostile regulation have affected the development of therapy at critical moments in its past. Thus, in the same year that Sigmund Freud published 'The question of lay analysis', a law was passed in New York prohibiting the practice of psychoanalysis by non-medically qualified practitioners (Abram, 1992; Kohon, 1986). Freud's own view, quoted with approval by the Foster Report, was that 'no one should practise who has not acquired the right to do so by a particular training. Whether such a person is a doctor or not seems to me immaterial' (1971: 179; Freud, 1926/1993; 1927/ 1993). The other well-known example concerns Carl Rogers' development of the term 'counselling' to describe his approach when use of the term psychotherapy was restricted to medical practitioners (Thorne, 1990: 106).

A further example of hostile regulation of therapy is provided by a case in Virginia, USA, in 1972, where the Board of Psychology attempted to restrain a counsellor from using the tools of a psychologist in his private practice as a career counsellor. This attempt at hostile regulation actually gave the impetus for counsellors to attain their own separate certification and state recognition or licensure (Lee and Six, 1992: 94; Roberts et al., 1994). Where consensus on regulation measures is hard to achieve, the end-result of prioritising statutory regulation may be that certain professional groupings, such as psychologists and psychotherapists, may well achieve a degree of legal protection for their own practice or title, but one that is achieved at the expense of less powerful groupings such as counsellors or complementary therapists, who are then evicted from their competitive position as a result.

The final part of the argument concerns the existence of alternative adequate remedies to statutory control. Mowbray makes the point that psychotherapy is *not* totally unregulated in the UK, because it is covered by common law, and by the laws of contract and trade description. His suggestion is for consumer and practitioner reliance on clear contracting and full disclosure by the therapist. 'In my opinion the greatest source of difficulty for the "customer" derives from not knowing on what basis to make their judgement' (Mowbray, 1995: 204). His proposed alternative to statutory regulation would be in the form of a more open system of voluntary registration, where the right to practise would be withdrawn in the event of serious or repeated complaint against a practitioner.

Issues of client protection
Mowbray makes a well-documented case against statutory regulation of therapists in the UK, which seems to have some resonance with certain practitioners, such as those belonging to the Independent Practitioners' Network. However, in stressing the alternative approach of promoting consumer choice and reliance on the use of complaints or contract law, the central issue of client protection remains unresolved. As argued elsewhere in this book, tort law requires a high threshold of proof for clients to overcome in bringing cases against therapists. Action against a therapist for breach of contract may prove to be an intimidating and frustrating experience for a client to initiate and bring to a successful conclusion. Complaints procedures can also prove to be problematic for clients who feel aggrieved over the therapy they have received. Ideally, consumers of therapy need to be fully informed of their rights, of the nature of the service they are receiving and to feel able to challenge or complain about unsatisfactory performance. In reality, clients may well be emotionally vulnerable, lacking in information about best practice, and unsure how to go about making their voice heard if unhappy about their experience of therapy.

The usual analogy made for the advantages of statutory control for therapy is made with reference to the medical profession. However, the evidence suggests that regulation alone does not automatically lead to higher status for the profession concerned. The continuing subordinate position of nurses and midwives relative to doctors would be a case in point here. The advantages to the consumer of statutory self-regulation may also be overstated, according to Stacey's analysis of the General Medical Council, given that 'no more than a small number of complaints ever reach the formal procedures' (1994: 118). She is critical of what she sees as 'the failure of the GMC hitherto to consider any except the grossest cases of incompetence as "serious professional misconduct"' (1994: 120). The *power* accruing to the medical profession does not result from it possessing professional traits such as its code of ethics or control over selection, training and discipline, but from external factors, such as the '"state-medical alliance" of which the GMC is the crucial medical ingredient' (1994: 122).

Stacey's conclusion is pessimistic both for the efficacy of the General Medical Council as a model of self-regulation, and as an example for other professional groupings to emulate: 'my evidence about the GMC . . . suggests that it has not been very thorough in protecting the public' (1994: 129). Furthermore, 'the whole question of professional regulation should be thought through very carefully before any new pieces of legislation, whether relating to the GMC or to other health care occupations, are put on the statute book' (1994: 131).

Therapy, professional power and society

The debate about statutory regulation of therapy goes to the heart of the problematic status of therapy in society at the present time. However, even its staunchest defenders acknowledge that it may be some way away from convincing the wider public of the rightness of its claims to full professional status. 'Despite aspirations to acceptance and respectability, psychotherapy as a whole does not yet present the public with the unity and ideological coherence that are the landmarks of a profession' (Holmes and Lindley, 1989: 204). Part of the paradox is that therapy is undeniably growing in popularity, despite its uneven and often critical treatment by the media. The media's sceptical treatment of therapy does not seem to undermine its increasing appeal and application, however, in employment, post-trauma situations or for facilitating personal growth. Giddens suggests that the increasing demand for therapy reflects the pressures on individuals in a post-modern society, where former support systems of community, family and established values have been eroded. This has led to the growth of 'expert systems'. Problems of coping with modernity have led to a reliance by individuals on expert systems, such as psychotherapy and counselling, to manage and cope with

problems concerning intimacy, trust and interpersonal relationships. He refers to 'the transformation of intimacy', and the
widening interest in self-reflection and self-actualisation in modern
society (Giddens, 1990: 124). Increasingly, individuals come to
rely on 'experts of the personal', whether therapists or lawyers, to
help them negotiate and resolve problems in living in a complex
and ever-changing society.

Yet increasing levels of demand for therapy do not necessarily
translate into a dynamic process which ends with the achievement
of full professional status for therapists. What is sometimes lacking
in discussions about the professionalisation of therapy is placing
such a process in its wider social context. Critics of professionalisation argue that it is fundamentally about *power relationships*
relative to the client, and to other professional groups. Becoming
a profession is not a gradual process of refining *Codes of Ethics*, or
of improving selection and training, but is fundamentally a
question of *power and occupational control*. The new profession
needs to possess and maintain a monopoly of a crucial form of
expertise and decision-making power (Johnson, 1972: 37–8).

Furthermore, professionalisation is a historically specific
process. The period following the Industrial Revolution which
enabled the emergence of this form of social power for doctors
and lawyers has quite possibly passed. New aspiring professions
now have the disadvantage of competing for power with other
more powerful and well-established social groupings, which do
not wish to cede power to newcomers.

Finally, there is the social policy argument. Moves to recognise
the professional status of new professional groups form part of a
wider political canvas. Recognition depends upon the gaining of
wide public support, and upon gaining the backing of powerful
groups in society. This is suggested by the example of social work
as another aspiring professional group. The slow process of social
workers in acquiring a modest exercise of power, since dimin-
ished, hinged in the first stage on the revelation of public care
scandals in 1944. In the second stage, it was accelerated by
government departments wishing to extend their influence in
1970, following a major government report by the Seebohm
Committee. This led to the growth of social work as a major
resource controller in local and national government (Packman,
1975). The reduction of the legal and resource powers of social
workers has shown this model working in reverse, following the

unrelenting series of child care enquiries in the 1970s. For therapists to be granted full professional status, there would need to be other supporting interests who would benefit from this development, by acquiring organisational power or prestige as a result. It is not yet clear who these interests might be, or how they would benefit from devolving professional status to therapists.

Summary

The model of professional status which the therapeutic community seems to have adopted is that of a 'trait' approach. This model focuses on the main qualities of established professional groups such as medicine and the law. Each stage in the group's development, such as producing a detailed *Code of Ethics*, represents a step towards achieving recognition by society as a fully fledged profession.

Movement towards statutory recognition has taken the form of a regrouping of psychotherapy organisations, and of the launching of parallel voluntary registers of qualified practitioners. The process of working towards statutory recognition has been challenged by certain critics. These point to the absence of a supposed European agenda for state control of therapy, the uproven nature of alleged benefits to clients, and to the existence of alternative regulatory measures, such as the use of existing contract law.

Conclusion

At various stages, this book has emphasised the contrasting and even conflicting natures of therapy and the law. They are concerned with different dimensions of human experience, with private as opposed to public spheres of discourse and interaction, and with the dimensions of feeling and experience versus those of evidence and logic. However, these opposing elements may sometimes be overstated. Bond (1993a) has suggested that the law is a crucial cornerstone of safe, ethical and competent therapeutic practice. According to Giddens (1990), therapy, like the law, is an 'expert system' which helps people to make sense of their experience, and to adapt more purposefully to the challenge of contemporary living. Both law and therapy are crucially concerned with the ideas of rights, justice and the peaceful resolution of conflict. One possible danger may be the accelerating process of the 'legalisation of therapy'. It is hoped that, rather than this scenario occurring, therapeutic values and experience may reach some kind of closer interplay and co-existence, influencing and informing the quality of justice in the future.

Discussion points

1 Is the 'trait' model of professionalisation an accurate way of describing therapists' efforts to achieve statutory recognition? What characteristics of an established profession does therapy lack at present, and how might these be acquired?

2 What are the advantages and disadvantages of statutory recognition of therapy? Consider the ten points listed in the opening section of this chapter, and add further points to both sides of the argument.

3 Should therapists aim to follow the medical model of statutory control of their profession? How would this prove to be of benefit to clients and to society at large?

4 In seeking statutory regulation, should therapists opt for a Practice Act or a Title Act? What working definition of counselling or psychotherapy could you suggest as the basis for such legislation?

5 What other professional groups in society would actively welcome and support therapists in gaining full professional status? What other professional groups might seek to oppose this development?

Resources

Insurance for therapists

Bartlett Insurance
Broadway Hall
Horsforth
Leeds LS18 4RS
(0113-258 5711)

Devitt Insurance Services Ltd
Central House
32–66 High Street
Stratford
London E15 2PF
(0181-519 0202)

Psychologists' Protection Society
Standalane House
Kincardine
Alloa FK10 4NX
(01259-730785)

Smithson Mason Ltd
SMG House
31 Clarendon Road
Leeds LS2 9PA
(0113-294 4000)
(Fax: 0113-294 4100)

Official organisations

Advertising Standards Authority (print
    and cinema adverts)
Brook House
2–16 Torrington Place
London WC1E 7HN
(0171-580 5555)

Broadcasting Complaints Commission
7 The Sanctuary
London SW1P 3JS
(0171-233 0544)

Commission for Racial Equality
Elliott House
10–12 Allington Street
London SW1E 5EH
(0171-828 7022)

Court of Protection
Stewart House
24 Kingsway
London WC2B 6JX
(0171-269 7000)

Criminal Injuries Compensation Board
Blythswod House
200 West Regent Street
Glasgow G2 4SW
(0141-221 0945)

Crown Prosecution Service
50 Ludgate Hill
London EC4M 7EX
(0171-273 8152)

Data Protection Registrar
Wycliffe House
Water Lane
Wilmslow
Cheshire SK9 5AF
(Enquiries: 01625-545745)
(Admin: 01625-535711)

Employee Assistance Programme
    Association (EAPA)
2 Dovedale Studios
465 Battersea Park Road
London SW11 4LN
(0171-228 6768)

Equal Opportunities Commission
Overseas House
Quay Street
Manchester M3 3HN
(0161-833 9244)

Health Service Ombudsman
Church House
Great Smith Street
London SW1P 3BW
(0171-276 3000)

Home Office
50 Queen Anne's Gate
London SW1H 9AT
(0171-273 3000)

Law Commission
Conquest House
37–38 John Street
Theobald's Road
London WC1N 2BQ
(0171-453 1213)

Law Society
50–52 Chancery Lane
London WC2A 1SX
(0171-320 5764)

Legal Aid Board
85 Grays Inn Road
London WC1X
(0171-813 1000)

Lord Chancellor's Department
Selborne House
54–60 Victoria Street
London SW1E 6QW
(0171-210 0618)
(Fax: 0171-210 0725)

Mental Health Act Commission
Floor 3
Maid Marian House
56 Houndsgate
Nottingham NG1 6BG
(01602-504040)

Press Complaints Commission
1 Salisbury Square
London EC4Y 8AE
(0171-353 1248)

Secretary, European Commission of
    Human Rights
Council of Europe
BP 431 R6
F-67006 Strasbourg Cedex
France
(00-3388-614961)

Voluntary Organisations Consultancy
    Service (criminal records checks)
Unit 4
Pride Court
80/82 White Lyon Street
London N1 9PF

Therapists' organisations

British Association for Counselling
1 Regent Place
Rugby
Warwickshire CV21 2PJ
(01788-578328)

British Confederation of Psychotherapists
37a Mapesbury Road
London NW2 4HJ
(0181-830 5173)

British Psychological Society
St Andrew's House
48 Princess Road East
Leicester LE1 7DR
(01162-549568)

General Medical Council
44 Hallam Street
London W1N 6AE
(0171-580 7642)

Independent Practitioners' Network
326 Burley Road
Leeds LS4 2NZ
(01532-755984)

Royal College of Psychiatrists
17 Belgrave Square
London SW1X 8PG
(0171-235 2351)
(Fax: 0171-245 1231)

United Kingdom Council for
    Psychotherapy
167–9 Great Portland Street
London N1 5SB
(0171-436 3002)

Advocacy or consumer support organisations

Accuracy About Abuse
PO Box 3125
London NW3 5QB
(0171-431 5339)
(Fax: 0171-433 3101)

ASC (Advocacy Services for Children)
Canterbury House
1–3 Greengate
Salford
Manchester M3 7NN
(0161-839 8442)
(0800-616101)

British False Memory Society
Belcombe Croft
Bradford-on-Avon
Wiltshire BA15 1NA
(01225-868682)
(Fax: 01225-863262)

Children's Legal Centre
University of Essex
Wivenhoe Park
Colchester
Essex CO4 3SQ
(Office: 01206-874416)
(Advice line: 01206-873820)

Citizen Advocacy Alliance
Douglas House
26 Sutton Court Road
Sutton
Surrey SM1 4SY
(0181-643 7111)

Consumers' Association (publishers of
    Which)
2 Marylebone Road
London NW1 4DF
(0171-830 6000)

Freedom to Care (whistleblowers)
PO Box 125
West Molesey
Surrey KT8 1YE
(0181-224 1022)

Immunity Legal Centre (HIV+/AIDS)
1st Floor
32–38 Osnaburgh Street
London NW1 3ND
(0171-388 6776)

Inquest (campaign on Coroner's Courts)
Ground Floor
Alexandra National House
330 Seven Sisters Road
Finsbury Park
London N4 2PJ
(0181-802 7430)

Institute of Mental Health Law (training)
Murrayfield House
The King's Gap
Hoylake
Wirral L47 1HE
(0151-632 4115)
(Fax: 0151-632 0090)

IRCHIN (Independent Representation for
    Children In Need)
1 Downham Road South
Heswall
Wirrall LT60 5RG
(0151-342 7852)

Law Centres' Federation
Duchess House
18–19 Warren Street
London W1P 5DB
(0171-387 8570)

Legal Action Group
242–244 Pentonville Road
London N1 9UN
(0171-833 2931)

MIND (National Association for Mental
    Health)
Granta House
15/19 Broadway
Stratford
London E15 4BQ
(0181-519 2122)
(Fax: 0181-522 1725)
(Information Line: 0181-522 1728)

National Centre for Volunteering
Carriage Row
183 Eversholt Street
London NW1 1BU
(0171-388 9888)
(Fax: 0171-383-0448)

National Consumer Council
20 Grosvenor Gardens
London SW1W 0DH
(0171-730 3469)
(Fax: 0171-730 5851)

Network for the Handicapped (free
    specialist legal advice for people with
    physical or learning disability)
16 Princeton Street
London WC1R 4BB
(0171-831 8031)
(0171-831 7740)

POPAN (Prevention of Professional Abuse
    Network)
1 Wyvil Court
Wyvil Road
London SW8 2TG
(0171-622 6334)
(Fax: 0171-622 9788)

Public Law Project (support for judicial
    review procedures)
17 Russell Square
London WC1B 5DR
(0171-467 9800)

Refugee Legal Centre
Sussex House
39–45 Bermondsey Street
London SE1 3XF
(0171-827 9090)

Rights of Women (legal advice on
 domestic violence)
52–54 Featherstone Street
London EC1Y 8RT
(0171-251 6577)

Survivors Speak Out (mental health
 survivors)
34 Osnaburgh Street
London NW1 3ND
(0171-916 5472)
(Fax: 0171-916 5473)

Suzy Lamplugh Trust (protection at work)
14 East Sheen Avenue
London SW14 8AS
(0181-392 1839)

United Kingdom Advocacy Network
 (mental health survivors)
Suite 417
Premier House
14 Cross Burgess Street
Sheffield S1 2HG
(01142-753131)

VOICE (support in court for
 victims with learning disabilities)
PO Box 238
Derby DE1 9JN
(01332-519872)

Witness Support Programme
Victim Support
Cranmer House
39 Brixton Road
London SW9 6DZ
(0171-735 9166)
(Fax: 0171-582 5712)

Complaints concerning
legal representation

General Council of the Bar (barristers)
3 Bedford Row
London W1CR 4DB
(0171-242 0082)

Legal Services Ombudsman
22 Oxford Court
Oxford Street
Manchester M2 3WQ
(0161-236 9532)

Office for the Supervision of Solicitors
Victoria Court
8 Dormer Place
Leamington Spa
Warwickshire CV32 5AE
(01926-820082)
(Helpline: 01926-822007-9)

Mediation

Advisory, Conciliation and Arbitration
 Service
Clifton House
83 Euston Road
London NW1
(0171-388 5100)

Divorce Conciliation and Advisory Service
38 Ebury Street
London SW1 0LU
(0171-730 2422)

Mediation UK (alternative dispute
 resolution)
82A Gloucester Road
Bishopston
Bristol BS7 8BN
(01179-241234)

National Family Mediation Charity Base
50 Westminster Bridge Road
London SE1 7QY
(0171-721 7658)

Family Mediators' Association
The Old House
Rectory Gardens
Henbury
Bristol BS10 7AQ
(01179-500140)

The Cambridge Family and Divorce
 Centre
162 Tenison Road
Cambridge CB1 2DP
(01233-460136)

Glossary of Terms and Abbreviations

actus reus Guilty act; combined with guilty intent (*mens rea*), an indication of a crime having been committed.

ACPC Area Child Protection Committee; local body linking police, health and social services to coordinate responses to child abuse.

amicus curiae Friend of the court; adviser to the court on specialist points of law.

Analytic treatment Shorthand for psychoanalytic therapy, based on an exploration of unconscious drives.

Anton Piller order Court order for seizure of documents or property.

Approved Social Worker Social worker authorised to make compulsory admissions of patients under the Mental Health Act 1983.

Arbitration Dispute resolution process, where parties agree to the outcome decided by an independent body.

Assault Reasonable fear of violence or threat of uninvited physical contact.

BAC British Association for Counselling; the main body representing the interests of counsellors and those using counselling skills.

Barrister Qualified advocate, specialising in legal representation in higher courts.

Battery Actual violence or uninvited physical contact, other than everyday touching.

BCP British Confederation of Psychotherapists: broadly psychoanalytic grouping of therapists, distinct from UKCP.

BMA British Medical Association; the main representative body for doctors as a profession.

BPS British Psychological Society; the main body representing interests of psychologists; holds the Royal Charter.

Chartered Psychologist Member of the British Psychological Society, holding a degree plus three years supervised clinical work.

Child Legal term for a person aged under 18 years.

Child in need Target group for services provided under Children Act 1989.

Childline Confidential telephone helpline for children.

Circuit judge Judge at Crown Court or County Court level.

Civil law Law dealing with disputes between private individuals or organisations.

Cognitive therapy Form of treatment focusing on client's thinking patterns.

Common law Body of law based on tradition; law made by judges, rather than law made by Parliament.

Conciliation Voluntary process for resolving disputes, concerning custody or contact with children in divorce or separation.

Conditional fee Legal representation with the fee calculated as a proportion of the damages if the client is successful with the case; also known as contingency fee, 'no win, no fee'.

Contract   Legally binding agreement to exchange goods or services for payment.

Counselling   Contracted therapeutic work with a group or individual.

Counselling skills   Use of defined responses, such as active listening, paraphrasing, often as part of another work-role.

Court order   Authoritative decision of the court, requiring, for example, a person to attend court and give evidence.

Criminal law   Law relating to offences against the person, property or the state.

Cross-examination   Questioning of a witness's evidence by the opposing lawyer, after the examination-in-chief.

De Clerambault's syndrome   An erotic obsession with a therapist.

Defamation   Comment which is damaging to the reputation or interests of its subject.

Deliberate self-harm   Damaging behaviour such as overdosing with medication, probably intended to fall short of suicide.

DES   Department of Education and Science.

DfEE   Department for Education and Employment.

DHSS   Department of Health and Social Security.

Discovery   Legal term for the process requiring the release of confidential documents relevant to court proceedings.

DoH   Department of Health.

DoE   Department of the Environment.

DSM   *Diagnostic and Statistical Manual:* main assessment and treatment manual in use for mental health problems; currently in its fourth edition; see also *ICD.*

EAP   Employment Assistance Programme; professional counselling firm contracted to provide a service to an organisation's workforce.

Eating disorders   Severe problems in maintaining a normal diet or body weight, associated with anorexia nervosa or bulimia nervosa.

EC   European Community (formerly Common Market; European Economic Community).

ECHR   European Court of Human Rights.

ECT   Electro-convulsive therapy; also known as electric shock treatment; treatment used for moderate to severe depression.

Egg-shell skull or personality   Person with an added physical or psychological vulnerability to damage caused by another person, which is not obvious at first sight.

Emergency Protection Order   Power authorising a social worker to remove a child at risk, authorised by a magistrate under s.44 Children Act 1989.

EU   European Union (formerly Common Market; European Economic Community).

Evidential privilege   Legal protection from the requirement to give evidence about confidential matters in a court of law.

Examination-in-chief   Main presentation of the body of evidence by a witness, via responding to questions by a lawyer representing the party calling the witness.

ex parte   Court hearing in the absence of one party, such as the defendant.

Expert witness   Witness accepted by the court as qualified to give opinion on matters before the court, based on special knowledge, qualifications or experience.

False memory   Contested memory of earlier childhood sexual abuse, returning in therapy, but lacking supporting evidence.

Fiduciary   Relationship of trust and responsibility, as in professional contract with a therapist.

Forensic Relating to crime and offenders, as in forensic psychiatry.

Foster Report 1971 Report of Inquiry into the Church of Scientology, recommending the regulation of psychotherapy.

GMC General Medical Council; regulatory body for doctors.

GP General practitioner; family doctor.

Gillick Court decision in 1986 indicating when a child under 16 could be treated in a confidential relationship by a doctor or a therapist without requiring parental permission.

Hearsay evidence Second-hand observation or recounting of what another person has seen or experienced.

HFEA Human Fertilisation and Embryology Authority.

HMI Her Majesty's Inspectorate; inspects schools and colleges.

Hypnotherapist Therapist using hypnosis as main treatment.

ICD *International Classification of Diseases*; manual for the assessment and treatment of mental health, similar to *DSM*; currently in its tenth edition.

Indemnity insurance Coverage against the cost of legal representation and payment of damages in case of court action.

Informed consent Client's voluntary agreement to treatment, based on a knowledge of the risks and benefits involved.

Injunction Court order requiring the subject to follow certain action, such as to stop harassment of a former marital partner.

in loco parentis In place of the parent; body, such as school, holding the temporary responsibility of parent to protect and care for the child.

Interlocutory Hearing held before a judge.

Judicial review Legal process where decisions of courts or public bodies are examined for procedural fairness.

Law Commission Reform body set up in 1965 to simplify and modernise the law.

Law Society Body representing solicitors.

Legal Aid State-funded assistance with costs of legal representation.

Liability Responsibility to act according to a certain standard; failure to do so determines vulnerability to legal action.

Libel Permanent form of defamation, as in an article or on TV.

Litigation Taking civil legal action, such as suing another person for breach of contract.

Litigant in person Person acting without legal representation.

Malpractice Lack of care to client involving the use of an actively damaging approach, such as sexual contact.

Manic depression Mental illness characterised by violent mood swings between elation and profound sadness.

McKenzie Legal term for the unofficial adviser for a party in court.

McNaughten rules Procedure for making legal defence based on insanity.

ME Myalgic Encephalomyelitis: extreme disabling fatigue, also referred to as chronic fatigue syndrome.

Mediation Voluntary agreement to resolve disputes using an outside negotiator, as in financial matters following divorce.

Memorandum interviewing Video interview with a child to present evidence of sexual abuse to a court in criminal proceedings against the alleged abuser.

mens rea Guilty mind or criminal intent; required with guilty act (*actus reus*) to qualify as a crime.

Munchausen's by Proxy Adult deliberately producing symptoms in, or inflicting abuse on, a dependent child in order to get medical attention.

Negligence Lack of care to client involving failure to follow accepted professional standards.

Nervous shock Dated legal term for psychiatric damage.

NHS National Health Service.

NLP Neuro Linguistic Programming; therapeutic approach which pays particular attention to a client's behavioural forms of expression.

NSPCC National Society for the Prevention of Cruelty to Children; leading voluntary organisation in the field of child protection.

Paradoxical injunction Technique in therapy of highlighting a problem area for the client by appearing to give contradictory advice about it.

Passing-off actions Legal challenge to another party's use of an established trade name or one very similar to it.

Personality disorder Psychiatric term for abnormal, deeply ingrained behaviours causing distress to the patient or client, and disruption to relationships with others.

Person-centred Form of therapy concentrating on exploration of the client's feelings, based on the work of Carl Rogers.

Post-Traumatic Stress Disorder Legally recognised term for the state where a person relives a distressing incident such as a disaster via flashbacks or persistent intrusive images.

Precedent Legally binding decision by a higher, more authoritative court on the same issue.

prima facie Based on the immediate known facts of the case.

Private law Action taken by a citizen to pursue his or her rights or seek redress, for example by suing an individual or organisation.

Privilege Legally recognised form of confidentiality.

Privity of contract Rule that persons not directly party to a contract cannot sue for breach of that contract.

Professional protection society Defence organisation providing legal advice and representation for its members.

Psychoanalysis Form of therapy focusing on the exploration of unconscious material, based on the work of Sigmund Freud.

Psychiatrist Medically qualified therapist, able to diagnose mental illness, prescribe medication and authorise treatment.

Psychodynamic As in psychoanalysis; may be short-term; sometimes shortened, as in 'dynamic therapy'.

Psychotherapy Contracted therapeutic work with a group or individual.

Psychologist Term for wide range of therapists, academics and researchers covering all aspects of human interaction and behaviour.

Psychosis Form of mental illness characterised by delusions, a seriously flawed perception of reality.

Public interest Judicial standard for deciding issues such as breaking confidentiality.

Public interest immunity Form of legal protection claimed for documents or confidential sources of information.

Public law Statute and case law concerning the responsibilities of local and central government bodies.

Qualified privilege Limited form of legal protection against defamation for professionals in releasing information or reporting a colleague's misconduct.

QC Queen's Counsel: elite barrister.

Ramona Key false memory case in California in 1994, where therapists were successfully sued by a third party, the client's father.

Relate   Formerly National Marriage Guidance Council.

Samaritans   Major voluntary telephone crisis befriending service.

Sectioning   Compulsory admission of patient to a psychiatric hospital under Mental Health Act 1983.

Schedule One offender   Person convicted of serious offences against children under Schedule 1, Children and Young Persons Act 1933.

Schizophrenia   Serious form of mental illness, involving disintegration of personality and reduced social functioning.

Sieghart Report   1978 response to the Foster Report by a broad range of psychotherapy associations on the need for statutory regulation.

Significant harm   Trigger for the investigation of child abuse by social workers, under s. 47 Children Act 1989.

Slander   Damaging statement about another person made in temporary form, such as speech.

Small Claims Court   Branch of the County Court providing access to civil action over claims up to £3,000 without requiring a lawyer.

Solicitor   Qualified lawyer; may be specialist in particular area, such as medical negligence.

Specialling   Placing a possibly suicidal psychiatric patient under special observation, such as constant nursing supervision.

Spent convictions   Convictions no longer requiring disclosure after a prescribed lapse of time for certain occupations.

SSD   Social Services Department; social work division of local government.

'Stalking'   Intrusive following, contact or attention, which is covered by civil and criminal law under the Prevention of Harassment Bill (1997).

Statutory duty   Compulsory requirement under Act of Parliament.

Statutory Instrument   Secondary legislation, under powers delegated to relevant government minister.

Statute   Act of Parliament, such as Mental Health Act 1983.

Strict liability   Responsibility for damage held by the manufacturer or distributor of a product, once the fact of damage is proven by the claimant.

Subpoena   Court order requiring action, such as attending court as a witness.

Tarasoff   Key legal case in California, requiring therapists to take reasonable steps to warn intended victims of the danger posed by a client.

Therapy   General term for psychological treatment.

Therapeutic privilege   Potential for withholding certain information from a client or patient in establishing informed consent, to avoid harm to the client caused by that information.

Third party   Interested party who is not directly involved in the primary relationship between the client and the therapist, such as a parent or partner.

Tort   Civil wrong; legal term for a broad range of actions, such as defamation, libel, slander.

Transference   Arousal of powerful emotion directed at the therapist during therapy, associated with psychoanalytic approaches.

UKCP   United Kingdom Council for Psychotherapy; major umbrella organisation for psychotherapists.

Vicarious liability   Liability or legal responsibility for the staff's actions held by an employer, such as the NHS.

References

A Child in Mind: Protection of Children in a Responsible Society (Report on Kimberley Carlisle) (1987). London: Borough of Greenwich.

'A government source' (1990) 'The EEC Directive on Higher Education Diplomas: effect on the alternative professions and complementary therapies', *Self and Society*, 18(1): 3.

Abram, J. (1992) *Individual Psychotherapy Trainings: A Guide.* London: Free Association.

Adirondack, S. and MacFarlane, R. (1992) *Getting Ready for Contracts: A Guide for Voluntary Organisations.* Second edition. Guildford: Directory of Social Change.

Alberding, B., Lauver, P. and Patnoe, J. (1993) 'Counselor awareness of the consequences of certification and licensure', *Journal of Counseling and Development*, September/October, 72: 33–8.

Alderson, P. (1993) *Children's Consent to Surgery.* Buckingham: Open University Press.

Alderson, P. and Montgomery, J. (1996) *Health Care Choices: Making Decisions with Children.* London: Institute for Public Policy Research.

Alexander, R. (1995) *Folie à Deux: An Experience of One-to-one Therapy.* London: Free Association.

Allen, N. (1992) *Making Sense of the Children Act.* Second Edition, Harlow: Longman.

American Counseling Association (ACA): Ethics Committee (1995) *Personal Communication.*

American Psychiatric Association (APA) (1994) *Diagnostic and Statistical Manual of Mental Disorders.* Fourth edition. Washington, DC: APA.

Anderson, R. (1996) 'Clinical system security: interim guidelines', *British Medical Journal*, 312: 109–11.

Appelbaum, P.S. (1993) 'Legal liability and managed care', *American Psychologist*, 48(3): 251–7.

Applebey, G. (1994) *A Practical Guide to the Small Claims Court.* Croydon: Tolley.

Armson, S. (1995) Chief Executive, Samaritans, *Personal Communication.*

Austin, K., Moline, M. and Williams, G. (1990) *Confronting Malpractice: Legal and Ethical Dilemmas in Psychotherapy.* London: Sage.

Bailey, S. (1988) 'A problem with discipline: The Nurses, Midwives and Health Visitors (Professional Conduct) Rules 1983', *Professional Negligence*, July/August: 108–11.

Balen, D. (1995) 'Professionalism in practice insurance', *The Therapist*, 3(2): 15–17.

Ball, V. (1995) *Guidelines for the Employment of Counsellors in General Practice.* Rugby: Counselling in Medical Settings/BAC.

Barclay Report (1982) *Social Workers: Their Role and Tasks.* National Institute for Social Work, London: National Council for Voluntary Organisations/Bedford Square.

Barkham, M. (1992) 'Research on integrative and eclectic therapy', in W. Dryden (ed.), *Integrative and Eclectic Therapy: A Handbook*. Buckingham: Open University Press. pp. 239–68.

Baron, J. (1993) 'Self discipline', *The Therapist*, 1(2): 10–11.

Baron, J. (1996) 'The emergence of counselling as a profession', in R. Bayne, I. Horton and J. Bimrose (eds), *New Directions in Counselling*. London: Routledge. pp. 16–24.

Bass, E. and Davis, L. (1991) *The Courage to Heal: A Guide for Women Survivors of Child Sexual Abuse*. London: Cedar.

Bawdon, F. (1994) 'Expert pioneers', *Supplement to Solicitors' Journal*, 3 June: 20–22.

Bazire, S. (1995) *Psychotropic Drugs Directory*. Quay: Salisbury.

BBC (1992) *Public Eye* documentary.

BBC (1994) *Inside Story* documentary, 15 June.

BBC (1996) *Watchdog*, 26 February.

Beauchamp, T. and Childress, J.F. (1989) *Principles of Biomedical Ethics*. Third edition. Oxford: Oxford University Press.

Bennett, C. (1994) 'Lend me your ears', *Guardian*, 5 May.

Bergin, A.E. and Garfield, S.L. (eds) (1994) *Handbook of Psychotherapy and Behaviour Change*. Fourth edition. Chichester: Wiley.

Berlin, M. and Dyer, C. (1990) *The Law Machine*. Third edition. Harmondsworth: Penguin.

Biggs, V. and Robson, J. (eds) (1992) *Developing Your Court Work Skills*. London: British Agencies for Adoption and Fostering.

Birley, J. (1994) *Psychiatric Scandals: Past, Present and Future*. Occasional Paper 24. London: Royal College of Psychiatrists.

Birley, J. (1996) 'Whistle blowing', *Advances in Psychiatric Treatment*, 2: 48–54.

Black, D., Wolkind, S. and Hendriks, J.H. (eds) (1991) *Child Psychiatry and the Law*. Second edition. London: Gaskell/Royal College of Psychiatrists.

Bloom, J., Gerstein, L., Tarvydas, V., Conaster, J., Davis, D., Kater, D., Sherrard, P. and Esposito, R. (1990) 'Model legislation for licensed professional counselors', *Journal of Counseling and Development*, May/June, 68: 511–22.

Bluglass, R. (1984) *A Guide to the Mental Health Act 1983*. London: Churchill Livingstone.

Bluglass, R. (1995) 'Preparing a medico-legal report', *Advances in Psychiatric Treatment*, I: 131–7.

Bolger, T. (1991) 'Research and evaluation in counselling', in W. Dryden, D. Charles-Edwards and R. Woolfe (eds), *Handbook of Counselling in Britain*. London: Routledge. pp. 385–400.

Bollas, C. and Sundelson, D. (1995) *The New Informants: Betrayal of Confidentiality in Psychoanalysis and Psychotherapy*. Karnac: London.

Bond, T. (1991) 'Suicide and sex in the development of ethics for counsellors', *Changes: An International Journal of Psychology and Psychotherapy*, 9(4): 284–93.

Bond, T. (1992a) 'Ethical issues in counselling in education', *British Journal of Guidance and Counselling*, 20(1): 51–63.

Bond, T. (1992b) Letter, *Counselling*, 3(4): 198–9.

Bond, T. (1992c) *HIV Counselling*. Second edition. Rugby: BAC/Department of Health.

Bond, T. (1992d) 'Confidentiality: counselling, ethics and the law', *Employee Counselling Today*, 4(4): 4–9.

Bond, T. (1993a) *Standards and Ethics for Counselling in Action*. London: Sage.

Bond, T. (1993b) 'Counsellor/client sex', in W. Dryden (ed.), *Questions and Answers on Counselling in Action*. London: Sage. pp. 103–7.

Bond, T. (1993c) 'Reporting a colleague's misconduct', in W. Dryden (ed.), *Questions and Answers on Counselling in Action*. London: Sage. pp. 108–12.

Bond, T. (1993d) 'HMI's powers to inspect student counsellors', *Counselling*, 4(3): 177–8.

Bond, T. and BAC Standards and Ethics Sub-Comittee (1994a) *Counselling, Confidentiality and the Law*. Rugby: British Association for Counselling.

Bond, T. (1994b) 'A new era for ethical standards for therapy', *The Therapist*, 4(1): 20–23.

Bond, T. (1996) Personal communication.

Bor, R., Miller, R. and Goldman, E. (1992) *Theory and Practice of HIV Counselling: A Systemic Approach*. London: Cassell.

Bowman, C.G. and Mertz, E.E. (1996) 'A dangerous direction: legal intervention in sexual abuse therapy', *Harvard Law Review*, January, 109(3): 551–639.

Bradbury, A. (1993) 'Therapists and data protection', *The Therapist*, 1(1): 4.

Bradley, J. (1989) 'Malpractice in psychiatry', *Medico-Legal Journal*, 57(3): 164–73.

Bray, J.H., Shepherd, J.N. and Hays, J.R. (1985) 'Legal and ethical issues in informed consent to psychotherapy', *American Journal of Family Therapy*, 13(2): 50–60.

Brayne, H. and Martin, G. (1995) *Law for Social Workers*. Fourth edition. London: Blackstone.

Brazier, M. (1992) *Medicine, Patients and the Law*. Second edition. Harmondsworth: Penguin.

Brinkley, A. (1993) 'Families hit by a wall of silence', *Legal Aid News*, October.

British Association for Counselling (BAC) (1984) *Code of Ethics and Practice for Counsellors*. Rugby: BAC.

British Association for Counselling (1989) *Code of Ethics and Practice for Counselling Skills*. Rugby: BAC.

British Association for Counselling (1992a) *Code of Ethics and Practice for Counsellors*. Rugby: BAC.

British Association for Counselling (1992b) *Complaints Procedure*. Rugby: BAC.

British Association for Counselling (1993a) *Code of Ethics and Practice for Counsellors*. Rugby: BAC.

British Association for Counselling (1993b) 'Membership Survey 1993', *Counselling*, 4(4): 243–4.

British Association for Counselling (1993c) *Recognition of Counsellor Training Courses*. Third edition. Rugby: BAC.

British Association for Counselling (1994a) *Complaints Procedure*. Rugby: BAC.

British Association for Counselling (1994b) 'A United Kingdom Register of Counsellors', *Counselling*, 4(4): 252–3.

British Association for Counselling (1995a) 'Prevention of child abuse – call to counsellors to give their views', *Counselling*, 6(2): 95–8.

British Association for Counselling (1995b) *Code of Ethics and Practice for Trainers of Counselling and Counselling Skills*. Rugby: BAC.

British Association for Counselling (1996) *Code of Ethics and Practice for Counsellors*. Rugby: BAC.

British Association for Sexual and Marital Therapy (BASMT) (1991) *Code of Practice*. Sheffield: BASMT.

British Association of Social Workers (BASW) (1995) 'Case book', *Professional Social Work*, January: 7–8.

British Confederation of Psychotherapists (BCP) (1994) *Newsletter*. Autumn.

British Confederation of Psychotherapists (1995a) *Publication Announcement of 1996 Register of Psychotherapists*, Autumn.

British Confederation of Psychotherapists (1995b) *BCP Conference Papers on Psychotherapy and the Law*. London: BCP.

British Medical Association (BMA) (1906) 'Railway signalman: professional secrecy', *British Medical Journal*, 15 December: 1753.

British Medical Association (1995) *Advance Statements about Medical Treatment*. London: British Medical Journal Publishers.

British Medical Association (1996a) 'Medical litigation faces British revolution', *British Medical Journal*, 312: 330.

British Medical Association (1996b) 'US court rules on confidentiality', *British Medical Journal*, 312: 1629.

British Medical Association (BMA), General Medical Services Comitee (GMSC), Health Education Authority (HEA), Brook Advisory Centres (BAC), Family Planning Association (FPA) and Royal College of General Practitioners (RCGP) (1993) *Confidentiality and People Under 16*. London: BMA.

British Psychological Society (BPS) (1995a) *Recovered Memories*. Leicester: BPS.

British Psychological Society (1995b) *Code of Conduct, Ethical Principles and Guidelines*. London: BPS.

British Psychological Society (1995c) 'Professional liability insurance', *The Psychologist*, February: 82–5.

British Psychological Society (1995d) *Expert Testimony: Developing Witness Skills*. Training Video.

Bromberger, B. and Fife-Yeomans, F. (1991) *Deep Sleep: Harry Bailey and the Scandal of Chelmsford*. East Roseville, NSW: Simon and Schuster.

Brown, D. and Pedder, J. (1979) *Introduction to Psychotherapy*. London: Tavistock.

Budd, S. and Sharma, U. (eds) (1994) *The Healing Bond: The Patient–Practitioner Relationship and Therapeutic Responsibility*. London: Routledge.

Bull, D. (1995) 'Interviewing children in legal contexts', in R. Bull and D. Carson (eds), *Handbook of Psychology in Legal Contexts*. Chichester: Wiley. pp. 235–46.

Burnell, A., Fitsell, A. and Reich, D. (1990) *Feeding the Hungry Ghost: A Framework for a Birth Records, Intermediary and Post-Reunion Counselling Service*. Discussion Paper No 6. September. London: Post-Adoption Centre.

Butler, K. (1994) 'You must remember this', *Guardian*, 23 July: 6–12, 53.

Butler-Sloss, E. (1988) *Report of the Inquiry into Child Abuse in Cleveland 1987*. Cm 412. London: HMSO.

Campbell, J.C. (1995) *Assessing Dangerousness*. London: Sage.

Campion, J. (1991) *Counselling Children*. London: Whiting and Birch.

Carolin, B. (1995) 'Working with children in a family and divorce centre', *Counselling*, 6(3): 207–10.

Carson, D. (1990) *Professionals and the Court: A Handbook for Expert Witnesses*. Venture: Birmingham.

Casemore, R. (1995) *Confidentiality and School Counselling*. Occasional Paper No. 1. Rugby: Counselling in Education/BAC.

Central Statistical Office (CSO) (1996) *Social Trends*. London: HMSO.

Chadwick, R. and Ngwena, C. (1992) 'The development of a normative standard in counselling for genetic disease: ethics and law', *Journal of Social Welfare and Family Law*, 4: 276–95.

Children Act Advisory Committee (CAAC) (1993) *Annual Report 1992/93*. London: HMSO.

Children's Legal Centre (CLC) (1994) *Mental Health Handbook*. Second edition. London: CLC.

Childright (1989a) No 57:. 7–10.

Childright (1989b) No 58: 11–14.

Childright (1989c) No 59: 19–20.

Civil, J. (1992) *Managing Student Services*. Coombe Lodge Report. Bristol: Further Education Staff College.

Clare, A. (1993) *In the Psychiatrist's Chair*. London: Mandarin.

Clinical Resource and Audit Group (CRAG) (1993) *Depressive Illness: A Critical Review of Current Practice and the Way Ahead*. Edinburgh: HMSO.

Clothier, C. (1994) *The Allitt Inquiry: An Independent Inquiry Relating to Deaths and Injuries on the Children's Ward at Grantham and Kesteven General Hospital During the Period February to April 1991*. London: HMSO.

Cohen, E.D. (1990) 'Confidentiality, counseling and clients who have AIDS: ethical foundations of a model rule', *Journal of Counseling and Development*, January/February, 68: 282–6.

Cohen, J. (1995) 'The independent?', *Supplement to New Law Journal*, 14 July.

Cohen, K. (1992) 'Some legal issues in counselling and psychotherapy', *British Journal of Guidance and Counselling*, 20(1): 10–26.

Colman, A.M. and Mackay, R.D. (1995) 'Psychological evidence in court: legal developments in England and the United States', *Psychology, Crime and the Law*, 1: 261–8.

Commission of the European Communities (CEC) (1993) *How to Combat Sexual Harassment at Work: A Guide to Implementing the European Commission Code of Practice*. EC: Luxembourg.

Cooper, C. (1995) 'The worrier mentality', *Management Today*, January: 14.

Cooper, C.L., Sadri, G., Allison, T. and Reynolds, P. (1990) 'Stress counselling in the Post Office', *Counselling Psychology Quarterly*, 3(1): 3–11.

Costa, L. and Altekreuse, M. (1994) 'Duty to warn guidelines for mental health counselors', *Journal of Counseling and Development*, March/April, 72: 346–50.

Counselling in Medical Settings (CMS) (1995) *Guidelines for Staff Employed to Counsel in Hospital and Health Care Settings*. Rugby: CMS/BAC.

Counselling in Medical Settings (1996) *CMS News*, 'Letters to the Editor', February: 6.

Craft, N. (1996) 'No touch technique', *British Medical Journal*, 3 February, 312: 318–19.

Crane, P. (1982) *Gays and the Law*. London: Pluto.

Criminal Injuries Compensation Authority (CICA) (1994) *Victims of Crimes of Violence: A Guide to Criminal Injuries Compensation*. Glasgow: CICA.

Crompton, M. (1992) *Counselling and Children*. London: Edward Arnold.

Croner's Europe (1991) 'Brussels Update', 1–425.

Croner's Europe (1995) 'Proposed Directives', 2–407.

Daines, B., Gask, L. and Usherwood, T. (1996) *Medical and Psychiatric Issues for Counsellors*. London: Sage.

Dale, P. (1995) *Counselling Adults Who Were Abused as Children*. Second edition. Rugby: BAC.

Dalton, J. (1993) 'Dropping like flies in academe', *Guardian*, 10 September.

Daly, R.J. (1993) 'Suicide in depressed patients: medico-legal issues', *British Journal of Psychiatry*, 163, (suppl. 20): 29–32.

Daniluk, J.C. and Haverkamp, B.E. (1993) 'Ethical issues in counseling adult survivors of incest', *Journal of Counseling and Development*, 72: 16–22.

Darley, B., Griew, A., McLoughlin, K. and Williams, J. (1994) *How To Keep a*

Clinical Confidence: A Summary of Law and Guidance on Maintaining the Patient's Privacy. London: HMSO.

Data Protection Registrar (DPR) (1992a) *Data Protection Act 1984: Guideline 1: Introduction to the Act*; (1992b) *Guideline 5: Individual Rights.* Wilmslow: DPR.

Data Protection Registrar (1995) *Annual Report 1994–95.* DPR: Wilmslow.

Davies, M. (1995) 'Debt counselling: the rise of a new profession and the professional negligence implications', *Professional Negligence*, 11(1): 27–31.

Davis, L. (1993) *Pastoral Care: Caring for Secondary School Pupils.* London: Janus.

De Cruz, P. (1987) 'Parents, doctors and children: the *Gillick* case and beyond', *Journal of Social Welfare Law*, March: 93–108.

De Tocqueville, A. (1840/1956) *Democracy in America.* London: New English Library.

Department for Education and Employment (DfEE) (1993a) *The Charter for Further Education.* DfEE: London.

Department for Education and Employment (1993b) *The Charter for Higher Education.* DfEE: London.

Department of Education and Science (DES), *Circular 1/89.* London: DES.

Department of Employment (DE) (1995) *How Equal Opportunities Can Benefit Your Business.* London: DE.

Department of the Environment, *Circular 12/88*, London: DoE.

Department of Health (DoH) (1991a) *Children Act 1989: Guidance and Regulations, Vol 2, Family Support, Day Care and Educational Provision for Young Children.* London: HMSO.

Department of Health (1991b) *Children Act 1989: Guidance and Regulations, Vol 3, Family Placement.* London: HMSO.

Department of Health (1991c) *Children Act 1989: Guidance and Regulations, Vol 4, Residential Care.* London: HMSO.

Department of Health (1992) *The Health of the Nation.* Cm 1986. London: DoH.

Department of Health (1994) *Being Heard: The Report of a Review Committee on NHS Complaints Procedures.* London: DoH.

Department of Health (1995a) *Health and Personal Social Services Statistics for England 1994.* London: HMSO.

Department of Health (1995b) *On the State of the Public Health: The Annual Report of the Chief Medical Officer of the Department of Health for the Year 1994.* London: HMSO.

Department of Health (1996) *The Protection and Use of Patient Information: Guidance from the Department of Health.* London: DoH.

Department of Health and Social Security (DHSS) (1976a) *Children Act 1975: Implementation of Section 26, Access by Adopted Children to Birth Records. LAC (76)21.* London: DHSS.

Department of Health and Social Security (1976b) *Access to Birth Records: Notes for Counsellors.* London: HMSO.

Department of Health and Welsh Office (DoH/WO) (1993) *Mental Health Act 1983: Code of Practice.* London: HMSO.

Devine, P. (1989) 'The professions and professional indemnity in the "Single European Market": problems and prospects, *Professional Negligence*, November/December: 185–93.

Division of Educational and Child Psychology (DECP)/BPS (1985) *Child Psychology and the Law.* Leicester: British Psychological Society.

Dobson, R. (1995) 'Increase in "false memory" insurance', *Independent on Sunday*, 12 February.

Dryden, W. (1991) *A Dialogue with Arnold Lazarus*. Buckingham: Open University Press.

Dryden, W. and Feltham, C. (1992) *Psychotherapy and Its Discontents*. Buckingham: Open University Press.

Dugdale, T. (1994) 'Negligence liability and public service professionals', *Professional Negligence*, 10(3): 81–5.

Dyer, C. (1994) 'Fishing for real abuses', *Guardian*, 15 November.

Dyer, C. (1995) 'Any complaints?', *Guardian*, 13 June.

Earwaker, J. (1992) *Helping and Supporting Students*. Buckingham: Open University Press.

East, P. (1995) *Counselling in Medical Settings*. Buckingham: Open University Press.

Eastman, N. (1987) 'Clinical confidentiality: a contractual basis', *Issues in Criminological and Legal Psychiatry*, 11: 49–57.

Eastman, N. (1995) 'Assessing for psychiatric injury and "nervous shock"', *Advances in Psychiatric Treatment*, I: 154–60.

Eaton, L. (1990) 'At the end of the line', *Social Work Today*, 21(48): 20–1.

Ebert, B. (1992), 'Mandatory child abuse reporting in California', *Forensic Reports*, 5: 335–50.

Echiejile, I. (1995) 'The business case for diversity', *Professional Manager*, July: 8–11.

Eldrid, J. (1988) *Caring for the Suicidal*. London: Constable.

Ellison, M. (1996) 'On the record', *Volunteering*, July, 20: 4.

Employment Assistance Programme Association (EAPA) (1995) *UK Standards of Practice and Professional Guidelines for Employee Assistance Programmes*. London: EAPA.

Enns, C.Z., McNeilly, C.L., Corkery, J.M. and Gilbert, M.S. (1995) 'The debate about delayed memories of childhood sexual abuse: a feminist perspective', *The Counseling Psychologist*, 23(2): 181–279.

Erickson, S. (1990) 'Counseling the irresponsible AIDS client: guidelines for decision making', *Journal of Counseling and Development*, March/April, 68: 454–5.

Etzioni, A. (1969) *The Semi-Professions and Their Organization*. New York: Free Press.

European Commission (1993) *Psychotherapy in the European Communities (Outline)*. 26 February.

Evans, R. (1993) *The Conduct of Police Interviews with Juveniles*. Royal Commission on Criminal Justice Research Study No. 8. London: HMSO.

Fasal, J. (1994) *Interview*. June.

Faulk, M. (1994) *Basic Forensic Psychiatry*. Second edition. Oxford: Blackwell.

Faust, D. and Ziskin, J. (1988) 'The expert witness in psychology and psychiatry', *Science*, July, 241: 31–5.

Feldman, D. (1985) 'Access to clients' documents after the Police and Criminal Evidence Act', *Professional Negligence*, January/February: 24–9; March/April: 67–72.

Feldman, S. and Ward, T. (1979) 'Psychotherapeutic injury: reshaping the implied contract as an alternative to malpractice', *North Carolina Law Review*, 58: 63–96.

Fennell, P. (1992) 'Informal compulsion: the psychiatric treatment of juveniles under common law', *Journal of Social Welfare and Family Law*, 4: 311–33.

Fennell, P. (1996) 'Medical law', in *All England Law Reports Annual Review*. London: Butterworth. pp. 354–96.

Fishwick, C. (1988) *Court Work*. Birmingham: Pepar.

Flaxman, R.H. (1989) *How to Protect Your Reputation: A Guide to Professional Indemnity Insurance.* Cambridge: ICSA.

Fleming, J. (1994) *Barbarism to Verdict: A History of the Common Law.* NSW, Australia: Angus and Robertson.

Fletcher, N. (1992) 'The Nurses, Midwives and Health Visitors Act 1992', *Professional Negligence,* 8(3): 94–8.

Flint, M.F. (1990) *A User's Guide to Copyright.* Third edition. London: Butterworth.

Fong, M.L. (1995) 'Assessment and DSM-IV diagnosis of personality disorders: a primer for counselors', *Journal of Counseling and Development,* July/August, 73: 635–9.

Foss, B. (1986) *Review of the Accreditation Scheme.* Rugby: BAC.

Foster, B. and Preston-Shoot, M. (1995) *Guardians-ad-litem and Independent Expert Assessments.* Manchester, Stockport, Tameside and Trafford Guardian-ad-litem Reporting Officer Service and the University of Manchester.

Foster, J.G. (1971) *Enquiry into the Practice and Effects of Scientology.* London: HMSO.

Francis, J. (1995) 'Cast aside', *Community Care,* 28 September.

Frankland, A. (1995) 'An invitation to accreditation: steps towards an emerging profession', *Counselling,* 6(1): 55–60.

Freud, S. (1906/1971), 'Psycho-analysis and the establishment of the facts in legal proceedings', *Jensen's 'Gradiva' and Other Works.* Vol. 9. Standard Edition Complete Works, London: Hogarth/Institute of Psycho-Analysis. pp. 103–14.

Freud, S. (1909/1991) *Case Histories 2: The 'Rat Man'; 'Schreber'; The 'Wolf Man'; A Case of Female Homosexuality.* Vol. 9. Penguin Freud Library, Harmondsworth: Penguin.

Freud, S. (1926/1993) 'The question of lay analysis', in *Psychoanalysis: Its History and Development.* Vol. 15. Penguin Freud Library, Harmondsworth: Penguin. pp. 282–353.

Freud, S. (1927/1993) 'The question of lay analysis: a postscript', in *Psychoanalysis: Its History and Development.* Vol. 15, Penguin Freud Library, Harmondsworth: Penguin. pp. 355–63.

Freud, S. (1931/1971), 'The expert opinion in the Halsmannn case', in *The Future of an Illusion: Civilisation and its Discontents.* Vol 21. Standard Edition Complete Works, London: Hogarth/Institute of Psycho-Analysis. pp. 251–3.

Gabbard, G. (1995) 'Transference and counter transference in the psychotherapy of therapists charged with sexual misconduct', *Journal of Psychotherapy Practice and Research,* 4(1): 10–17.

Gartrell, N.K. (ed.) (1994) *Bringing Ethics Alive: Feminist Ethics in Psychotherapy Practice.* NY: Harrington Park.

Gelder, M., Gath, D. and Mayou, R. (1989) *Oxford Textbook of Psychiatry.* Second edition. Oxford: Oxford University Press.

General Medical Council (GMC) (1992) *Professional Conduct and Discipline: Fitness to Practise.* London: GMC.

General Medical Council (1994) *Annual Report.* London: GMC.

General Medical Council (1995a) *Duties of a Doctor: Guidance from the General Medical Council.* London: GMC.

General Medical Council (1995b) *HIV and AIDS: the Ethical Considerations.* London: GMC.

Giddens, A. (1990) *The Consequences of Modernity.* Stanford, California: Stanford University Press.

Gomien, D. (1991) *Short Guide to the European Convention on Human Rights.* Strasbourg: Council of Europe.

Gooding, C. (1996) *Blackstone's Guide to the Disability Discrimination Act 1995*. London: Blackstone.

Gordon, P. (1993) 'Keeping psychotherapy white? Psychotherapy and equal opportunities', *British Journal of Psychotherapy*, 10(1): 44–9.

Goring, S. and Ward, R. (1990) 'Group work with sex offenders – the legal problem', *Journal of Social Welfare Law*, 3: 193–203.

Gray, L.A. and Harding, A.K. (1988) 'Confidentiality limits with clients who have the AIDS virus', *Journal of Counseling and Development*, 66: 219–23.

Grealis, K. and Coles, D. (1994) 'Inquests: redressing the balance', *Solicitors Journal*, 1 April: 321–2.

Green, J. (1989) 'Post-test counselling', in J. Green and A. McCreaner (eds) *Counselling in HIV Infection and AIDS*. London: Blackwell. pp. 29–68.

Grewal, H. (1988) *The Race Discrimination Handbook*. Harmondsworth: Sphere.

Grewal, H. (1990) *The Sex Discrimination Handbook*. Harmondsworth: Sphere.

Grunebaum, H. (1986) 'Harmful psychotherapy experience', *American Journal of Psychotherapy*, April, XL(2): 165–76.

Gulbenkian Foundation (1993) *One Scandal Too Many: The Case for Comprehensive Protection for Children in All Settings*. London: Calouste Gulbenkian Foundation.

Gunn, M. (1989) 'Sexual abuse and adults with mental handicap: can the law help?', in H. Brown and A. Craft (eds), *Thinking the Unthinkable: Sexual Abuse and People With Learning Difficulties*. London: Family Planning Association. pp. 51–72.

Gunn, M.J. (1991) *Sex and the Law: A Brief Guide for Staff Working with People with Learning Difficulties*, Third edition, London: Family Planning Association.

Halmes, E. and Timms, N. (1985) *Adoption, Identity and Social Policy*. Aldershot: Gower.

Halsbury's Laws of England (1974) Fourth edition. London: Butterworth.

Ham, C., Dingwall, R., Fenn, P. and Harris, D. (1988) *Medical Negligence*. Briefing Paper No. 6, Centre for Socio-Legal Studies. Oxford, London: King's Fund Institute.

Hamilton, A. (1995) 'The criminal law and HIV infection', in R. Haigh and D. Harris (eds), *AIDS: A Guide to the Law*. Second edition. London: Routledge. pp. 21–37.

Hansard (1993a) *House of Lords Education Bill Debate*, 26 June, Cols. 64–5; (1993b) Standing Committee, Education Bill 1992–1993, 9 February, Cols. 1511–1516.

Hansard (1995) House of Lords, 1622, WA 3, 6 February.

Hansen, O. (1994) *The Solicitors' Complaints Bureau: A Consumer View*. London: National Consumer Council.

Harding, A.K., Gray, L.A. and Neal, M. (1993) 'Confidentiality limits with clients who have HIV: a review of ethical and legal guidelines and professional policies', *Journal of Counseling and Development*, January/February, 71: 297–305.

Harpwood, V. (1994) 'Medical negligence claims and NHS complaints', *Professional Negligence*, 10(3): 74–81.

Harrar, W.R., VandeCreek, L. and Knapp, S. (1990) 'Ethical and legal aspects of clinical supervision', *Professional Psychology*, 21(1): 37–41.

Harris, B. (1976) *A Guide to the Rehabilitation of Offenders Act 1974*. London: Barry Rose.

Harris, D. and Haigh, R. (1995) *AIDS: A Guide to the Law*. Second edition. London: Routledge Kegan Paul.

Harris, N. (1993) *Law and Education: Regulation, Consumerism and the Education System*. London: Sweet and Maxwell.

Harrison, H. (1994) 'Childline UK: How children and young people communicate their experiences by telephone', in V. Sinason (ed.), *Treating Survivors of Satanist Abuse*. London: Routledge. pp. 171–3.

Harrop-Griffiths, H. and Bennington, J. (1985) *Professional Negligence*. Second edition, London: Fourmat.

Hawkins, C. (1985) *Mishap or Malpractice?* London: Blackwell Scientific Publications.

Hay, P. (1991) *An Introduction to US Law*. Second edition. New Hampshire, USA: Butterworth.

Hayman, A. (1965) 'Points of view', *The Lancet*, 16 October: 785–6.

Her Majesty's Government (HMG) (1991) *Citizens' Charters*. Cm 1599. London: HMSO.

Hervey, T. (1985) 'The immunity of expert witnesses', *Professional Negligence*, May/June: 102–5.

Higgs, R. and Dammers, J. (1992) 'Ethical issues in counselling and health in primary care', *British Journal of Guidance and Counselling*, 20(1): 27–38.

Hill, D. (1995) Relate, *Personal Communication*.

Hodgkins, P. (1991) *Birth Records Counselling: A Practical Guide*. London: British Agencies for Adoption and Fostering.

Hogan, D. (1979) *The Regulation of Psychotherapists*. Vols 1–4. Cambridge, Massachusetts: Ballinger.

Hoggett, B. (1996) *Mental Health Law*. Fourth edition. London: Sweet and Maxwell.

Hohensil, T.H. (1994) 'DSM-IV: What's new', *Journal of Counseling and Development*, September/October, 73: 105–7.

Holmes, J., Adshead, G. and Smith, J. (1994) 'An ethical dilemma in psychotherapy', *Psychiatric Bulletin*, 18(8): 466–8.

Holmes, J. and Lindley, R. (1989) *The Values of Psychotherapy*. Oxford: Oxford University Press.

Holmes, J. and Lindley, R. (1994) 'Ethics and psychotherapy', in R. Gillon (ed.), *Principles of Health Care Ethics*. Chichester: Wiley. pp. 671–80.

Home Office (1991) *Police and Criminal Evidence Act 1984 (s.66): Codes of Practice*. Second Edition. London: HMSO.

Home Office (1993) *Disclosure of Criminal Records for Employment Vetting Purposes*. Cm 2319. London: HMSO.

Home Office (1996a) *On the Record: The Government's Proposals for Access to Criminal Records for Employment and Related Purposes in England and Wales*. London: HMSO.

Home Office (1996b) *Stalking – The Solutions: A Consultation Paper*. London: Home Office.

Home Office Circular No. 66/1988 *The Use of Hypnosis by the Police in the Investigation of Crime*.

Home Office/Department of Health (1991) *Working Together: Under the Children Act 1989: A Guide to Arrangments for Inter-agency Cooperation for the Protection of Children from Abuse*. London: HMSO.

Home Office/Department of Health (1992) *Memorandum of Good Practice on Video Recorded Interviews with Child Witnesses in Criminal Proceedings*. London: HMSO.

Home Office/Scottish Education Department (1972) *Report of the Departmental Committee on the Adoption of Children*. Cmnd 5107. London: HMSO.

Honigsbaum, M. (1995) 'Dark side of the New Age', *Daily Mail*, 5 April.

Hopkins, B. and Anderson, B. (1990) *The Counselor and the Law*. Alexandria, VA: American Counseling Association.

Human Fertilisation and Embryology Authority (HFEA) (1993) *Code of Practice*. London: HFEA.

Hurwitz, B. (1995) 'Clinical guidelines and the law: advice, guidance, or regulation?', *Journal of Evaluation in Clinical Practice*, 1(1): 49–60.

Ingram, K. and Roy, L. (1995) 'Complaints against psychiatrists: a five year study', *Psychiatric Bulletin*, 19: 620–22.

Inquest (1995) *Victims Without a Voice Project*. London: Inquest.

Inquest (nd) *A Short Guide to Inquests*. London: Inquest.

Institute for Personnel Development (IPD) (1995) *Guide on Employee Data*. London: IPD.

J.M. Consulting Ltd (1996) *The Regulation of Health Professions: Report of a Review of the Professions Suplementary to Medicine Act (1960) with Recommendations for New Legislation*. Bristol: J.M. Consulting Ltd.

Jackson, J. (1995) 'Evidence: legal perspective', in R. Bull and D. Carson (eds), *Handbook of Psychology in Legal Contexts*. Chichester: Wiley. pp. 163–77.

Jakobi, S. (1995) *The Law and the Training of Counsellors and Psychotherapists*. Wealden College: Royal Society of Medicine.

Jakobi, S. and Pratt, D. (1992) 'Therapy notes and the law', *The Psychologist*, May: 219–21.

James, A.L. and Wilson, K. (1991) 'Marriage, social policy and social work', *Journal of Social Work Practice*, 5(2): 171–80.

Jeffs, T. (1995) 'Children's educational rights in a new ERA?' in B. Franklin (ed.), *Handbook of Children's Rights: Comparative Policy and Practice*. Routledge: London. pp. 25–39.

Jehu, D., Davis, J., Garrett, T., Jorgensen, L.M. and Schoener, G.R. (1994) *Patients as Victims: Sexual Abuse in Psychotherapy and Counselling*. Chichester: Wiley.

Jenkins, P. (1993a) *Children's Rights*. Harlow: Longman.

Jenkins, P. (1993b) 'Counselling and the Children Act 1989', *Counselling*, 4(4): 274–6.

Jenkins, P. (1995a) 'Advocacy and the 1989 United Nations Convention on the Rights of the Child', in J. Dalrymple and J. Evans (eds), *Having a Voice*. London: Venture. pp. 31–52.

Jenkins, P. (1995b) 'Two models of counsellor training: becoming a person or learning to be a skilled helper?', *Counselling*, 6(3): 203–6.

Jenkins, P. (1995c) *The Law and the Training of Counsellors and Psychotherapists*. Wealden College: Royal Society of Medicine.

Jenkins, P. (1996) 'Counselling and the law', in S. Palmer, S. Dainow and P. Milner (eds), *The BAC Counselling Reader*. London: Sage/BAC. pp. 451–7.

Jenkins, P. (1997) 'False or recovered memories? Legal and ethical dilemmas for therapists', *British Journal of Guidance and Counselling*, 25(2): 199–215.

Johnson, T.J. (1972) *Professions and Power*. London: Macmillan.

Jones, C. (1993) 'The complaints procedure – lessons from the past year', *Counselling*, 4(1): 14–15.

Jones, R. (ed.) (1997) *Mental Health Act Manual*. Fifth edition. London: Sweet and Maxwell.

Judicial Studies Board (JSB) (1994) *Guidelines for the Assessment of General Damages in Personal Injury Cases*. London: Blackstone.

Kennedy, H. (1992) *Eve Was Framed: Women and British Justice*. London: Chatto & Windus.

Kermani, E.J. (1989) *Handbook of Psychiatry and the Law.* London: Year Book Medical Publishers.

Kirkwood, A. (1993) *The Leicestershire Inquiry 1992.* Derby: Leicestershire County Council.

Kitching, A. (1995a) 'Contract counselling', *Counselling,* 6(1): 10–11.

Kitching, A. (1995b) 'Our duty of care goes beyond the grave', *Counselling,* 6(4): 269–70.

Kitching, A. (1995c) 'Practical approaches: counselling assurance', *Counselling,* 6(3): 188–9.

Kloss, D. (1989) 'Legal aspects', in J. Green and A. McCreaner (eds), *Counselling in HIV Infection and AIDS.* London: Blackwell. pp. 285–300.

Knight, B.H. and Palmer, R.N. (1992) *Medico-Legal Reports and Appearing in Court.* London: Medical Protection Society.

Kohon, G. (1986) *The British School of Psychoanalysis: The Independent Tradition.* London: Free Association.

Labour Research Department (LRD) (1994) *The Law at Work.* London: LRD.

Laing, R.D. (1985) *Wisdom, Madness and Folly: The Making of a Psychiatrist.* London: Macmillan.

Lambert, M.J., Bergin, A.E. and Collins, J.L. (1977) 'Therapist induced deterioration in psychotherapy', in A. Gurman and A. Razin (eds), *Effective Psychotherapy: A Handbook.* Oxford: Pergamon. pp. 452–81.

Law Commission (1981) *Breach of Confidence.* Cmnd 8388. London: HMSO.

Law Commission (1995a) *Liability for Psychiatric Illness.* Consultation Paper No. 137. London: HMSO.

Law Commission (1995b) *Damages for Personal Injury: Non-pecuniary Loss.* Consultation Paper No 140. London: HMSO.

Law Society, (1990) *A Survey of Complainant Satisfaction among Lay Complainants to the Solicitors' Complaints Bureau.* London: Law Society.

Leder, M. and Shears, P. (1991) *Consumer Law.* Third edition. London: Longman.

Lee, C.C. and Six, T.L. (1992) 'Counsellor licensure: the American experience', *Counselling,* 3(2): 93–5.

Lefébure, M. (1996) 'Who will count as a counsellor? Gleanings and tea leaves', in R. Bayne, I. Horton and J. Bimrose (eds), *New Directions in Counselling.* London: Routledge. pp. 5–15.

Lendrum, S. and Syme, G. (1992) *Gift of Tears: A Practical Approach to Loss and Bereavement Counselling.* London: Routledge.

Levine, M. and Doueck, H.J. (1995) *The Impact of Mandated Reporting on the Therapeutic Process.* London: Sage.

Levy, A. and Kahan, B. (1991) *The Pindown Experience and the Protection of Children: The Report of the Staffordshire Child Care Enquiry 1990.* Staffordshire County Council.

Lewis, J., Clark, D. and Morgan, D. (1992) *Whom God Hath Joined Together: The Work of Marriage Guidance.* London: Routledge.

Lindsay, D.S. and Read, J.D. (1994) 'Psychotherapy and memories of childhood sexual abuse: a cognitive perspective', *Applied Cognitive Psychology,* 8: 281–338.

Lindsay, M. (1991) 'Complaints procedures and their limitations in the light of the "Pindown" enquiry', *Journal of Social Welfare and Family Law,* 6: 432–41.

Littlechild, B. (1994) *The Social Worker as Appropriate Adult under the Police and Criminal Evidence Act 1984.* Birmingham: British Association of Social Workers Trading Ltd.

Litton, R. (1996) 'Professional liability insurance for counsellors', *Counselling*, 7(1): 19–24.

Lloyd-Bostock, S. (1988) *Law in Practice*. London: British Psychological Society/ Routledge.

Lord Chancellor's Department (1995) *Looking to the Future: Mediation and the Grounds for Divorce*. Cm 2799. London: HMSO.

Lord Chancellor's Department (1996) *Striking the Balance: The Future of Legal Aid in England and Wales*. Cm 3305. London: HMSO.

Malek, M. (1991) *Psychiatric Admissions: A Report on Young People Entering Residential Psychiatric Care*. London: Children's Society.

Malek, M. (1993) *Passing the Buck: A Summary: Institutional Responses to Controlling Children with Difficult Behaviour*. London: Children's Society.

Mandelstam, M. and Schwehr, B. (1995) *Community Care Practice and the Law*. London: Jessica Kingsley.

Mangalmurti, V.S. (1994) 'Psychotherapists' fear of *Tarasoff*: all in the mind?', *Journal of Psychiatry and Law*, Fall, 22(3): 379–409.

Manning, M. (1988) 'The implications of Clause 28', *Social Work Today*, 26 May: 14–16.

Marks. L. (1995) 'Adopted and at home in the world: a message for counsellors', *Counselling*, 6(1): 48–50.

Masson, J. (1992) *Against Therapy*. London: Fontana.

Matthews, A. (1995) *The Litigation Handbook: A Guide to the Civil Courts*. London: Fitzwarren.

McAllister, F. (1995) *The Law and the Training of Counsellors and Psychotherapists*. Wealden College: Royal Society of Medicine.

McEwan, J. (1995) 'Adversarial and inquisitorial proceedings', in R. Bull and D. Carson (eds), *Handbook of Psychology in Legal Contexts*. Chichester: Wiley. pp. 495–508.

McGee, A. (1992) 'Requirements of supervision in professional liability policies', *Professional Negligence*, 8(3): 113–14.

McHale, J.V. (1993a) 'Confidentiality and the Human Fertilisation and Embryology Act 1990 – a problem reconsidered', *Professional Negligence*, 9(2): 74–5.

McHale, J.V. (1993b) *Medical Confidentiality and Legal Privilege*. London: Routledge.

McLeod, J. (1993) *An Introduction to Counselling*. Buckingham: Open University Press.

McLeod, J. (1994) *Doing Counselling Research*. London: Sage.

McMahon, G. (1994) *Setting Up Your Own Private Practice in Counselling and Psychotherapy*. Cambridge: National Extension College.

Mearns, D. (1993) 'Against indemnity insurance', in W. Dryden (ed.), *Questions and Answers on Counselling in Action*. London: Sage. pp. 161–4.

Medical Protection Society (MPS) (1995) 'Psychiatrist harassed by former patient', *MPS Casebook No 5*. p. 16.

Megranahan, M. (1989) *Counselling: A Practical Guide for Employers*. London: Institute for Personnel Management.

Meyer, G., Landis, E. and Hays, J. (1988) *Law for the Psychotherapist*. New York: Norton.

MIND (1995) *Getting the Best from Your Counsellor or Psychotherapist*. London: MIND.

Mitchison, A. (1992) 'The boy who peaked too soon', *Independent Magazine*, 12 December.

Morgan, D. and Lee, R. (1991) *Human Fertilisation and Embryology Act 1990: Abortion and Embryo Research, The New Law*. London: Blackstone.

Mowbray, R. (1995) *The Case against Psychotherapy Registration*. London: Trans Marginal Press.

Mulholland, M. (1993) '*Re W*. (A minor): Autonomy, consent and the anorexic teenager', *Professional Negligence*, 9(1): 21–4.

Mullaney, N.J. and Handford, P.R. (1993) *Tort Liability for Psychiatric Damage: The Law of 'Nervous Shock'*. Sydney: Law Book Company.

Mullis, A. and Oliphant, K. (1993) *Torts*. London: Macmillan.

Munday, R. (1987) 'The admissibility of hypnotically refreshed testimony', *Justice of the Peace*, 151: 404–6.

Murray, S. (1995) *The Law and the Training of Counsellors and Psychotherapists*. Wealden College: Royal Society of Medicine.

Naish, S. (1994) *Counselling People with Fertility Problems*. Rugby: BAC.

National Association of Local Government Officers (NALGO) (1992) *Lesbian and Gay Organising Handbook*. London: NALGO.

National Children's Home: Action for Children (NCH) (1994) *Messages from Children: Children's Evaluations of the Professional Response to Child Sexual Abuse*. London: NCH.

National Consumer Council (NCC) (1993) *Getting the Best from Your Solicitor*. London: NCC.

National Medical Advisory Committee (NMAC) (1994) *Management of Anxiety and Insomnia*. Edinburgh: HMSO.

National Union of Teachers (NUT) (1991) *Lesbians and Gays in Schools: An Issue for Every Teacher*. London: NUT.

NHS Executive (1996) *Practice-Based Complaints Procedures: Guidance for General Practices*. London: DoH.

NHS Executive North-West (1994) *Report of Inquiry into Dr Maden*. NHS NW: Warrington.

Nijboer, H. (1995) 'Expert evidence', in R. Bull and D. Carson (eds), *Handbook of Psychology in Legal Contexts*. Chichester: Wiley. pp. 555–64.

Office of Fair Trading (OFT) (1994) *A Buyer's Guide*. London: OFT.

Orr, M. (1996) 'False memory law suits against therapists', *Counselling News*, March: 14–15.

Otto, R. and Schmidt, W. (1991) 'Malpractice in verbal psychotherapy: problems and some solutions', *Forensic Reports*, 4: 309–36.

Owen, I. (1993) 'Assesment for counselling and the psychiatric services', *Counselling*, 4(4): 287–9.

Owens, R.G. (1995) 'Legal and psychological concepts of mental status', in R. Bull and D. Carson (eds), *Handbook of Psychology in Legal Contexts*. Chichester: Wiley. pp. 315–28.

Packman, J. (1975) *The Child's Generation: Child Care Policy from Curtis to Houghton*. London: Basil Blackwell and Martin Robertson.

Packman, W.L., Cabot, M.G. and Bongar, B. (1994) 'Malpractice arising from negligent psychotherapy: ethical, legal and clinical implications of *Osheroff v. Chestnut Lodge*', *Ethics and Behaviour*, 4(3): 175–97.

Page, S. and Wosket, V. (1994) *Supervising the Counsellor: A Cyclical Model*. London: Routledge.

Painter, A.A. and Lawson, R.G. (1990) *Business Law*. London: Heinemann.

Palmer, S. (1991) 'Directive may affect counselling', *Counselling*, 2(2): 34.

Palmer, S. and Szymanska, K. (1994) 'How to avoid being exploited in counselling and psychotherapy', *Counselling*, 5(1): 24.

Palmer-Barnes, F. (1993) 'In the complaints chair', *Counselling*, 4(2): 84–6.

Palmer-Barnes, F. (1995) 'New directions in counselling: a roundtable', *Counselling*, 6(1): 34–40.

Pannett, A.J. (1992) *Law of Torts*. Sixth edition. London: Longman.

Panting, G.P. and Palmer, R.N. (1992) *Disclosure of Medical Records*. London: Medical Protection Society.

Parkinson, L. (1991) 'The split couple: conciliation and mediation approaches', in D. Hooper and W. Dryden (eds), *Couple Therapy: A Handbook*. Buckingham: Open University Press. pp. 217–37.

Parsloe, P. (1988) 'Social services: confidentiality, privacy and data protection', in P. Pearce, P. Parsloe, H. Francis, A. Maccara and D. Watson (eds), *Personal Data Protection in Health and Social Services*. Beckenham: Croom Helm. pp. 28–91.

Patients' Association (PA) (1995) *Advance Statements about Future Medical Treatment: A Guide for Patients*. London: PA.

Pearce, J. (1994) 'Consent to treatment during childhood: the assessment of competence and the avoidance of conflict', *British Journal of Psychiatry*, 165: 713–16.

Pearce, P. (1988) 'The law', in P. Pearce, P. Parsloe, H. Francis, A. Maccara and D. Watson (eds), *Personal Data Protection in Health and Social Services*. Beckenham: Croom Helm. pp. 1–27.

Pearson Commission (1978) *Royal Commission on Civil Liability and Compensation for Personal Injury*. Cmnd 7504. Report Vol. 1. London: HMSO.

Perry, J.C. and Jacobs, D. (1982) 'Overview: clinical applications of the amytal interview in psychiatric emergency settings', *American Journal of Psychiatry*, 139(5): 552–9.

Phillips, M. (1991) 'Violations of the ground rule of confidentiality in a counselling centre: the contribution of Langs', *Counselling*, 2(3): 92–4.

Phillips, R. and McWilliam, E. (1995) 'Developing a post-adoptive service for adoptive families', *Practice*, 7(3): 45–58.

Plotnikoff, J. (1990) 'Compensation and child abuse', *Journal of Law and Practice*, 1(3): 18–34.

Plotnikoff, J. and Woolfson, R. (1996) *Reporting to the Court under the Children Act*. London: DoH.

Public Law Project (PLP) (1994) *Challenging Community Care Decisions*. London: PLP.

Pugh, C. and Trimble, M.R. (1993) 'Psychiatric injury after Hillsborough', *British Journal of Psychiatry*, 163: 425–9.

Putnam, F.W. (1992) 'Using hypnosis for therapeutic abreactions', *Psychiatric Medicine*, 10: 51–65.

Radio Lancashire (1994) *Documentary on Dr Maden*, 27 August.

Randle, M. (1995) *How to Defend Yourself in Court*. London: Civil Liberties Trust.

Ratigan, B. (1991) 'Counselling in Higher Education', in W. Dryden, D. Charles-Edwards and R. Woolfe (eds), *Handbook of Counselling in Britain*. London: Tavistock/Routledge. pp. 151–67.

Read, J. (1995) *Counselling for Fertility Problems*. London: Sage.

Reamer, F.G. (1993) 'Liability issues in social work administration', *Administration in Social Work*, 17(4): 11–25.

Reddy, M. (1987) *The Manager's Guide to Counselling at Work*. London: Methuen/BPS.

Reed, D. (1976) *Anna*. London: Secker and Warburg.

Reid, B.R. (1986) *Confidentiality and the Law*. London: Waterlow.

Reynolds, M.P. and King, P.S.D. (1989) *The Expert Witness and his Evidence*. London: Blackwell Scientific Publications.

Reynolds, P. and Allison, T. (1996) 'Criminal assault at work', in S. Palmer, S. Dainow and P. Milner (eds), *The BAC Counselling Reader*. London: Sage/BAC. pp. 242–53.

Roberts, W., Schmid, R. and Blaine, B. (1994) 'The passage of counselor legislation in the 1991 Arkansas State Legislature', *Journal of Counseling and Development*, November/December, 73: 227–30.

Robertson, G. and Nicol, A. (1992) *Media Law*. Third edition. Harmondsworth: Penguin.

Robertson, G. and Tudor, K. (1993) 'Counselling in the context of community care', *Counselling*, 4(3): 188–90.

Roche, J. and Briggs, A. (1990) 'Allowing children a voice: a note on confidentiality', *Journal of Social Welfare Law*, 3: 178–92.

Rodger, B. (1995) 'Equal treatment among professions? Public policy and social workers' liability', *Professional Negligence*, 11(4): 114–20.

Rogers, A., Pilgrim, D. and Lacey, R. (1993) *Experiencing Psychiatry*. MIND/ Macmillan.

Rosenfield, M. (1996) *Counselling by Telephone*. London: Sage.

Roth, A. and Fonagy, P. (1996) *What Works for Whom? A Critical Review of Psychotherapy Research*. New York: Guilford.

Royal College of Psychiatrists (RCP) (1990) 'Position statement on confidentiality', *Psychiatric Bulletin*, 14: 97–109.

Royal College of Psychiatrists (1996) 'Advance statements about medical treatment', *Psychiatric Bulletin*, 20: 56–9.

Rozenberg, J. (1994) *The Search for Justice: An Anatomy of the Law*. London: Hodder and Stoughton.

Rudinger, E. (ed.) (1985) *Taking Your Own Case to Court or Tribunal*. London: Consumers' Association/Hodder and Stoughton.

Russell, J. (1993) *Out of Bounds: Sexual Exploitation in Counselling and Therapy*. London: Sage.

Rutter, P. (1991) *Sex in the Forbidden Zone*. London: Mandala.

Ryan, V. and Wilson, K. (1995) 'Child therapy and evidence in court proceedings: tensions and some solutions', *British Journal of Social Work*, 25: 157–72.

Scott, M. and Stradling, S. (1992) *Counselling for Post-Traumatic Stress Disorder*. London: Sage.

Scott, W. (1994) *The General Practitioner and the Law of Negligence*. Buckinghamshire: Business and Medical Publishers.

Sheppard, D. (1995) *The Appropriate Adult: A Review of the Case Law 1988–1995*. Hoylake: Institute of Mental Health Law.

Shield, J. and Baum, J. (1994) 'Children's consent to treatment', *British Medical Journal*, 7 May, 308: 1182–3.

Sieghart, P. (1978) *Statutory Registration of Psychotherapists: A Report of Professions Joint Working Party*. London: Tavistock.

Sinason, V. (1995) *Mental Handicap and the Human Condition: New Approaches from the Tavistock*. London: Free Association.

Slawson, P.F. and Guggenheim, F.G. (1984) 'Psychiatric malpractice: a review of the national loss experience', *American Journal of Psychiatry*, 141(8): 979–81.

Smith, R.G. (1995) *Medical Discipline: The Professional Conduct Jurisdiction of the General Medical Council 1858–1990*. London: Clarendon.

Sone, K. (1995) 'Whisle down the wind', *Community Care*, 6 July: 16–17.

Southern Derbyshire Health Authority and Derbyshire County Council (SHDA/

DCC) (1996) *Report of the Inquiry into the Care of Anthony Smith*. Derby: SDHA/DCC.

Stacey, M. (1994) 'Collective therapeutic responsibility: lessons from the GMC', in S. Budd and U. Sharma (eds), *The Healing Bond: The Patient–Practitioner Relationship and Therapeutic Responsibility*. London: Routledge. pp. 107–33.

Stanard, R. and Hazler, R. (1995) 'Legal and ethical implications of HIV and duty to warn for counselors: does *Tarasoff* apply?', *Journal of Counseling and Development*, March/April, 73: 397–400.

Stanton, K. (1986) 'Obtaining leave to bring a negligence action: Section 139 of the Mental Health Act 1983', *Professional Negligence*, July/August: 106–7.

Stone, J. and Matthews, J. (1996) *Complementary Medicine and the Law*. Oxford: Oxford University Press.

Straus, S. (1996) 'Chronic fatigue syndrome', *British Medical Journal*, 5 October, 313: 831–2.

Striano, J. (1988) *Can Psychotherapists Hurt You?* Santa Barbara: Professional Press.

Stuart-Smith, S. (1996) 'Teenage sex', *British Medical Journal*, 17 February, 312: 390–91.

Sugarman, L. (1992) 'Ethical issues in counselling at work', *British Journal of Guidance and Counselling*, 20(1): 64–75.

Sumerling, R. (1994) 'Therapeutic responsibility and the law', in S. Budd and U. Sharma (eds), *The Healing Bond: The Patient–Practitioner Relationship and Therapeutic Responsibility*. London: Routledge. pp. 134–50.

Sumerling, R. (1996) 'Violence and harassment against medical practitioners', *Medical Protection Society Casebook*, No 8: 8–10.

Sutherland, S. (1977) *Breakdown*. St Albans: Paladin.

Syme, G. (1994) *Counselling in Independent Practice*. Buckingham: Open University Press.

Thompson, A. (1983) *Ethical Concerns in Psychotherapy and Their Legal Ramifications*. Lanham: University Press of America.

Thompson, H. (1994) 'When therapists are the problem', *The Times*, 26 April.

Thoreson, R.W., Shaughnessy, P., Heppner, P.P. and Cook, S.W. (1993) 'Sexual contact during and after the professional relationship: attitudes and practices of male counselors', *Journal of Counseling and Development*, March/April, 71: 429–34.

Thorne, B. (1987) 'Beyond the core conditions', in W. Dryden (ed.), *Key Cases in Psychotherapy*. London: Croom Helm. pp. 48–77; also published in Thorne, B. (1991) *Person-Centred Counselling: Therapeutic and Spiritual Dimensions*. London: Whurr.

Thorne, B. (1990) *Carl Rogers*. London: Sage.

Thorne, B. (1992) 'Psychotherapy and counselling: the quest for differences', *Counselling*, 3(4): 244–8.

Thorne, B. (1993) 'Body and spirit', in W. Dryden (ed.), *Questions and Answers on Counselling in Action*. London: Sage. pp. 113–17.

Tolley, K. and Rowland, N. (1995) *Evaluating the Cost-Effectiveness of Counselling in Health Care*. London: Routledge.

Trayner, B. and Clarkson, P. (1992) 'What happens when a psychotherapist dies?', *Counselling*, 3(1): 23–4.

Triseliotis, J. (1973) *In Search of Origins: The Experience of Adopted People*. London: Routledge and Kegan Paul.

Tyndall, N. (1986) *Relate: Marriage Guidance Counselling*. Rugby: National Marriage Guidance Council.

Unell, J. (1992) *Criminal Record Checks Within the Voluntary Sector: An Evaluation of the Pilot Scheme*. London: Volunteer Centre.

UNICEF (1989) *The United Nations Convention on the Rights of the Child 1989*. London: Children's Rights Development Unit.

United Kingdom Central Council for Nursing, Midwifery and Health Visiting (1987) *Confidentiality: An Elaboration of Clause 9 of the Second Edition of UKCC's Code of Professional Conduct for the Nurse, Midwife and Health Visitor*. London: UKCC.

United Kingdom Council for Psychotherapy (UKCP) (1995) *Ethical Guidelines of the UKCP*. London: UKCP.

Urwin, J. (1992) 'Re R.: the resurrection of parental powers?', *Professional Negligence*, June: 69–73.

Utting, W. (1991) *Children in the Public Care: a Review of Residential Care*. London: HMSO.

van Deurzen-Smith, E. (1991) '1992 and all that: BAC conference 1991', *Counselling*, 2(4): 133–4.

Van Hoose, W.H. and Kottler, J.A. (1985) *Ethical and Legal Issues in Counseling and Psychotherapy*. Second edition. London: Jossey-Bass.

Ward, S. (1995) 'Laying down the law on medical evidence', *BMA News Review*, June: 21–2.

Warnock, W. (1985) *A Question of Life: The Warnock Report on Human Fertilisation and Embryology*. Oxford: Basil Blackwell.

Weishaar, M.E. and Beck, A.T. (1990) 'The suicidal patient: how should the therapist respond?', in K. Hawton and P. Cowen (eds), *Dilemmas and Difficulties in the Management of Psychiatric Patients*. Oxford: Oxford University Press. pp. 65–76.

Weldon, F. (1993) *Affliction*. London: Harper Collins.

Weldon, F. (1994) 'The threats in therapy?', *The Therapist*, 4(1): 24–9.

Wells, C. (1994) 'Disasters: the role of institutional responses in shaping public perceptions of death', in R. Lee and D. Morgan (eds), *Death Rites: Law and Ethics at the End of Life*. London: Routledge. pp. 196–222.

Whimster, P. (1995) *A Straightforward Guide to Small Claims in the County Court*. London: Straightforward Publications.

White, T. (1996) *The Nearest Faraway Place: Brian Wilson, the Beach Boys and the Southern California Experience*. London: Macmillan.

Wilkins, P. (1994), 'Sexual relationships between counsellors and ex-clients: can they ever be right?', *Counselling*, 5(3): 206–9.

Williams, B. (1996) *Counselling in Legal Settings*. Buckingham: Open University Press.

Williams, C. (1995) *Invisible Victims: Crime and Abuse Against People With Learning Difficulties*. London: Jessica Kingsley.

Wise, E.A. (1988) 'Issues in psychotherapy with EAP clients', *Psychotherapy*, 25(3): 415–19.

Wood, D. (1993) *The Power of Words: Uses and Abuses of Talking Treatments*. London: MIND.

Woolf, J. (1991) *Contracts and Small Voluntary Groups*. London: Voluntary Service Council.

Woolf, J. (1992) *Beginner's Guide to Contracts*. London: Voluntary Service Council.

Woolf, Lord (1995) *Access to Justice: Interim Report to the Lord Chancellor on the Civil Justice System in England and Wales*. London: Lord Chancellor's Department.

World Health Organisation (WHO) (1992) *ICD-10: Classification of Mental and Behavioural Disorders*. Geneva: WHO.

Yalom, I. (1991) *Love's Executioner and Other Tales of Psychotherapy*. Harmondsworth: Penguin.

Yapko, M.D. (1994) *Suggestions of Abuse*. London: Simon and Schuster.

Table of Cases

Note: Law references follow a format which may be unfamiliar to most therapists. Case reports are written in the following way:

R. v. Emery (1993), Criminal Appeals Reports (Sentencing) 14 394-400;
Page v. Smith [1994] 4 All ER 522.

The first case is a criminal case. The second case, probably more relevant to therapists, is a civil case, with the full report available in Volume 4 of the *All England Law Reports* (All ER) for 1994, starting at page 522. Where a number of judges comment on a case, the style of quotation will be 'per Lord Ackner at 569', rather than the usual Harvard system (such as, Egan, 1990: 214). Most public reference libraries will have Acts of Parliament, and either the *All England Law Reports*, or *Weekly Law Reports* (*WLR*), together with CD-ROM access to newspaper reports and relevant government publications referred to in this text. On-line computer access to unreported cases can be made via Lexis, but this will only be available to paying subscribers, such as law firms or university law departments. Journals which carry up-to-date commentary on the law include *Childright*, *Community Care* and *New Law Journal*. Two useful guides in finding cases are: N. Smith (1987) *Legal Research Techniques* (Hebden Bridge: Legal Information Resources Ltd); and J. Dane and P. Thomas (1987) *How to Use a Law Library* (Second edition, London: Sweet and Maxwell).

UK

Table of Statutes

Index